Woolf Studies Annual

Volume 24, 2018

PACE UNIVERSITY PRESS•NEW YORK

Copyright © 2018 by
Pace University Press
41 Park Row, 15th Floor, Rm. 1510
New York, NY 10038

All rights reserved
Printed in the United States of America

ISSN: 1080-9317
ISBN: 978-1-935625-25-4

Member

Council of Editors of Learned Journals

♾ Paper used in this publication meets the minimum requirements of American National Standard for Information Sciences–Permanence of Paper for Printed Library Materials, ANSI Z39.48–1984

Editor

Mark Hussey — Pace University

Associate Editor

Vara Neverow — Southern Connecticut State University

Book Review Editor

Amanda Golden — New York Institute of Technology

Editorial Advisory Board

Tuzyline Allan	Baruch College, CUNY
Judith Allen	Kelly Writers House, University of Pennsylvania
Morris Beja	Academy Professor Emeritus, Ohio State University
Pamela L. Caughie	Loyola University Chicago
Kimberly Engdahl Coates	Bowling Green State University
Sarah Cole	Columbia University
Kristin Czarnecki	Georgetown College
Emily Dalgarno	Boston University (Emeritus)
Beth Rigel Daugherty	Otterbein University
Claire Davison	Université Paris III–Sorbonne Nouvelle
Jane de Gay	Leeds Trinity University
Erica Gene Delsandro	Bucknell University
Madelyn Detloff	Miami University
Jeanne Dubino	Appalachian State University
Jane Goldman	University of Glasgow
Elizabeth Willson Gordon	King's University, Canada
Leslie Kathleen Hankins	Cornell College
Alice Keane	Queens College, CUNY
Emily Kopley	Concordia University Library
Karen V. Kukil	Special Collections, Smith College
Michael Lackey	Distinguished McKnight University Professor, University of Minnesota, Morris
Jane Lilienfeld	Curator's Distinguished Professor of English, Lincoln University of Missouri
Maren Linett	Purdue University
Gill Lowe	University of Suffolk
Celia Marshik	Stony Brook University
Ann Martin	University of Saskatchewan
Gabrielle McIntire	Queen's University, Canada
Toni A. H. McNaron	University of Minnesota (Emerita)
Eleanor McNees	University of Denver
Jeanette McVicker	SUNY Fredonia
Jean Mills	John Jay College, CUNY
Patricia Moran	London City University

Editorial Advisory Board (continued)

Steven Putzel	Penn State Wilkes-Barre
Beth C. Rosenberg	University of Nevada, Las Vegas
Victoria Rosner	Columbia University
Derek Ryan	University of Kent
Randi Saloman	Wake Forest University
Bonnie Kime Scott	University of San Diego (Emerita)
Urmila Seshagiri	University of Tennessee
Drew Shannon	Mount St. Joseph University
Kathryn Simpson	Unaffiliated
Anna Snaith	King's College London
Helen Southworth	Clark Honors College, University of Oregon
Elisa Sparks	Clemson University (Emerita)
Peter Stansky	Stanford University
Alice Staveley	Stanford University
Diana L. Swanson	Northern Illinois University
Janine Utell	Widener University
Julie Vandivere	Bloomsburg University
Susan Wegener	Purdue University
Michael Whitworth	University of Oxford
Alice Wood	De Montfort University
John Young	Marshall University

Many thanks to readers for Volume 24 (in addition to the Editorial Board): Amy Elkins (Macalester C); Evelyn Haller (Doane C); Gary Leonard (U of Toronto); Elizabeth Outka (U of Richmond); David Sherman (Brandeis U); Heidi Stalla (Yale-NUS); Elizabeth Wright (Bath Spa U)

Woolf Studies Annual is indexed in *Humanities International Complete*, *ABELL*, and the *MLA Bibliography*.

Contents

Woolf **S**tudies **A**nnual

Volume 24, 2018

	viii	Abbreviations
		Essays in honor of Jane Marcus
Linda Camarasana, J. Ashley Foster, Robin Hackett, Clara Jones, & Jean Mills	1	Jane Marcus in the Archives: Politics and Pleasures
Jane Marcus	5	Flirting with the HRC
Paulina Pająk	11	"Echo Texts": Woolf, Krzywicka, and *The Well of Loneliness*
Margot Kotler	35	After Anger: Negative Affect and Feminist Politics in Virginia Woolf's *Three Guineas*
Matthew Cheney	55	The Reader Awakes: Pedagogical Form and Utopian Impulse in *The Years*
		ARTICLES
Robin Adair & Ann Martin	75	A Driving Bloomsbury: Virginia Woolf, Vanessa Bell, and the Meaning of the Motor-Car
Siân White	101	The Dramatic Modern Novel: Mimesis and The Poetics of Tragedy in *Mrs. Dalloway*
Brett Rutherford	135	Virginia Woolf's Egyptomania: Echoes of *The Book of the Dead* in *To the Lighthouse*

Darin Graber	165	*H.M.S. Orlando:* The Metamorphosing Imperial Vessel
	185	**GUIDE** Guide to Library Special Collections
		REVIEWS
Erica Gene Delsandro	207	*Tense Future: Modernism, Total War, Encyclopedic Form* by Paul K. Saint-Amour
		Writing Against War: Literature, Activism, and the British Peace Movement by Charles Andrews
Emily James	212	*At the Mercy of Their Clothes: Modernism, the Middlebrow, and British Garment Culture* by Celia Marshik
Sarah E. Cornish	215	*Modernism, Fashion, and Interwar Women Writers* by Vike Martina Plock
Jennifer Sorensen	218	*Cheap Modernism: Expanding Markets, Publishers' Series, and the Avant-garde* by Lise Jaillant
Annalisa Zox-Weaver	221	*Ordinary Matters: Modernist Women's Literature and Photography* by Lorraine Sim
Kathryn Laing	225	*Fresca: A Life in the Making. A Biographer's Quest for a Forgotten Bloomsbury Polymath* by Helen Southworth
Drew Patrick Shannon	228	*Virginia Woolf's Modernist Path: Her Middle Diaries & the Diaries She Read* by Barbara Lounsberry
Gabriel Hankins	231	*Scholarly Adventures in the Digital Humanities: Making the Modernist Archives Publishing Project* by Claire Battershill, Helen Southworth, Alice

		Staveley, Michael Widner, Elizabeth Willson Gordon, and Nicola Wilson
Margaret Konkol	**234**	*The Sky of Our Manufacture: The London Fog in British Fiction from Dickens to Woolf* by Jesse Oak Taylor
Kristin Czarnecki	**236**	*Virginia Woolf Writing the World: Selected Papers from the Twenty-fourth Annual International Conference on Virginia Woolf* Pamela L. Caughie and Diana L. Swanson, eds.
Kathryn Holland	**240**	*Virginia Woolf and Her Female Contemporaries: Selected Papers from the Twenty-Fifth Annual International Conference on Virginia Woolf* Julie Vandivere and Megan Hicks, eds.
Madeleine Davies	**242**	*Virginia Woolf & Heritage: Selected Papers from the Twenty-Sixth Annual International Conference on Virginia Woolf* Jane de Gay, Tom Breckin, and Anne Reus, eds.
	247	Notes on Contributors
	249	Submission Guidelines

Abbreviations

AHH	*A Haunted House*
AROO	*A Room of One's Own*
BP	*Books and Portraits*
BTA	*Between the Acts*
CDB	*The Captain's Death Bed and Other Essays*
CE	*Collected Essays* (4 vols.)
CR1	*The Common Reader*
CR2	*The Common Reader, Second Series*
CSF	*The Complete Shorter Fiction*
D	*The Diary of Virginia Woolf* (5 vols.)
DM	*The Death of the Moth and Other Essays*
E	*The Essays of Virginia Woolf* (6 Vols.)
F	*Flush*
FR	*Freshwater*
GR	*Granite & Rainbow: Essays*
JR	*Jacob's Room*
L	*The Letters of Virginia Woolf* (6 Vols.)
M	*The Moment and Other Essays*
MEL	*Melymbrosia*
MOB	*Moments of Being*
MT	*Monday or Tuesday*
MD	*Mrs. Dalloway*
ND	*Night and Day*
O	*Orlando*
PA	*A Passionate Apprentice*
RF	*Roger Fry: A Biography*
TG	*Three Guineas*
TTL	*To the Lighthouse*
TW	*The Waves*
TY	*The Years*
VO	*The Voyage Out*

Jane Marcus in the Archives: Politics and Pleasures
Linda Camarasana, J. Ashley Foster, Robin Hackett,
Clara Jones, & Jean Mills

Jane Marcus, more than anyone else, shared with us the joy of that serendipitous moment when something significant or worth noting quite literally falls out from in between the pages of a book. It is entirely appropriate, then, that such is the case with Marcus's own "Flirting with the HRC," a typescript dated January 1985, about her love affair with the Harry Ransom Center at the University of Texas, Austin. On a rainy day, in a dimly lit study, "Flirting with the HRC" floated to the floor from between the pages of a book and is now published here in *Woolf Studies Annual*, possibly for the first time. Could it have fallen out of Nancy Cunard's *These Were the Hours* or was it *Essays on Race and Empire*? It couldn't have been inside "Poems for France"; the trim size is too small and it would have been detected sticking out, announcing itself. But there it lay on the floor, with its heading strangely pointing the way: the words "for Discovery," typed at the top, seemed to indicate the essay's destination, but the status of its publication history, at this writing, after rigorous inquiry, has yet to be, well…discovered.

In the late 1980s, Jane Marcus was just beginning her research into the activism and political journalism of Nancy Cunard and made extensive use of the Cunard materials at the Harry Ransom Center. The essay included here, however, chronicles her earlier forays into women's suffrage—the Pankhursts, Elizabeth Robins, and later, Ethel Smyth—figures who informed decades of Marcus's pioneering feminist scholarship. Perhaps Marcus re-read this piece, reflecting on it to contextualize her new project on Cunard, when she sighed (there's a great deal of sighing in research), and stuck it into one of her books. Who knows?

The discovery of the typescript echoes another happy accident of research featured in the piece: the "accidental" acquisitions of the Ransom Center's extensive collections on women's literature and history, which Marcus seeks to promote. On one level, the essay foregrounds her passionate and personal relationship to intellectual inquiry, but then it telescopes out to become a multi-tiered critique of what it means to be a woman, any woman, conducting research. Framed somewhat comically as her illicit affair with a research institute, the essay has all the hallmarks of Marcus's distinctive prose style as well as glimpses into areas of inquiry and activism about which she was passionate: women's poverty; women's history; the importance of mentorship; creating and maintaining the archive; pedagogy; research process; funding. These and many other subjects arise, as they often do in a Jane Marcus essay, as if we're sharing in her ideas as she's coming up with them for the first time. There are many gems of insight here, each one meant to be generative, left as clues, or rather, as possibilities, for succeeding generations of scholars.

Marcus's criticism and teaching often coalesced under the sign of 'Discovery.' That signifier—discovery—was pressed upon her students; discovery in the archives, in the classroom, in the text, in one's past, history, and story. It is felicitous, then, that as a student of Jane Marcus what one often "discovered" was Marcus's own monumental scholarly reach. Her scholarship surfaced even when one wasn't looking for it. This happened recently, and mirrors the fortuitous finding in Jane's study that was stamped "for <u>Discovery</u>," on a different hunt for scholarship, this time on a sunny day in a library, to research Sylvia Townsend Warner's understudied Spanish Civil War text, *After the Death of Don Juan*. I (and here "'I' is only a convenient term for somebody who has no real being. … call me Mary Beton, Mary Seton, Mary Carmichael or by any name you please" [Woolf 4-5]) went looking for a chapter in a book by Barbara Brothers and found Jane, not in the Brothers chapter, but infused into the whole book. Upon opening the first pages of the volume *Women's Writing in Exile*, I was greeted with and struck by the dedication page: "This book is for Jane Marcus, without whom it wouldn't have started." Further into the acknowledgements, it becomes clear that Marcus was the impetus behind the entire collection, which came out of the 1986 MLA conference, three sessions whose organization was attributed to Jane Marcus. Shari Benstock, Susan Stanford Friedman, Sneja Gunew, and Gayatri Chakravorty Spivak are on the list of contributors.

Marcus's own essay in the volume, "Alibis and Legends: The Ethics of Elsewhereness, Gender and Estrangement," published in 1989, eerily, prophetically, and disappointingly, still speaks to the present moment. It could have been written today, in the midst of the current global refugee crisis. In this chapter, Marcus reminds us that women are always already in exile from their own language, that "estrangement seems built into the female condition" and that "all women artists are strangers—though some women are stranger than others" (276). As such, she asks that while we remember exile as a lived, literal, and physical experience of displacement for some, exile is experienced in a multiplicity of ways and takes many expressions. In classic Jane Marcus style, the essay traverses Virginia Woolf, June and Jennifer Gibbons, Elaine Showalter, Alice Walker, and Sylvia Townsend Warner. She seeks to create "a new kind of compass" (271), to rescale the "legends of exile on women's maps" (272), and calls on us to read "exilic art"—both figuratively and literally exilic—as a form of "homemaking" (275). This homemaking and reconstruction holds subversive potential from its very (Freudian) *uncanniness*: "In exile the woman rejects her role as representation of home/the mother's body to male desire and so is a threat to patriarchy as well as to the state" (273). How to attend to this subversion, how to account for the "alibis" provided by exile status from the crimes of the patriarchy, how not to let ourselves, as women and feminist critics, off too easily, are the subjects of this essay. Marcus closes with a powerful indictment of our own role in social structures, and observes that Townsend Warner "asks us to examine our own complicity in 'othering' even when we think we are working to expand the canon" (291). Our scholarly activities, our writing, does not give us a pass to innocence, and "as critics we surely should beware of a stance and a practice that gives us an alibi for so many cultural crimes" (292). Jane confronts us with the most "dangerous alibi," "the one that excuses us from political action because we are engaged in writing criticism" (292), calling on us to perhaps do the hardest thing of all, but one that she was very good at as an activist and author, teacher and critic: to live our convictions. This essay, found accidentally in a volume dedicated and attributed to her, signals so much of Jane Marcus's legacy: the way in which she has underwritten all of our feminist modernist scholarly endeavors; how she marries art and activism, criticism and teaching; her concern for creating collaborative feminist networks; and the considerable range of her work.

The essays featured in this special section speak to Marcus's substantial reach as teacher and scholar. They chart different elements of her theories, from affect, to "echo texts," to radical pedagogy. Because mentoring was so important to her and because Jane insisted upon a reciprocal exchange between her pedagogy and her research, we are proud to assemble here three essays by emerging scholars. All three build on Marcus's Virginia Woolf scholarship and, in our view, make significant contributions to the discourse in their respective fields of inquiry.

Paulina Pajak's "Echo Texts: Woolf, Krzywicka and *The Well of Loneliness*," in addition to introducing the work of Polish feminist writer and activist Irena Krzywicka, offers an inspiring example of scholarly sleuthing. Pajak, a doctoral candidate and lecturer at the University of Wroclaw, writes to us that she was "particularly inspired by [Marcus's] works from the 1980s, written during the 'battles' between the Woolfians and the 'defenders' of the 'non-feminist' and 'apolitical' Woolf." Pajak's moving essay is testimony to the breadth of Marcus's influence. Her books and edited collections on Woolf had a formative role in shaping the critical imaginations of many feminists working in English Studies today who never had the privilege of meeting her. In an email to the editors, Pajak reports that "*Virginia Woolf and the Languages of Patriarchy* [is] particularly relevant to the contemporary Polish culture, in which Emancipationists (Polish Suffragettes)'s legacy and modernist writers' feminist engagements are recently re-discovered and researched." The essay offers a window into the trans- and LGBTQ- experience under fascism, as well as to its historical importance, engaging with archival materials and revealing the *nom de plume* of a mysterious translator of Woolf's work.

Margot Kotler's "After Anger: Negative Affect and Feminist Politics in Virginia Woolf's *Three Guineas*" makes an important contribution to affect theory, as well as to feminist theoretical approaches and strategies for the twenty-first century. Taking on one of Jane Marcus's favorite subjects, anger, particularly the politics of women's anger, Kotler's essay follows Marcus and other critics to note, "the value of anger as a strategy of resistance" as it also offers a refreshing and original reading of Woolf's use of the impersonal as "an effective mode of feminist methodology."

The third essay, Matthew Cheney's "The Reader Awakes: Pedagogical Form and Utopian Impulse in *The Years*" deploys Marcus's insights into reading practices across Woolf's work; Cheney's essay is a reconsideration of *The Years'* aesthetics from a pedagogical standpoint. The essay investigates the novel's "subversive pedagogy," which, Cheney argues, "teaches readers to imagine new alternatives to old forms and exhausted ideologies." His essay makes effective use of Marcus as both reader and teacher, as he persuasively outlines the novel's utopian aspects and subversive politics embraced by Woolf and re-enacted by Marcus.

All three essays are meaningful, generative tributes to Jane Marcus and her pioneering body of work. We hope you will be taught by each of them individually, as we were. We hope, as well, that together with the newly discovered essay by Marcus, this collection inspires to action the communities of feminist scholarship Marcus's work helped call into being.

Works Cited:

Marcus, Jane. "Alibis and Legends: The Ethics of Elsewhereness, Gender, and Estrangement." *Women's Writing in Exile*, edited by Mary Lynn Broe and Angela Ingram, North Carolina U P, 1989, pp. 269-94.

Woolf, Virginia. *A Room of One's Own*, annotated and introduced by Susan Gubar, edited by Mark Hussey, Harcourt, 2015.

Flirting with the HRC
Jane Marcus

Fifteen years is a long time for a love affair, a long time to keep secret from one's husband and children, one's colleagues and friends, the great passion of one's life. Perhaps it's time to confess. I'm in love with a library. Its name, when I first conceived this passion as a graduate student, was the Humanities Research Center. Later it became the Harry Ransom Center. Now it has the double-barreled initials of HRHRC. Changing its name is entirely characteristic of its role as my mysterious lover. It always keeps me guessing. The HRC is my Humphrey Bogart. In all my dealings with it, I am not really a Virginia Woolf scholar or a historian of the British Women's Movement. I am really Lauren Bacall. It's hard to tell, I know, when you see trudging across campus a middle-aged professor with circles under her eyes and a brief-case laden with student papers. But when I'm on my way to a brief hour's tryst with my lover on the fifth floor between classes or on a Saturday morning snatched from the insistent call of the family wash, I feel like Lauren Bacall meeting Bogie in Morocco. Sometimes I stand in the window of Parlin Hall and gaze wistfully across the courtyard at my beloved. If only I could skip the committee meetings, the students, the Senate. But the HRC is very understanding and greets me with open arms whenever I can get away, never chiding me for my absences, tolerant of my marriage and my teaching. For, deep down, we both know, my real self, the scholar, is faithful. I'm just burdened with other responsibilities. What a never-ending supply of treasures is revealed to me on each visit.

It all began in Chicago, when I was doing research on feminist writers in the English suffrage movement. We could only meet by mail and phone. How excited I was when those enormous packages of xeroxed sheets arrived with their familiar vertical red stripes marking the pages "Property of the Humanities Research Center, University of Texas at Austin." Little did the former librarian, Ellen Dunlap, know, as she patiently answered my questions, that she was aiding and abetting an illicit passion.

I had spent a year in England, tracking down the American feminist writer, Elizabeth Robins. She was a playwright, a novelist, a great actress who introduced Ibsen to English audiences in the 1890s. She had written some brilliant feminist tracts and had joined the elite board of the Pankhursts' militant Women's Social and Political Union early in the suffrage campaign. I had been working in the Fawcett Women's Library in London. There was precious little on the Pankhursts. Then housed in a small dusty building near Victoria tube station, the Fawcett Library could not afford a professional staff. The priceless collections of women's papers were yellowing and fading in boxes and bins. The light was dim; it was freezing cold and there was no xerox machine. Volunteer veterans of women's struggle for the vote kept the library open. For most of the year I was the only visitor. Some days, cold and cramped from copying all day, I would carry the enormous purple, white and green bound copies of the suffragettes' newspaper, *Votes For Women*, down the street to the Army and Navy Stores and stand in line with the secretaries to use the copying machine. On those trips Virginia Woolf's arguments in *A Room of One's Own* came home to me. "Women have always been poor." Women's history and women's literature have been lost because for so long women could neither own nor bequeath property; they could not endow colleges or libraries. Their work was not valued by men, not kept by male institutions.

The contemporary women's movement has changed all this. The Fawcett Library is now decently housed and professionally staffed in a London Polytechnic. (The British Library refused to accept the collection when the Fawcett Society could no longer afford to maintain it.) Scholars from all over the world pour in to use the archives. Feminist scholarship is not only an accepted field in most disciplines, it is where the scholarly action is, the cutting edge, as administrators say, as if research were a plow in the fields of history.

Back in Chicago in a cozy library carrel, I puzzled over the gaps in what I had learned. We had no real records of the suffragettes' formation of policy, of how they arrived at their effective tactics of huge and colorful demonstrations, chaining themselves to the railings in the House of Commons, hunger-striking in prison. Like all historians of movements for social change, I cursed the police. They had raided the offices of the Women's Social and Political Union and made off with most of the records. Legend has it that they also emptied the safe of thousands of pounds worth of women's jewelry. For Mrs. Pankhurst's huge afternoon suffrage meetings filling the Albert Hall often resulted in mobs of well-dressed women throwing their diamond bracelets and rings on to the stage as contributions to the cause. For even well-to-do Edwardian women had little access to money and were dependent on their husbands. Their diamonds financed the women's movement.

Checking American collections for information, I wrote to the HRC. Elizabeth Robins had saved all the letters written to her by Emmeline, Christabel, and Sylvia Pankhurst. Scribbled in haste as they toured the country from meeting to meeting, these letters constitute the most important source we have, outside of their published speeches and editorials, of the thinking of the women who fought for the vote in England. They are not literary masterpieces but they show Emmeline Pankhurst at her most determined. We see her courage and her sense of humor. We see her convince Elizabeth Robins to use her power as an actress on the platform for women's suffrage.

Later, while working on a book about Dame Ethel Smyth, the brilliant and eccentric English composer, I again checked the HRC. Sure enough, my lover never failed. While Dame Ethel had published several of Mrs. Pankhurst's letters to her (much to the annoyance of her daughter, Christabel) Dame Ethel's letters to her leader revealed a whole new dimension to the movement and to the personal relations between the women. Dame Ethel had pledged two years of her life in devotion to the cause. She wrote "The March of the Women" which became their anthem, and was observed conducting suffragette prisoners in Holloway Gaol in a rousing chorus with her toothbrush serving as a baton. I have some snapshots taken by Elizabeth Robins of Dame Ethel teaching the elegant and ladylike Mrs. Pankhurst, who always wore the latest Paris dresses and hats, how to throw rocks, once the group had decided to break all the windows in Bond Street Shops in a suffrage protest. After the two years were up, Ethel went to Egypt to finish her opera. But she felt guilty writing music, while Mrs. Pankhurst and the suffragettes were risking their lives daily. Forbidden to speak, they spoke and were jailed. In prison they hunger-struck and were forcibly fed by prison doctors in a brutal policy which brought them to the edge of death. Mrs. Pankhurst would be freed, recover her health, speak again and the whole process was repeated. Ethel agonized with daily telegrams to "My darling Em," and Emmeline shared with her her doubts about her daughter Sylvia's loyalty, since she kept falling in love with men. Ethel told her not to worry, that the movement had produced many "amazons like us" who would carry on the work. Despite Dame Ethel's support for suffrage, she was a general's daughter, a snob, and a racist. Her descriptions of the Arabs are appalling. She amused Mrs. Pankhurst by tracking down and taking photos of a hermaphrodite. She travelled by caravan to meet a "woman" who had once been in a harem but had left to perform tricks with horses and now had wives of her own. It's a pity the pictures did not survive the journey home, but the letters are hilarious and must have amused the indomitable Mrs. P. while she tried to gain back her strength after each bout in prison.

Last week I agreed to edit and write an introduction to an edition of the Pankhurst papers from the Fawcett Library in London for a British publisher. The editors will be very surprised to learn that the contents of a second and third volume reside at The Humanities Research Center, and that they are even more exciting. For this lover of mine, the HRC, is a real ladies' man, has always had a soft spot for women, but he has kept up his macho image, and virtually no one knows his secret.

In 1981 when I first came to the University of Texas to teach and to build a Women's Studies program, the first papers I wanted to see at the HRC were the Bloomsbury papers, an enormous collection of papers and letters by Virginia Woolf, E. M. Forster, Lytton Strachey, and all the brighter and lesser lights of the modern literary movement. Ellen Dunlap, Sally Leach, and I pored over the collection, thinking we might be able to mount an exhibition in conjunction with our Virginia Woolf and Bloomsbury Centenary Celebration, sponsored by the College of Liberal

Arts in 1982. But the collection was too vast to catalogue so quickly and we had to be content with making the papers available to scholars who came to participate in the seminar and graduate students interested in the subject. Many of the papers had already been used by scholars, but different scholars have different perspectives. Michael Holroyd had used the Leonard Woolf/Lytton Strachey correspondence. As his interest was mainly in Strachey he had made little use of Leonard Woolf's papers. But I cared about Leonard. He bound and kept his correspondence with Lytton during their King's College Days. Both had been members of the elite secret society, the Apostles, and he had kept the slips of paper on which members had voted for the inclusion of Virginia's brother, Thoby, in the group. Their letters revealed how low they were all ranked in their graduating class, and yet the myth of their genius survives. Saddest of all was Leonard's outsidership as a Jew. Just down from Kings, he wrote to Strachey that he planned a career as a teacher in one of the "public" schools. He conferred with his uncles, and Lytton made inquiries. There was no hope. Jews simply did not teach in British public schools. I hope the salt from my tears did not corrode the pages of this correspondence. The only career for Leonard Woolf was the Civil Service. He would go out to Ceylon. Jews were presumably suitable for governing the natives. But there was one drawback. Gentlemen civil servants were expected to ride. Leonard had never been on a horse. He entertained Lytton with tales of his riding lessons. There is much in these papers which does not appear in the books about Bloomsbury, despite their number. They await the right scholar to tap them. There is much to be done here on the relations between class and race in Britain and in the colonies.

    When I began to teach our basic Introduction to Women's Studies in the Humanities, I wanted the students to do research on women from primary documents. The field is such a new one that students should be able to experience the thrill of discovery reserved in other fields for only a few lucky scholars. For the Women's Studies students, the HRC has been an invaluable resource, a seemingly limitless source of original materials for study. It has not been perfect, of course. No one would ever argue that the acquisition of thousands of papers of women writers and persons of historical interest was a deliberate policy on the part of some mute, inglorious crypto-feminist librarian secretly building one of the best women's manuscript collections in the country. The building and acquisition of these materials appears to have been an historical accident. Contemporary policy on acquisition certainly confirms this belief. For when I asked the HRC to buy a fine (and inexpensive) collection of women's musical manuscripts, books, letters, and diaries including Clara Schumann, Fanny Mendelssohn, and Dame Ethel Smyth, they were not interested, so I have had to travel to the University of Michigan to use the collection.

One splendid accident occurred in the acquisition of a set of ledgers from the 1890s containing the records of a home for unwed mothers (called "Homes of Hope" in London) in the Winerip Collection. Two students in Women's Studies worked on these documents for a year and produced a remarkable study. It is obvious to the contemporary reader that the Evangelical women whose "charity work" brought them to interview these unfortunate girls, salved their consciences by blaming the victim and used the homes as a source of cheap domestic labor. The admission forms contain categories such as "Fallen?", "Age of Fall," "Cause of Fall," and should give some idea of the thinking of early social workers. The stories of poverty, incest, drink, abuse, and suffering contained in the pages and commented upon by high-minded Victorian lady philanthropists are more melodramatic than even fiction could bear and are a more graphic illustration of social attitudes toward women than feminist theory and philosophy discussed in the abstract.

Another "accidental" find were the papers, both British and American, for the landmark obscenity trials of Radclyffe Hall's *Well of Loneliness* (1928). When the British case was lost, the American lawyers acquired the materials from that case to prepare their own. The judge in England had refused to allow "literary merit" as an issue, and consequently the letters in defense of the novel by many famous writers, including Virginia Woolf, were never published. The defense of the lesbian novel was a cause for celebration and some of the letters are wonderful. No one argues that it was a great novel. Many were quick to remark on its lugubrious religious character and pointed out that it certainly would never convince anyone that there was any happiness to be found in such a life. Edna Ferber disliked the novel but defended free speech, hoping that the New York Society for the Suppression of Vice didn't get their hands on the Bible. Both Professor Angela Ingram and I are using these materials in our current work on women in the '20s.

Cathy Henderson, Special Collections Librarian at the HRC, has been especially attentive to our needs. Perhaps because I have sent so many students and visiting feminist scholars to her she has prepared a staggering list of women whose papers are in the HRC. I am sure she was driven to produce the list by the exigencies of her profession, but its existence has been a tremendous boon to the future of Women's Studies at The University of Texas. Last fall Beverly Stoeltje called an informal meeting at the home of Jean Andrews Smith of community women and non-faculty friends of Women's Studies. As we went around the room discussing our hopes for the future, for a formal program at the university, for a statewide conference on a feminist topic, I found myself saying without any forethought, "I have a dream. I have a dream of an Institute for Research on Women at The University of Texas. An institute like the ones at Radcliffe, Wellesley, Brown and Stanford—based on possibilities for research at the HRC, the Barker Library and all the other campus libraries and collections." Cathy Henderson's list is the source of my dream. Though few people know it, the HRC has one of the best women's collections in the country. It is not listed in the standard source books because it was not acquired as a "women's collection." But in terms of individual writers and historical figures, it is stupendous. I dreamed out loud of a first step toward such an Institute, an annotated bibliography, a book called "Opportunities for Research on Women at The University of Texas."

Everyone in that room shared my dream and the women have met again and begun their plans. That very day Jean Andrews wrote a sizeable check, and other women have followed her lead. The first step is a small one, to hire a researcher to finish the bibliography and get it printed. There is apparently no way for the university to fund women's studies so the group is raising the money to pay a researcher. Sally Leach of the HRC and Jean Andrews Smith are co-chairing Friends of Women's Studies and have begun the work in earnest. Simultaneously Mrs. Marion Mark, the wife of the new chancellor, has joined forces with Prof. Beverly Stoeltje's group to plan a conference on Women, Work and Society which will bring the best feminist scholars in the country to campus along with the women's studies people and interested community women from all over the state.

We're not flying yet, but we're off the ground. Every first-rate Women's Studies program in the country has been built by the joint efforts of women in the community and faculty experts in feminist scholarship. Those who benefit are the next generation of women students. It will take many years and many books and articles to tap the HRC's secret collection of women's materials. The library is resourceful and generous, able to support many mistresses, and carry on many scholarly flirtations like mine.

The HRC is like many men I know who are public patriarchs, but in private they support and encourage the careers of their wives and daughters. Someday I'd like to devote full time to our relationship, but in the meantime, each stolen afternoon is a joy, not only to me but to excited graduate students planning dissertations. And Texas women who share our dream of an Institute have begun to use Virginia Woolf's strategy for saving women's history. The HRC's collections show how rich our heritage is—now we must eliminate women's poverty by providing opportunities for feminist scholars to use that heritage.

———January 1985

Printed by permission of Michael Marcus and the Jane Marcus Collection at Mount Holyoke College Archives and Special Collections.

"Echo Texts": Woolf, Krzywicka, and *The Well of Loneliness*
Paulina Pająk

I

The nature of literary and existential survival is one of the constant themes in Virginia Woolf's writing. In *A Room of One's Own*, Woolf explores the connection between the cultural vitality of texts and their intellectual honesty: "what holds [novels] together in these rare instances of survival...is something that one calls integrity, though it has nothing to do with paying one's bills or behaving honourably in an emergency. What one means by integrity, in the case of the novelist, is the conviction that he gives one that this is the truth" (*AROO* 61). As Jane Marcus has shown, in this seminal essay Woolf responded to the censorship of Radclyffe Hall's *The Well of Loneliness,* one of the first novels with an undisguised lesbian/transgender theme, both persecuted and praised for its honesty. When in 1928, Sir Chartres Biron judged the book obscene and all copies were burned, it seemed probable that the novel would fall into obscurity (Doan and Prosser 1-3). Indeed, *The Well*[1] was not published in Britain until 1949. Nevertheless, Hall's novel not only survived destruction and censorship, but also traveled across countries and continents, both in the original version and in numerous translations. The translated book entered the Polish culture in 1933.

This article seeks to compare the reception of *The Well* in Britain and Poland, juxtaposing two important statements by public intellectuals: Woolf's *A Room of One's Own* and Irena Krzywicka's preface to *Źródło samotności,* the Polish translation of Hall's novel. I look at *Źródło* through the lens inspired by Marcus's scholarship, situating it within the biographical and political contexts of interwar Poland. The Polish reception of *The Well* casts light on the way this novel became the "bible of lesbianism" in different cultures for at least half a century and reveals new networks of transnational modernism.

While Hall's trial has become one of the most studied events in British LGBTQ history, the fascinating story of *The Well*'s early global reception has remained unwritten, despite fruitful areas of research enabled by the transnational turn in Modernist studies.[2] Already in 1929, the novel became a bestseller in the United States, and it was also translated into Danish and German. Promptly, other publishers followed: in 1931 *The Well* was available in Czech, a year later in French,

---

[1] I use the following abbreviations for works frequently cited: *The Well, WL* for Radclyffe Hall's *The Well of Loneliness* and *Źródło, ZS* for its Polish translation, *Źródło samotności.*
[2] A case in point is Marcus's search for the lost legacy of African, West Indian, and South Asian public intellectuals in her book *Hearts of Darkness: White Women Write Race* (2003).

and in 1933 in Polish. Although many factors are responsible for the global popularity of Hall's novel, there are two most probable explanations that I will briefly explore: the all-embracing character of the novel challenging various categories of identity, and the efforts of intellectuals within transnational modernist networks.

The Well is an emancipatory landmark and an important legacy to a whole LGBTQ community, raising issues still relevant today, such as marriage equality or stress that members of marginalized groups experience, and inspiring new scholarship. Among the recent critical voices interpreting *The Well*, Nadine Tschacksch[3] investigates the emergence of queer identities in the Great War, Hannah Roche[4] examines the camp aesthetics of lesbian romances, and Katherine A. Costello[5] juxtaposes various approaches to the identity of the protagonist Stephen Gordon. This last issue sparked a heated debate on the eve of the twenty-first century, when queer studies witnessed a transgender turn, resulting in research questioning the lesbian interpretations of *The Well*.[6] Elizabeth English underlines that this process has profoundly influenced the scholarship on *The Well*: "Melanie A. Taylor and Jay Prosser...question the established reading of the novel as a key lesbian text by arguing that this interpretation is founded upon a critical conflation of inversion and homosexuality. For both, *The Well* is not a narrative of emerging lesbian identity but rather one of transgenderism" (50). Furthermore, new critical guidelines were formulated by Jack Halberstam, who called the researchers "to account for historical moments when the difference between gender deviance and sexual deviance is hard to discern. The history of inversion and of those people who identified themselves as inverts (Radclyffe Hall, for example) still does represent a tangle of cross-gender identification and sexual preference that is not easily separated out" (303). While the novel has played a vital role in lesbian culture, its transgender interpretations are well grounded, and I deeply appreciate in Stephen what Madelyn Detloff has called "borderland status between identity categories" (94).[7] As a proto-queer hero(ine) Stephen becomes an Every(wo)man, who "transgresses" all identities. S(he) is an exile deprived of a stable national identity, a Christian not entitled to belong to the religious community, and finally, a person who challenges

---

[3] See Tschacksch, Nadine. "Sexual Identities and Patriotism in Wartime Britain: Literary No-Man's Land." *English Literature in Transition, 1880-1920* vol. 60, no. 4, 2017, pp. 449-70.
[4] See Roche, Hannah. "An 'ordinary Novel': Genre Trouble in Radclyffe Hall's *The Well of Loneliness*." *Textual Practice*, 2016, pp. 1-17, http://dx.doi.org/10.1080/0950236X.2016.1238001. Accessed 8 November 2017.
[5] See Costello, Katherine A. 2017. "A No-Man's-Land of Sex: Reading Stephen Gordon and 'Her' Critics." *Journal of Lesbian Studies*, 2017, pp. 1-20, http://dx.doi.org/10.1080/10894160.2017.1342457. Accessed 8 November 2017.
[6] The first attempts were studies by Gillian Whitlock (1987), Sandra Gilbert and Susan Gubar (1989).
[7] Although Detloff notes in the essay cited that *The Well* is a text "of transgender/ FtM subjectivity" (89).

both gender and sexual identity. Consequently, Hall's novel has been read and discovered by generations of diverse readers around the world.

The Well survived extreme censorship and entered other cultures due to the efforts of modernist networks, created around the world by intellectuals striving to preserve fragile peace and demanding rights for various groups in the increasingly hostile war cultures of the 1930s. Since, as Jessica Berman proposes, transnational modernism was "a dynamic series of aesthetic relationships or responses to the problematics of modernity in which we can see worldwide textual correspondences and intersections among its social and political commitments" (30), the censorship of Hall's novel sparked a global response. Among those voices were Woolf and Krzywicka, who as public intellectuals played vital roles in preserving Hall's emancipatory message, embodying it in their "echo texts," to use Marcus's term.

It was Marcus who first showed that in *A Room of One's Own*, Woolf responded—both forcefully and cautiously—to the censorship of *The Well*. For years, Marcus was "storming the toolshed," critically exploring feminist methodology and undermining the divinity of various "Bogeys," or distorted portrayals of Virginia Woolf. Finally, Marcus succeeded in her brave attempt at redefining the role that in Woolf's oeuvre plays two tabooed currents, "on one hand her lesbian identity, woman-centered life, and feminist work, and on the other, her socialist politics" (Marcus "Storming," 629), both essential for current Woolf studies. If, as Marcus notes, "Judith Shakespeare was, to contemporary audiences, very clearly a portrait of Radclyffe Hall" ("To the" 19), then Woolf herself became a custodian of the banned novel.

Similarly in Poland, Irena Krzywicka (1899-1994), a feminist writer and journalist, whose memoirs were tellingly titled *Wyznania gorszycielki* [*Confessions of a Scandalizer*], advocated and popularized *The Well*. When, in 1933, *Źródło* was issued by the Publishing Society "Rój," she wrote a preface to the novel. The implications of Krzywicka's text for Polish LGBTQ culture are enormous, as when in May 1933 this emancipatory manifesto was reprinted as a feature in the "Wiadomości Literackie" [Literary News], both Hall's novel and lesbianism literally made headlines.

Yet, in Poland, taboo still surrounds the history of marginalized groups' emancipation—since the lost poetry of Sappho, their past has survived only in fragments and echoes. When I started my search, I came across the views of some scholars who believed that *The Well* was translated, but it had never been distributed. As the 1933 press reviews were not discovered, Krzywicka's preface was considered the only remaining trace. How could a novel survive, if it has never truly existed? And I thought about the pertinent question asked by Marcus: "Does notoriety still ensure ignomiy and social ostracism in those women's lives, and then, perhaps, posthumous honor by historians?" ("Middlebrow" 164). Yet, oblivion

Figure 1: Irena Krzywicka. 1925. The National Digital Library Polona, F.33147.

was apparent—*The Well* was obscured, but it did not disappear. On the basis of internet reviews, it can be established that Hall's novel has been read by the modern Polish LGBTQ community—though the copies are scarce and locked up in the National Library. Moreover, after sixty-seven years, the extracts of *Źródło* and Krzywicka's preface were republished in the issues No. 3-4/5 (1999/2000) of the "Furia Pierwsza" [Fury First], a "literary feminist lesbian magazine."

Shortly after finding the reprints in the internet archives of the British Embassy in Poland, I came across a poignant epilogue to the story of *Źródło*. In 2011, Ric Todd, the Ambassador to Poland, and Clare Dimyon, an activist of PRIDE Solidarity, visited the National Library to see the Polish translation. Their homage was inspired by Joan Nestle, a co-founder of the Lesbian Herstory Archives in New York, who recalled the story of a Polish Jewish woman who had survived the Holocaust: "I had a chance to read *The Well of Loneliness* that had been translated into Polish before I was taken into the camps. I was a young girl at the time, around 12 or 13 and one of the ways I survived in the camp was by remembering that book. I wanted to live long enough to kiss a woman" (LGBT History Month).

Not often can we have such a proof—paraphrasing Czesław Miłosz—that literature (disregarding its "brow" status), *does* save people and nations. Not often can we hear the voice of a lesbian Holocaust survivor. And yet, the questions are numerous, starting with the name of the woman who gave that testimony. As Dimyon comments, "this is what lesbian history often looks like ... tiny fragments that escaped destruction, the most tenuous of connections.... These two or three sentences and this book are the only fragments we have of this woman and this astonishing story of survival" (LGBT History Month).

These words have been echoing in my mind during the time I have been researching the publications of Modernist and LGBTQ scholars. *Źródło* is never mentioned in the few studies of "Rój" Publishing, nor in the monographs on Polish Modernism, nor in publishers' memoirs. A few feminist and LGBTQ scholars (as for example Ewa Chudoba and Krzysztof Tomasik) have briefly discussed the fact that Hall's novel was published in 1933, but they do not mention the translator; others probably are not aware that it has been translated, as they use its English title or translate it literally as "Studnia samotności." Furthermore, while some Krzywicka scholars discuss her preface to *Źródło*, they are obviously not interested in Hall as an author, writing her name as "Radcliffe Hull" (a spelling that appeared in Krzywicka's reprinted preface). For several months I have been also researching the diaries, memoirs and letters of Polish writers and I have not found a single word about the novel nor about the Polish translation. It seemed that for the critics and writers, *Źródło* was tabooed and forgotten.

Such (self-)censorship, as Marcus has shown in her ground-breaking book *Virginia Woolf and the Languages of Patriarchy*, "makes the reader mistrust the

Figure 2: Irena Krzywicka dressed as a page. 1914. The National Digital Library Polona, F.33146.

published text" and encourages the researcher to immerse herself in the "drafts of novels, letters, and diaries, proceedings of political meetings, and newspapers" (*Languages* xii). Following in Marcus's footsteps while undertaking broad archival and press research on *Źródło*, I have discovered that its interwar fate can be partly reconstructed, as the novel was reviewed, advertised in publishing catalogues and in press, and finally, mentioned in the publishers' postwar letters. Yet, the story of *Źródło* told by the archive is full of "blank pages"—censored, forgotten or lost fragments.

The Well first entered Polish culture when the echoes of Hall's trial were reverberating throughout the world. The daily "Gazeta Lwowska" [Lviv Newspaper] in October 1928 covered the story: "In London a book made a lot of noise, provoking lengthy discussion and comments about the censorship and freedoms of the written word. A renowned author, Miss Margaret Radclyffe-Hall wrote a book…, in which she raises the question of some abnormal tendencies in women"[8] (5). The journalist also mentioned the hostility of the *Sunday Express* and the withdrawal of the first British edition. After the trial, Biron's judgment must have also been

---

[8] All translations are mine unless otherwise indicated.

Figure 3: Irena Krzywicka dressed as a page. 1914. The National Digital Library Polona, F.39704.

known to some Polish intellectuals—because, as Celia Marshik notes, it was extensively covered: "The printed transcript of his words indicates that Biron could not separate his anger at Hall's insult to war workers from his horror at Mary's 'debauchery' at the hands of Stephen....Biron's comments on Hall's ambulance drivers were widely reported" (152).

Surprisingly, the influential and progressive "Wiadomości Literackie" ["Literary News"] was silent about *The Well* and its trial. This literary weekly, "whose intellectual patrons were George Bernard Shaw, H. G. Wells and Bertrand Russell" (Zawiszewska 109), frequently informed readers about instances of literary censorship in Europe. Nonetheless, in December 1928, the journal published Tadeusz Boy-Żeleński's feature about Narcyza Żmichowska, a founder of the Polish women's rights movement, sentenced to prison for independence activism. Yet what Żeleński explored in his essay electrified some audiences—it was Żmichowska's lesbianism and the story of her love for Paulina Zbyszewska, presented in a heterosexual disguise in her novel *The Heathen* (*Poganka* 1846, Eng. transl. 2012). Even though it is possible that the essay was provoked by Hall's trial, it clearly belonged to Żeleński's project, concerning morality reform, to which this writer, interpreter of French literature and journalist committed himself—supported both privately and publicly by Irena Krzywicka.

In 1928 Żeleński started a "Bloomsbury affair" with Krzywicka, as they were both married—the spouses tolerated their relationship. Krzywicka recalls in her memoirs that for their first date she bought a hat, in order to mask her shabby coat. When she came to the meeting point, she saw Boy, waving to her with a hat and shouting, "Look! It's crazy, things I do for you. I have just bought a hat!" (193). Krzywicka and Boy-Żeleński inspired each other in their public activity: she persuaded him to write about women's reproductive rights, he convinced her to support his efforts concerning "sexual minorities." However, Wojciech Śmieja cautions against overestimating their role: "Even though the liberal publicists (partially) take the blame from homosexuality..., still, those who 'know better' speak on behalf of the homosexual. Yet, what they say not always corresponds with the facts.... This phenomenon is particularly visible in the journalism of Tadeusz Boy-Żeleński or Irena Krzywicka" ("Topografia" 87). Nonetheless, as Krzysztof Tomasik observes, "homosexuality became discussed in an open forum thanks to the heterosexuals: the first emancipatory texts were formulated by Tadeusz Boy-Żeleński, a preface to Radclyffe Hall's *Źródło samotności* was written by Irena Krzywicka.... Their numerous homosexual colleagues did not resume the topic, rather hold it to ridicule" (16). Boy-Żeleński was also an important author of "Rój" Publishing (Kister 41-42), and thus could have inspired the publication of *The Well* in Poland.

In the publishing history of *Źródło*, the pivotal role was played by the Publishing Society "Rój," one of the most important Polish modernist publishers. In 1924 "Rój" was initiated in Warsaw by Melchior Wańkowicz, a writer, reporter, and at that time a government official, soon joined by Marian Kister, a bookseller and publisher (Wańkowicz "Wspomnienia," 16; Okopień 176-77). Because of Wańkowicz, the company was initially close to the ruling Sanation camp, gathered around Józef Piłsudski, who later advocated the authoritarian system. However, the "Rój" political profile was diverse as among its authors were Irena Krzywicka, a liberal feminist; Wanda Wasilewska, a communist activist; Adolf Nowaczyński, a nationalist and anti-Semite; as well as Sholem Asch (שלום אש), a Yiddish writer.

This diversity of "Rój's" endeavor is already visible in its beginnings: "the company started off with a brochure series, 'Library of History and Geography.' With the innocent slogan 'To entertain without lying. To teach without boring,' it published books by such eminent writers as Julian Tuwim, Zofia Kossak, Maria Kuncewiczowa" (Pytlak 172). Among "Rój" authors were numerous Nobel Prize winners, such as Sigrid Undset, Thomas Mann, John Galsworthy, Roger Martin du Gard, Pearl Buck, and many others listed in Wańkowicz's memoirs (*Tędy* 42-44). Ewa Gisges-Zwierzchowska, who has analyzed the few "Rój" catalogues that survive, underlines that translations constituted a significant part of its publications,

Figure 4: Tadeusz Boy-Żeleński. Ca. 1910. The National Digital Library Polona, F.397.

and their average print run is estimated at 1200-1500 copies. In 1938 alone, almost sixty percent of 360 new books were translations (among them fifty-three from English) (Giseges-Zwierzchowska 45).

The "Rój" catalogues do not usually reveal the publishing histories of individual books. As the company books and documents were burnt or lost, the search for archival materials concerning the "Rój" translating endeavor resembles looking for a needle, not in a haystack, but in a pile of ashes. During the Second World War many Polish libraries and archives were completely destroyed—the National Library alone lost forever almost 800,000 registered items of the most valuable part of its holdings.

The situation is further complicated by the postwar conflict between the "Rój" publishing partners, Wańkowicz and Kister. In her memoirs Hanna, Kister's wife, briefly mentions Wańkowicz and does not write a single word about his wife, Zofia, who in the 1940s tried to rescue "Rój" (Ziółkowska-Boehm *passim*). In a poignant letter to Wańkowicz, dated 17th October 1945, Zofia relates the fates of their daughter Krysia, other relatives and the "Rój":

> The orderlies and colleagues said that Krysia died on 6th August.... we have buried many of her colleagues, but we have not found her group yet. Rom was killed.... Bisia, who was last seen in the Gestapo...disappeared without a trace. The Germans shot Tol....
>
> I wrote to Kister about the "Rój," but I do not know whether he received my letter. The Germans burned down the book warehouses.... So far we have not resumed the "Rój".... Our little house has burnt down and I stayed literally in one dress, without even a coat.... I live from hand to mouth. (Ziółkowska-Boehm 32)

The Nazis burned 70,000 books published by "Rój" (Kister 88) and the company has never been rebuilt in Poland. However, "Rój" was reopened as "Roy Publishers" in New York by Hanna and Marian Kister, who escaped to the United States, and since 1943 were publishing translations of Polish literature (Kister *passim*).

Surprisingly, it was in the letters of the "Roy Publishers" from 1944-68 that I found the only instance in which the "Rój" publishers mentioned the publication of *Źródło*. In the papers preserved with the letters, Marian Kister and Aleksander Janta, a writer and journalist, reconstruct the scope of "Rój" interwar endeavors. Among the most popular British authors were E. M. Forster, James Joyce, D. H. Lawrence, Daphne du Maurier, Bertrand Russell, and Lytton Strachey. On the long list of writers, there is also "R. Hall" with a symbol plus used for "literature," and not with a circle, indicating "entertainment" (*Listy Roy Publishers*, cards 43-44). I consequently assume that the publishers considered *The Well* to be an interesting example of modern prose, and not a scandalous novel for the less discerning readers.

The analysis of press advertisements for *Źródło* tends to confirm these conjectures. It seems that "Rój" tried to follow a strategy similar to that of Jonathan Cape, the British publisher of *The Well*, who "pitched the publicity, pricing, and reviews not to Hall's usual middlebrow following but to a more highbrow readership" (Doan and Prosser 4). The Polish publishers launched a reviewing and advertising campaign for *Źródło* in the prestigious "Wiadomości Literackie," the journal of the literary world, which published two reviews of the novel, as well as "Rój" advertisements, in which the novel appeared. A case in point is an advertisement, published in July, in which only *Źródło* is visually singled out with a frame and recommended as "the latest publication" among "the most eminent new European books" (The "Rój" 6). Both the advertisement and the 1933 "Rój" catalogue show

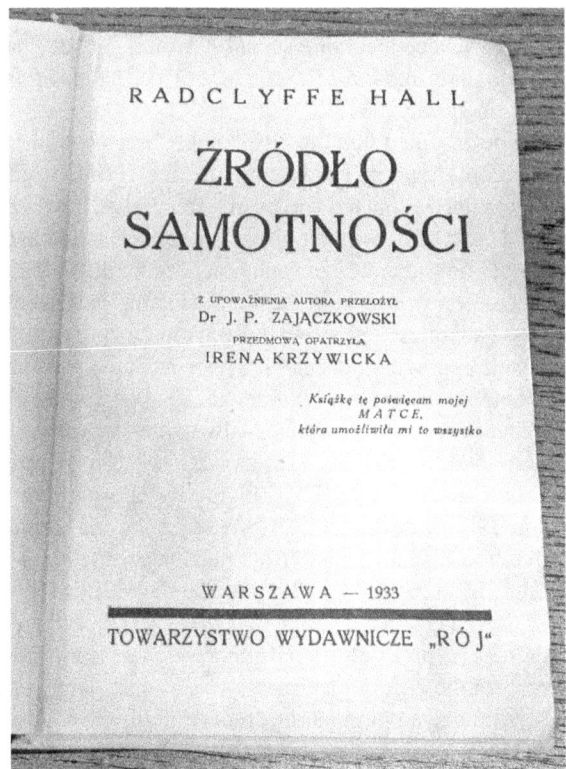

Figure 5: Title page. Radclyffe Hall, and Irena Krzywicka. Źródło samotności. Towarzystwo Wydawnicze Rój, 1933.

that initially Hall's novel was relatively expensive, as it was sold for 10 zloty, while the average price of the "Rój" foreign novels was 7 zloty. Nonetheless, in the late 1930s when the "Rój" held massive book sales announced in the press, *Źródło* became more available for the middlebrow audience, as it then cost 2 zloty.

While looking through the 1931 and 1932 "Rój" catalogues, I made a startling discovery. It turns out that "Rój" wanted to publish *The Well* as early as 1931, announcing it under the title "Męka samotności" [The Agony of Solitude]; a year later it appeared under its final title "Źródło samotności" (Polish "źródło" means both "a well" and "a source"), though the only two copies preserved in the National Library were published in 1933. It is possible that this delay was caused by ongoing changes in the Polish law concerning homosexuality. Although homosexuality was never penalized in independent Poland, in the years 1795-1918, when the country was conquered by three partitioning powers (Austria, Prussia, and Russia), it was a criminal offence. In interwar Poland, the authorities must have united the judicial systems of former partitions. Finally, in 1932, the new Criminal Code was completed and it was decided that homosexuality would not be penalized (Śmieja "Boy," 65). The Code came into force in September 1932 and *Źródło* was published almost immediately in spring 1933.

Could it then be assumed that the "Rój" publishers were afraid of the confiscation of *Źródło* copies and its costly consequences? Similarly to Britain, the censorship system in interwar Poland was mostly repressive; however, instances of censorship occurred more often with the rise of authoritarian rule in the 1930s, and the press drew the public's attention to such practices by publishing the censored blank pages. Ryszard Nycz observes that the censorship "affected primarily the avant-garde writers—anarchist, leftist and those sympathizing with communism… yet it has been as well imposed on the authors connected to the ruling camp" (14). Among the most notable instances of literary censorship was the confiscation of the short story "Zenobia Palmura" by Jarosław Iwaszkiewicz for an offence against "the sense of shame and beauty" in 1920, as well as the forfeiture of the novel *Wspólny pokój* [The Common Room] by Zbigniew Uniłowski, due to its alleged "moral offence" in 1932 (Zawada 202). However, only one example of official censorship interference appears in the "Rój" publishers' memoirs—in 1934, the novel "Oblicze dnia" [The Face of the Day] by Wanda Wasilewska was published without several censored chapters (Kister 41).

Although there is no proof of official suppression of Hall's novel in Poland, the mysterious story of the *Źródło* translator(s) casts some light on the fundamental role that censorship played in the Polish reception of *The Well*. Officially, *The Well* was translated into Polish by the enigmatic Dr J. P. Zajączkowski, who cannot be found in biographical dictionaries. Yet, he was described by Wańkowicz as "a renowned and highly regarded interpreter, an expert on the Napoleonian epoch,

Figure 6: Źródło samotności. 1933. The National Library.

spying, the Great War, famous trials, aviation, a connoisseur of ladies' fashion, a chronicler of Australian rams, as well as an authority on ballet" ("Wspomnienia" 201). Certainly, nobody knows Dr Zajączkowski better than Wańkowicz, who created both this unmistakable figure and pseudonym. It became both a *nom de plume* adopted by the authors and a group pseudonym for the "Rój" translators and editors (Wańkowicz "Wspomnienia," 199), who used it when the publication was prepared in haste, or if they were disappointed either with the original text or the results of publishing processes (Kister 57-58).

The National Library notes that in the case of *Źródło*, Dr Zajączkowski was used as a pseudonym for "Karolina Beylin, Jerzy Pański, Andrzej Stawar, Adam Ważyk, Lucjan Szenwald (the editors of 'Rój')." Possibly, Pański, Stawar, and Ważyk could have worked on Hall's novel as editors, since they translated from French and Russian. It may be assumed that the most probable translator of Hall's novel was Karolina Beylin, a writer, journalist, Varsavianist, as well as Dickens's translator.[9] However, the question is more complicated, since Szenwald, a poet

---

[9] Regrettably, Beylin's interwar years in the "Rój" are not documented. Her private archive was preserved by Marek Beylin, the son of her nephew, and then handed down to Joanna Olczak-Ronikier, who was working on her book *In the Garden of Memory: A Family Memoir*

and communist activist, was also an accomplished translator of British poetry and crime novels (Tarczałowicz *passim*). Moreover, Kister (not surprisingly in view of other omissions) in her memoirs hardly mentions Beylin, who translated at least nine "Rój" books.

Whether Beylin translated Hall's novel or not, a close examination of *Źródło* reveals possible reasons for using the pseudonym, and yields important new insights into Polish reception of *The Well*. Before publication, the translation was considerably censored—almost all excerpts concerning "inversion" and the Great War were omitted or manipulated. From the very first pages, Hall draws Stephen's portrait as a "congenital invert," based upon the theories formulated by early sexologists (English 37-38). Hall carefully structured this theme: in the novel first appears the word "invert," denoting the individual, then its plural form "inverts," suggesting a community, and finally, from chapter 48 to the end, she uses the word "inversion" to embrace the phenomenon. This scheme is completely destroyed in the Polish translation, since for nine occurrences of the word "invert," only one survives in Polish; of five "inverts," two survive; and of seven uses of "inversion," four survive. Moreover, even when the words "invert/inversion" occur in Polish, they are rendered as pejorative "zboczeniec/zboczenie" ("pervert/perversion"). More serious is the omission of the passages on lesbian/transgender visibility and emerging community in the chapters on the First World War. These Chapters (34 to 37) are seriously cut and manipulated. While in *The Well*, for example, the fourth part of Chapter 34 consists of five paragraphs (*WL* 319-21), in *Źródło* only two survived (*ZS* 265).

---

about the Horowitz family—among them Regina Beylin, Karolina's sister, whose premature death ended her career as a follower of Wanda Landowska, a Polish-French harpsichordist and member of Natalie Clifford-Barney's lesbian circle, portrayed as Wanda in *The Well*. As Marek Beylin informs me, Karolina's interwar papers have not survived. Yet, he recalls that she belonged to the progressive intelligentsia in the spirit of Boy-Żeleński and the "Wiadomości Literackie" (conversation with Marek Beylin). Beylin, a Polish Jewish woman, could have easily perished in the Holocaust: "Karola was caught, arrested and imprisoned for a few months. Miraculously she escaped on the first day of the ghetto liquidation, when everyone was transported to the gas chambers" (Olczak-Ronikier 303, transl. A. Lloyd-Jones). Later Beylin was rescued by the Wołk Family, awarded the title Righteous among the Nations (Rytlowa). After the war, she belonged to the literary world—the famous writers Maria Dąbrowska and Jarosław Iwaszkiewicz wrote about her in their memoirs. Interestingly, Dąbrowska also praised Beylin's novel *Mieszkamy na Puławskiej* [Living at Puławska Street]—though she was not aware of her authorship, as it was published under a *nom de plume*. In her lifetime, Beylin used at least nine pen-names and thirty journalist pseudonyms. Why was she so secretive? Juliusz Gomulicki suggests that Beylin was ashamed of certain interwar publications, produced to eke out a meager existence (1985 10). In a recollection "The Woman-Institution," Alicja Wielgoławska wrote, "It was hard to know her.... Her life was her own and she felt completely fulfilled. And yet, she was always detached" (20).

Since there is no proof of official censorship, it seems that the publishers decided to suppress themselves the "sensitive" extracts of Hall's novel, using Biron's statements from the trial as guidance—an ironic turnabout in the publishing history of *The Well*. Andrzej Zawada explains that such practices were common in the interwar publishing houses, as "the editors mediated with the authors to minimize the losses by convincing them to tone down the controversial extracts of their manuscripts" (203). Translators might not have wanted their names on the title pages of censored books, which could explain why Dr Zajączkowski was the official translator of *Źródło*.

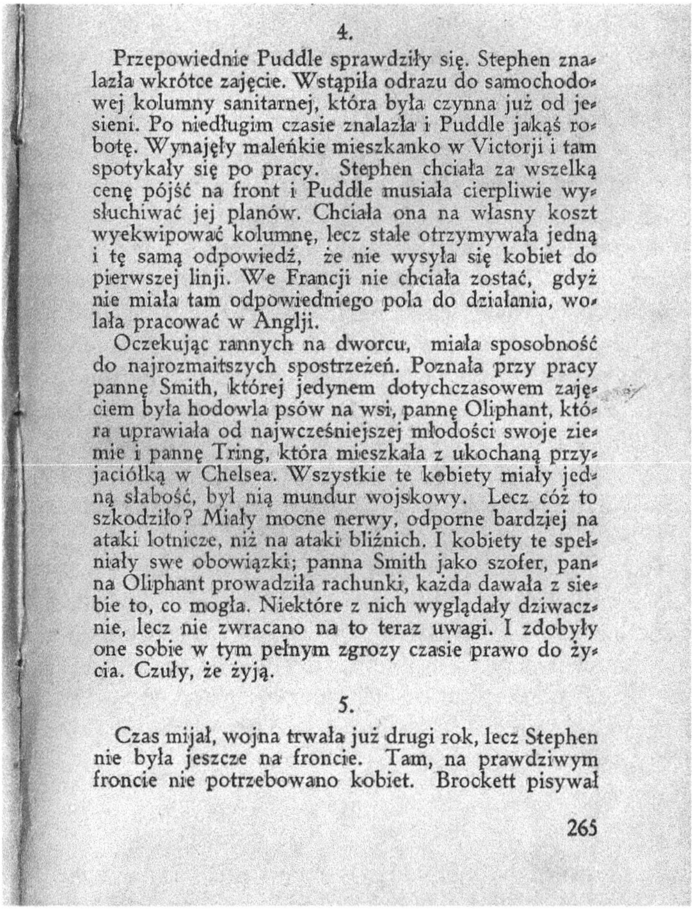

4.

Przepowiednie Puddle sprawdziły się. Stephen znalazła wkrótce zajęcie. Wstąpiła odrazu do samochodowej kolumny sanitarnej, która była czynna już od jesieni. Po niedługim czasie znalazła i Puddle jakąś robotę. Wynajęły maleńkie mieszkanko w Victorji i tam spotykały się po pracy. Stephen chciała za wszelką cenę pójść na front i Puddle musiała cierpliwie wysłuchiwać jej planów. Chciała ona na własny koszt wyekwipować kolumnę, lecz stale otrzymywała jedną i tę samą odpowiedź, że nie wysyła się kobiet do pierwszej linji. We Francji nie chciała zostać, gdyż nie miała tam odpowiedniego pola do działania, wolała pracować w Anglji.

Oczekując rannych na dworcu, miała sposobność do najrozmaitszych spostrzeżeń. Poznała przy pracy pannę Smith, której jedynem dotychczasowem zajęciem była hodowla psów na wsi, pannę Oliphant, która uprawiała od najwcześniejszej młodości swoje ziemie i pannę Tring, która mieszkała z ukochaną przyjaciółką w Chelsea. Wszystkie te kobiety miały jedną słabość, był nią mundur wojskowy. Lecz cóż to szkodziło? Miały mocne nerwy, odporne bardziej na ataki lotnicze, niż na ataki bliźnich. I kobiety te spełniały swe obowiązki; panna Smith jako szofer, panna Oliphant prowadziła rachunki, każda dawała z siebie to, co mogła. Niektóre z nich wyglądały dziwacznie, lecz nie zwracano na to teraz uwagi. I zdobyły one sobie w tym pełnym zgrozy czasie prawo do życia. Czuły, że żyją.

5.

Czas mijał, wojna trwała już drugi rok, lecz Stephen nie była jeszcze na froncie. Tam, na prawdziwym froncie nie potrzebowano kobiet. Brockett pisywał

265

Figure 7: The most censored part of chapter 34. Radclyffe Hall, and Irena Krzywicka. Źródło samotności. Towarzystwo Wydawnicze Rój, 1933.

Undoubtedly, the mysterious person who translated *The Well* into Polish took great pains to convey Hall's original message. The most important emancipatory conversations between Stephen, Adolphe Blanc, and Valérie Seymour are rendered faithfully. For example, Blanc's hopeful visions for the future, as well as his idea of "invert's messiah," who can "make the ignorant think," "bring home the sufferings of millions" (*WL* 455), are only shortened in the Polish version, yet their message is played down by the translation of "an invert" as "a pervert." Thus, Hall's novel survived another censorship and entered Polish culture. Yet, the values of *The Well* could have been lost, if not for its contemporary preservers, Woolf and Krzywicka, who embodied them in their own—to use Marcus's term—echo texts.

While *Źródło* was forgotten by critics and writers, the delayed reception of Virginia Woolf in Poland may have resulted in the rediscovery of Hall's novel by Polish readers. When in 1997 *A Room of One's Own* was finally brought into Polish by Agnieszka Graff, followed in 2002 by a composite edition of *A Room of One's Own* and *Three Guineas* translated by Ewa Krasińska, Woolf became an icon for Polish feminist thinkers and activists. Ewa Kraskowska claims that they "made Virginia Woolf a canonical author in Poland. Moreover, the phrase of the essay's title as well as such expressions as 'Shakespeare's sister', 'a woman's sentence' or 'an androgynous mind' have become firmly established in contemporary Polish feminist discourse.... [Woolf] was recognized as one of the first politically engaged feminist women writers" (2). Interestingly, in the Polish translations of *A Room of One's Own* (1997, 2002), while both translators Agnieszka Graff and Ewa Krasińska, as well as Izabela Morska in the preface, retell the story of *The Well*, they use its original title—unaware (at that time) that the novel was translated into Polish.

A few years later, Krzywicka's intellectual prose has been rediscovered by feminist and LGBTQ scholars. In 2008 Agata Zawiszewska published *Kontrola Współczesności* [The Control of the Present], a volume of Krzywicka's selected essays and publicity, including her preface to *Źródło*. The role of Krzywicka, both as the Polish "custodian" of Hall's novel and the author of the first emancipatory texts, has been briefly acknowledged by Krzysztof Tomasik (16). Yet, there is to date almost no scholarship on the publication of *Źródło* in Poland. Therefore, it seems that while *Źródło* became forgotten after the Second World War, Hall's novel has lived primarily in Krzywicka's echo text, and later also in the Polish translation of Woolf's *A Room of One's Own*.

II

Having presented the publishing history of *Źródło*, I would like now to look at the reception of Hall's novel in Britain and Poland from a unique perspective offered by two public intellectuals: Virginia Woolf and Irena Krzywicka. In the comparison of Woolf's *A Room of One's Own* with Krzywicka's preface to *Źródło*,

I explore their discussion of Hall's novel and its trial, as well as their textual strategies used to structure their own writing on "inversion" around the themes of censorship and social norms. Finally, as there is a substantial amount of research on press reaction to *The Well* and *A Room of One's Own*, I will discuss only the responses of the Polish press.

The legislative contexts in which Woolf and Krzywicka defended the novel could not have been more different. While attending the exhibition "Queer British Art 1861-1967" at Tate Britain (5 April-1 October, 2017), I could stand right in front of the door to Oscar Wilde's cell in Reading prison, and I thought about the writers like Woolf or Hall who needed to "face" that door and find their own strategy of survival. In the United Kingdom, (male) homosexuality was severely penalized and remained illegal until 1967 (Moran *passim*), while in independent Poland it has never been mentioned in the Criminal Code. Though the censorship in both countries was repressive, it seems that its chilling effect was more profound for British intellectuals.

Consequently, in Britain, self-censorship was a matter of survival—allowing the writer only allusions, which could turn into echoes if their readers joined the conspiracy. In *Virginia Woolf and the Languages of Patriarchy*, Marcus presents a captivating interpretation of *A Room of One's Own* as "an echo chamber, in which Echo, the woman artist, who transgressed both sexually and verbally in the myth… may speak in her own words" (164), and creates the term "Sapphistry" to denominate Woolf's subversive narration.

The chilling effect casts a shadow over Woolf's brilliant essay, which is one of the first attempts at analyzing the social and material circumstances of women's creative activity. As Hermione Lee notes, "while she committed herself publicly to the protest against censorship which the Radclyffe Hall case aroused…she carried out a telling piece of self-censorship in those cancelled pages of *A Room of One's Own*" (519). Lee refers to Woolf's draft note on a passage that begins with "Chloe liked Olivia. They shared a…" thus quoted in Marcus's analysis:

> The words covered the bottom of the page: the pages had stuck. While fumbling to open them there flashed into my mind the inevitable policeman… the order to attend the Court; the dreary waiting: the Magistrate coming in with a little bow… for the Prosecution; for the Defense—the verdict; this book is called obscene + flames sing, perhaps on Tower Hill, as they compound (?) that mass of paper. Here the paper came apart. Heaven be praised! It was only a laboratory. (*Languages* 186)

Woolf's ominous vision of her own persecution reveals how difficult it is for the modern author, say "Mary Carmichael," to tell this story. Consequently, the fragmented scene "Chloe liked Olivia" is revived several times—first in the "flirtatious passage" (Marcus *Languages*, 169), which subtly alludes to lesbian attraction:

> I turned the page and read...I am sorry to break off so abruptly. Are there no men present? Do you promise me that behind that red curtain over there the figure of Sir Charles Biron is not concealed? We are all women you assure me? Then I may tell you that the very next words I read were these—"Chloe liked Olivia..." Do not start. Do not blush. Let us admit in the privacy of our own society that these things sometimes happen. Sometimes women do like women. (*AROO* 70)

In the final part of her essay, Woolf, playing on the word "like" used in the story of Chloe and Olivia, comes back to the lesbianism: "The truth is, I often like women. I like their unconventionality. I like their completeness. I like their anonymity. I like—but I must not run on in this way. That cupboard there—you say it holds clean table-napkins only; but what if Sir Archibald Bodkin were concealed among them?" (*AROO* 96). The allusion to Hall's trial must have been clear to her audience, as the Director of Public Prosecutions Bodkin (together with the Home Secretary William Joynson-Hicks) "successfully" opposed the novel.

If, as Marcus says, *A Room of One's Own* "sings sisterhood in homoerotic tones, slyly seducing the woman reader and taunting patriarchal law just this side of obscenity" (*Languages* 163), then it is important to notice that all allusions to lesbianism are accompanied by the ubiquitous censors. While Hall's name does not appear in Woolf's essay, all the patriarchal figures involved in the trial are identified and ridiculed: Biron eavesdrops behind the red curtains, Hicks is summoned to give evidence on the apparently non-platonic relationship of writers, and finally, Bodkin hides in the cupboard. As Leslie Kathleen Hankins underlines, "Woolf's lesbian signatures, messages, and strategies were shaped by the brooding presence of the censor, for no lesbian writer in 1928 was immune from the perils of censorship" (182-83).

In Woolf's essay, there is no "inversion," yet there are passages on canonical writers, like William Shakespeare, whose androgynous mind allows for gender and sexual transgressions in his art. As Marcus has shown, Woolf's subversive textual strategies of "Sapphistry"—ellipses, pauses, broken sequences, a whole discourse of interruption— successfully creates the women's community, a precursor to her Outsiders' Society. Importantly, this conspiracy empowers her readers to write the blank pages of *Orlando* with their own experience and enables the rebirth of *The Well* in new literary shapes.

Writing in a very different cultural and legal context, Irena Krzywicka was more explicit in her preface to *Źródło*. Zawiszewska in her monograph on Krzywicka's "modern intellectual prose" characterizes her idiosyncratic style of reviewing.

While in the early reviews the writer discussed the literary works from a perspective similar to Woolf's "common reader," in the 1930s, she adopted "the role of popularizer and advocate" and used free indirect speech to render the meaning and poetics of reviewed texts (Zawiszewska 155), thus creating her own echoes.

In the preface to *Źródło*, she introduces Hall as an author of a "notoriously and provocatively lesbian novel" (*ZS* vi), yet asserts that it is not pornographic, but on the contrary, "full of love poetry" (*ZS* vi) and "profoundly reverential about religion" (*ZS* x). However, she treats Hall's literary talent with reserve: "Radclyffe Hall is not a great writer. Yet, she is courageous and conscientious, loyal and honest" (*ZS* ix).

It is interesting that for Krzywicka inversion emerges as an amalgam of identities, close to Halberstam's "tangle of cross-gender identification and sexual preference." On the one hand, she describes Stephen as "a type of modern girl," "a new woman," "with little breasts and the good brains" (*ZS* vi), on the other hand, she calls the protagonist "a boy, an unhappy boy" (*ZS* vii). Furthermore, from the very first words, Krzywicka restores the word "inversion," completely lost in the Polish translation:

> Sexual inversion? I do not want to translate this word as "perversion." Perversion suggests pathology. Yet, it is rather a shift, a reversal of instinct. This reversed instinct could be completely normal at its core. Nobody will call a left-handed a pervert. Therefore, in accordance with the rules of contemporary knowledge, it is high time people stopped to consider these…sexual "lefties" to be degenerates, and understood how many fine full people are among them. (*ZS* v)

In her preface, Krzywicka uses several strategies to oppose the prejudices faced by LGBTQ people. She refers to the scientific authorities ("contemporary knowledge"), juxtaposes "inversion" with more familiar left-handedness ("sexual lefties"). Moreover, she questions the social norms, when she underlines that the ideal woman of the 1930s would have been considered "a freak and born spinster" (*ZS* vi) in the past. Krzywicka challenges also the conventional notions about lesbian/transgender women: "good writers are few, yet lesbians are numerous" (*ZS* vii), "this two women couple is a common marriage" (*ZS* ix) and speaks up for common "inverts": "What could a woman do, if she resembles Stephen, but could not tell the people to their face a well-known name?" (*ZS* vii).

It is also worth noting that rhetorically Krzywicka starts with the mistranslation of the word "inversion" as "perversion," then experiments with neologisms such as "sexual lefties" and "majoritians" ("większościowcy"), and towards the end of her text repeats the words "normal," "human being(s)," and "love." She concludes the preface calling for the change of attitudes towards "people like Stephen" (*ZS* xi), and in a moving manifesto opposes the censorship of the novel:

> Love, true love, is the most demanding test of morality on the heart. Where there is no love, there are boredom, abomination, and dissolution, yet where there is love all becomes pure and bright. This novel, confiscated in England as "immoral" in the common meaning of this word, propagates the sanctity of feeling and all noble impulses of the human heart. (*ZS* xi)

The implications of Krzywicka's preface for LGBTQ culture in Poland are enormous. When in May 1933 the text was published as a feature in "Wiadomości Literackie," both Hall's novel and lesbianism literally made the headlines.

The feature provoked a debate within the "Wiadomości Literackie" and some brutal attacks from the conservative press. A case in point is the article by Adolf Nowaczyński, a radical right-wing journalist and writer, entitled "Safona z Y.P.S.U.," which appeared in "Myśl Narodowa" [National Thought] in June 1933. He used the polemics to promote anti-Semitic and homophobic views; thus he attacked the echo of Hall's religious views and Krzywicka's Jewish identity:

> Not for this purpose, in hospitable and tolerant Poland hundreds and thousands of Goldbergs [Krzywicka's maiden name] were rescued from the foul smelling abyss of Ghetto, taught not to use the Yiddish jargon, taught to use the Polish language,…so that colleague Krzywicka might write in Polish similar *cochonneries* and…her godless, trivial and anti-Catholic shmontzes. (Nowaczyński 399)

Two months later, "Wiadomości Literackie" published the review of *Źródło*, written by Wanda Melcer, a writer and journalist. Her reaction to Hall's novel reminds us of that of Leonard Woolf's mother[10]: she was moved by the story of Stephen's horse and awkwardly admired Krzywicka's skill in writing about "these matters." Yet, homosexuality is for Melcer perversion, and she mentions in her text "the hospitals for homosexuals…so stuffy that it is difficult even for nurses" (3). In September 1933, Bolesław Dudziński, a literary critic and activist, formulated the most positive response to the novel, published in the papers of the Polish Socialist Party, Cracow "Naprzód" [Forward] and Lviv "Dziennik Ludowy" [People's Daily]:

---

[10] Cf. In a letter to Vanessa Bell, Woolf parodied Marie Woolf's long monologue on *The Well*: "I am seventy-six—but until I read this book I did not know that such things went on at all. I do not think they do. I have never heard of such things…But I think much of Miss Radclyffe Hall's book is very beautiful. There is the old horse—that is wonderful—when she has to shoot the old horse…All that about the old horse and the old groom is very beautiful. But the rest of the book I did not care for" (*L* 525-26).

> Describing courageously and with gravity, the matters, which are not trifles, yet are usually kept under the hat, Miss Hull [sic!] with fiery faith and almost religious (Yes!) passion defends the right to existence and happiness of creatures similar to Stephen. She understands well their personal tragedies and is aware that "the intellect and courage often go together" with what the majority see as "physical perversion". (4)

The role of Dudziński's review cannot be overestimated, since the socialist press was read by the intelligentsia and social leaders, who may have educated the working class communities and fostered tolerance.

III

"Every burned book or house enlightens the world; every suppressed or expunged word reverberates through the earth from side to side," says Ralph Waldo Emerson in his essay "Compensation" (299). This dream of global solidarity has come true for Hall's *The Well of Loneliness,* one of "these rare instances of survival" cherished by Woolf in *A Room of One's Own*. Woolf repeatedly stressed in her diary and correspondence that while the act of writing was vital for her existence as an individual, readers were essential for her survival as an artist (Snaith 42).

In the context of the dramatic trajectory of Hall's, Woolf's, and Krzywicka's[11] lives, the concept of surviving in writing overlaps with existential survival. These three women writers have embodied Woolf's ideal, described by Jane de Gay as "the custodians of literary culture," who manifest their "power to foster survival and renewal" (93). Modernism cherished this unique ability, enhancing the networks of solidarity and hospitality. As numerous scholars, inspired by Marcus's groundbreaking research in all four corners of the world, assure us, these are also key values in academia.[12] In one of her last published works, the critic warns us that "the whole weight of the war culture is working against us. So the bonds of scholars working together as 'communal modernists' studying 'communal modernisms' are fragile and we must work to keep them alive" (Marcus "Afterword," 179).

A possibility for strengthening these bonds is a "trans critical optic," recently proposed by Jessica Berman during a Comparative Modernisms Seminar held at the University of London in June 2017. Thus, the perspective adopted in this article and inspired by Marcus's transgressive insights, "serves to decenter the 'national tradition' as an object of inquiry, exploring texts in relation to other, comparative

---

[11] During the Second World War Krzywicka witnessed the deaths of her son Piotr, Boy-Żeleński executed by the Nazis, and her husband Jerzy Krzywicki, murdered by the Soviets (Krzywicka *passim*).

[12] Cf. among others the tributes to Jane Marcus published in *Virginia Woolf Miscellany* (Spring/Summer 2015).

and transnational horizons of expectations" (Berman "Trans Reading"). In Poland, transnational works such as *The Well* and *A Room of One's Own* remind us that while the Solidarity movement has brought us freedom, the Polish word "gościnność" (hospitality), or rather as Paweł Leszkowicz and Tomek Kitliński propose "gość-inność" (hospit-alterity), still asks us to embrace otherness (279).

Works Cited

Berman, Jessica S. *Modernist Commitments: Ethics, Politics, and Transnational Modernism*. Columbia UP, 2012.

———."Trans Reading and Comparative Modernism." Comparative Modernisms Seminar. 26 June 2017. Abstract. Web. 7 September 2017.

Beylin, Marek. Personal interview. 28 May 2017.

De Gay, Jane. *Virginia Woolf's Novels and the Literary Past*. Edinburgh UP, 2007.

Detloff, Madelyn. "Gender Please, Without the Gender Police: Rethinking Pain in Archetypal Narratives of Butch, Transgender, and FtM Masculinity." *Journal of Lesbian Studies*, vol. 10, no. 1-2, 2006, pp. 87-105.

Doan, Laura L, and Jay Prosser. *Palatable Poison: Critical Perspectives on the Well of Loneliness*. Columbia UP, 2002.

Dudziński, Bolesław. "Z nowych książek." *Naprzód* XLII.204 (1933): 4.

Emerson, Ralph W. *Essays and Lectures*. The Library of America, 1984.

English, Elizabeth. *Lesbian Modernism: Censorship, Sexuality and Genre Fiction*. Edinburgh UP, 2017.

Gisges-Zwierzchowska, Ewa. *Rój 1924-1945: próba monografii*. Oficyna Pod Wiatr, 2015.

Gomulicki, Juliusz Wiktor. *Aleje czarów*. DiG, 2000.

Halberstam, Jack. "Transgender Butch: Butch/FtM Border Wars and the Masculine Continuum." *GLQ: a Journal of Lesbian and Gay Studies*, vol. 4, no. 2, 1998, pp. 287-310.Dół formularza

Hall, Radclyffe, and Havelock Ellis. *The Well of Loneliness*. Pegasus Press, 1929.

Hall, Radclyffe, and Irena Krzywicka. *Źródło samotności*. Towarzystwo Wydawnicze Rój, 1933.

Hankins, Leslie Kathleen. "Orlando: 'A Precipice Marked V' Between 'A Miracle of Discretion' and 'Lovemaking Unbelievable: Indiscretions Incredible'." *Virginia Woolf: Lesbian Readings*, edited by Eileen Barrett, and Patricia Cramer. New York UP, 1997, pp. 180-202.

Kister, Hanna. *Pegazy na Kredytowej. Wspomnienia*. PIW, 1980.

Kitliński, Tomek, and Paweł Leszkowicz. "Miłość odmieńcow, myśl, gość-inność i inne uczucia. Afektywność fotografii Roberta Mapplethorpea i Nan Goldin?" *Teksty Drugie,* vol. 1-2, 2007, pp. 272-83.

Kraskowska, Ewa. "On the Circulation of Feminist Discourse via Translation (V. Woolf, S. de Beauvoir, J. Butler)." *Ruch Literacki,* vol. 1, 2010, pp. 1-14.
Krzywicka, Irena, and Agata Tuszyńska. *Wyznania Gorszycielki.* SW Czytelnik, 1995.
Lee, Hermione. *Virginia Woolf.* Vintage, 1997.
"LGBT History Month" *National Archives* 28 Feb. 2011. Web. 31 May 2017.
Listy Roy Publisher w Nowym Yorku do Aleksandra Janty i inne materiały. Special Collections Rps BN 12961 IV, cards 43-44, recto, verso. National Library of Poland, Warsaw.
Marcus, Jane. "Middlebrow Feminism." *Tulsa Studies in Women's Literature,* vol. 27, no. 1, 2008, pp. 159-65.
———. "Afterword: Some Notes on Radical Teaching". *Communal Modernisms,* edited by Emily M. Hinnov, Laurel Harris, and Lauren M. Rosenblum. Palgrave Macmillan, 2013, pp. 189-98.
———. "Storming the Toolshed." *Signs,* vol. 7, no. 3, 1982, pp. 622-40.
———. "To the Women's Review of Books (letter)." *The Women's Review of Books,* vol. 11, no. 3, 1984, pp. 18-19.
———. *Virginia Woolf and the Languages of Patriarchy.* Indiana UP, 1987.
Marshik, Celia. "History's 'Abrupt Revenges': Censoring War's Perversions in *The Well of Loneliness* and *Sleeveless Errand.*" *Journal of Modern Literature,* vol. 26, no. 2, 2003, pp. 145-59. Początek formularza
Melcer, Wanda. "Dwie powieści kobiece." *Wiadomości Literackie,* vol. 36, no. 507, 1933, p. 3.
Moran, Leslie J. *The Homosexual(ity) of Law.* Routledge, 1996.Dół formularza
Nowaczyński, Adolf. "Safona z Y.P.S.U." *Myśl Narodowa,* vol. XIII, no. 27, 1933, p. 399.
Nycz, Ryszard. "Literatura polska w cieniu cenzury: wykład." *Teksty Drugie,* vol. 3, 1998, pp. 5-27.
Okopień, Jan. "Towarzystwo Wydawnicze "Rój"." *Poczet wydawców książki polskiej: Książka Wyzwolona 1918-1950,* edited by Jan Okopień, and Joanna Czarkowska. Inicjał, 2015. 176-89.
Olczak-Ronikier, Joanna. *In the Garden of Memory: A Memoir.* Transl. Antonia Lloyd-Jones. London: Phoenix, 2005.
Pytlak, Magdalena. "Polish Women Translators outside the Canon. On a Forgotten Translation of Dostoyevsky's *The Devils.*" *Przekładaniec,* vol. 24, 2010, pp. 163-78.
The "Rój". Advertisement. *Wiadomości Literackie,* vol. 29, no. 500, 1933, p. 6.
"Rój" 1930-1938. Special Collections BN 2.607.508. National Library of Poland, Warsaw.

Rytlowa, Jadwiga. "Rodzina Wołków." *Polish Righteous/Polscy Sprawiedliwi* Jan. 2011. Web. 15 July 2017.

Snaith, Anna. *Virginia Woolf: Public and Private Negotiations.* Palgrave, 2000.

Śmieja, Wojciech. "Boy i homoseksualizm. Literatura, prawo i ten przerażający homoerota we własnej osobie." *Teksty Drugie,* vol. 5, 2008, pp. 64-74.

———. "'Topografia pożądania' - konstruowanie przestrzeni wokół homoseksualnych bohaterów polskiej prozy międzywojennej (Iwaszkiewicz, Choromański, Gombrowicz, Breza)." *Pamiętnik Literacki,* vol. 103.4, 2012, pp. 83-99.

Tarczałowicz, Jacek. *Lucjan Szenwald: życie i twórczość.* PIW, 1977.

Tomasik, Krzysztof. *Homobiografie.* Wydawnictwo Krytyki Politycznej, 2014.

Wańkowicz, Melchior. "Wspomnienia wydawcy." *Za i Przeciw,* vol. 45, 1968, p. 16.

———. *Tędy i owędy.* Iskry, 1961.

Wielgoławska, Alicja. *Dziennikarze. Byli wśród nas. Są z nami.* Akson, 2014.

Woolf, Virginia. *A Room of One's Own and Three Guineas.* Vintage, 2001.

———. *The Letters of Virginia Woolf, Vol 3,* edited by Nigel Nicolson, and Joanne Trautmann. Harcourt Brace Jovanovich, 1978.

Zawada, Andrzej. *Dwudziestolecie literackie.* Wydawnictwo Dolnośląskie, 1995.

Zawiszewska, Agata. *Życie świadome.* Wydawnictwo Naukowe Uniwersytetu Szczecińskiego, 2010.

Ziółkowska-Boehm, Aleksandra. *Na tropach Wańkowicza po latach.* Prószyński Media, 2009.

After Anger: Negative Affect and Feminist Politics in Virginia Woolf's *Three Guineas*

Margot Kotler

Jane Marcus ends her 1978 essay, "Art and Anger: Elizabeth Robins and Virginia Woolf" by exhorting women writers and critics to "spit out" their "rage and savage indignation" in order to guarantee the future for feminism (153). The idea that the expression of an emotion is a strategy of resistance to patriarchy informs the subject of her essay, which concerns the techniques that Virginia Woolf and Elizabeth Robins used to conceal and eventually reveal their anger, but it also constitutes a methodology for Marcus's feminist intervention. Marcus uses the example of these women writers' anger, expressed late in life—"Why wait until old age, as they did, waiting long to let out their full quota of anger?"—as a warning for and inspiration to women (153). There is an ethical imperative behind Marcus's demand, one that will secure the future for the next generation: "When the fires of our rage have burnt out, think how clear the air will be for our daughters. They will write in joy and freedom only after we have written in anger" (154). Contemporary readers who are removed from Marcus's fiery demand by several decades might be skeptical of the idea that emotional expression leads to freedom. Marcus was aware that her call to action sounded polemical—but that was her intention. Her language, mode of address, and faith in the power of emotion exemplify strategies of feminists of her generation, who asserted the validity of personal feelings, and anger in particular, as an effective political strategy and as a response to a male-dominated critical establishment. Marcus explains, ten years later, in the introduction to *Art and Anger: Reading Like a Woman*, that her earlier essays on Woolf were meant as "opposition and objection to the official view of [Woolf's] work" at the time and "grew out of [her] own anger and the anger of [her] generation of feminist critics, who were trying to change the subject without yet having developed a sophisticated methodology" (xv, xxi). Marcus thus justifies the necessity of her project while anticipating a question that future generations of feminist scholars would face: What comes *after* anger? After "the fires of our rage have burnt out"? While Marcus hoped that the "daughters of anger" would not have any use for it and would "write in joy and freedom," anger continues to be an important source of feminist politics, especially considering the role of anger and other emotions in fueling feminist activism after the 2016 presidential election. However, Marcus's question remains helpful in thinking about how a more "sophisticated methodology" of anger might be developed, one that makes anger a more sustainable source of feminism that does not burn out. Indeed, Marcus recognized the eventual obsolescence of anger in a narrative where feminist affect moves teleologically toward joy and happiness. When anger is immediate and personal, and must be "spit out" and purged in order to be useful, one only has a certain "quota" of emotion to unleash on the world.

This article follows Marcus in asserting that anger and other negative feelings continue to have political currency, while complicating her claims by questioning the idea that feminist emotions are authentic only when they emerge from personal experience. The problem of women's personal anger—how and when, if ever, to express it and in what context—has been a major concern of Woolf scholars and of feminist critics more generally. The expression of the personal, whether it implies the exposure of autobiographical information, emotion, or personality, is a historically fraught issue for women writers who have felt and continue to feel pressure to adhere to masculine standards of intellectual objectivity in order to avoid accusations of writing from a subjective, gendered place. Beginning in the 1970s, feminist scholars such as Elaine Showalter, Sandra Gilbert and Susan Gubar, and Kate Millett demonstrated that gender and the personal are serious categories of literary analysis, while others later applied this idea to critical writing, with Nancy K. Miller arguing that "autobiographical performance" within personal criticism is not just political, but also inherently theoretical (1). Jane Marcus, Brenda Silver, and others pioneered the exploration of Woolf's work in relation to these questions, establishing the narrative of Woolf's anger as suppressed early in her career and in *A Room of One's Own* until it was unleashed in the form of "an angry old woman" or a "guerilla fighter in a Victorian skirt" in *Three Guineas* (*Art and Anger* 123, 73). This narrative establishes what I believe to be a specious relationship between personal, feminist politics, and the expression of emotion in Woolf's nonfiction, one which implicitly suggests that her early "impersonal" writing is an avoidance of gendered subjectivity, or one which insists that Woolf's instances of anger in *Three Guineas* are personal. Here, formulating impersonality as an affective and political stance that strategically embraces "weak" emotional states and avoids autobiography, I propose an alternative reading, locating impersonal anger and other negative emotions as essential to Woolf's feminist project in *Three Guineas*. Indeed, despite feminist scholars' efforts to destigmatize the personal, the notion of impersonality continues to carry gendered associations and this affects many critical readings of Woolf. When the term is applied to a woman, it often suggests that she is insufficiently warm or emotional, and that she is avoiding autobiography and the performance of "personality" often required of women. In short, it is a way of accusing a woman, sometimes even in feminist discourse, of failing to use an appropriately gendered affective register—a failing from which feminist critics have tried to "save" Woolf, even as they implicitly accuse her of it.

In contrast to the idea that Woolf's anger represented a "submerged truth" or was (intentionally or not) concealed, I will argue that in *Three Guineas* she conveys anger impersonally in a challenge to conventional gendered understandings of the relationship between politics and affect. My understanding of feminist emotions and impersonality as compatible builds upon recent work in affect theory that attends to the politics of minor and negative affects. Sianne Ngai's *Ugly Feelings* follows Martha Nussbaum and Brian Massumi in defining emotion as intentional (expressed by a subject toward an object) and defining affect as "less object- or goal-oriented," "intentionally weak," and as associated with a less specific, global perspective (26). Ngai refuses to lean on this theoretical distinction, however, understanding emotion and affect as existing on a continuum of degree, which makes possible an analysis of "weaker," less passionate emotions— such as envy, irritation, and anxiety—that have more in common with affect than with "grander passions like anger and fear" and "morally beatific states like sympathy" (6). I am interested in Woolf's engagement with negative emotions, that is feelings, unlike desire or fear, that involve a turning away from an object, or, in Ngai's terms, those that are "organized by trajectories of repulsion rather than philic strivings 'toward'" (11).

The idea of impersonal anger might seem to defy the logic of an affective continuum of degree, as it suggests that it is possible to approach a traditionally passionate emotion, one that involves an attachment to an object of anger, with an impartial stance. However, in contending that anger can work impersonally, I am aligning anger with those less passionate emotions that Ngai associates with affect. Following Sara Ahmed's theorization of feminist unhappiness in *The Promise of Happiness*, I suggest that it might be possible to formulate a feminist political response that begins with affective disengagement from objects understood in the dominant culture as "good," such as patriotism and nationalism. To contextualize my approach to impersonal anger, I turn to feminist theories of anger that use a cognitivist approach to emotions and to Woolf's impersonal method, through which she avoids personal narrative, speaks for the collective of the "daughters of educated men" and the Society of Outsiders, and explicitly demonstrates her narrator's imperviousness to emotional appeal. Focusing on "weaker," negative feelings is not meant as an avoidance or invalidation of Woolf's anger, but as an attempt to shift the focus from discovering its sources to paying close attention to the way that she uses language to convey affect as part of a feminist methodology. In the second and third parts of the essay, I turn from anger to other negative feelings in *Three Guineas* that have received less critical attention, such as indifference and lack of sympathy. I read the negative emotional stance of the Society of Outsiders alongside Sara Ahmed's concept of the "feminist killjoy" and argue that Woolf's juxtaposition of images and text allows her to reveal the limitations of sympathy in forming a political response to injustice. This essay ultimately suggests that Woolf provides a model for a collective feminist politics that complicates the teleological narrative of feminism in which emotion operates as a site of truth.

Impersonality, Anger, and Feminist Methodology

Feminist reassessments of anger and other emotions during the 1970s sought to assert their value as tools of the oppressed. The understanding of emotions that supported this trend involved a particular understanding of how emotions operate. Sara Ahmed explains that this debate has historically been split between those who believe that emotions are tied to bodily sensations, involving an "immediacy [which] suggests that emotions do not involve processes of thought, attribution or evaluation," and a cognitivist approach, which understands that emotions "involve appraisals, judgments, attitudes or a 'specific manner of apprehending the world'" ("Introduction" 5). While the bodily view of emotions understands them as producing automatic reactions, such as an instinctual flight from a situation caused by fear, the cognitivist view recognizes emotions as having intentional objects. The relationship between these two views is more complex than it is possible to illustrate here, but my purpose is to show that the cognitivist approach to emotions has allowed feminists to challenge the notion that the emotions of women and other oppressed groups are "out of control," instead representing them as rational, less immediate, responses to injustice. Naomi Scheman's "Anger and the Politics of Naming" argues that the discovery and naming of emotions transforms them into political acts, as the recognition "that some state of affairs counts as oppression or exploitation" involves attributing anger to external circumstances, rather than mere personal dissatisfaction, and therefore calls attention to the need to address collective forms of injustice faced by all women (181). Elizabeth V. Spelman historicizes oppressed groups' access to discourses of anger and, like Scheman, affirms anger's potentially subversive power. Spelman traces the idea that anger is an appropriate response to injustice, rather than an irrational emotion, back to Aristotle's *Nicomachean Ethics*, but explains that anger has only been associated with justice and reason when it is expressed by politically and culturally dominant groups (264). Dominant groups use emotion to maintain unequal power relations by associating women and other oppressed groups with unruly emotional expression and the body, which maintains their own association with reason and the mind. Drawing a distinction between anger and other emotions, Spelman writes that though oppressed groups are "expected to be emotional...the possibility of their being angry will be excluded by the dominant group's profile of them" (264). She suggests that in keeping anger for themselves, dominant groups demonstrate their understanding of anger's difference from other "irrational" emotions and the potential danger it poses to them in the hands of the oppressed. Adhering to a cognitivist approach that involves recognizing the role of judgments and beliefs in shaping emotions, Spelman asserts that "being angry involves judging that some wrong or injustice has been done," which contrasts with the idea that emotions are mere "dumb events" (265). This view of emotions understands the anger of oppressed groups as a "negative evaluative judgment" about a person or situation, transforming it into an "act of insubordination" (266). Spelman cites Peter Lyman's "The Politics of Anger" in asserting that "anger is the 'essential political emotion,' and to silence anger may be to repress political speech" (272).

Feminist theories of anger, then, claimed the power of anger as a political tool by reevaluating its epistemological status. When anger is informed by a judgment, it also has an object, and can therefore address personal experiences of injustice that affect collective groups. As Brenda Silver explains, this shift in understanding anger changed the conversation about *Three Guineas*, transforming earlier critics' charges of Woolf's "'resentment,' 'grievance,' and 'complaint' into collective public concepts associated with social and political change" (361). Silver notes that this change occurred in the late 1970s, with the publication of several critical essays "that explore the increasing recognition of Woolf's political vision" in 1978 alone (361). Marcus's call for feminist anger in "Art and Anger" is part of the wave of criticism that developed out of feminist reassessments of the political value of anger, asserting the subversive potential of women's collective expression of emotion, while also suggesting that this expression of emotion is validated by its personal source. Indeed, Marcus's deployment of Woolf's anger as an example for—and warning to—younger women contains two claims that are common in one of the predominant second-wave feminist approaches to understanding anger. The first is the implication that women's anger is repressed and in need of expression and the second is the related notion that anger almost always has a deeply personal and gendered source. The repetition of these ideas occurs on multiple levels of feminist discourse: while one of the primary concerns of feminist literary criticism has been the project of reclaiming and uncovering women's writing of the past in an effort to establish a canon, a similar process of unearthing and reclaiming occurred at the level of the unconscious, as women uncovered and expressed their feelings of anger, unhappiness, and resentment. An essential aspect, then, of the feminist project has been conceptualized in psychoanalytic terms, as women's "truth" has been understood as hidden deep in archives and minds conditioned by patriarchy.

The idea that women's expression of the repressed truths of their personal experience, through emotions such as anger, would not only allow them to claim power and authority, but could also be a source of creative and political energy, is an essential contribution of feminist theory and activism. However, these ideas, despite Woolf's investment in describing the sources of women's oppression and her interest in depicting women's interiority, do not align with her beliefs about the expression of the author's personality and emotions. Woolf maintained that the personal is inappropriate to both the essay and fiction in several of her essays, beginning with "The Decay of Essay Writing" in 1905, which accuses contemporary essayists of using their writing as a vehicle for the unnecessary display of personality, writing that the essay, "owes its popularity to the fact that its proper use is to express one's personal peculiarities so that under the decent veil of print one can indulge one's egoism to the full" (4). In "The Modern Essay" Woolf similarly argues that personality is the essayist's "most dangerous and delicate tool" and that when it is misused, "[w]e are nauseated by the sight of trivial personalities decomposing in the eternity of print" (217). Woolf expressed related ideas about personality in literature, praising Greek literature as the "impersonal literature" because it is free from authors' personal association, which has "preserved them from vulgarity" ("On Not Knowing Greek" 23). Woolf most explicitly demonstrates her stance on the relationship between personality, gender, and the emotions in *A Room of One's Own*, where she criticizes literature that is tainted by personality or emotion. The narrator explicitly warns women against writing "in rage" or of themselves through the example of Charlotte Brontë's distraction by "some personal grievance" (AROO 68, 72). Critical evaluations of Woolf's impersonality often focus on this aspect of *A Room*, with Elaine Showalter describing Woolf's impersonality and her argument for androgyny as an avoidance of gendered subjectivity and the body (263-64). However, Woolf's impersonality has also been considered in relation to modernist impersonality, which is usually associated with formalism and the authoritative aesthetics of T.S. Eliot and other male modernists. Rochelle Rives' and Christina Walter's recent work attempts to complicate the story of modernist impersonality by showing how the impersonal might also serve as the site for a radical critique of subjectivity.[1] Lisa Low challenges the idea that Woolf's impersonal style indicates her avoidance of gendered subjectivity by arguing that she used it "not for its authoritarian potential, as Eliot might, but because it is empathetic and democratic" (259).

Critical evaluations of Woolf's anger are in tension with her actual use of impersonality. The application of feminist theories of anger to *Three Guineas* was widespread in second-wave criticism, even though there is danger in suggesting that Virginia Woolf, a notoriously impersonal writer, sought to make her previously repressed personal anger public. In her essay, "Feminist Killjoys (And Other Willful Subjects)," Sara Ahmed maintains that a "feminist call might be a call to anger, to develop a sense of rage about collective wrong," but warns against making "feminist emotion into a site of truth," as assuming the universality and authority of personal emotions often undermines attempts at collectivity.[2] Marcus argues that

---

[1] See Rochelle Rives' *Modernist Impersonalities: Affect, Authority, and the Subject*, Palgrave Macmillan, 2012, and Christina Walter's *Optical Impersonality: Science, Images, and Literary Modernism*, Johns Hopkins UP, 2014, for alternative accounts of modernist impersonality.
[2] Ahmed cites Audre Lorde's and bell hooks's accounts of exclusion from white feminist spaces based on their alienation from ostensibly collective emotional experiences, as explored in *Sister Outsider: Essays and Speeches*, Berkeley: Crossing Press, 2007, and *Feminist Theory: From Margin to Center*, Cambridge: South End Press, 1984.

Woolf "first learned to say 'we' as a woman…thinking back through her mothers gave her her first collective identity and strengthened her creative ability. Her whole career was an exercise in the elimination of ego from fiction in author, characters, and readers" (83-84). Despite this, Marcus and other second-wave feminist critics, a generation that solidified Woolf's iconic status as a feminist and a canonical woman writer, have tended to represent Woolf's anger as a repressed source of personal truth. Indeed, accusations that Woolf was too angry or not angry enough continue to proliferate, revealing the extent to which the appropriate expression and use of anger continues to anger feminists. Although she is writing about *A Room*, Adrienne Rich finds Woolf's anger inadequate: "It is the tone of a woman almost in touch with her anger, who is determined not to appear angry, who is *willing* herself to be calm, detached, and even charming in a roomful of men…" (37). Rich assumes that Woolf censored herself by using an "objective" tone, as opposed to an emotional or angry one, to sound less threatening to men, implying that Woolf would have been more candid, more personal if she had not been repressed. Brenda Silver, however, argues that for Woolf, anger was a source of her text's authority, and the act of recognizing and writing about her tone in literary criticism is a political one. At the same time, Silver implies that the source of anger's authority is its previous repression, both by Woolf herself and by earlier male critics who failed to recognize it. Silver asks, "what voice would be 'natural,' what tone 'appropriate,' for a woman writing a feminist complaint or critique of her culture, a feminist polemic?" (358). Marcus compares Woolf's anger to Adrienne Rich's poem, "The Phenomenology of Anger," arguing that "the burning rage produces a kind of angry truth-telling, fulfilling, one feels, Woolf's demand that women *tell the truth*. That 'the truth' is synonymous with anger is testimony to its power and the rich history of its suppression" (152). Contemporary criticism continues to perpetuate similar ideas about Woolf's anger, with Kathleen Helal, for example, arguing that anger is Woolf's "submerged truth" (78). While these critics have been essential to the project of feminist efforts to assert the epistemological validity of the emotional and personal, the dominance of their ideas and their application to Virginia Woolf's anger might prevent critics from recognizing that anger and impersonality are not necessarily irreconcilable aspects of a feminist project. Indeed, the notion of impersonality as divestment of personality and a turning away from emotional immediacy pervades Woolf's oeuvre, and its manifestation in *Three Guineas* presents an opportunity to think of impersonality and other negative feelings, not as attempts at assuming a "neutral" masculine subjectivity, but as a potential source for feminist politics.

The Personal is Factual

Three Guineas has been considered primarily in relation to anger since its publication because it is Woolf's most explicitly feminist text, in which she argues that an essential aspect of pacifist politics involves the recognition that fascism and the gender relations associated with it emerge from fundamental structures of patriarchal society, namely, the family and public institutions. Written in the context of the Spanish Civil War and the rise of European fascism, Woolf begins her epistolary essay as a response to a gentleman's letter asking her, "How in your opinion are we to prevent war?"; however, before answering this letter or giving money to his cause, Woolf must first respond to a request from a woman's college and a society for professional women (5). The responses to these requests allow Woolf to articulate the idea that women must first achieve independence through emotional, material, and intellectual disengagement from British patriarchal institutions in order to consider the problem of war. Woolf speaks for the specific class of the "daughters of educated men" and a "Society of Outsiders" through the epistolary essay, a complication of public and private distinctions that allows her to simultaneously write in a traditionally personal and private genre while speaking for a collective group of women. Woolf bolsters the effect of her essay through her inclusion of photographs and evidence drawn from newspapers and journals; women's biographies, memoirs, and letters; and historical and academic texts. What Jessica Berman refers to as Woolf's "documentary impulse" is evident in her creation of scrapbooks of documentary materials clipped between 1932 and 1938 (63). Indeed, Jane Marcus suggests that Woolf's composite text and her "erudite set of notes and references" provide "a reading list for an alternative history" (*TG* lix). I argue that Woolf resists using the personal and the emotional as sources for intellectual authority, both in the methodology she employs to support the evidence for her feminist claims and the language she chooses to present that evidence. I demonstrate how Woolf inverts the gendered binaries of the personal and factual and of emotion and reason, allowing her to suggest that women's anger is factual, while men's anger is inseparable from their personal emotions. This allows for a differentiation between two forms of anger: anger that comes from personal injury, which can only respond with its own concerns, and anger about injustices affecting groups.

 Although Woolf's letters and diaries demonstrate that she felt incredible rage about women's lack of education and professional opportunities, she does not draw from these personal empirical sources, but channels her emotions into an argument that refuses to rely on her own lived experience. Instead, Woolf takes her facts from biography, a "largely untapped aid to the understanding of human motives," to the exclusion of her own lived experience: "There is thus no longer any reason to be confined to the minute span of actual experience which is still, for us, so narrow, so circumscribed. We can supplement it by looking at the picture of the lives of others" (*TG* 9). Woolf demonstrates that she regards biography as an important resource because it provides a variety of experiences from multiple real women's lives for use as evidence, which transforms the individual personal lives of women into collective facts, and allows biography to stand for authoritative history. In a letter to Ethel Smyth, Woolf describes her inability to include in *A Room* her personal experience of the injustice of not receiving an education, explaining that if she had said, "'Look here, I am uneducated because my brothers used all the family funds'—which is the fact—they'd have said, 'she has an axe to grind'" (*L5* 195). Even though this story and the anger behind it is a "fact," it will not be treated as one because it is "personal," so Woolf transforms it via biography from an angry-sounding anecdote to an impersonal fact in *Three Guineas* with the example of Mary Kingsley, whose only paid-for education is "being allowed to learn German" (6). Woolf explains that "Mary Kingsley is not speaking for herself alone; she is speaking, still, for many of the daughters of educated men...she is also pointing to a very important fact about them, a fact that must profoundly influence all that follows: the fact of Arthur's Education Fund" (*TG* 7). Indeed, throughout the text Woolf relies on the facts of biography, using phrases such as "biography provides us," "biography informs us," and "the evidence of biography" so often that the genre itself becomes imbued with the authority Woolf herself avoids (33, 95). Biography is the mediator that translates the personal into fact and the singular into the universal, allowing Woolf to transform the personal testimony of subjects of biography into evidence for an argument about a collective, capturing the anger-inducing injustice women experience.

Contrary to Woolf's treatment of women's experiences, which are transformed into a collection of facts, her descriptions of men's anger do the opposite, revealing that what appears to be motivated by reason and logic is often caused by petty emotions and personal fear, the type of emotion Elizabeth Spelman calls a "dumb event." Interestingly, the word "anger" appears in *Three Guineas* only in Woolf's discussion of men, and the word "emotion" is concentrated in the part of the third chapter that focuses on men's "infantile fixation."[3] Woolf applies a psychologist's description of men's "infantile fixations"—which "betray their presence, below the level of conscious thought, by the strength of the emotions to which they give rise"—to several "cases" of men's "strong feeling" or "strong emotion" getting in the way of them allowing women to enter the professions or receive education (150). Woolf mimics the tone of the detached scientist in her examination of the source of "our fear and your [men's] anger" and turns once again to biography, but does not in this case transform the personal experiences of its subjects into facts, insisting instead on a psychoanalytic approach, which reduces seeming facts to emotions and their causes. In Woolf's analysis of Mr. Barrett, the

---

[3] Vara S. Neverow notes that the Freudian term "infantile fixation" was not used by his English translators at the time and that Woolf might have acquired it from Professor Grensted, one of the narrator's sources in *Three Guineas* (61, 68).

Rev. Patrick Brontë, and Mr. Jex-Blake, she explains that the anger of their prohibitions on their daughters' behavior is not rational or justified, as they believe it is, but has its source in "a very strong emotion and an emotion which also seems to have its origin in the levels below conscious thought," which is jealousy and the related fear that their daughters will no longer be dependent on them (156). Woolf goes on to explain that in the case of Sophia Jex-Blake and her father, he "had recourse to one of the commonest of all evasions; the argument which is not an argument but an appeal to the emotions" (158). In this case, it is men's emotions, not women's, which are an enemy to reason and justice, and are a cause of the distortion of facts. Woolf reverses conventional understandings of the gendered nature of anger, where men's anger is characterized as factual and justified and women's is irrational and personal, evidence of an "axe to grind." Indeed, Woolf subjects men's personal emotions to the same level of scrutiny women's usually receive, inverting the situation Spelman describes, in which dominant groups associate themselves with reason and their subordinates with emotion. This reversal does not demonstrate that Woolf believed that women should fear or hide the personal, but that anger and impassioned argument are not more valid for having come from a personal place. Woolf suggests that the personal, at least for men, implies the translation of narrow and distorting emotional instincts into truths to support the oppression of women; while for women, the personal or autobiographical is fact and must be treated as such, rather than as a repressed, and therefore irrational emotion. Implicit in Woolf's methodology in *Three Guineas*, then, is a critique of emotional immediacy, and, as we shall see, a defense of emotional detachment.

Attributed Anger and Collective Indifference

Contemporary feminist theorists, such as Sara Ahmed, acknowledge anger's indispensability to feminist political struggles, but problematize the idea that its naturalness and personal source validate it. Indeed, Ahmed's work continues the feminist project of reclaiming negative affects, while refusing the teleology of a feminist politics in which the ultimate result of anger is happiness. In *The Promise of Happiness*, Ahmed explains how feminist scholarship and activism has historically "expose[d] the unhappy effects of happiness, teaching us how happiness is used to reinscribe social norms as social goods" (2). Ahmed refers here to the work of feminists like Jane Marcus and Adrienne Rich, who, as we have seen, encouraged women to recognize and express their anger in the belief that its causes—the reinscription of oppressive conditions, such as patriarchal marriage and gender norms, as the apotheosis of happiness—could be eradicated, resulting in a situation where, "they [the next generation of feminists] will write in joy and freedom" (Marcus 154). In contrast, Ahmed follows black feminists such as bell hooks and Audre Lorde in emphasizing how some women have never had access to the fantasy of happiness feminism wants to discredit and recognizes that both the past *and* future projects of feminism involve "refusing to follow other people's goods, or by refusing to make others happy" (60). Woolf makes a similar argument about the future of feminism in *Three Guineas* in a section of the text that proposes inventing a new ceremony to celebrate the "freedom" Woolf's correspondent assumes women enjoy:

> What more fitting than to destroy an old word, a vicious and corrupt word that has done much harm in its day and is now obsolete? The word 'feminist' is the word indicated. That word, according to the dictionary, means 'one who champions the rights of women.' Since the only right, the right to earn a living, has been won, the word no longer has a meaning. (120-21)

Woolf ironically suggests the obsolescence of feminism, now that its purported goal been achieved and women are "free," which not only allows her to reiterate the necessity of feminism to the projects of fighting patriarchy and fascism, but also to emphasize the continuity of the feminist project over generations, as Ahmed does much later. Woolf goes on to clarify by explaining that what "those queer dead women in their poke bonnets and shawls" were working towards in the nineteenth century is "the very same cause for which we are working now" (121).

Woolf suggests that negative feelings are essential to the feminist project, but that they are also the source of feminists' vilification as "those queer dead women in their poke bonnets and shawls," because their enduring refusal to let go of unhappiness and anger is viewed as pathological. This describes the condition of Ahmed's "feminist killjoy," who also repeatedly "spoils" the happiness of others and is therefore "attributed as the origin of bad feeling" (65). Ahmed's description of the feminist killjoy and the source of her anger is useful for conceptualizing alternatives to the personal anger that supports a teleological narrative of feminism. Ahmed explains the process through which reasonable anger becomes personal anger: "Reasonable thoughtful arguments are dismissed as anger (which of course empties anger of its own reason), which makes you angry, such that your response becomes read as the confirmation of evidence that you are not only angry but also unreasonable!" (68). In this scenario, reasonable anger, derived from a "judgment that something is wrong," is read as "unattributed anger" that comes from a personal place (68). Ahmed's differentiation between reasonable and unattributed anger, which follows Spelman's differentiation between understanding emotions as judgments and "dumb events," reveals how the prioritization of the personal source of anger can erase the reasoning behind it and make it susceptible to attack. Additionally, separating anger from the personal voids the requirement that it eventually be replaced by "joy and freedom." If the feminist killjoy is not an angry *person* but a person who is angry *about* injustice, she is better able to address those injustices beyond the scope of personal injury and through a project that does not end when she is "free" from anger but continues on as an essential aspect of a feminist genealogy.

Indeed, Woolf's use of the personal and the biographical as fact, and her use of evidence to demonstrate the facts behind women's anger (as opposed to men's emotionally-motivated arguments) in *Three Guineas* demonstrate her support for a version of feminist politics supported by the attributed, reasonable anger Ahmed describes. Woolf's characterization of men's anger as rooted in "infantile fixations," which are "strong emotions" hidden "below the level of conscious thought," is thus a personal form of anger that cannot be attributed to a rational source. Women's anger, however, is revealed to be rational when they are not subject to the process Ahmed describes, where reasonable anger about injustice is transformed by those it threatens (men) into unattributed anger, creating the figures of the feminist killjoy and the "queer dead women in their poke bonnets and shawls." Woolf's argument for impersonal feminist anger, however, exceeds her formal interest in establishing the factual source of women's anger through the facts of biography and a scientific analysis of men's feelings. Woolf's suspicion of the evidentiary value of personal anger extends to her understanding of the collective political potential of the personal. Indeed, in "Thinking Back Through Our Mothers: The Collective Sublime," Marcus maintains that the "elimination of the ego" was an essential aspect of Woolf's oeuvre, part of her participation in "a democratic feminist 'collective sublime'" that included past, present, and future women writers (84, 82). Although Marcus's claims might conflict with her idea that Woolf's personal anger, and therefore her identity, permeated her work, it is useful for understanding the Society of Outsiders, which embraces the value of impersonal and dispassionate argument and reflects a concern with collective justice in its rejection of identity and ego. Woolf's Society makes use of "weaker," negative feelings that are closer to affect in their association with detachment and turning away.

Woolf's description of the Society of Outsiders, which does not emerge until her final chapter, follows her earlier characterization of women throughout the text as not only separate from the concerns and interests of men and patriarchal society but as interested in eschewing the personal in favor of the collective. This occurs through Woolf's transformation of personal biographical material into collective facts and her contention that the women she writes about constitute their own class as the "daughters of educated men." As Christine Froula argues, Woolf "pragmatically" limits her analysis to one class of women, declining to speak for working class women, even as "*Three Guineas* envisions all women as an emerging economically independent collective that might conceivably exert diffuse social power against barbarism, tyranny, and war" (275). Woolf's language in her response to her correspondent highlights the differences in power and identity between "your

[his] class" and the collective perspective ("our class") from which Woolf writes. For Woolf, "we" means "a whole made up of body, brain and spirit, influenced by memory and tradition," demonstrating her conceptualization of the collective of women as one being (*TG* 22). Similarly, the Society of Outsiders emphasizes the daughters of educated men's impersonal attitude toward the concerns of her correspondent and the society he represents. The Society abides by the notion that "it seems both wrong for us rationally and impossible for us emotionally to fill up your form and join your society," illustrating their refusal to be emotionally or personally manipulated into supporting a cause that does not align with the pursuit of "liberty, equality, and peace" (125, 126). The Society maintains a rational indifference to the types of emotionally motivated arguments made by men who suffer from the "infantile fixation" described earlier. The place of women, Woolf argues, is "not to incite their brothers to fight, or to dissuade them, but to maintain an attitude of complete indifference," a quality that she maintains must be "given a firm footing upon fact": "As it is a fact that she cannot understand what instinct compels him, what glory, what interest, what manly satisfaction fighting provides for him…as fighting thus is a sex characteristic which she cannot share" (127).

    The Society's refusal to understand and share in the personal and emotional motivations for the political causes of others that do not align with one's values resonates with Ahmed's notion of the "affect alien." Ahmed describes the sense of alienation that arises when we do not, for example, "experience pleasure from proximity to objects that are attributed as being good," creating a gap that can lead to anger (41-42). A feminist perspective, then, can lead to alienation from happiness. Woolf's Society of Outsiders is alienated from the dominant affects of British patriarchal society because war and nationalism do not make them feel happy or sympathetic; however, rather than fill this gap with anger, they respond with indifference. Indeed, when they do support a cause, they do so not out of sympathy, but out of the carefully formulated conclusion that their behavior is just and indifferent to personal influences, which is guaranteed by their vows of "poverty, chastity, derision, and freedom from unreal loyalties" (97). The last of these vows—which requires ridding oneself of "national, religious, collegiate, sex and familial pride"—is essential to Woolf's vision of an ideal form of politics as one that abandons personal identity, which leaves one susceptible to irrational, emotional appeal, in favor of an indifferent collective (97). Woolf demonstrates how women are already, by default of their sex, collectively excluded from these attachments, as they "have no country," "want no country," and therefore have the ability to oppose war, as a group, through their indifference (129). As Marcus argues in "Thinking Back Through Our Mothers," Woolf imagines a collective that exceeds the bounds of time and space, and even includes common readers in a "collective audience" that strips them of individual identity (82).

Emotional Immediacy, Unsympathetic Response, and "those dead bodies and ruined houses"

As we have seen, Woolf establishes her stance on the relationship between emotion and feminist politics through her transformation of women's lived experiences into collective facts and her description of the Society of Outsiders' attributed anger and indifferent form of critique. Both of these strategies challenge the idea that Woolf privileged her own anger or believed that women's emotional responses to injustice are the key to their freedom. Woolf's understanding of the role of affect in politics also allows her to conceptualize a future for feminist politics that can embrace negative feelings without disappointment in the failings of a narrative that was supposed to end in joy and happiness. A third fundamental aspect of Woolf's suspicion of the power of personal emotions to formulate a rational response to injustice is evident in her inclusion and exclusion of particular photographs in the text. Woolf's narrator references absent photographs of "dead bodies and ruined houses," which are images from the Spanish Civil War, sent by the Spanish government "with patient pertinacity about twice a week" to alert British supporters to the violence of the fascists (14). Marcus's notes reveal that while Woolf was writing *Three Guineas*, socialist and communist newspapers and pamphlets arrived at the Woolf household on a regular basis (*TG* 228). However, it is the contrast between these photographs of "dead bodies and ruined houses," mentioned seven times in the text, and the photographs of a General, Heralds, a University Procession, a Judge, and an Archbishop that suggests Woolf's critique of sympathy as an impetus for action.

The photographs of patriarchal figures that Woolf originally included in the text were absent for decades before they were restored to the text with Michèle Barrett's 1993 Penguin edition and Jane Marcus's 2006 Harcourt edition. Marcus notes that it is "not known how the photographs were dropped from the English and American editions for so many decades, or why," but emphasizes that reading them with the text brings out, as Woolf intended "the connection between them" (*TG* 229). While the majority of this criticism has focused on the included photographs, some critics have addressed the absent images and their affective role in particular. In her introduction to the 2006 edition, Marcus argues that although the images are absent, they are nevertheless "visually very present to us as we read" as Woolf "never lets us forget that they are the occasion of her outburst" (lxiv). Indeed, Woolf provides a detailed description of the photographs she chooses not to include: "They are not pleasant photographs to look upon. There are photographs of dead bodies for the most part. This morning's collection contains the photograph of what might be a man's body, or a woman's; it is so mutilated that it might, on the other hand, be a body of a pig" (14). Furthermore, Marcus suggests that Woolf's exclusion of the violent photographs is part of her pacifism, as "[a]trocity photographs would incite us to fight and she refuses to show them" (lxiii). Maggie Humm also attends to their implicit presence by reading the play between the visible and absent photographs as evidence of the juxtaposition between a masculine narrative of public events with the "feminine 'affect' of the narrator's visual memories" (646). Humm's analysis echoes earlier psychoanalytic readings of Woolf's personal relationship to the text when she argues that the absent photographs feature "the narrator's memory and her bodily responses to the photographs," which allows them to "produce sexual difference and represent the ideological effects of sexual difference" (647-48). Finally, one of the most widely read analyses of the absent photographs appears at the beginning of Susan Sontag's *Regarding the Pain of Others*, where she close-reads Woolf's first invocation of the absent Spanish photographs, in which she tells her correspondent that "we are seeing with you the same dead bodies, the same ruined houses" as a way of revealing their shared opposition to war (14). Sontag argues that Woolf "professes to believe that the shock of such pictures cannot fail to unite people of good will," accuses her of "allow[ing] her interlocutor to take a 'we' for granted," and claims that "into this 'we,' after the pages devoted to the feminist point, she [Woolf] then subsides" (6). While Humm argues that the Spanish photographs operate as the text's feminine unconscious, Sontag takes umbrage with the implication that images of war affect people emotionally in the same way, an argument supported by her later critique of the idea that the sympathy evoked by images has the power to prevent war. Although Sontag herself argues that "[a] narrative seems likely to be more effective than an image" in its ability to force people to pay attention for a prolonged period of time, she does not acknowledge that Woolf does not in fact make visible the violent photographs Sontag accuses her of using cheaply, and indeed only references them throughout the narrative of the text, as Marcus points out (Sontag 110).

Sontag is correct in claiming that Woolf assumes the universality of her response to the absent images, but Woolf's description of it reveals her skepticism of a politics forged from emotional response. Woolf transitions to the photographs, which are "pictures of actual facts," by comparing them with "pictures of other people's lives," or history and biography (13). However, she also writes that they "are not arguments addressed to the reason; they are simply statements of fact addressed to the eye" (14). These statements seem to conflict as Woolf suggests that the photographs are factual and realistic, as opposed to the more interpretive genres of history and biography, but they are also addressed to the eye, rather "than arguments addressed to reason." Woolf creates a nuanced opposition between fact and argument and between eye and reason in a place where one would perhaps expect an opposition between emotion or body and reason. While the use of the word "eye" implies a direct bodily interpretation, Woolf goes on to clarify that "the eye is connected with the brain; the brain with the nervous system," which in turn creates "sensations" of "horror and disgust" (14). Although the photographs enter the eye as facts, they become sensations, and finally emotions as they move through the body, which leads to a dead end. Woolf seems to say that although "we" are affected by the photographs in the same way, "we" (Woolf and her correspondent) do not share the same politics, so let us move on from looking at these images, which she goes on to describe in rather straightforward language, to the facts of women's experience, which will do a better job of convincing you why war should be prevented. Indeed, at the end of this section, Woolf abruptly moves on to her own argument, which relies not on the sensational and emotional immediacy of "statements of fact addressed to the eye," but "arguments addressed to the reason."

Before examining the photographs that Woolf includes in *Three Guineas*, it is necessary to understand how she might have tried to explore alternatives to the sympathetic use of war images, as they rely, like personal anger, on emotional immediacy. Judith Butler argues that affect, and sympathy in particular, can create a "differential distribution of grievability across populations," which points to the necessity of attending to the way that affective response is not always organic but is conditioned by political forces (24). Indeed, she argues that affective responses are regulated and censored by regimes of power, in efforts to prevent war or to support war by preventing people from reacting with the "horror and disgust" that could incite both pacifist and nationalist sentiments. While also attending to the political nature of affective response, Ahmed reveals the exclusionary nature of sympathy and its limitations as a source of action. In challenging the "routinisation of sympathy as a mode of responding to loss," Ahmed argues that it is not just a feeling of extension, but also one of restriction: "You might be sympathetic *to the extent* that you can be in accordance with others. Maybe you are more kind to those you feel are more of your kind" ("Becoming Unsympathetic"). Like Butler, Ahmed points to the political implications of deeming a particular group of people unsympathetic, but she also attends to the way that sympathy excludes those who do not share in dominant *positive* feelings, like happiness. Ahmed returns to the concept of the "affect alien" to describe the way that "[w]hen others expect sympathy from you, they might also be expecting your feeling to be in accordance with theirs," which means that the feminist killjoy is "unsympathetic" in the sense that she does not sympathize with the happiness of others when that happiness is derived from damaging social norms ("Becoming Unsympathetic").

Butler's and Ahmed's work on sympathy can help us understand Woolf's invocation of the "dead bodies and ruined houses" and her inclusion of the photographs of the patriarchal figures. As Butler points out, photographs of war elicit powerful affective responses, but they do not always produce consensus. Woolf might have been aware of the fact that although "we" (Woolf and her interlocutor) have the same emotional response, she can neither guarantee that other viewers and readers will respond the same way, nor that their emotions will be transformed into political action. Woolf recognized the danger of groups experiencing a collective emotional response to the images because she understood that sympathy, as a "fact" that is transformed into a "sensation," can prevent thinking, or rational response. Indeed, Jessica Berman argues that Woolf intentionally avoids including the Spanish photographs because she is aware of their "inevitable mobilization within an immoderate, emotional, and in many ways, unethical propaganda argument," ultimately suggesting that *Three Guineas* allows Woolf to explore the limits of ethical connection (68). Woolf works according to what Berman refers to as a "narrative politics of hiatus, involution, and substitution"; thus, she not only avoids including the Spanish photographs, but, in a move that might seem characteristic of the feminist killjoy in its indifference to being viewed as unsympathetic, also subjects photographs of patriarchal figures to her own and the reader's gaze (63).

The five photographs in *Three Guineas*—of a General, Heralds, a University Procession, a Judge, and an Archbishop—were excised from the text from the mid-1960s to the 1990s in the British and American editions (Wisor 1). Since then, critics have examined the cultural and historical meaning of the photographs, with Alice Staveley first describing, in 1998, the meaning that they would have had for contemporary viewers. Staveley's archival research confirmed that contemporary readers "would probably have identified all of the famous men, as much by their faces as by their raiments," meaning that "far from comprising a series of faded and anonymous snapshots of late great men—a misperception enhanced by the distance of time or place...these men were not only very much alive in June 1938, they were also the reigning 'chiefs' of the patriarchal enterprise" (4-5). Staveley goes on to provide the names and titles of the men, which include Lord Baden-Powell ("A General"), Stanley Baldwin ("A University Procession"), Lord Hewart ("A Judge"), and William Cosmo Gordon Lang, Archbishop of Canterbury ("An Archbishop") (4). Unlike Humm, who contends that in contrast to the "absent photographs, whose contingent, affective scenes electrify Woolf's bodily synapses, the public photographs lack affect," contemporary readers might have been shocked by Woolf's inclusion of photographs of such eminent men (657). Woolf knew that replacing the expected anti-war photographs of the "dead bodies and ruined houses" with representatives of British patriarchal power was a highly political decision, one that would incite a different kind of emotional response.

The inclusion of the photographs of these pillars of British civilization, situated in the context of the absence of photographs of foreign victims of war, amplifies Woolf's argument that the source of fascism and tyranny is the nation and the home. Woolf's decision to include these particular photographs challenges the reader to subject them to a higher level of scrutiny than usual. The photographs themselves are close shots of some of the most important British men alive, which depict them decked out in the clothing that symbolizes their power and in official processions that are reminiscent of fascist imagery. Only in the photograph of a General is the subject smiling and facing the camera in a pose that would usually elicit identification, and perhaps sympathy, from a viewer. Woolf, however, sarcastically emphasizes these official displays' inability to evoke her emotions and distract her from her focus on women's education:

> Here, too, we marvel at the brilliance of your clothes; here, too, we watch maces erect themselves and processions form, and not with eyes too dazzled to record the differences, let alone explain them…we must cease to hang over old bridges humming songs; we must attempt to deal with the question of education, however imperfectly. (30-31)

Once again showing her skepticism of "facts addressed to the eye," Woolf makes it clear that she and her Society of Outsiders are not "too dazzled" by the spectacle of these processions of men to think reasonably about what they represent. Woolf does not merely dismiss these men's official regalia and titles as superfluous and outdated, but also reveals that these images are insidious in their ability to conceal, through the emotional response they coerce, the injustices they support. While these photographs might traditionally elicit affective responses that include feelings of patriotism, nationalism, safety, and faith in venerable institutions spanning Empire, Government, Justice, and Religion, their seemingly haphazard pairing with Woolf's text highlights their contrast and encourages the reader to take an unsympathetic view of them—to refuse to be dazzled. Just as Woolf subjects the emotional "infantile fixations" of Mr. Barrett, the Rev. Patrick Brontë, and Mr. Jex-Blake to the level of scrutiny women's usually receive, the objectifying gaze is reversed in the photographs from depicting the victims of war to the perpetrators of the sentiments that lead to it.

If readers follow the example of Woolf's own rational textual analysis, the Society of Outsiders, and the feminist killjoy, they can refuse to feel with, or sympathize with, the dominant positive affects these photographs usually produce by remaining unsympathetic and indifferent to them. Woolf does not include the absent Spanish photographs, which might have provoked an unthinking sympathetic response, but replaces them with the photographs of the patriarchal figures because her readers are able to resist their emotional call, as they have been indoctrinated in the impersonal affective strategies of the Society of Outsiders. One way to resist tyranny, Woolf suggests, is to become unsympathetic to it by understanding that it exploits emotional immediacy to transform, as Ahmed contends, "social norms into social goods." Woolf thus demonstrates the danger of a feminist politics that uncritically exploits the personal and the emotional as a source of truth and makes them the first step of a political project that will end in its own obsolescence.

Instead, Woolf maintains that feminists would be better served by both transforming personal emotions into collective negative feelings, as shown in her use of impersonal anger as a feminist methodology, and harnessing this *attributed* anger and unhappiness to launch a collective critique, via unsympathetic and indifferent response, of the emotionally exploitative rhetoric and imagery of the fascist and patriarchal state. A project grounded in negative, but impersonal, affect does not conceptualize anger as a personally exhausting emotion to overcome, but as a critical methodology that supports a more sustainable feminist politics. That is to say, writing "in joy and freedom" need not remain a future that is only possible after feminism becomes obsolete; Woolf implies that the project will never be complete because there is no "after" to anger.

Works Cited

Ahmed, Sara. "Becoming Unsympathetic." *Feminist Killjoys,* 16 April 2015, https://feministkilljoys.com/2015/04/16/becoming-unsympathetic. Accessed 22 November 2016.

———. "Introduction: Feel Your Way." *The Cultural Politics of Emotion*, Edinburgh UP, 2014, pp. 1-19.

———. "Feminist Killjoys (And Other Willful Subjects)." *The Scholar & Feminist Online*, 8.3, 2010, pp. 1-8.

———. *The Promise of Happiness*. Duke UP, 2010.

Berman, Jessica. "Intimate and Global: Ethical Domains from Woolf to Rhys." *Modernist Commitments: Ethics, Politics, and Transnational Modernism*, Columbia UP, 2012, pp. 39-89.

Butler, Judith. *Frames of War: When is Life Grievable?* Verso, 2009.

Froula, Christine. "St. Virginia's Epistle to an English Gentleman: Sex, Violence, and the Public Sphere in *Three Guineas*." *Virginia Woolf and the Bloomsbury Avant-Garde*, Columbia UP, 2005, pp. 259-84.

Helal, Kathleen M. "Anger, Anxiety, Abstraction: Virginia Woolf's 'Submerged Truth.'" *South Central Review,* vol. 22, no. 2, 2005, pp. 78-94.

Humm, Maggie. "Memory, Photography, and Modernism: The 'dead bodies and ruined houses' of Virginia Woolf's *Three Guineas*." *Signs*, vol. 28, no. 2, 2003, pp. 645-63.

Low, Lisa. "Refusing to Hit Back: Virginia Woolf and the Impersonality Question." *Virginia Woolf and the Essay*, edited by Beth Carole Rosenberg and Jeanne Dubino, 1997, pp. 257-74.

Marcus, Jane. *Art and Anger: Reading Like A Woman*. Ohio State UP, 1988.

Miller, Nancy K. "Getting Personal: Autobiography as Cultural Criticism."

Getting Personal: Feminist Occasions and Other Autobiographical Acts, Routledge, 1991, pp. 1-30.
Neverow, Vara S. "Freudian Seduction and the Fallacies of Dictatorship." *Virginia Woolf and Fascism: Resisting the Dictator's Seduction*, edited by Merry M. Pawlowski, Palgrave, 2001, pp. 56-72.
Ngai, Sianne. "Introduction." *Ugly Feelings*, Harvard UP, 2005, pp. 1-38.
Rich, Adrienne. "When We Dead Awaken: Writing as Re-Vision." *On Lies, Secrets, and Silence,* Norton, 1979, pp. 33-49.
Scheman, Naomi. "Anger and the Politics of Naming." *Women and Language in Literature and Society*, edited by Sally McConnell-Ginet, Ruth Borker, and Nelly Furman, Praeger, 1980, pp. 174-87.
Showalter, Elaine. "Virginia Woolf and the Flight Into Androgyny." *A Literature of Their Own,* Princeton UP, 1999, pp. 263-97.
Silver, Brenda R. "The Authority of Anger: *Three Guineas* as Case Study." *Signs,* vol. 16, no. 2, 1991, pp. 340-70.
Sontag, Susan. *Regarding the Pain of Others*, Penguin, 2004.
Spelman, Elizabeth V. "Anger and Insubordination." *Women, Knowledge, and Reality: Explorations in Feminist Philosophy*, edited by Ann Garry and Marilyn Pearsall, Unwin Hyman, 1989, pp. 263-74.
Staveley, Alice. "Name That Face." *Virginia Woolf Miscellany,* 51, 1998, pp. 4-5.
Wisor, Rebecca. "About Face: The *Three Guineas* Photographs in Cultural Context." *Woolf Studies Annual,* 21, 2015, pp.1-49.
Woolf, Virginia. "The Decay of Essay Writing." *Virginia Woolf: Selected Essays,* Edited and with an introduction by David Bradshaw, Oxford UP, 2008, pp. 3-5.
———. *The Letters of Virginia Woolf: Volume Five, 1932-1935*. edited by Nigel Nicolson and Joanne Trautmann, Harcourt, 1979.
———. "The Modern Essay." *The Common Reader*, Harcourt, 1984, pp. 211-22.
———. "On Not Knowing Greek." *The Common Reader*, Harcourt, 1984, pp. 23-38.
———. *A Room of One's Own*. Annotated and with an introduction by Susan Gubar, Harcourt, 2005.
———. *Three Guineas*. Annotated and with an introduction by Jane Marcus, Harcourt, 2006.

The Reader Awakes: Pedagogical Form and Utopian Impulse in *The Years*
Matthew Cheney

Reading was a vital activity for Virginia Woolf not only for its own pleasures, or even for the knowledge it provided, but for its pedagogies: through reading, we learn to think more fully and astutely than we would otherwise, and we train our imagination to think beyond the world as we find it. Woolf's is an active reading practice, one that enlivens and enlightens the reader who is able to approach texts with both an openness to unforeseen possibilities and a skepticism about the many forces that limit possibilities—social forces such as patriarchy and nationalism, certainly, but also our own individual foibles, such as ignorance, unexamined assumptions, or the inevitable prejudices of personal taste.

Anne Fernald has written that Woolf sought and demonstrated a type of reading "that is at once generous and critical," a type of reading that then "teaches us how to read her" (15). One of the readers who read Woolf's texts both generously and critically was Jane Marcus, who similarly praised the generosity she saw in Woolf's stance as an "enraptured reader, egoless and open to the text, rather than aggressively attacking it" (*Art & Anger* 225). While Marcus was a writer and scholar, it is at least equally valuable to consider her as a reader and teacher, for it is through her always passionate, generous, and yet specific reading of Woolf that she teaches us new ways of imagining the text, imagining the world of the text, and imagining the world in which we read the text.

Beginning with some implications from Marcus's insistence on the radicalism of Woolf's form as well as content, we can work toward reading *The Years* as a novel with a subversive pedagogy, a text that teaches readers to imagine new alternatives to old forms and exhausted ideologies. Seeing *The Years* as infused with utopian impulses means reading it not as a plan for a perfect world, but rather as a novel of quietly utopian desires, a novel that yearns for an ever-shifting unity of senses and sensibilities that could resist and perhaps even triumph over the threats of authoritarianism, patriarchy, nationalism, and militarism. As such, the novel may fit within Gayatri Spivak's notion of an aesthetic education in an era of globalization, a frame congruent with many of Marcus's concerns, for Spivak is a reader who values how close attention to the language and structure of texts can train readers toward new ways of using their imaginations, ways necessary for liberty and justice to have any hope of flourishing. "The literary imagination," Spivak writes, "is programmed to fail but can figure the impossible" (*Aesthetic* 116). The literary imagination has no escape from the inevitable failure of language's aspiration to encompass all the possible representations of the world, nor can such imagination rise free from the histories of imperialism and patriarchy that shape its articulations, but nonetheless it is *the literary*, with all its polyphonies, that offers what Spivak (discussing Woolf) calls "the impossible possible of 'perhaps'" (117) available only to fictionality. Through the figurations of fiction, the impossible becomes imaginable; once imaginable, it may move beyond the realm of dreams and into discourse, the realm of analysis, thus narrowing the chasm between the possible and impossible.

Figuring the impossible is a task that unites Marcus with Woolf and Woolf with Marcus, and both women valued the act of reading as indispensable to that task. "Reading," Woolf wrote in 1931, "has changed the world and continues to change it" (*E5* 274)—a statement of great hope and optimism if we assume that the change reading allows is toward liberty and justice. Woolf and Marcus knew that for such an assumption to be valid, we must also assume that readers possess certain skills and habits of imagination, and thus the relationship between text and reader is paramount, because texts can encourage readers toward either an active or passive relationship to their words, structures, and ideas.

The Pedagogy of Form

Throughout her career, Jane Marcus elucidated the ways experimental form could aid radical meaning, and in such essays as "Britannia Rules *The Waves*" (in *Hearts*) she pushed against the many critics who argued for social realism as the only valid aesthetic for radical fiction: "When a text like *The Waves* situates itself in the oppositional framework of minority discourse but is refused a place among the countercanonical classics of the thirties by a certain set of cultural guardians, one senses their fear of 'poetic' language and experimental structure as vehicles for radical politics" (*Hearts* 60). Valuing experimental form, she was not only sensitive to *what* texts mean, but to *how*. Of *The Years*, she said, "The freedom is in the form ... Our experience of pleasure comes from the artist's handling of aesthetic barriers ... The content of this novel happens to be as radical as its form" (*Languages* 54).

In the introduction to her annotated edition of *Three Guineas*, Marcus makes a convincing argument that not only the text but the solid object of the book itself is designed to encourage a particular experience, one that teaches skills of critical, skeptical reading:

> Much noisy page turning is required to read this book, as one moves from the page to Virginia Woolf's own notes, to this editor's notes, and then to the bookshelves or the Internet to chase an undocumented allusion or a puzzling phrase. Woolf's genius lies in her commitment to experimental writing: *Three Guineas* is an interactive text. ... Part of Woolf's advanced

project in experimental writing was to involve the reader in both the reading and the "writing" of the script for her books. (xlvii-xlviii)

For Marcus, such experimental form is an inextricable expression of the book's political purpose: "Virginia Woolf's political commitment to undermining authority is enacted in the structure and voice of her writing. Her style and her politics are equally antiestablishment" (xlix). To make any sense of *Three Guineas*, we not only must flip back and forth between Woolf's main text and her footnotes (as well as any editor's notes in an annotated edition), but we must also sort through the various characters and voices Woolf brings in. The polyphony may become overwhelming, making us yearn for an authoritative narrative voice to clear things up and give us a packaged meaning, but it is exactly such authority that Woolf subverts.

While less "noisy page turning" is required of *The Years*, the style and the politics of the novel are no less antiauthoritarian than those of *Three Guineas*, no less demanding that readers stay aware, active, skeptical, and willing to imagine connections and conclusions for themselves.[1] *The Years* is less openly in dialogue with the reader (who is not directly addressed), but even a reader who has never heard the name Bakhtin will likely wonder which voices, utterances, and details to pay most attention to in the novel's rich tapestry. Each chapter begins with a prelude presenting a (seemingly) objective, distant view of places and people, few clearly related to the family story that follows by anything other than geography; throughout the novel, characters' thoughts and dialogue are often elliptical and fragmentary; objects, colors, sounds, and sights appear and reappear in ways that suggest significance and symbolism, but the patterns are inconclusive. In contrast to many family sagas, the story of the Pargiters is not teleological, it does not move from glory to ruin (or vice versa); but neither is it static: time passes, people change, some characters find success and others don't, memories haunt and fade, life goes on. The novel scrupulously resists declaring an unambiguous meaning for any of it, but the construction is also far from random. Readers, like the characters, must choose how to make sense of the patterns, what to value and what to discard.[2] The reader seeking narrative authority is endlessly frustrated, just as the reader seeking slogans from *Three Guineas* is going to have to do some real violence not only to the book, but to its polyphony.

---

[1] Charles Andrews explores the ways the novel's "elliptical, allusive form" and "fragmentary assemblage of voices ... require active readership" (67). Andrews reads *The Years* as an example of "literary activism" and (borrowing from Nancy Knowles) "narrative pacifism," a reading that fits with my own emphasis on Woolf's pedagogical form.
[2] For a particularly thorough accounting of the novel's repetitions of ideas, images, and objects, see Wheare 140-71.

Of Woolf's *oeuvre* generally, Susan Stanford Friedman has written that "Each text sets the ground for its own experiments, which it teaches its readers to interpret" (105).[3] This is no less true of *The Years* than of Woolf's other novels. The frustrations that *The Years* produces in readers expecting a type of novel it evokes but does not enact are central to its pedagogy: a project of teaching the reader to take an active role with the text rather than to assume a passive, unquestioning stance toward authoritarian novelistic conventions.[4] What Woolf sought with *The Years* was, in part, as Liisa Saariluoma states, to write a book that "deconstructs the family novel mode from within" (290). To do so, it had to resemble a family novel, and thus invite the reading conventions of that subgenre so that the text could then frustrate, challenge, and retrofit those conventions, training the reader toward a new way of reading and, with luck, of seeing the world.

Generational sagas about families had been popular at least from the time of Zola's Rougon-Macquart novels; after the first decades of the twentieth century, though, they came to be seen as a rather dusty genre. For all her critiques of outmoded novel forms, Woolf was a writer obsessed with time and memory, and she must have felt an inescapable attraction to the family saga's possibilities, and particularly to how she could use the conventions of the genre for her own purposes. Conventions regulate readers' expectations, and the subversive writer invokes those conventions, then shapes them either to guide the reading experience toward new effects or to surprise the reader into some new awareness. Readers may expect, for instance, that a novel of generations, which is a type of historical novel, will make note of important historical events, and *The Years* does (British colonialism, the death of Charles Stewart Parnell, the women's suffrage movement, the death of King Edward VII, World War I), but these events are often noticed only in passing,

---

[3] Friedman makes the case for the pedagogical aspects of Woolf's texts and pays close attention especially to scenes in Woolf's novels (particularly *The Voyage Out*) in which characters read. While Friedman's psychoanalytic approach to Woolf is not at all my own, her essay is further evidence for the centrality of reading to Woolf's aesthetic and for pedagogy as part of her project.

[4] An anti-authoritarian, active stance was one Woolf desired for education generally, and Natasha Periyan has shown that Woolf, who was quite familiar with debates about education and social class, didn't simply want to abolish institutions, but was interested in how educational institutions could be restructured to better foster egalitarian democracy — an interest that Periyan demonstrates is present throughout *The Years*. Similarly, Rod C. Taylor writes about Woolf's ideas for radical new schools and notes the importance of the reading experience itself to *Three Guineas*: "The experience that Woolf offers her readers gives them a chance to test out the benefits of her pedagogy, which in turn puts them in direct dialogue with the author" (74). Taylor links the pedagogy that Woolf advocates in the book to the critical pedagogy made famous by Paolo Freire, but if, as Jane Marcus proposes, the reading experience is one key to Woolf's pedagogy, then *how* Woolf elicits, organizes, controls, and liberates that experience must also be key. Benjamin D. Hagen explores some of this *how*, but his focus is on Woolf's nonfiction, particularly "A Sketch of the Past."

or their drama is muted, and many major events of the sort that would be prominent in a traditional historical novel are skipped over altogether. Woolf's focus is on the everyday details of life, the steady changes of technology that affect how people communicate with each other and move around in their lives, how money is attained and accounted for, who gets to go to school and who gets to go to work, and what sort of schools and what sort of work they get to go to. The private, quotidian world is emphasized and the public world is radically de-emphasized, shifting what is assumed to be important in historical writing. Woolf's technique, though, is not simply a shifting of emphases or a change in content; what the text shows or doesn't show is inextricable from how it shows or doesn't show it. Conventions are legible because of patterns, and in *The Years* Woolf creates new patterns, building a complex structure within the exhausted form, paying close attention to the repetition of particular phrases, colors, sounds, and objects through the book, making *The Years* into something like a novelistic pantoum.[5]

For the critique of patriarchy and family that was so important to Woolf's project in the 1930s, she needed to pull apart the novel form from the inside.[6] She had gathered, she said, "enough powder to blow up St Pauls" (*D4* 77), but for the most effective demolition, she needed to place that powder inside the structure itself. The normalizing discourse of *the family* that generational sagas support was a discourse Woolf knew to be highly compatible not only with that particular subgenre of novel, but with traditional novel form generally. Instead of rejecting traditional novelistic discourse for *The Years,* though, Woolf overloads it, exploding the family novel from within and reconstructing it so that any reader who begins *The Years* expecting to be able to put the reading protocols of the conventional novel to use soon becomes confused, bored, or frustrated, and those feelings offer the first step toward the reader beginning to understand Woolf's project. If such readers are to

---

[5] Before the rise of feminist scholarship, much Woolf criticism was formalist, and though *The Years* received less attention than the novels of the 1920s, critics who did discuss it recognized many of the features we still value in its structure. The repetitions in particular attracted attention from the first reviews written when the book was published; they were an important focus for such critics as Harvena Richter in *Virginia Woolf: The Inward Voyage* (Princeton UP, 1970), and they continue to be central to critics' perception of this novel's form. Marcus wrote that "In a sense *The Years* is *about* repetition as well as repetitive in style" (*Languages* 37-38), while Tamar Katz has stated that "Repetition, for *The Years*, establishes not just the continuity of figures or images that repeat across time, but the potential and the discomfort, for characters and readers, of repeated suspense ... in which we anticipate the shape of the world becoming clear" (9-10).

[6] Woolf's use in *The Years* of the family novel form to subvert patriarchal assumptions has been well established by numerous critics since the 1970s. See, for example, Chapters 2 and 3 of Marcus's *Virginia Woolf and the Languages of Patriarchy*, as well as Laura Moss Gottlieb's *"The Years:* A Feminist Novel." For a compelling exploration of Woolf and concepts of family generally, see Alex Zwerdling's *Virginia Woolf and the Real World*, especially chapters 6 and 7. For more recent scholarship, see Amidon, Saariluoma, and Suh.

do much more than dismiss the novel, they must change their assumptions and expectations so that they can practice different reading strategies.

To Learn, To Dream

The attentive reading practice that novels such as *The Years* elicit is part of what Gayatri Spivak has advocated as an aesthetic education for ethical imagination. We must, Spivak says, read the literary text for its literariness, we must pay close attention to its textual moves, and "we cannot read if we do not make a serious linguistic effort to enter the epistemic structures presupposed by a text" (*Aesthetic* 452). As Marcus and others have shown, the epistemic structures presupposed by *The Years* are ones that reject all totalizing ideology, whether the ideology of dominant literary practice, the ideology of patriarchy, the ideology of nationalism, or the ideology of fascism. They are also structures that question epistemology itself, and so, if we agree with Spivak, then to read this text means to enter into an attitude of skepticism, to be receptive to resonance, to tolerate contradictory judgments of characters and events, and to accept—or even, ideally, to enjoy—the lack of an authoritative narrative voice.

Woolf is thus what Spivak would call an activist of the imagination, a label Spivak insists must be embraced by teachers: "It is not a question of just producing correct descriptions, which should of course be produced, but which can always be disproved ... There must be, at the same time, the sense of how to train the imagination, so that it can become something other than Narcissus waiting to see his own powerful image in the eyes of the other" (*Readings* 54). Here we have the Woolfian idea of *fact* ("correct descriptions") versus *vision* (imagination), but like Woolf, Spivak does not simply create a binary opposition: correct descriptions must be produced, just as facts must be accounted for and the bark of guns must be heard, but facts are not sufficient, nor is it sufficient to ask how to prevent war without also asking how to create peace.[7] For the ideal of peace, and for the ideal of aesthetic perfection, multiple voices must be brought into play, reaching toward what Marcus dubbed "the collective sublime of Woolf's narrative voice" (*Art & Anger* 83), a voice that refuses the narcissistic desire to see nothing but a self in the other. This is polyphony, but it is not simply a collection of varied voices; the voices are assembled, they each speak from their own point of view, their differences are not elided, the selves are not erased, yet the assemblage creates a whole that speaks more powerfully than any voice alone. As Marcus suggests, Woolf asks us to imagine that specific narrative voices can become a single voice united through literary form, and so to imagine then what such unity might imply not only within the realm of the literary, but beyond it. Woolf challenges the reader to

---

[7] Spivak, in a rather Woolfian footnote, writes: "The absence of war cannot be defined as democracy" (*Aesthetic* 518).

wonder whether there might be a way to assemble a unity that is not the authoritarian unity she so despised.

Woolf never drafted a plan for a utopia, but a utopian impulse is present in *The Years* both as allusions within the text itself and, more substantially, in the characters' persistent yearning for a new world.[8] If the novel may be said to have a politics, that politics is both an extension of the frustrations produced by the world's failures and of the hopes inspired by imagining that those failures may be transcended. The pedagogy of *The Years* encourages readers to learn how to imagine such transcendence. Traditional utopian novels offer methods of transcending the world's injustices, but their pedagogy is that of a lecturer in a large auditorium, with the reader left to do nothing but take notes on Great Ideas. Woolf was skeptical of such an authoritarian approach, and she makes her skepticism explicit in "Character in Fiction," declaring: "There are no Mrs. Browns in Utopia. Indeed I do not think that Mr. Wells, in his passion to make her what she ought to be, would waste a thought upon her as she is" (*E3* 428).[9] Yet if Woolf seeks to encourage readers to become activists of the imagination, then she must find a way to reconcile with utopianism and build a critical pedagogy into it, because utopian impulses are fundamental for any politics that seeks to be more than *realpolitik*. Leonard Woolf himself said in *Framework for a Lasting Peace* in 1917, "Everything is Utopian until it is tried" (58). What Virginia Woolf needed to solve was the problem of writing from a utopian impulse without getting caught by the traps of the utopian novel, and to do so without turning away from the ever-growing horrors of the world in the 1930s. She needed, as Loretta Stec proposes in regard to *Three Guineas*, "to chart the range of possible responses to utopian impulses in a dystopian age" (180).

While numerous utopian novels were published throughout the 19th century, the 1930s were more dominated by dystopias than utopias, including various works by Katherine Burdekin, Storm Jameson, and others.[10] The most famous of these

---

[8] Fredric Jameson (following Ernst Bloch) identifies, in contrast to explicitly utopian programs, "an obscure yet omnipresent Utopian impulse finding its way to the surface in a variety of covert expressions and practices" (3), which is a good description for what it seems to me Woolf is up to in *The Years*.

[9] H.G. Wells, who was friends with Leonard Woolf and published some essays with the Hogarth Press, was a particularly apt foil for Virginia Woolf's ideas, since he was a prominent writer both of utopian texts and of the sort of traditional novel Woolf disdained. In 1918, she reviewed his *Joan and Peter: The Story of an Education*, criticizing it for being more interested in conveying ideas about education than in its characters and story (*E2* 294-98). It is also worth noting that one of Wells's most popular works of nonfiction was titled *New Worlds for Old* (1908), which was praised by both Galsworthy and Bennett. The book was popular enough that its title is cited by Leopold Bloom in Chapter 15 of *Ulysses*, and given the repetition of the yearning for new worlds in Woolf's novel, it would make a fine alternate title for *The Years*.

[10] "If the nineteenth century was not *the* Golden Age of utopianism," Kenneth M. Roemer writes, "it was certainly *a* golden age" (79), and this was especially true for literary utopias.

novels was *Brave New World* (1932) by Woolf's friend Aldous Huxley, whose fiction Woolf considered too didactic, his novels exemplars of a type for which she declared she had "a horror," and so she cautioned herself that Huxley's mode of fiction was one she must avoid (*D4* 281). Though Woolf did not want to write utopian or dystopian fiction, and often disparaged the kind of political idealism required of any utopian writer, she nonetheless understood (and felt herself) the yearning for a new world. This is most apparent during the 1930s in Woolf's proposal in *Three Guineas* for a society of outsiders, a proposal that extends some of what is implicit in *The Years* via what Laura Moss Gottlieb calls "Woolf's vision of a feminist utopia" (225). The "Outsiders' Society" was as programmatic in its utopianism as Woolf ever got: the outsiders must be pacifists who not only refuse to fight, but also "refuse in the event of war to make munitions or nurse the wounded" and who "maintain an attitude of complete indifference" (*TG* 126-27). The attitude of indifference requires women outsiders "to take no share in patriotic demonstrations; to assent to no form of national self-praise; to make no part of any claque or audience that encourages war; to absent herself from military displays, tournaments, tattoos, prize-givings and all such ceremonies as encourage the desire to impose 'our' civilization or 'our' dominion upon other people" (*TG* 129).

The utopian vision of *Three Guineas* is clear—Woolf's anti-militarist, anti-nationalist, and anti-imperialist ideas were at least as utopian when *Three Guineas* was published as they are today. But that vision is not absent from *The Years*, where the utopian impulse most clearly arises in the various musings on a (brave?) "new world," the first of which appears in the 1917 chapter after the air raid, when Sara raises a glass and everyone toasts "To the New World!" (277). Eleanor later asks, "About the new world…Do you think we're going to improve?" (280), but though Nicholas says yes, Eleanor continues to wonder: "When, she wanted to ask him, when will this new world come? When shall we be free?" (281). In the "Present Day" chapter, remembering the air raid, Eleanor recalls the toast "they had drunk to a new world. 'A new world—a new world!' Sally had cried" (312). The final use of the phrase is not by Eleanor, but by North, her nephew who has been to both war and colonial Africa, and whom Marcus identifies as a "potential poet-priest" (*Languages* 41), a member of the society of outsiders and "the incarnation of the Year-Spirit" (*Languages* 64). He is asked to speak for the younger generation, and he endorses Peggy's earlier outburst ("'You'll write one little book, and then another little book,' she said viciously, 'instead of living…living differently, differently'"

Though the utopian novels of the late nineteenth century are well known, dystopias were also published, such as Walter Besant's 1882 anti-feminist story *The Revolt of Man*. See also *Utopian Spaces of Modernism* edited by Rosalyn Gregory and Benjamin Kohlmann for more context, including "'The Strange High Singing of Some Aeroplane Overhead': War, Utopia and the Everyday in Virginia Woolf's Fiction" by Christina Britzolakis (pp. 121-40), which explores utopian impulses in *Jacob's Room* and *Mrs. Dalloway*.

[371]). *To live differently* becomes a kind of mantra for him. "It was what she meant that was true...her feeling, not her words. He felt her feeling now; it was not about him; it was about other people; about another world, a new world" (401). As an outsider who is also a member of the younger generation, North may be able to live into a new world of the future that is better than the future that has arrived for Eleanor and her generation.

The Years is a novel of utopian inclinations not in the sense of providing descriptions and prescriptions for a new world, but in its careful limning of what Fredric Jameson dubs "the desire called Utopia" (xiv). Utopia as desire and impulse prefigures or even opposes utopia as system. The utopian appears not in plans for a future society but in the hope for change, the yearning to inhabit a new world for which the need is vivid and immediate, but which is itself less vision than feeling, less blueprint than wish. Woolf's utopia is glimpsed in hints, glances, allusions, and the occasional brief moments where lives are connected through links invisible to the individuals themselves. The future stays unknown to the present, but within each chapter's present the yearning for a better world, a world of freedom and peace, persists for many of the characters. While in the first essay chapter of *The Pargiters*, Woolf indicates that she planned to span the years 1800 to 2032 (9), *The Years* did not become a novel of the future—it ends in a present that was past from the moment of publication—but it is a novel in which the future is, in every sense, always present in yearnings for different ways of living and dreams of new worlds.

The future is also present via allusion, though it is not the future itself that the allusion most vividly evokes, but rather imagined futures from the past. In the "1914," "1917," and "Present Day" chapters, Woolf repeats the word *sleepers* and the fear of waking them, first with Martin and Maggie (where the sleepers are Maggie's baby and Sarah), next in the air raid scene where Eleanor lowers her voice "as if she were afraid of waking sleepers" (280), then when Maggie enters Sara's room and stands staring at Sara and North "as if she had wakened sleepers" (328), and finally when Eleanor falls asleep at Delia's party and North and Maggie talk around her: "She looked peaceful, far from them, rapt in the calm which sometimes gives the sleeper the look of the dead" (360). At the end, the figure of the sleeper and the yearning for a new world are united when North wakes from a doze and is suddenly able to feel his way into a new sense of community (401). Woolf uses the figure of the sleeper for various purposes, most explicitly to signal the carving out of privacy within a public space, but sleep is also the realm of dreams, the place where, in times of crisis, hope and imagination may find release.

Given how vexing Woolf often found H.G. Wells (indeed, reading his thoughts on women helped inspire *Three Guineas* [*D4* 75]), she would likely have been aware at least of the title of his novel *When the Sleeper Wakes* (originally serialized in 1898/99, revised and printed as *The Sleeper Awakes* in 1910), wherein a man tries to cure his insomnia and ends up sleeping until the year 2100, waking up in an authoritarian plutocracy. Though Wells's novel was fundamentally a dystopia, the conceit of a sleeping person awaking had also been used in various utopian stories, most prominently Bellamy's *Looking Backward* (1888) and Morris's *News from Nowhere* (1890), and the phrase that supplied Wells's novel's title was familiar from the English translation of Philip Nicolai's Lutheran hymn "Wachet auf, ruft uns die Stimme" and J.S. Bach's cantata using its lyrics. Such use of the word *sleeper* applied to a person (rather than a train carriage) was by the 1930s, though, a bit odd or at least faintly archaic, a word drawing some slight attention to itself, so that a reader familiar with Wells's book, or any other story about a "sleeper" awaking in a new world, may think of that other text and wonder what sort of new world Woolf's sleepers will awake in.

The repetition of the word *sleeper*, and more importantly the access sleep allows to dreaming, is important to the novel's presentation of characters yearning for different lives and new worlds, a presentation that reaches full flower in the final chapter, where the "Present Day" is filled with memories of the past and dreams of times to come. Within the frame of pedagogy, the final chapter could be seen as the reader's final exam, though it isn't a test so much as a culminating lesson. Our skills of attention have been shaped and strengthened through the previous chapters, we sense the epistemological structure of the text, and we arrive at the last chapter with a bank of memories, some of which are hazy, some of which might even be unconscious. If, as the prelude of the 1891 chapter told us, the year begins in October, then the summer evening of "Present Day" is nearing the end. The sun sets, and "an edge of light surrounded everything." Red and gold are the dominant colors; colors don't have simple symbolic meanings in the novel, their implications shift and shimmer, but there is passion in red and beauty and wealth in gold. Gentler, more delicate, fragile, and peaceful colors (lilac and pink) appear in flowers and "shone veined as if lit from within" (290).[11] After fractured conversations and fragmented memories, Eleanor slips again and again into dreaming, and the final chapter brings her into the first hours of a new day. James Haule reads this progress as demonstrating that Eleanor "sees a better human existence which may now be within reach since the darkness of war, like the night itself, is finally over" (241), but this may be a hopeful reading, as the narrative provides no evidence that Eleanor herself believes that a better life (never mind utopia!) has come closer. The novel's pedagogy does not require Eleanor to see a new world,

---

[11] Marcus notes that Eleanor's name is associated with light: "'Eleanor' is 'Helen,' from Helios, the sun; she puts the sunflower symbol on the houses she builds" (*Languages* 40). (The sunflowers are first mentioned in the 1891 chapter [91], when they are called a "symbol of her girlish sentiment" that "amused her grimly" [95], and then briefly remembered as Eleanor reflects on her life [348].) Throughout the novel, war, violence, ignorance, and oppression are associated with darkness; possibility, hope, and enlightenment are associated with light.

however. We need only to be able to imagine that a better world is possible, and to imagine what such a world might include.

A Unity of Liberation

A yearning for a new world is tied in *The Years* to a yearning for a certain communal feeling, a unity that brings together incomplete bits and broken shards. Constructing a whole from fragments had been an aesthetic concern of Woolf's from early in her career, and unity and wholeness were thus guiding concepts for her desires and ideals. These concepts were key not only to her aesthetics, but to her politics. Alex Zwerdling, in a discussion of Woolf's pacifism, sees the effect of the many scenes in Woolf's novels of parties and other social occasions as one that works toward a kind of empathy: "Such events are the set pieces of Woolf's novels, and they always serve to test the characters' capacities for identifying emotionally with others toward whom they initially feel indifference or hostility" (278). Zwerdling notes that a "vision of the possibility of human unity affects not only the larger elements of Woolf's fiction (plot, time scheme, characterization) but also the sentence and paragraph" (280) to the extent that Woolf's "style is an instrument of coherence that refuses to compartmentalize or exclude, a verbal expression of the ideal of human unity" (281).

Woolf stages the quest for unity, and the frequent failure to find it, within the diegeses of her novels as well as through their aesthetics, thus achieving her desired melding of form and content. This is visible from the structure of *Jacob's Room* all the way to *Between the Acts*, where characters are concerned throughout with questions of unity, harmony, fragmentation, and discord. In *The Years*, characters yearn for various sorts of unity and the text itself unifies through its narrative voices. The distant, seemingly objective voice of the preludes (and, occasionally, elsewhere) can be read as a prose corollary to a landscape painting, a wide-angle photograph, or a long shot in a movie.[12] Again and again, the text demonstrates that the wholeness desired by such different characters as Eleanor and Peggy cannot be achieved only through words or only through an elite view — these characters seldom finish their thoughts, seldom even complete a conversation. Fragments of experience and philosophy fill each scene, though, requiring a perspective that can see a system, a distance (like the distance of the preludes) that delineates the movement of groups. Aside from the prelude narrator, the only force capable of such a distance is the reader's own imagination. It is the long final chapter that brings together the main characters who are still alive, dramatizing the harmonies

---

[12] Some of the most compelling recent writing on *The Years* has read it cinematically: see *The Tenth Muse: Writing about Cinema in the Modernist Period* by Laura Marcus (Oxford UP, 2007) and *Literature, Cinema and Politics 1930-1945: Reading Between the Frames* by Lara Feigel (Edinburgh UP, 2010).

and discords that have been set up in the previous chapters, ultimately finishing with the characters all uncertain. But the reader, who unifies the book by turning its last page, is left with a new day and the words "beauty, simplicity, and peace" (412). We can imagine the peaceful, simple, beautiful new day, and as the only observer of all the characters' encounters and ideas we may then be able to imagine how such encounters and ideas could contribute to a greater whole.

Unity remains in *The Years* a question of possibility more than reality, and the possibility is primarily available to the reader, not the characters. For instance, though physical spaces offer opportunities for moments of unity throughout the novel, those opportunities are mostly visible only to a perspective broader than that of any individual. Houses, in particular, bring characters together and hold them for a few hours or days or years, creating concrete markers of time. But without perception, time and space aren't unified. Abercorn Terrace signifies meaning for all of the Pargiters because they consistently associate it with moments of family life, but Number 30 on the street under Westminster Abbey's shadow remains un-unified by perception: Colonel Pargiter visits it at the beginning of the novel to see his mistress, Mira; then the 1917 section mostly takes place there, but the characters don't know the history, and no connection is made. Or, rather, no connection is made within the diegesis—alert readers can note the link, can flip from page 264 to page 6 and back again, and so the unity is left to the text's traces in the reader's perception. The act of reading can be an act of unification, the reader's imagination a unifying force.

At the end of *Three Guineas*, the narrator sees a relationship between the concepts of multiplicity and unity:

> Even here, even now your letter tempts us to shut our ears to these little facts, these trivial details, to listen not to the bark of the guns and the bray of the gramophones but to the voices of the poets, answering each other, assuring us of a unity that rubs out divisions as if they were chalk marks only; to discuss with you the capacity of the human spirit to overflow boundaries and make unity out of multiplicity. (169)

In this passage, *unity* is the ultimate goal of the dream of peace, and *multiplicity* is a step along the way. The narrator is not oblivious to the threat of fascism—not only is it a subject of the book, but it is present in the reference to chalk marks, which we know from *The Years* may "decorate academic lintels" (54), may be elements of children's games (108), or may indicate the British Union of Fascists (294). (It is vital, Woolf implies, to be able to read the signs well.) In the next paragraph in *Three Guineas*, she writes: "And since we are different, our help must be different. What ours can be we have tried to show—how imperfectly, how superficially there is no need to say" (169), which receives the final footnote of the book, one leading to a discussion of Coleridge, Whitman, and George Sand, all advocating unity as both an aesthetic and ethical concept. Unity, like chalk, can be an instrument of scholars, children, artists, poets, dreamers, and advocates of peace; it can also be an instrument of fascists. Woolf recognized the seductions and dangers of the concept of unity, particularly as a political concept, all the way back to *The Voyage Out*, where Richard Dalloway advocates it and Rachel Vinrace wrestles with the idea. As an aesthetic concept, though, it is usually positively inflected, e.g. with Jinny Carslake in *Jacob's Room*, who says if you look at a box of ordinary pebbles carefully, "multiplicity becomes unity, which is somehow the secret of life" (137). In her essays, Woolf consistently valorizes unity as an artistic achievement, as in her *Second Common Reader* essay on Hazlitt: "He seldom reaches the perfection of these great writers or their unity" (*E5* 497-98).

A key technique of the pedagogy of *The Years* and *Three Guineas* is first to present readers with some form of polyphonic multiplicity within which flows a yearning for liberatory, communal, anti-authoritarian unity, and then to leave the unifying to each reader's imaginative work. While Woolf insists that the totalitarian unities of fascism and patriarchy must be resisted and destroyed, she also shows that another type of unity is possible: the unity of paratactic meaning.

Spivak has claimed of Jamaica Kincaid's *Lucy* that what "mainly happens in this novel is, I believe, parataxis" (*Aesthetic* 354) and we could say the same for *The Years*. On a grammatical/rhetorical level, parataxis simply means the coordination of clauses without conjunctions, but if we extend the word beyond its technical meaning to refer also to the placement of images, objects, and ideas beside each other without overt explanation of the relationship between them, we can see parataxis as one of Woolf's basic strategies in *The Years* (as well as many of her other writings). Once she abandoned the essay-novel form of *The Pargiters*, where the expository prose explaining gaps and disjunctions reduced paratactic meaning, Woolf decided that one of her tasks was "to contract: each scene to be a scene, much dramatised; contrasted" (*D4* 261). Her strategy of contraction and contrast creates gaps and juxtapositions requiring readers to supply connections of their own between the chapters and between the scenes within each chapter, between the shifting narrative voices and floating points of view, between the panoply of characters, between history and fiction, between the many repeated words and phrases, between the barrage of sensory images (colors, sounds, smells). Each chapter's prelude is perhaps the most obviously paratactic element, with few of the preludes referencing any of the novel's characters or events and thus immediately requiring readers to speculate on how the prelude connects to the chapter that follows, but parataxis operates at every level in *The Years*. After its prelude, the first chapter begins like a more-or-less conventional family novel, with Colonel Pargiter introduced in his club, talking with "men of his own type" (4) about imperial deeds past, then wandering off to visit his mistress, Mira. Then, just as the Colonel begins to undress Mira with his three-fingered hand, the scene ends and we read a short paragraph in the same mode as the prelude (a brief impression of rain, a street singer, then sunlight) before jumping to the Pargiter children at home in a scene that requires readers to pay attention to a panoply of character names for which we do not yet have associations. The chapter ends with Mrs. Pargiter's funeral, and the next chapter jumps eleven years ahead to 1891, creating the first paratactic relationship between the chapters. Some of what happened between 1880 and 1891 will be referenced in the text, but much will be left for the reader to imagine. Between the scenes within the chapters, there are also gaps, for instance in the 1891 chapter, where Eleanor prepares to give her opinion at a committee meeting but the scene ends with, "She cleared her throat and began" (91), then a space break jumps us to a description of smoke and houses before returning us to Eleanor. It is not until pages later that we learn "she had won her scrap with Judd" (95) at the meeting; later, she will speak of the argument in an exaggerated way that is also not described (98). The absence of a dramatization of Eleanor's argument requires us as readers to imagine it for ourselves, and it focuses our attention not on the content of the debate but on Eleanor's own memory and presentation of it.

In addition to shaping attention and inspiring imagination, parataxis presents us with multiplicity that we must then make the effort of unifying within our imagination. We inescapably feel the need for such effort between the individual chapters, between the prelude sections and what follows, and between the many scenes separated from each other by space breaks (particularly in the "Present Day" chapter), but there is a similar effort necessary when moving between points of view within the same scene. Shifts in point of view are generally signaled by a space break between scenes, but not always, as, for instance, in the moment when Eleanor returns home from the committee meeting. As Colonel Pargiter waits for her, the narrative provides a few paragraphs of the Colonel's thoughts on whether to tell Eleanor about his relationship with Mira, and then, with only a paragraph break, the narrative shifts from the Colonel ("He began to carve the chicken") to Eleanor ("She was very hungry"), a shift smoothed only by the link of food (98). The chapter then stays with Eleanor's point of view until shifting to a one-paragraph objective scene before returning the narrative to the Colonel's point of view (109), breaking it only for a brief scene with Eugénie's servants (110). The chapters continue in this manner, shifting between perspectives until "1917," where the narrative presents actions and dialogue via Eleanor's point of view alone, and then "1918," the only single-scene chapter, limited to Crosby's point of view. "1918" is followed by "Present Day," in which numerous scenes and points of view are juxtaposed and brought together at Delia's party, and the novel ends with one last paratactic leap between the question "And now?" and the rising of the sun over a peaceful morning.

One particularly subtle example of Woolf's paratactic shifts between perspectives occurs in the 1907 chapter, as Sara tries to read her cousin Edward's translation of *Antigone*. She grows tired and hears the world outside: "Everything—the music, the voices—became stretched and generalized. The book fell on the floor. She was asleep" (128). The point of view then moves to a young woman and man outside.[13] They have a brief conversation, then the point of view shifts again: "The moon which was not clear of clouds lay in a bare space as if the light had consumed the heaviness of the clouds and left a perfectly clear pavement, a dancing ground for revelry. For some time the dappled iridescence of the sky remained unbroken. Then there was a puff of wind; and a little cloud crossed the moon" (129). The progression from Sara to an unknown and unnamed couple and then to the moon, sky, and clouds occurs in four paragraphs of fewer than 200 words. The passage moves our imagining first away from a familiar character to strangers and then from strangers to the nonhuman world above. The second part of the movement (from people we don't know to features of the landscape and nature) is similar to many of the prelude sections, but now it is anchored to the people of the main narrative.

In parataxis, Spivak says, "the absence of conjunction is felt as absence, if we read for singularity of language, respecting literature as fiction" (*Aesthetic* 357). If we read in such a way, seeking out, through a mix of reason and imagination, the absent connections, then the experience of "an overwhelming sense of parataxis (and how the relatively more connected passages negotiate it)" allows us to perceive "a formal description, a homology for what the language describes" (355). A lack of conjunction or transition between textual items increases the possibility of the reader becoming confused, and even frustrated, but as we seek paths out of our confusion and frustration, we train ourselves to bridge the gaps. As the paratactic structure continues, revealing the fractal logic in the chaos, we not only continue to practice certain ways of imagining, but we now extend that practice across more and more of the text and simultaneously strengthen previous habits of reading and thinking while also building new habits. Those habits may then be extended beyond this particular novel, thus functioning as a kind of immunization against the ideological force of the conventional novel.

---

[13] McNees's edition for Harcourt, which I have used for citations through this article, inserts a space break between Sara falling asleep and the shift to outside, creating a greater separation between the points of view. However, this break is not present in either the Oxford World's Classics edition edited by Hermione Lee or the authoritative edition edited by Anna Snaith for the Cambridge Edition of the Works of Virginia Woolf. While many readers would, like McNees, likely read the lack of a space break as an error, the evidence of both this specific scene in the novel and Snaith's meticulous edition suggests that Woolf wanted the point of view changes here to be between paragraphs without added space between them.

Immunity is a concept Woolf explored in a July 1932 diary entry: "To be immune, means to exist apart from rubs, shocks, suffering; to be beyond the range of darts; to have enough to live on without courting flattery, success; not to need to accept invitations; not to mind other people being praised… Immunity is an exalted calm desirable state, & one I could reach much oftener than I do" (*D*4 117). It's a feeling Eleanor has in the "1917" chapter when she rests and feels a sense of timeless, egoless calm. A traditional picture (perhaps of Italy) has no effect on her: "She lay back in the chair. Everything seemed to become quiet and natural again. A feeling of great calm possessed her. It was as if another space of time had been issued to her, but, robbed by the presence of death of something personal, she felt — she hesitated for a word; 'immune?' Was that what she meant? Immune, she said, looking at a picture without seeing it. Immune, she repeated. It was a picture of a hill and a village perhaps in the South of France; perhaps in Italy. There were olive trees; and white roofs grouped against a hillside. Immune, she repeated, looking at the picture" (278). The idea of a work of art possessing (and perhaps conveying) immunity reappears in the "Present Day" chapter, this time through Peggy's perception: "She looked at the picture of her grandmother as if to ask her opinion. But she had assumed the immunity of a work of art; she seemed as she sat there, smiling at her roses, to be indifferent to our right and wrong" (310).

While parataxis offers one strategy for immunization, we can see another in what Woolf does with the sorts of regular details so essential to the verisimilitude conjured by conventional social realism. The array of details in *The Years* could be assumed, on first reading, to be representing a status quo of ordinary life and things as they are, but they fail to work that way — they feel somehow unmoored, even random, and soon the reader may grow as frustrated as Phyllis Rose, who complained about "Woolf's refusal to define a central character or to shape a narrative, while heaping upon us the kind of detail that demands such a shape" (213), or Pamela Transue, for whom the novel becomes "tedious in its attention to trivialities which often seem dwelled upon to no purpose" (165). The sense of the details as trivial and purposeless is tied to an idea of what a novel like this one should do and be — the shape it demands — and *The Years* will inevitably frustrate such assumptions. The normal (and normalizing) imperatives of the traditional novel simply do not fit. If, however, the reader does not give up, and instead seeks out a new way of thinking about the purpose and effect of the apparently trivial or random details, then that reader may discover new frameworks to apply to what they read.

As the novel progresses, conversations become more fragmentary and interrupted (usually it is men interrupting women), memories drift, and communication itself seems, inevitably, to fail. Yet Woolf is not Beckett. Failure and silence are present, but they are not the end point. In a world of fascism, silence can too easily become consent or complicity (normalizing discourses don't mind silence).

We must remember the prelude narrator. Without that narrative voice, it would be more difficult to make sense of the many scattered moments that make up *The Years*. The prelude narrator doesn't do this work for us, but rather, like a good teacher, suggests some possibilities and then lets us try things on our own.[14] The prelude narrator has the freedom to dart from perspective to perspective, fact to fact, moment to moment. As readers, we must free ourselves to do the same. Only with such freedom of movement and such open, flexible perspective will we be able to make meaning from the text that follows each prelude.

The "1880" prelude begins with a description of the season and weather, of country and city. It then starts, slowly, to zoom in: spring becomes April; all the people of London become shop assistants, "ladies in flounced dresses"; "shoppers in the West End"; businessmen; people mailing letters; people standing at the windows of clubs in Piccadilly; "ladies in many-coloured dresses wearing bustles, and … gentlemen in frock coats carrying canes"; the Princess; "servant girls in cap and apron"; "diners-out, trotting over the Bridge in hansom cabs" (3-4). The mass becomes comprehensible as we see how it is made up of individual groups, and how each of those groups is made up of individuals. The narrator then pulls back to describe the moon and the clouds above it all, the world of nature beyond the constructions of human society. The sky unites perception: each person who looks up sees that sky and that moon from their own vantage point. The sky and moon may be indifferent to human life and action, but they are as enmeshed in time as the humans are: "Slowly wheeling, like the rays of a searchlight, the days, the weeks, the years passed one after another across the sky" (4). Despite the floating perception of the prelude narrator, though, there is no unifying perception in the novel. The narration does not do the reader's work; instead, it reminds us to think beyond the immediate perspective in any scene, to imagine the world outside the walls of any one room, to imagine lives lived outside the text.

At the beginning of the novel, Delia and Eleanor stand at a window and watch a cab stop two doors down, and so, too, at the end, Eleanor stands and watches a cab stop two doors down, while Delia admires the loveliness of roses.[15] The moment is circular within the novel's structure, but Woolf's repetition is like jazz, always with some bit of difference, some revision. At the window, Eleanor asks a question to end the long night, a question that was previously asked by Kitty in 1910 as she watched *Siegfried* and by Sara in 1917 when everyone went into the cellar for

---

[14] Taylor notes that Woolf and Freire's approaches are both "problem-posing pedagogies" (73), and the approach is true of Woolf's novels, as well.
[15] In her "Letter to a Young Poet," Woolf advised: "All you need now is to stand at the window and let your rhythmical sense open and shut, open, and shut, boldly and freely, until one thing melts in another, until the taxis are dancing with the daffodils, until a whole has been made from all these separate fragments" (*E5* 315).

the air raid, and the words are ones Martin stuttered to Sara in 1914 when trying to get her to speak to him, and they remain a question for all of us: "And now?"

A blank space follows, and then only the final sentence: "The sun had risen, and the sky above the houses wore an air of extraordinary beauty, simplicity, and peace." Eleanor's question isn't answered. The gap, that blank space, stands between the individual characters (trapped in their time and circumstances) and the egoless, enraptured moment of the sky's beauty, simplicity, and peace. "We are forced to lay down our weapons as readers," Jane Marcus wrote of Woolf's work. "All our egotism and individuality, the swords and shields of the hated 'I, I, I' must be abandoned outside the doors of her fiction" (*Art & Anger* 82). If we can imagine a way to bridge the gap, then we have learned what we needed to learn. Our readerly weapons have not only been laid down, but reconfigured into new tools, the sharp edges now set to plow the soil rather than shed blood, preparing us to imagine fresh growth rather than more death. The narrative voice of this novel is no patriarch laying an outline of history before us; our lessons are over, we have gained immunization against authoritarianism by strengthening our imaginations with paratactic practice, we have escaped the prison of "I, I, I," and we are left to do our own work, to shape our own world, to explore limits, to imagine new worlds, and to figure the impossible.

Works Cited

Amidon, Stevens. "*The Years*: Mapping a Genre." *The CEA Critic*, vol. 71, no. 3, 2009, pp. 85-99.

Andrews, Charles. "'Beauty, Simplicity and Peace': Faithful Pacifism, Activist Writing, and *The Years*." *Virginia Woolf: Writing the World*, edited by Pamela L. Caughie and Diana L. Swanson, Clemson UP, 2015, pp. 63-67.

Fernald, Anne E. *Virginia Woolf: Feminism and the Reader*. Palgrave Macmillan, 2006.

Friedman, Susan Stanford. "Virginia Woolf's Pedagogical Scenes of Reading: *The Voyage Out*, *The Common Reader*, and Her 'Common Readers.'" *MFS: Modern Fiction Studies*, vol. 38, no. 1, Jan. 2009, pp. 101-25.

Gottlieb, Laura Moss. "*The Years*: A Feminist Novel." *Virginia Woolf: Centennial Essays*, edited by Elaine K. Ginsberg and Laura Moss Gottlieb, Whitston Pub. Co, 1983, pp. 215-29.

Gregory, Rosalyn, and Benjamin Kohlmann, editors. *Utopian Spaces of Modernism: British Literature and Culture, 1885-1945*. Palgrave Macmillan, 2012.

Hagen, Benjamin D. "Feeling Shadows: Virginia Woolf's Sensuous Pedagogy." *PMLA*, vol. 132, no. 2, Mar. 2017, pp. 266-80.

Haule, James. "Reading Dante, Misreading Woolf: New Evidence of Virginia Woolf's Revision of *The Years*." *Woolf Editing/Editing Woolf: Selected Papers from the Eighteenth Annual Conference on Virginia Woolf*, edited by Eleanor McNees and Sara Veglahn, Clemson UP, 2009, pp. 232-54.

Jameson, Fredric. *Archaeologies of the Future: The Desire Called Utopia and Other Science Fictions*. Verso, 2007.

Katz, Tamar. "Pausing, Waiting, Repeating: Urban Temporality in *Mrs. Dalloway* and *The Years*." *Woolf and the City: Selected Papers from the Nineteenth Annual Conference on Virginia Woolf*, edited by Elizabeth F. Evans, Clemson U Digital P, 2010, pp. 2-16.

Marcus, Jane. *Hearts of Darkness: White Women Write Race*. Rutgers UP, 2004.

———. *Art & Anger: Reading Like a Woman*, Ohio State UP, 1988.

———. *Virginia Woolf and the Languages of Patriarchy*. Indiana UP, 1987.

Periyan, Natasha. "'Altering the Structure of Society': An Institutional Focus on Virginia Woolf and Working-Class Education in the 1930s." *Textual Practice*, Jan. 2017, pp. 1-23.

Roemer, Kenneth M. "Paradise Transformed: Varieties of Nineteenth Century Utopias." *The Cambridge Companion to Utopian Literature*, edited by Gregory Claeys, Cambridge UP, 2010, pp. 79-106.

Rose, Phyllis. *Woman of Letters: A Life of Virginia Woolf*. Harcourt Brace Jovanovich, 1987.

Saariluoma, Liisa. "Virginia Woolf's *The Years*: Identity and Time in an Anti-Family Novel." *Orbis Litterarum*, vol. 54, no. 4, Aug. 1999, pp. 276-300.

Spivak, Gayatri Chakravorty. *An Aesthetic Education in the Era of Globalization*. Harvard UP, 2012.

———. *Readings*. Seagull Books, 2014.

Stec, Loretta. "Dystopian Modernism vs Utopian Feminism: Burdekin, Woolf, and West Respond to the Rise of Fascism." *Virginia Woolf and Fascism: Resisting the Dictators' Seduction*, edited by Merry M. Pawlowski, Palgrave, 2001, pp. 178-93.

Suh, Judy. "The Comedy of Outsiders in Virginia Woolf's *The Years*." *Fascism and Anti-Fascism in Twentieth-Century British Fiction*, Palgrave Macmillan, 2009, pp. 138-82.

Taylor, Rod C. "Narrow Gates and Restricted Paths: The Critical Pedagogy of Virginia Woolf." *Woolf Studies Annual*, vol. 20, 2014, pp. 55-81.

Transue, Pamela J. *Virginia Woolf and the Politics of Style*. State U of New York P, 1986.

Wheare, Jane. *Virginia Woolf: Dramatic Novelist*. Palgrave Macmillan, 1989.

Woolf, Leonard. *The Framework of a Lasting Peace*. G. Allen & Unwin Ltd., 1917.

Woolf, Virginia. *The Diary of Virginia Woolf.* Edited by Anne Olivier Bell and Andrew McNeillie, Harcourt Brace Jovanovich, 1977-84. 5 vols.

———. *The Essays of Virginia Woolf.* Edited by Andrew McNeillie and Stuart N. Clarke, Hogarth P, 1986-2011. 6 vols.

———. *Jacob's Room.* 1922. Edited by Vara Neverow, Annotated ed., Harcourt, 2008.

———. *The Letters of Virginia Woolf.* Edited by Nigel Nicolson and Joanne Trautmann Banks, Harcourt Brace Jovanovich, 1975-80. 6 vols.

———. *The Pargiters: The Novel-Essay Portion of The Years.* Edited by Mitchell A. Leaska, Harcourt Brace Jovanovich, 1978.

———. *Three Guineas.* 1938. Edited by Jane Marcus, Annotated ed., Harcourt, 2006.

———. *The Years.* 1937. Edited by Eleanor McNees, Annotated ed., Harcourt, 2008.

Zwerdling, Alex. *Virginia Woolf and the Real World.* U of California P, 1986.

Articles

A Driving Bloomsbury: Virginia Woolf, Vanessa Bell, and the Meaning of the Motor-Car[1]
Robin Adair & Ann Martin

The materialization of modernity in literary, aural, and visual forms has been recognized in its corollary: modernism's expression through both mass-marketed and bespoke consumer goods. In the shift of critical attention to this dynamic interplay between cultural registers, the motor-car has emerged as a signifier not just of technological innovation, individualism, and accelerated motion, but of modernist experience itself. In its status as commodity, it speaks to the liberating aspects of early twentieth-century consumerism, representing an appeal to an "affordable individual mobility" (Daly 114) that promises the crossing of social lines. It is no coincidence that Orlando's fast-paced shopping trip to Marshall & Snelgrove's in "the present moment" is enabled by an automobile: "She ran downstairs, she jumped into her motor-car, she pressed the self-starter and was off" (284, 285). As her driving demonstrates, the car is a form of personalized, mechanized speed that enables the modern subject "to experience space in a new way" (Duffy 19), that changes "the mode of organization of human sensory perception" (Minow-Pinkney 178), and that alters "subject/object relations" (Goldman 51). By thus mediating "new forms of perceptual experience" (Sim 122), the motor-car "grounds a more abstract sense of flux and change that many modernist writers attempted to articulate in their texts" (Thacker 8), where the physical and cognitive shifts with which the automobile is associated are reflected in the artistic experimentations of the day.

There is a tension, of course, between the motor-car as a privileged "metaphor for modernity" (Thoms, Holden, and Clayton 1) and the motor-car as an object that is itself open to interpretation. To regard motoring in the early twentieth century as a singular experience or universal aesthetic is to overlook the meaning of a given car: the significance of its engine, chassis, and coachwork; of its styling, ornamentation, and interior; of the marque, model, and year, all of which determine the vehicle's socioeconomic and cultural implications. The specifics of that given vehicle's use— the roads driven or tracks raced; the physical demands of driving according to the car and the conditions; the legal particulars of production, importation, taxation,

---

[1] We are extremely grateful for generous advice provided by the two anonymous reviewers of this article. We are also indebted to Gill Lowe, Helen Wussow, and Keith Bell. Our project was funded in part by a Graduate Catalyst Award through the College of Arts and Science, University of Saskatchewan. This essay is for Jennifer.

and ownership; the cost of tires, petrol, parking, maintenance, insurance, accidents, and so on—further situate motoring as a complex interplay of experiences, associations, and desires that vary according to time, place, manufacturer, owner, driver, and automobile. In other words, while motor-car production "came to stand as a symbol of manufacturing industry" in the interwar period (Benson 39) and to represent one of "the two most spectacular consequences of the second industrial (or techno-scientific) revolution" (Trotter, "Techno-Primitivism" 151), the local, material histories of actual vehicles complicate the car's identification as a general reference point for the processes and outcomes of modernization.

Because the significance of the automobile shifts according to contexts of use, it invokes significantly different connotations within the same cultural moment. Through these various affiliations—with mechanical innovation, with new experiences and perceptions, with modernist experimentation, with early twentieth-century commodity culture, with performed identities, with the feelings that arise at driving and being driven, with the affective dimensions of advertisement and patriotic landscapes—motor-cars link what only appear to be dissimilar elements of modernity. In so doing, they illuminate a pattern of discourses through which the vehicles are understood, and whose stakes are enunciated with terrible clarity in the military applications of what is ostensibly civilian technology. The companies that enabled interwar Britain to drive are the same companies that produced aeroplane engines, small arms, and armoured vehicles during World War One,[2] and that developed new adaptations of automotive machines for the Spanish Civil War and World War Two. Articulating such national and global investments, as well as individual desires and subjectivity, motor-cars exist at the intersection of personal and public modes of signification, illustrating the complexities and instabilities that attend technology's integration into daily, modern life.

Even within Bloomsbury, interpretations and implementations of the motor-car's potential blur a clear distinction between the democratic and the hierarchical, or the freeing and the fettering connotations read into or out of modern machines.[3] The most immediate association between driving and Bloomsbury may, indeed, be its members' unmodern automotive incompetence; and yet cars sustained connections (and reiterated divisions) among the members of this variously defined circle of artists and intellectuals clustered around members of the Stephen family (see Rosenbaum x). Their automobiles meant that travel to the Continent need not follow train schedules or involve hired cars, with the result being a "wonderful

---

[2] See Ann Martin's "Sky-Haunting: The British Motor-Car Industry and the World Wars."
[3] As Tony Pinkney points out, "whereas today revolution and the commodity, political activism and technological novelty, responsibility and 'post-modernist' hedonism are a rigid binary opposition we can hardly think our way out of, for the early-twentieth-century metropolis they fruitfully interbreed: mass-production is 'democratic', technology sweeps away vestigial feudal survivals, and socialism will liberate a dynamism that capitalism fetters" (16).

feeling of liberation," as Leonard Woolf put it (179). Their automobiles facilitated the painting, writing, hosting, and sightseeing that took place in France, Italy, and Germany during a time of artistic and political upheaval. They enabled exploration of a rapidly changing English countryside as well as self-determined movement between Tavistock Square and Monk's House, Gordon Square and Charleston. Motoring was also a medium for sibling rivalry, as Virginia Woolf and Vanessa Bell asserted the superiority of their respective cars in letters aimed to tease and provoke. Even so, their automobiles represented a common mode of financial agency. Christine Froula has discussed the early role of "paid work" in freeing the Stephen sisters from the expectations of the "marriage market" (572). More than twenty years after their symbolic move to Gordon Square, a different kind of license arrives in the form of the motor-car, "the greatest agent for freedom" in the modern era (Dunn 233)—and a consumer good made accessible to the sisters through their participation in the markets of modernism.

Where the motor-car has the potential to liberate bodies and minds, and thus to reflect the revolutionary impulses of modernity for women as for men, it can—subsequently or simultaneously—create new restrictions and exclusions, or be used to reassert familiar social relations in different forms.[4] Virginia Woolf's and Vanessa Bell's interactions with the complex social imaginary that informed the status of automobiles in interwar Britain illustrate that "the modernist present is always saturated with various pasts and futures" (Driscoll 160). Those layered impulses inform the discourses that characterize the sisters' representations and uses of automobiles. Woolf's references to motor-cars and motoring in her diaries, letters, essays, and prose fiction illustrate her engagement with modern technology and thus undermine assumptions that she "had no interest in cars" (Holroyd, *On* 64). Her inclusion of details such as the puncture on Bond Street that shocks Clarissa Dalloway (*MD* 14) and the actions of the chauffeur as he replaces the tire (16) speaks to her familiarity with automobile maintenance and the demands of car ownership.[5]

---

[4] David Trotter emphasizes the importance of the "overlapping and mutually definitive appearances on the market and in social and cultural view" of commodities in his study of materials—rubber, glass, plastics—out of which consumer goods were manufactured ("Modernism's" 58). We use his position here with regard to the manufactured goods that are automobiles, but with a similar intention: "to avoid the assumption that they were once widely understood, and they should still be understood, as in some uncomplicated fashion a 'sign of the new' (Brown, 2009, p.152)" (Trotter, "Modernism's" 58).

[5] Woolf's knowledge is signaled by the figure of Miss Pym (*MD* 14), who recognizes the sound of a punctured tire: a not-uncommon occurence before the widespread adaptation of balloon tires, which could be inflated to a much lower pressure, and during a period in which horse traffic would leave horseshoe nails on roads. However, the noise in this scene is often misinterpreted as a backfire. Backfiring indicates a problem with the fuel-air ratio: the engine is running rich. The sound is of raw fuel combusting in the exhaust. Backfiring is now rare because of fuel-injected engines, but in the past would require an adjustment of

However, she pairs that knowledge of the mechanical aspects of cars with her recognition of their signification of social status. Thus, just as Sir William Bradshaw is placed by the "sober suavity" of his "low, powerful, grey" car (103), so Woolf's descriptions in her personal writings of her own automobiles derive from the classed language of automotive advertising and the social hierarchy of owner-drivers. The tension between driving as a personally and artistically inspiring act, and driving as a reiteration and consolidation of position within "the patriarchal power game" (Minow-Pinkney 161) is evident too in the work of Vanessa Bell, whose attempts at balance and rhythm in her life and art were both mediated and problematized by the cars that moved her (and others) to the spaces in which she painted. Her participation in the marketing of British motoring through the Shell-Mex advertising campaign, as well as her seemingly insular resistance to the encroachment of car culture in East Sussex—and the encroachment of fellow Bloomsberries on her working life at Charleston—is, however, of a piece with Woolf's unresolved navigations of motoring and its class connotations. Within Bloomsbury, as within interwar Britain, the motor-car exerts a material influence on lived experience that arises from its multifaceted cultural and symbolic currency. With the coming of another war, the automobile's role in daily life takes on an additional and perhaps unexpected weight, as motoring continues to enact a more than metaphorical shift for Woolf and Bell.

In the summer of 1927, and within weeks of each other, Woolf and Bell buy their first automobiles, begin their first driving lessons, and embark upon sightseeing trips through the English landscape, coming to store their motor-cars, it would appear, in the same Judd Street garage (*L3* 497, 509). Motoring was a form of connection between the two. In practical terms, it fuelled the "constant physical movement" between Monk's House and Charleston that Nuala Hancock has viewed as "a material enactment of Woolf's and Bell's reciprocity" (50), and that Diane Gillespie has noted as central to Woolf's writing: in "identifying with her sister as closely as she did, Virginia felt more certain of her own artistic gifts" (10).

---

the choke, which would be located on the dashboard. Alternatively, it could be a question of timing (i.e. of the ignition), which was often adjustable through a lever, also on the dash. Neither would require the driver to stop the vehicle or get out of the car. A possible reason for the chauffeur to get off "the box" (16) might be to adjust the carburetor in order to make the fuel mix leaner. This would entail a significant amount of time and work: opening the hood to access the engine; using a screwdriver to adjust a difficult-to-reach part in the internals; testing the fix. It seems highly unlikely that the driver would conduct such sensitive and detailed mechanical labor (best done in a garage) on the side of a noisy, busy London street, let alone so very quickly. He could, however, change a flat tire quite readily using the tools and spare that he—like many drivers—would carry in the trunk of the vehicle, and which would involve him "opening something, turning something, shutting something" according to the view that Rezia has of his actions (16).

But motoring was a mode of rivalry too. In their continual attempts to articulate their defining attributes as artists in relation to each other, the motor-car became a medium for assertions of difference and distinction. Just as the sisters determined their success according to their comparative artistic standings and contributions to modernist innovation, so Woolf and Bell compared their skills behind the wheel and distinguished themselves through their performative choice of vehicles. Where the Woolfs chose British marques—two Singers in 1927 and 1928 respectively, and a 1933 Lanchester—Vanessa and Duncan Grant drove a Renault and a Citroën, though they used Julian's Baby Austin as well (V. Bell, *SL* 332, 365).

It would appear that Vanessa was the first sister to buy a car. On 7 July 1927, Vanessa Bell sent a letter to her eldest son, Julian, telling him that she had meant to write earlier but that she had "been frightfully busy lately": Fred Pape, on his holidays, had been providing her with driving lessons in her "own car. I have had it nearly a week now," she writes, "and so far have killed no one and done the car no damage" (*SL* 319). On 23 July, just a few days after Virginia and Leonard had bought their first automobile, Woolf writes to her sister about taking driving lessons with another Fred:

> my whole life is spent motoring with Harris. Not that I've had as many lessons as I should like. I'm now competent to drive alone in the country, he says. I think it is a very exciting employment. [*sic*] and he says (but this may be flattery) that I'm well above the average. We both have the same fault—you and I—we keep too much to the left. But my gear changing is very good. (*L3* 401)

She informs Vanessa cheekily that Harris will be driving with the Woolfs to Charleston that Sunday: "Then you will see me take the wheel and return—It is an awesome sight."

All that summer, Woolf used her letters and diary to express her excitement about the car. To Janet Case: "We have bought a motor car (this is the cut of the Lighthouse) and I have been wobbling round and round Windmill Hill, every day, trying to avoid dogs and children" (*L3* 403). To Saxon Sydney-Turner: "We drive over to Charleston and find Nessa has driven somewhere else. Clive to protect himself is going to learn to drive; because we talk of nothing but gears and cylinders" (*L3* 411). To Ethel Sands she confesses that "We still do nothing but talk about motors" (*L3* 417), and in early September, she conveys the same hyperbolic combination of pride, self-parody, and enthusiasm in a letter to Lytton Strachey:

> All the rest of the news is motor car gossip. We flash through Sussex almost daily; drop in after dinner; visit ruins; muse by retired moats, of which Sussex is full; surprise Colonels—it is a perfect invention. What we did without it

> passes comprehension. Most of the Victorian horror seems explicable by the
> fact that they walked, or sat behind stout sweating horses. (*L3* 418)

Woolf's delight for driving, and especially for excursions into the countryside, is echoed by Vanessa, who writes to Roger Fry of "various expeditions" on "heavenly days" to see castles and moats, and of having "a pic-nic with the Woolves the other day, each driving our rival cars" (*SL* 322).

The speed with which the vehicles became part of Woolf's and Bell's daily lives is not surprising, given the automobile's potential to facilitate the personal interactions at the heart of Bloomsbury. During Christmas 1927, for example, Vanessa writes to her sister of her intention to motor to Ham Spray to see Lytton, and then to drive "to Snow [Margery Snowden] at Cheltenham for the night," before heading back to London (*SL* 325). The place of the car in these trips through social and familial networks, as well as in both sisters' regular travel to the Continent,[6] suggests that their relationship to machines was as influential as that of any modernist. Anne Herrmann's assertion of the contrast between Woolf and Gertrude Stein, where "Woolf never learns to drive, never flies, and never goes to America" (88), would thus seem to overlook the enthusiasm with which the British writer embraces not just her travels to France—"This is the way to live, I assure you. Driving all day; an hour or two for lunch; a few churches perhaps to be seen" (*L3* 479)—but also the technical discourse of car ownership[7] and the driving lessons that she took with Vita Sackville-West in Regent's Park (Glendinning, *Vita* 179). And though Hermione Lee indicates that, by the time that Woolf returns to Cassis in the Spring of 1928, Leonard is at the wheel of the Singer, "which she was now not allowed to drive" (550), such wording seems at odds with Lee's earlier statement that "Virginia gave up driving" (509). Given Woolf's reference to "insufficient lessons" in a diary entry from 10 August 1927, in which she calls the car "the joy of our lives" (*D3* 151), and given Jan Morris's sense that "Virginia never learnt to drive properly, *leaving* that to Leonard" (7 emphasis added), it may be more accurate to view Woolf as a passenger who decides, in Quentin Bell's words, "to let herself be driven" (*Virginia* 129). It may have been in part because she had received less instruction than Leonard; in part, because being driven allowed for sightseeing and the kind of ruminations she expresses in "Evening over Sussex: Reflections in a Motor Car"; and, in part, perhaps, because she drove into a hedge.

---

[6] While "Vanessa Bell, Duncan Grant, and Roger Fry spent long periods living and painting in Southern France, particularly during the 1920s" (Caws and Wright 3), Jan Morris's sketch of Woolf's travels suggests the breadth of her experience, echoed by Vanessa's, as she went to The Netherlands, France, Italy, Spain, Greece, Turkey (13). In Leonard Woolf's view, Virginia "had a passion for travelling" (178).

[7] An example is her fascination with the Daimler transmission, the fluid fly-wheel, which was a prominent element of Lanchester marketing. See Ann Martin's "'Unity-Dispersity': Virginia Woolf and the Contradictory Motif of the Motor-car."

A rather younger Quentin collaborated with Woolf to parody her incompetence as a driver—and to joke about Vanessa's lack of skill, too—in the *Charleston Bulletin* of July 1927:

> The less said about July the better.
> Mrs. Bell drove from Hyde Pk-Corner to Marble Arch.
> Mr. Woolf drove from Marble Arch to Hyde Park Corner.
> Mrs. Woolf knocked a boy of [sic] his bicycle.
> Mrs. Bell killed a cat.
> The less said the better. (Woolf and Bell 113)

Two years later, Virginia would in turn critique her nephew's driving to Vanessa: "I thought we were smashed again and again, as the car is very stiff still, and he hasn't quite got the hang of it and doesn't know one street from another" (*L4* 53). Leonard was no prodigy either. Woolf notes that he "knocked a bit off the car getting it into the shed" in late July 1927 (*L3* 405) and "bumped the back of the car on the gate post" in September (*D3* 155). And when Woolf writes to Vanessa in January 1928 that "You will be sorry, but not surprised, to hear that Leonard passed his [driving] test at Brighton without any difficulty first shot," she makes sure to add "I never thought he would. We almost collided with a bus, and then ran into a culdesac unexpectedly" (*L3* 452).

Woolf's "you will be sorry to hear" is part of an on-going exchange with Vanessa and Duncan regarding their own attempts at the driver's test, which was not truly official in Britain until 1934. As she wrote on 29 September 1927, "We were amused, indeed pleased, at least Leonard was, to hear you had both failed at your [driving] exam" (*L3* 424). Though Vanessa became a regular motorist—be it in London, at Charleston, or at La Bergère, the villa in Cassis that she and Duncan leased from Colonel Teed—her accounts of motoring suggest that driving was a work in progress. During a trip to Marseilles, for example, where Duncan was rattled by the presence of a police officer, he turned the wheel over to Vanessa. "I considered I did very well," she writes to her sister. "It's true that at one moment we found ourselves in a narrow passage with no possible exit and I had to go back between large heaps of stones on one side and a car standing on the other to get out of it. We held up a good sized crowd for some time while I made my way out and received a great deal of good advice from experts who crowded round" (*SL* 329). It is in France in March 1928 that she has a minor collision with a bus (*L3* 472), but she seems rather more accomplished than Duncan, whose inept approach to mechanical matters is noted by Woolf in a letter to Julian from February 1928: "Duncan turns the screws the wrong way and mechanics have to be wired for from Marseilles to turn them the right way" (*L3* 465). Frances Spalding notes tactfully, even euphemistically, that, as a driver, "(Duncan was always in a class of his own)" (232), but his friends were not so far behind. Lytton Strachey had bought a car in 1922, and "since neither Carrington nor he understood it," Ralph Partridge took the wheel (Holroyd, *Lytton* 511). Roger Fry's "energetic mode of doing everything caused him to frighten passengers, other motorists, and passersby" (Caws and Wright 212). Indeed, when Bunny Garnett decided to land his private aeroplane on the field behind Charleston, Fry was so distracted coming up the drive "that he ran slap into a gate post" (Q. Bell, *Bloomsbury* 114). Adrian Stephen and his wife Karin ran their new car into a truck in London in May 1928 (*L3* 499). Almost 20 years later, when Leonard put the Lanchester "back on the road" following the war, he received a series of tickets, including one "for driving after midnight without lights" (Glendinning, *Leonard* 354). As Angelica Garnett remarks, for the Bloomsberries, "machinery appeared to take control of them rather than the other way around" (101).

As important as *how* Bloomsbury drove, however, is their sense of *what* they drove, for the social significance they perceived in owning and operating automobiles reflects the complicated dynamics of the group and, especially, the performance of identity that was central to the relationship between Woolf and her sister. It's significant, then, that Vanessa bought a used Renault for her first car. Though its purchase was contemplated in France, the automobile was acquired in London (Woolf and Bell 110),[8] and while Vanessa does not specify the make in a letter to Julian, she is clearly taken with the vehicle: "The car is a beauty and I think a great bargain. It's practically new, being a 1927 model, and has been very little used. It's extremely comfortable and can really hold 5 people quite well" (*SL* 319). Woolf's diary entry of 11 July 1927 describes Vanessa arriving at Tavistock Square "rather nervously in control of a roomy shabby Renault with Fred beside her" (*D3* 146), and the same make is the topic of Vanessa's letter to Leonard Woolf in February 1928. "If you know anything about the clutch of a Renault," she writes, "you will know that it is necessary for the 'male cone to penetrate further and further into the female cone, pushing the tongues back until it is gripped perfectly.' Our male cone failed to do this. The leather got worn and finally burnt to shreds" (*SL* 327). The clutch is fixed in Cassis by a neighbor who used to race cars, but Virginia's response focuses more on the sexual side of things: "I can't believe your amazing stories of the Male and Female parts of the Renault. Do the French sexualise their engines? The Singer I know for a fact to be hermaphrodite, like the poet Cowper" (*L3* 463).

---

[8] Renault had had a British presence since the turn of the century, but, "taking a leaf from Citroën's book at Slough," the company expanded and established a large factory in "Acton where limited assembly took place in order to reduce the effects of the increased McKenna import duties levied from July 1925" (Baldwin 149). Given these duties, as well as tax ratings on horsepower, a Renault purchased by a British citizen in Britain would have been less costly than one bought in France.

Singer was a British marque, and the Woolfs bought their first on 15 July 1927, after much deliberation. Indeed, in *The Charleston Bulletin*, Quentin and his Aunt characterize the choice as an all-consuming process that boiled down to a series of oppositions:

> ... Citroën or Singer?
> Buick or Renault?
> Saloon or Touring?
> Four Cylinder or Six? (Woolf and Bell 113)

The Woolfs settled on a second-hand Singer "with 7,500 miles on the odometer," for which they paid £275 (Glendinning, *Leonard* 244) and which Leonard, writing decades later, refers to repeatedly as "old" (181). By September, "The Renault & the Singer new took the roads together, & it was found unnecessary for either car to use its horn, since the driver of each never ceased to trumpet the praises of his own conveyance" (Woolf and Bell 113-15). Woolf was tremendously proud of the car. David Bradshaw notes that, following Quentin Bell's pointed commentary on the rivalry that ensued, it is Woolf who added "But impartial observers were unanimously of the opinion that the SINGER WAS THE BEST" (ix). And indeed, the same spirit of automotive competition underpins her representations of the Woolfs' 1928 motor trip to Cassis. Even before they leave, Woolf writes to Julian that the Singer "is absolutely sublime" (*L3* 464). In April, she writes to Quentin from La Bergère that "We arrived here before our time, owing to the impetuous and fiery nature of the Singer, which went quicker and quicker, so that we were almost run away with through France" (*L3* 480). Upon returning to England, she records in her diary that "We have been across France & back—every inch of that fertile field traversed by the admirable Singer" (*D3* 179). In a letter to Quentin, however, Julian points out that Leonard was argumentatively exacting in his determination to split the costs of fuel with Vanessa and Duncan (Glendinning, *Leonard* 245), and after the Woolfs have gone home, Vanessa writes to Quentin that the Woolfs' car "had innumerable punctures": "The Old Umbrella"—the nickname for the Singer[9]—"was badly shaken on these roads and drank up several gallons of water a day, while our brave Renault is on its native heath and behaves beautifully. But no doubt you've had a prejudiced account of that" (*SL* 331).

The rivalry between the sisters and their cars—British and French—pales, however, in relation to their jointly constructed and not entirely playful scorn for John Maynard Keynes and his wife, Lydia Lopokova, whose vehicles draw forth the underlying class consciousness of Bloomsbury motor culture. The Keyneses

---

[9] In turn, Woolf refers to Vanessa's Renault as "the old char's bonnet" (*L3* 478), perhaps because of the "coalscuttle" hood of pre-war and 1920s Renaults.

had taken a lease on Tilton near Charleston in 1926 (Mackerell 227), very much to Vanessa's chagrin, whose attitude is noted by Woolf in a diary entry in which she deliberates on buying a motor-car:

> It will I think demolish loneliness, & may of course imperil complete privacy. The Keynes' have one too—a cheap one. Nessa thinks it will break down at once. Nessa takes a very sinister view of the Keynes'. She anticipates ruin of every sort for them, with some pleasure too. (*D*3 147)

A similar theme is evident in a September letter from Woolf to Ethel Sands:

> We motor all over Sussex—to Bodiam, Herstmonceaux, and so on, and have motor picnics, and compare our engines, and deride the Keynes'—who have a Morris Cowley, secondhand. You can imagine Nessa's derision. But my engine runs sweeter than hers—tell her so, please, with my love, next time you see her. (*L*3 417)

While it appears to have been a common pastime in late summer and early Fall to "buzz about the country in our cars, and abuse the Keynese's" (*L*3 518), by December 1929, the grounds for abuse have shifted. In her diary entry of the 28th, Woolf notes "the Keynes's have just wrecked my perfect fortnight of silence, have been over in their Rolls Royce—& L. made them stay, & is a little inclined to think me absurd for not wishing it" (*D*3 276). A motor-car is still the vehicle for resentment here, but the Rolls has replaced the Morris in Woolf's critique of the financially ascendant Keyneses. Her letter to Vanessa the next day emphasizes her distaste for both the car and its driver:

> What should we find at the gate, coming back to tea on Saturday in the rain, but a seedy grey Rolls-Royce; with the detestable Edgar [chauffeur], and the Keynes'. I dont see that ones friends have any right to mutilate one's life in this way. … But of course I admit they were amiable in the extreme. But then, curse them, we have to lunch at Tilton tomorrow. Leonard and I argued for an hour this morning—he says we are snobs and exaggerate. (*L*4 118)

Woolf's position slips and slides in this excerpt, as in so much of her personal writing; it prefigures in particular her tone in "Am I A Snob?" in which she condemns her own "egotism" (205) through its contrast to the modesty of Keynes: "Pigs, plays, pictures—he will talk of them all. But never of Prime Ministers and peerages. Alas and alas—Maynard is not a snob" (206). But the exclusivity of Bloomsbury (particularly where Lydia Lopokova was concerned) emerges nevertheless in her resistance to the invasion of her quiet and to the disruption of her sense of identity brought about by the chauffeur-driven Rolls-Royce.

The issue here is not that Maynard Keynes "of course had a motorcar" (Glendinning, *Leonard* 245), but that Woolf was attuned to the kind of motor-car Maynard Keynes had, and that she understands and mobilizes her cultural knowledge of both of his cars in her diaries and letters as those vehicles signify his status. Keynes's 11.9hp Morris Cowley was significantly less powerful than any popular Rolls engine of the 1920s, which would have had a Treasury rating of at least 40hp (Baldwin 133, 155). The gap in performance was attended by an equally significant gap in price. Where the cost of the Cowley had been dropped in 1921, so that, by 1925, the model sold for just over £160, most Rolls-Royces would have priced at least £1000 higher—and that sum would not have included the custom bodywork contracted to "specialist coachbuilders" for all 1920s and 1930s models (Baldwin 156). Though Keynes had bought the Rolls-Royce used from Samuel Courtauld (Skidelsky 217), the prestige of the marque—even a "seedy grey" example of the marque, through which Woolf both invokes and undermines the significance of Bradshaw's automobile from *Mrs. Dalloway*—becomes fuel for her ire. Indeed, Woolf's characterization of the Keyneses moves them into Sibyl Colefax territory, a social landscape summarized by Sibyl's chauffeur-driven Rolls and attempts "to impress me with the fact that she had known Henry James" ("Snob" 220).

Of course, the Woolfs had been undergoing their own social transformation, having sold the Old Umbrella and purchased a new Singer Sunshine Saloon in February 1929. This was a convertible known as the "As-U-Drive" to indicate the convenience of its retractable hood (*L4* 25). Where their first Singer had been purchased through advance sales of *To the Lighthouse*, "the Sunshade" (*L4* 57) was enabled by sales of *Orlando* and had cost them £270. Unfortunately, by April it proved to have a problematic clutch, which was, Virginia wrote to Vanessa, "a profound sorrow to Leonard. He thinks of buying a second car to keep in case of emergency. Now I daresay your Citroen is a perfect angel" (*L4* 41). This was the "smart new Citroën" that Vanessa and Duncan "shared with Colonel Teed" (Spalding 229), their landlord at La Bergère, and which had been bought in or around April 1929 as a replacement for the Renault, what with its mechanical issues. In a letter to Roger Fry from 15 August 1929, Vanessa, longing for Cassis, includes the Citroën in a list of what has been most on her mind: "our own house that can be heated, and books to read in the evenings, with our car" (qtd. Caws and Wright 223). A popular brand in the British market as well as the French, the Citroëns built at Slough in the mid- to the late-1920s sold in the £150-£190 range (Baldwin 58, 59), though the 12/20 Saloon was priced as high as £225. Regardless, it appears that Vanessa's vehicles—be they Renault or Citroën, or even the Morris that was in a shed at Charleston in 1931 (*SL* 366)—would have been less expensive than either of the Woolfs' Singers—and of course, both sisters' cars would have cost significantly less than the Keyneses' Rolls-Royce.

The class connotations of Bloomsbury's vehicles take on a new dimension in 1932 when the Woolfs buy a Lanchester 15/18 and when Woolf comes not merely to use but to revel in language derived from the classed and patriotic discourse of automotive marketing. Lanchester was owned by BSA (Birmingham Small Arms), the same company that had made the Lewis gun and military motorcycles for Britain in World War One and that had taken over Daimler, the automotive maker associated with the Royal Family from their first motoring.[10] The four-seater Lanchester 18 saloon, which had a retractable Tickford hood, was listed for £595 at the 1932 Olympia Motor Show in London ("The Olympia" 9). At less than half the price of a Rolls, such a vehicle would have allowed Woolf to remain distanced from the Keyneses and her perception of the privilege and authority associated with that marque: the Rolls-Royces of the "city magnates," for instance, who are depicted as being "furious" at the inconvenience of a traffic jam in "Flying Over London" (211). At the same time, and as she notes exaggeratedly in a letter to Ethel Smyth, the car links Woolf to a higher socioeconomic caste: "I feel ever so rich, conservative, patriotic, religious and humbuggish when I drive in it, and I enjoy this new Virginia immensely. She's one of the nicest people I know, and would love a party at Lady Roseberys above everything" (*L5* 154). As significantly, the car would seem to enable Woolf to connect with Vita Sackville-West. In a diary entry from August 1929, Woolf recalls driving to Long Barn with Vita and Dorothy Wellesley, and how she "had sat shyly in the motor observing their endearments rather awkwardly, & how they stopped the Rolls Royce[11] to buy great baskets of strawberries; & again I felt, not provincial, but ill-dressed, under-equipped" (*D3* 243). That shyness is gone when Woolf addresses one of her most exultant letters about the arrival of the Lanchester to Vita on 14 February 1933:

> I was going to say our car has come—silver and green, fluid fly wheel, Tickford hood—Lanchester 18—well what more could you want? It glides

---

[10] Daimler is a marque mentioned by Woolf several times, and usually in conjunction with tradition and formality. Reflecting on Jane Harrison's funeral in April 1928, for example, she writes: "Distinguished people drag up such queer chains of family when they die. They had hired Daimlers too, which succeeded the coffin at a foots pace" (D3 181). During the 1929 election, she notes the marque's role in a contemporary enactment of *noblesse oblige*: "We voted at Rodmell. I saw a white gloved lady helping an old farm couple out of her Daimler" (D3 231).

[11] This may have been Wellesley's, who had driven it to meet Vita, back from Persia, at Victoria Station in May 1926 (Glendinning, *Vita* 161). Even so, Sackville-West learned to drive, and learned that she loved to drive, in 1911, just a year before her mother bought a Rolls-Royce for £1450 (41, 45), and four years before Baroness Sackville bought Vita and Harold their own chauffeur-driven Rolls (77).

with the smoothness of eel, with the speed of a swift, and the—isn't this a good blurb?—the power of a tigress when that tigress has just been reft of her young in and out up and down Piccadilly, Bond Street. The worst of it is we cant live up to it. I've had to buy a new coat. But whats the good? Theres my hat. Thats all wrong—thats a Singer saloon hat. (*L*5 157)

The performative dimension of car ownership provides a sphere for the enactment of Woolf's success, literary as well as social, and the exaggeration of the persona—conveyed theatrically through her imagined body language, clothes, diction, and syntax—is again typical of Woolf's parodic self-positioning. She presents here a moving tableaux: experiencing the fascination of what it is like to be the Lanchester owner, and stepping into an alternative worldview to imagine the contradictory implications, both real and imagined, that this new perspective might unveil.[12]

Woolf's use of language from "blurbs" is, of course, an ironic recognition of the performance of identity to which advertisements appeal, but the sale and marketing of automobiles resonate powerfully with her position as "a literary professional"—a professional whose production of best-selling novels as author and as co-owner of the Hogarth Press suggests an "uncomfortable" proximity to the production of "mass culture" and the sale and marketing of art for popular consumption (Dubino 3). In "Reviewing," Woolf explores the tension between modern writers, situated as if "in the shop window, doing their work under the curious eyes of reviewers," and the reviewers who are more focused on "advertis[ing] [their] skill" than in "disinterested discussion" (152, 162). It is an image that has much in common with that of the vehicles behind "the plate-glass window of a motor-car manufacturer in Victoria Street," which Peter Walsh reflects upon as he reassures himself by thinking about his own mechanical abilities (*MD* 53). In such scenes, there is a distinction between the vehicle, be it writer or motor-car, and that object as situated within advertisement; that is, within social discourses of value and of identity performance. Woolf's "ambivalent" relationship to the modernist marketplace (Dubino 3) is signalled in these moments of staging and looking, as it is in her acknowledgement of the Lanchester as a commodity that has and speaks to a

---

[12] Both Virginia and Vanessa shared a lasting interest in role-playing, as evidenced by "the large variety of pieces performed in Bloomsbury" (Wright 77). Their ability to blur the line between life and art was, in part, shaped by their childhood and a communal domestic sphere, where they sought ways to process experiences of family trauma and transformation through imaginative play, storytelling, photography, and drawing and painting. Such creativity was surely informed by the artists connected to the Stephen household, such as Julia Margaret Cameron. Richard Shone notes the "curious continuity between Cameron's fantastic, contrived and mood-pervaded figure and the later artists' propensity to create just such tableaux of their own, whether in fine or applied art or in family theatricals in both London and Sussex" (Art 27-28).

consuming audience. The balance here between disinterested art and commercial interests is reflected in Woolf's not entirely secure distinction between quality—the aristocratic air of Vita, expressed even while driving[13]—and pretentiousness, as conveyed by the *nouveau riche* in their expensive cars.

The class consciousness of Woolf's car ownership is, in fact, an integral part of the discourse of modern motoring, as marques such as Lanchester were marketed through a deliberate invocation of tradition and patriotism, as well as of British engineering. Advertisements for the more expensive BSA vehicles feature visual cues and written references to the leisured classes, especially in conjunction with copy that draws attention to the Fluid Fly-Wheel transmission, a key element of the 1930s Daimler and Lanchester campaigns. According to a 1933 advert, the two marques are "designed to give you rest and relaxation—even if you are driving yourself" ("Silent Partners" 15). The implied figure of a chauffeur establishes the status of both the owner-driver and the company, denoting a reputation and thus a class history for a brand founded fewer than thirty years before. The company's technological advances are aligned with this language in what seems a slightly forced tone of reassurance: in one of the first magazine advertisements for the Lanchester 15/18, for example, the vehicle is described as "upholding all the finest Lanchester traditions but setting altogether new standards in economical luxury motoring" ("At Olympia").

The nostalgia that softens technological innovation, or perhaps the desire for tradition within the moment of modernity, underpins R. E. Davidson's review of the Lanchester 18 in the "About Motoring" column for the *New Statesman and Nation* on 10 October 1931.[14] Though established in 1903, Lanchester's hoary place in British automotive history is set by Davidson against a current "age of vulgarity," during which "clever advertising became more important than sound quality" (452). His characterization of Lanchester invokes the "supposedly non-commercial values" discernible in a number of modern marketing campaigns (Outka 4), as the cultural connotations of an apparently authentic, reliable, and respectable British marque are reinforced by Davidson's lament for an era in which a "blue-blooded gentleman who automatically ordered an extra Lanchester for each scion of the old stock, as the age for a driving licence was attained, is now reduced to buying one Ford for the entire family" (452). In contrast, the newly rich, "who draw their £10,000 a year as the reward of selling more gramophones or rayon pants than anyone can sell,

---

[13] Leonard Woolf's oft-quoted characterization of Vita is anchored in his appreciation at being "driven by Vita on a summer's afternoon at the height of the season through the London traffic—she was a very good, but rather flamboyant driver," and of hearing "her put an aggressive taxi driver in his place," which "made one recognize a note in her voice that the Sackvilles and Buckhursts were using to serfs in Kent 600 years ago, or even in Normandy 300 years before that" (112).

[14] We are indebted to Martin Winquist for this reference.

prefer something more lurid than the Lanchester" (452). The unfortunate consequence is that Lanchester "has at last been forced to produce a comparatively small and cheap car," though Davidson perceives a silver lining: "True to its traditions, it resolved to build the finest 15 h.p. in the world" and, in the writer's estimation, "has actually succeeded" (452). Lanchester is praised in particular for pairing the 15-18hp rated engine with "the most advanced transmission in the world" and one that is "British in design and British in workmanship" (452), a depiction of the motor-car that reiterates the mixture of patriotism, history, technological innovation, and class performance typical of representations of the brand.[15]

It's more than possible Leonard Woolf read Davidson's piece, "A New Lanchester Car"; it's certain that he and Virginia attended London's Olympia Motor Show in October 1932, where two Lanchester 18 models were on display ($L5$ 112). By November, they had purchased their own Lanchester, which was delivered in January 1933 and was driven by Leonard with pleasure for the next twenty-two years. But the advertisements, Davidson's newspaper column, the motor show, and Virginia Woolf's layered performance of class identity point to the complex relationship between the automobile's use-value and its exchange value; between the personal pleasure it brought to the Woolfs and the public performance of a classed and codedly English identity that may have informed their choice and that certainly marked their social standing. Its purchase enabled by Woolf's successful participation in "a literary marketplace wherein the counterfeit and authentic signs of cultural capital had become indistinguishable from one another" (Latham 94), the Lanchester suggests the car and driver's shared place in the market—as well as the uncertainties of the object/artist's status according to the vagaries of that economy. In this regard, her understanding of the cultural connotations of different marques is layered with Woolf's recognition of the less desirable implications of mobility, financial and cultural, as her investment in both car and consumer culture becomes less a marker of distinction and more a form of inevitable participation. The importance, the prominence of the motor-car in everyday experience—the peformativity not just the deliberate performance of hegemonic identity that those vehicles entail—signal the pervasiveness of commodity culture in Bloomsbury.

The presence of increasingly affordable vehicles and of business opportunities that surrounded the marketing, driving, and touring of motor-cars changed the social, commercial, and physical landscapes of interwar English art—and thus Bloomsbury's relationship to all three. Given their homes in the South Downs, and given the increasingly accessible drive to London from Monk's House and

---

[15] Equally important are the gender implications of the car. According to Davidson, the servo brake means that "weak women need not tread on the brake pedal as an Oxford stroke thrusts at his stretcher when Cambridge begin to steal their inevitable lead" (apparently he was a Cambridge man), and yet the brake still "operates manfully when the engine is dead" (454).

Charleston, the act of owning and operating a car was glossed for Woolf and Bell by the effects of automobilism on the countryside—a countryside that was becoming more accessible to day tourists and visitors alike. Thus, at the same time that their vehicles represented a certain level of financial independence and enabled a freer movement between different workspaces—their own and each other's—cars were also involved in their work as hosts, as they shuttled guests to and from the Lewes train station and the Newhaven docks. Indeed, even as her cars allowed her to travel to La Bergère or return to her Charleston studio, where Bell could focus on her art in a domestic space, that space was increasingly affected by the presence of car-borne visitors to Charleston and the demands of family and friends. The effects of technology for Bell, including her understandings of and experiences with this new form of mobility, threatened to disperse established modes of consciousness in multiple directions. Like Woolf, she was faced with reconciling, on one hand, the demands of her art and the pressures of commercialism with, on the other, her own desire to maintain her footing in a personal and domestic life. In this sense, Bell's attempts to find an equilibrium that would allow her to develop as a painter while meeting the needs of her household are connected powerfully to the effects of the motor-car, and especially to its role in her participation within a shifting art market.

Through the 1920s, Bell had developed strategies for balancing the domestic and creative aspects of her life. Aesthetically, her painting methodology had moved away from experimentation and minimalist formal constructions—as seen in works such as "Studland Beach" (1912)—to depictions of the figures and spatial arrangements found in her most intimate surroundings.[16] The effects of driving rather than taking the train between London and East Sussex are evident in her paintings of this period, especially if a symptom of her physical mobility as a driver was Bell's attempt to anchor herself in the everyday moments of her life at Charleston; a place which, she notes in a letter to Duncan, was "almost too full of associations ...crammed into a very short time" (qtd. in Spalding 190). While remaining anchored in a limited range of subjects and themes, Bell's paintings during the initial period of the motor-car's rise represent a remarkably productive tension between the traditions of the past and the conceptualizations of a new era. As an artist who had the means to move between the city and the countryside, she had different vantage points from which to choose: interior and exterior, urban and rural. That she persistently focused on subjects found in the confined spaces of the household sphere—of rooms replete with objects of comfort, and where living members of the home spent the majority of their times—suggests a desire to capture a quality

---

[16] As Frances Spalding describes, "[b]eauty had once again become fashionable and Vanessa no longer felt the need to apologize for painting that which merely appealed to the eye. She began to paint the view of the garden through the French windows, or the children seated in the window-seat in the dining-room, catching effects of light and atmosphere which Post-Impressionism, at its most severe, had tended to ignore" (189).

of being that is defined by silence, repose, immobility, and inner reflection. That quality is evident in the series of portrait paintings that Bell began in 1934, in which she depicted close friends and family members, most notably Duncan Grant, Virginia Woolf, Leonard Woolf, and Clive Bell (Shone, *Art* 224). *Interior with the Artist's Daughter* (1935-36) features Angelica seated in an armchair. Angelica's head is resting on her palm and her attention is absorbed in the action of reading a book. Interestingly, Bell gives as much attention to the objects and architecture in the represented space as she does to the human subject. Gillespie observes that in Bell's portrait studies "[p]eople appear indoors among solid objects that embody their interests and statuses or outside in landscape settings that suggest states of mind or that transcend individual egos" (12). In *Interior with the Artist's Daughter*, Bell uses a variety of formal elements to establish a consistency and stability in the overall composition of an interior scene. The subject's relaxed positioning in the armchair harmonizes with the overall color palette of yellow-ochres transitioning into deep violets and umbers. Similarly, the striped patterns represented by the book spines reference the abstract designs displayed on the textile draperies and arm chair coverings arranged throughout the painting. This thoughtful organization of elements echoes the composed state of mind of the subject, who later described the space as "'the sanctuary in which I spent the most treasured hours of my life'" (qtd. in Shone, *Art* 224).

There is, however, more at stake in *Interior with the Artist's Daughter* than the mere presentation of a harmonious effect. Like all of her works of this period, this portrait is a ground-breaking design that references and reassembles the fractured and forward-moving thrust of the modernist sensibility into a visual taxonomy of senses, memory, and thought. The subject is situated in an alcove, with a wall of books acting as a backdrop. A round end table positioned in the extreme foreground holds a vase of flowers, a pair of scissors, and a book lying at a dramatic angle. One corner of the book butts up against the corner of a striped rug angled immediately below Angelica's feet, making the foreground and background spaces converge to surround and hedge in the human subject. Shone suggests that "[t]his consciously arranged still life fronts the absorbed intimacy of the figure" (*Art* 224). In this way, the space depicted in Vanessa's painting is indeed a sanctuary, but one which must be viewed from an implied distance. In a subtle assertion of a resistance to exterior forces, such as the Keyneses and their Rolls, *Interior with the Artist's Daughter* advocates for a private condition augmented and encapsulated by the psychological and social parameters of the domestic sphere. The compromises inherent in such an enterprise suggest the always-threatened balance that Bell maintains in the face of the encroaching aspects of modernity. Like the experience of riding in a motor-car, she is tasked with staying focused while perpetually moving forward against a shifting landscape.

And indeed, Bell's reputation and position in the art world had itself shifted. By the 1930s, her career was largely shaped according to the commodity market. At the same time she was producing domestic-based works of art, she was taking on private commissions, some quite extensive and several that brought her into close contact with the most commercial dimensions of design. In 1930, for instance, she won third place in a competition offered by the *Architectural Review*, in which "[c]ompetitors were asked to design a modern yet discreet apartment for a wealthy, sporting widower" (Shone, *Bloomsbury* 244). In collaboration with Duncan, she designed sets for ballet companies and painted murals for interior spaces, and they accepted contracts from larger public and corporate entities, such as Royal Wilton, Wedgwood, and the Post Office. One of their largest commissions was to "decorate a lounge with three large panels for the R.M.S. Queen Mary" (249). The tension between Bloomsbury artistic practice and "the materialistic and fashionable values flaunted throughout the ship"—and espoused by the Chairman of the Cunard-White Star company, Sir Percy Bates—led to a highly unpleasant public dispute (Spalding 283). While Bell's panel was deemed acceptable, though displayed in an incongruously small room, Grant's work was rejected outright, an outcome that "would not only damage his reputation but lose him the valuable advertisement which the ship's main lounge provided" (283).

A certain amount of insecurity seemed typical for modernist artists who had gained recognition through their membership in the more exclusive clubs and societies founded over a decade earlier, including the London Group, the London Artists' Association, and the Seven and Five Society. By the time Bell and Grant had resigned from the London Artists' Association in July of 1931, they "were among the most widely known painters in England, but no longer could they be thought of as among the country's leading innovators" (Shone, *Bloomsbury* 231). Vanessa was still painting at Charleston, in the studios at Fitzroy Street in London, and at La Bergère, and a handful of London art dealers continued to sell her paintings: still-lifes, intimate portraits, and interior scenes of domestic life. Rarely, though, were her works exhibited in galleries. Even so, Bell's and Grant's reputations as modernist *avant-garde* painters still had a profound effect for the art-conscious British consumer drawn to the aura of experimentation. That aura was a reason they were among the first to become involved in the Shell-Mex advertising campaign of the 1930s.

A corporate incentive, the "See Britain First" advertising campaign was designed to encourage Shell-fuelled motoring. According to John Hewitt, Shell hired Jack Beddington in 1929 to shift the oil company's promotional strategy "from traditional commodity advertising to publicity and a concern for public relations" (125). The result was highly patriotic branding that encouraged petrol use through the commercialization of both modern art and the countryside. For "See Britain

First," Beddington hired a number of contemporary artists to depict a picturesque England, and while many of these works were shown at the new Burlington Galleries (Hewitt 134), they were also "reproduced by colour lithography as lorry bills" or advertisments on the sides of trucks (Spalding 259). Paul Nash created *Kimmeridge Folly, Dorset* in 1937, advising viewers that "To Visit Britain's Landmarks You Can Be Sure of Shell." Grant painted *St. Ives, Huntingdon* for a 1932 poster with the tagline "Everywhere you Go You Can Be Sure of Shell." Bell's contribution to the series took as its focus a village less than five miles from Charleston. With the title "See Britain First on Shell," her 1931 painting *Alfriston* depicts recognizable scenic landmarks: a field with a small stream running through the foreground and a parish church in the background. The image is composed of a minimalistic arrangement of sections harmonized by a consistent application of broken brush strokes. In its "pointillist technique" (Spalding 259), it resembles many of the dust-jacket designs Bell made for books such as *The Waves* and *To the Lighthouse*, as well as some of her illustrations in *Kew Gardens* (Humm 112). Unlike her book illustrations, however, the Shell poster has a more naturalistic color scheme and a more conventional, less abstracted perspectival view of a landscape. As Maggie Humm suggests, in much of Bell's decorative and commissioned work there is a sophisticated balance between, on the one hand, a Post-Impressionist preoccupation with experimentation and unconventional compositional structures and, on the other, a sensibility for a design that was attractive to a broader, more commercially-minded art viewership (112-13).

Bell's ability to create a poster design that combined artistic innovation and traditional subject matter complemented Beddington's strategy to promote petrol sales by marrying the modern obsession with freedom and mobility with the widespread consciousness of a British landscape. That the countryside was being encroached upon by urban and industrial development had generated a reactionary push towards preservation of rural Britain, especially with the founding of the Council for the Preservation of Rural England in 1926 (Hussey 9). The expansion of suburbs, the growth of intrusive billboard advertising, and the rise of car tourism in the country were seen to threaten rural ways of life and to entail not just noise and dust but also danger, as pedestrians and cyclists made up the majority of road fatalities through the 1920s and 1930s. The fact that "many cars were used solely for leisure" during this time gave "accidents involving the car a different complexion to those involving goods or public-service vehicles" (O'Connell 116), as roads traditionally used for foot, horse, and, later, bicycle traffic were being straightened to accommodate the startling rise in motoring. The speed of cars led Woolf to criticize "the baneful effects" of increasingly affordable automobiles (Thacker 172). In 1924's "The Cheapening of Motor-Cars," published in the *Nation and Athenaeum*, she excoriates the apparently suburban drivers who are "in perpetual and frantic haste not to be late for dinner" (*E3* 440). While her own motoring is later enabled by the very paving of the roads that she critiques in the piece, the distinction made between locals and tourists, between the traditional and the temporary, speaks to the complexities of British motoring culture represented by the Shell-Mex campaign.

With motoring magazines and other advertisers, Shell used the preservationist impulse in their publicity, be it through posters or the Shell Guides that were established in 1933 and that, as Ian Walker explains, "were integral to that central if paradoxical element in interwar Englishness whereby, as Matless put it, 'Motoring became styled as a modern practice in pursuit of an older England'" (33).[17] The contradiction that arose for these patriotic, newly mobile Britons—that to appreciate the beauty of rural England, one must take a sightseeing day-trip through the countryside in the very machines that were threatening the landscape—echoes the experiences of Bell and Woolf too, as those modernists would seem to embrace the isolation and seeming autonomy of rural life even as their place in the countryside was enabled by their use of motor-cars and participation in class-conscious discourse of British motoring. More to the point, however, were the effects on the Stephen sisters of this larger social shift to car ownership. As Bell wrote to Roger Fry, "Cars, I see, are a mixed blessing. One's own, I think, when enough people can drive, will be almost entirely a gain, but other people's are a terror. Now that everyone owns them one is never safe" (*SL* 322). A reminder in part of the 1924 car accident that involved her daughter Angelica and Angelica's nurse (Spalding 200), Bell's letter speaks directly to the more mundane horrors posed by visitors who arrived by car at Charleston unexpectedly. In a gesture that must have inspired Woolf's written resentment of the Keyneses' visit in late December, Bell had in 1927 "painted a large notice and stuck it up at the bottom of the field to say 'To Charleston. OUT'" (*SL* 322).

Bell's reaction to the influx of car traffic coming and going at Charleston was symptomatic of a more general condition brought about by the ubiquitous presence of this commodified machine. The motor-car dissolved boundaries among disparate physical and psychological and cultural spheres, and the different layers of meanings that Woolf and Bell perceived in the motor-car speak to such blurring of, among others, the high art and the commercial dimensions of modernism and modernity; the natural Sussex celebrated in motoring magazines and adverts, and yet altered by the presence of new technologies; and the tension between the privacy of the rural home and the "visitations" of motoring friends (V. Bell, *SL* 322). Rather than a clear sense of mechanized agency or an embrace of "the new," their

---

[17] In 1935, Nash wrote the Shell motoring guide to Dorset, which was aimed in part at introducing the "discerning visitor" to the, as yet, untainted British countryside (Walker 33), and in part for the connoisseur of modern art: "The book, then, is an odd mix of traditionalism and modernity, a duality which is also to be found in the photographs, clear and undemonstrative yet with echoes of the new photography which Nash had seen coming from Europe" (35).

representations of and responses to motoring reflect the contradictory attitudes implicit in Bloomsbury's machine age. And yet, despite their shared ambivalence toward "the complicated flows of social and cultural capital" (Latham 63), by the early 1930s, their motor-cars and modernism alike mark the sisters' participation in a landscape saturated with discourses not just of personal freedom and innovation, but also of tradition and nationalism, as the language of car and petrol advertisements foreshadowed the patriotic messaging that drew the country into war.

The implications of automobilism reached beyond Bloomsbury, then, even as it involved its members in local and lived experiences of global conflict. Automotive technology and the investment of motor-car companies in developing engines and vehicles for wartime use was an integral aspect of Britain's military, and it is the connection between the international and the interpersonal that makes such patterns visible. Vanessa had car trouble when trying to drive Julian to Newhaven in the summer of 1937, where he would depart for Spain; ironically, she went to the Keyneses at Tilton "to find alternative transport" (Spalding 294). Her eldest son had been trained as an ambulance driver and a mechanic for the Republican side of the Spanish Civil War, and thus the technology behind the sisters' countryside jaunts and trips to Europe becomes inextricably tied to the martial conflict that takes his life. It is not merely that Rolls-Royce sold engines to Junkers for use in a prototype of the Stuka bomber, which became central to Germany's Condor Legion in Spain; it is that Julian's death in July 1937 prefigures so many other deaths as well as the destruction of the British landscapes that the sisters had explored in their art and automobiles. Even as the petrol shortages of World War Two limited their visits to each other's homes (Dunn 293), other machines are piloted across the Channel. Rather than Renaults and Singers, Citroëns and Lanchesters, they are Dorniers and Heinkels: German bombers powered by Daimler-Benz and BMW engines, just as Britain's Lancaster bombers were powered by Rolls-Royce and Packard. This is the technology that destroys the Woolfs' house in Tavistock Square, its murals painted by Vanessa and Duncan, and sets fire to Bell and Grant's Fitzroy Street studios. And this is the often tacit link between the lived experience of interwar technology and the material effects of its military adaptation. Through war, the motor-car again connects disparate spaces and experiences, as different meanings and discursive placements of the automobile speak to the power not just of metaphor but of the historical, historicized machine.

Works Cited

"At Olympia—the New 15/8." *The Autocar,* 16 October 1931, p. 73. Ebay.com. Accessed 16 August 2016.

Baldwin, Nick. *A-Z of Cars of the 1920s.* Bayford, 1994.

Bell, Quentin. *Bloomsbury Recalled*. Columbia UP, 1995.
———. *Virginia Woolf: A Biography*. 1972. Random/Pimlico, 1996.
Bell, Vanessa. "Alfriston." Shell Heritage Art Collection, The National Motor Museum Trust. *National Motor Museum*, http://www.nationalmotormuseum.org.uk/?location_id=216&item=197.
———. *Selected Letters of Vanessa Bell*. Ed. Regina Marler. Bloomsbury, 1993.
Benson, John. *The Rise of Consumer Society in Britain, 1880-1980*. Longman, 1994.
Bradshaw, David. Preface. *The Charleston Bulletin: Supplements*, by Virginia Woolf and Quentin Bell, edited by Claudia Olk, British Library, 2013, pp. vi-ix.
Caws, Mary Ann and Sarah Bird Wright. *Bloomsbury and France: Art and Friends*. Oxford UP, 2000.
Daly, Nicholas. *Literature, Technology, and Modernity, 1860-2000*. Cambridge UP, 2004.
Davidson, R. E. "A New Lanchester Car." *New Statesman and Nation* ns 33, 10 October 1931, pp. 452, 454.
Driscoll, Catherine. *Modernist Cultural Studies*. UP of Florida, 2010.
Dubino, Jeanne. Introduction. *Virginia Woolf and the Literary Marketplace*, edited by Jeanne Dubino, Palgrave Macmillan, 2010, pp. 1-23.
Duffy, Enda. *The Speed Handbook: Velocity, Pleasure, Modernism*. Duke UP, 2009.
Dunn, Jane. *A Very Close Conspiracy: Vanessa Bell and Virginia Woolf*. Pimlico, 1990.
Froula, Christine. "On French and British Freedoms: Early Bloomsbury and the Brothels of Modernism." *Modernism/modernity*, vol. 12, no.4, 2003, pp. 553-80.
Garnett, Angelica. *Deceived with Kindness: A Bloomsbury Childhood*. Harvest/HBJ, 1984.
Glendinning, Victoria. *Leonard Woolf: A Biography*. Free Press, 2006.
———. *Vita: The Life of V. Sackville-West*. Knopf, 1983.
Gillespie, Diane. *The Sisters' Arts: The Writing and Painting of Virginia Woolf and Vanessa Bell*. Syracuse UP, 1988.
Goldman, Jane. *The Feminist Aesthetics of Virginia Woolf: Modernism, Post-Impressionism, and the Politics of the Visual*. 1998. Cambridge UP, 2009.
Grant, Duncan. "St. Ives, Huntingdon." Shell Heritage Art Collection, The National Motor Museum Trust. *National Motor Museum*, http://www.nationalmotormuseum.org.uk/?location_id=216&item=87.
Hancock, Nuala. *Charleston and Monk's House: The Intimate House Museums of Virginia Woolf and Vanessa Bell*. Edinburgh UP, 2012.

Herrmann, Anne. *Queering the Moderns: Poses/Portraits/Performances.* Palgrave, 2000.
Hewitt, John. "The Nature and Art of Shell Advertising in the Early 1930s." *Journal of Design History,* vol. 5, no. 2, 1992, pp. 121-39. *JSTOR,* www.jstor.org/stable/1315823.
Holroyd, Michael. *Lytton Strachey: The New Biography.* Farrar, Straus and Giroux, 1994.
———. *On Wheels: Five Easy Pieces.* Chatto and Windus, 2012.
Humm, Maggie. *Modernist Women and Visual Cultures: Virginia Woolf, Vanessa Bell, Photography and Cinema.* Edinburgh UP, 2002. Print.
Hussey, Mark. *"I'd Make It Penal": The Rural Preservation Movement in Virginia Woolf's* Between the Acts. London: Cecil Woolf, 2011.
Latham, Sean. *"Am I a Snob?": Modernism and the Novel.* Cornell UP, 2003.
Lee, Hermione. *Virginia Woolf.* 1996. Vintage, 1997.
Mackerell, Judith. *Bloomsbury Ballerina: Lydia Lopokova, Imperial Dancer and Mrs John Maynard Keynes.* Weidenfeld & Nicolson, 2008.
Martin, Ann. "Sky Haunting: The British Motor-Car Industry and the World Wars." *Virginia Woolf: Writing the World,* edited by Pamela L. Caughie and Diana L. Swanson, Clemson UP, 2015, pp. 49-53.
———. "'Unity-Dispersity': Virginia Woolf and the Contradictory Motif of the Motor-Car." *Virginia Woolf: Twenty-First-Century Approaches,* edited by Jeanne Dubino, Gill Lowe, Vara Neverow, and Kathryn Simpson, Edinburgh UP, 2015, pp. 93-110.
Minow-Pinkney, Makiko. "Virginia Woolf and the Age of Motor Cars." *Virginia Woolf in the Age of Mechanical Reproduction,* edited by Pamela L. Caughie, Garland, 2000, pp. 159-82.
Morris, Jan. *Travels with Virginia Woolf.* Pimlico, 1997.
Nash, Paul. "Kimmeridge Folly, Dorset." Shell Heritage Art Collection, The National Motor Museum Trust. *National Motor Museum,* http://www.nationalmotormuseum.org.uk/?location_id=216&item=145&filter=paul%20nash&filter_from=artist&match_all=true.
O'Connell, Sean. *The Car in British Society: Class, Gender and Motoring 1896-1939.* Manchester UP, 1998.
"The Olympia Show." *The Times* 19 Oct. 1932, p. 9. Gale Group. Accessed 19 Aug. 2013.
Outka, Elizabeth. *Consuming Traditions: Modernity, Modernism, and the Commodified Authentic.* Oxford UP, 2009.
Pinkney, Tony. Introduction. 1989. *The Politics of Modernism,* by Raymond Williams. Verso, 1996.

Rosenbaum, S.P. Foreword. *The Bloomsbury Group*, edited by S. P. Rosenbaum. 1975, U of Toronto P, 1977.
Shone, Richard. *The Art of Bloomsbury: Roger Fry, Vanessa Bell and Duncan Grant*. Princeton UP, 2002.
———. *Bloomsbury Portraits: Vanessa Bell, Duncan Grant, and Their Circle*. Phaidon, 1976.
"Silent Partners." *The Autocar*, 23 June 1933, p. 15. "Daimler Advertisements," *British Car Brochures*. Accessed 15 August 2016.
Sim, Lorraine. *Virginia Woolf: The Patterns of Ordinary Experience*. 2010. Routledge, 2016.
Skidelsky, Robert. *John Maynard Keynes*. Vol. 2, Allen Lane/Penguin, 1992.
Spalding, Frances. *Vanessa Bell*. Weidenfeld and Nicolson, 1983.
Stephanson, Andrew. "'Strategies of Situation': British Modernism and the Slump c. 1929-1934." *Oxford Art Journal*, vol. 14, no. 2, 1991, pp. 30-51. *JSTOR*. www.jstor.org/stable/1360523.
Thacker, Andrew. *Moving Through Modernity*. Manchester UP, 2003.
Thoms, David, Len Holden, and Tim Claydon. Introduction. *The Motor Car and Popular Culture in the 20th Century*, edited by David Thoms, Len Holden, and Tim Claydon, Ashgate, 1998, pp. 1-5.
Trotter, David. "Modernism's Material Futures: Glass, and Several Kinds of Plastic." *Utopian Spaces of Modernism: British Literature and Culture, 1885-1945*, edited by Rosalyn Gregory and Benjamin Kohlmann, Palgrave Macmillan, 2012, pp. 52-70.
———. "Techno-Primitivism: Á Propos of *Lady Chatterley's Lover*." *Modernism/modernity*, vol. 18, no. 1, 2011, pp. 149-66.
Walker, Ian. *So exotic, so homemade: Surrealism, Englishness, and documentary photography*. Manchester UP, 2007.
Woolf, Leonard. *Downhill All the Way: An Autobiography of the Years 1919-1939*. Hogarth, 1967.
Woolf, Virginia. "Am I a Snob?" *Moments of Being: A Collection of Autobiographical Writing*, edited by Jeanne Schulkind, Harvest, 1985, pp. 203-20.
———. "The cheapening of motor-cars." 1924. *The Essays of Virginia Woolf*, vol. 3, 1919-24, edited by Andrew McNeillie, Hogarth, 1988, p. 440.
———. *The Diary of Virginia Woolf*. Edited by Anne Olivier Bell and Andrew McNeillie, vol. 3, Hogarth, 1980.
———. "Evening over Sussex: Reflections in a Motor Car." *Selected Essays*, edited by David Bradshaw, Oxford UP, 2008, pp. 204-6.
———. "Flying over London." *Selected Essays*, edited by David Bradshaw, Oxford UP, 2008, pp. 208-12.

———. *The Letters of Virginia Woolf.* Edited by Nigel Nicolson and Joanne Trautmann, 6 vols., Hogarth, 1975-80.
———. *Mrs Dalloway*. Edited by Stella McNichol, Penguin, 1992.
———. *Orlando: A Biography*. Edited by Rachel Bowlby, Oxford UP, 1992, 2000.
———. "Reviewing." *The Crowded Dance of Modern Life*, edited by Rachel Bowlby, Penguin, 1993, pp.152-63.
Woolf, Virginia, and Quentin Bell. *The Charleston Bulletin: Supplements*, edited by Claudia Olk. British Library, 2013.
Wright, Elizabeth. "Bloomsbury at Play." *Woolf Studies Annual,* vol. 17, 2011, pp. 77-107.

The Dramatic Modern Novel: Mimesis and The Poetics of Tragedy in *Mrs. Dalloway*

Siân White

Elizabeth Bowen called Virginia Woolf "a master of the dramatic Now" namely because of Woolf's use of "that extraordinary simultaneousness in which a number of things may be made dramatic by happening close to each other" (135-36).[1] Bowen likely was not referring literally to the dramatic genre in a classical sense. What she admired, however, was Woolf's ability to produce an immediacy of the narrative moment, with a dramatic effect achieved through formal juxtaposition that is felt by both the citizen of the 1923 story world and the reader of modernist narrative in the reading present. That ability has its roots in a more direct association Woolf herself makes between classical Greek drama and the changing modern novel. In her notes written while reading James Joyce's *Ulysses*, Woolf posits, "It's possible that the novel to us is what the drama was to the Greeks" ("Modern Novels (Joyce)" 645). She converts that possible connection into a concrete and purposeful plan in her notes for revision of "The Hours": "The book to have the impression of a play: only in narrative" (*VW "The Hours"* 412). For Woolf, the dramatic seems to have a crucial role in rethinking the novel form, the success of which is measured in terms of its relation to audience reception, i.e., the impression that it conveys. That *Mrs. Dalloway*—the final title for "The Hours"—is set on one day in essentially one place with a coherent development of action suggests that Woolf drew on Aristotle's dramatic unities of tragedy in *Poetics*, not adopting his neat formula wholesale but rather adapting it as a constraint to achieve a dramatic quality in her narrative.[2] Aristotle's ideal poetics thus inspires Woolf not to a single form but to experiment with formal rigor in the interest of reconfiguring modern narrative. Woolf's reworking of Aristotle's classical unities and "verse-form" in the

---

[1] Bowen made this declaration in a broadcast given on the B.B.C. Home service in 1956 called "Truth and Fiction," subsequently published in *Afterthought: Pieces About Writing* (1962).
[2] Other of Woolf's friends value formal constraints when addressing the relation between artist and art. Clive Bell argues that appropriate form concentrates the "heat of artistic emotion" in such a way that it preserves the aesthetic energies in the artistic product, and the challenge lies in trying to find that form: "For the artistic problem, which limits the artist's freedom, fixes his attention on a point, and *drives his emotion through narrow tubes*, is what imports the conventional element into art" (104-5, my italics). In the same year, T. S. Eliot likens the artistic process to a chemical reaction, distinguishing the artist's emotion from that of the art: "it is not the 'greatness,' the intensity, of the emotions, the components, but *the intensity of the artistic process, the pressure,* so to speak, under which the fusion takes place, that counts" ("Tradition" 8, my italics). Bell's narrow tubes and Eliot's pressure describe productive formal constraints.

context of modernity generates experimental forms of the modern novel.[3]

Woolf's experiments with narrative form long precede her reading of excerpts of *Ulysses*, of course,[4] and this close examination of the dramatic in *Mrs. Dalloway* zeroes in on one moment in a much longer time span in which she was thinking about the relationship between life and generic forms. Steven Putzel's *Virginia Woolf and the Theater* and a "Woolf and Literary Genre" special issue of *Virginia Woolf Miscellany* (Sullam and Kopley), both published in 2013, reflect recent scholarly interest in Woolf's relationship to genre. Her main subjects of study in the last years of the nineteenth-century were the classics and classical languages (Lee 141). In her notes for an early lecture, "The Dramatic in Life and Art" (1902), Woolf addresses the different relationship of thought and feeling to action in drama, fiction, and life more broadly. Her notes suggest a distinction between the drama genre and a "dramatic" quality: whereas in drama, emotion and thought are perceivable only through action or plot, "the 'dramatic' in a novel is closer to the experience of the 'liver,' Woolf claims, because 'the dramatic moments in life…come mostly from the emotions without definite action'" (qtd. in Putzel "VW and Distance," 440). S.P. Rosenbaum comments of this early writing, "Clearly she had not yet read her Aristotle" (166); indeed, Aristotle's *Poetics* does not appear explicitly in her reading notebooks until 1927, well after the publication of *Mrs. Dalloway*. *Poetics* is the primary point of reference, however, for Leonard

---

[3] No scholar has offered a sustained reading of the intersections of the modern novel with Aristotelian poetics of tragedy and the three unities, though David Higdon cites letters by authors Mervyn Jones and Brian Moore who each express interest in the challenge of writing a novel within the constraints of the unities (59). In addition, scholars have noted that Aristotle's poetics does not have much influence on modern drama. Martin Puchner asserts that modern drama is widely considered to have turned away from Aristotle, arguing that Plato's dramatic dialogues are a more apt classical source for comparison (73). For the influence of tragedy on modern literature, and the distinction between Aristotle's poetics of tragedy and the philosophy of tragedy developed by the German Idealists, see K. M. Newton. Franco Moretti sees a fundamental incongruity between the tragedy (with its focus on truth) and the novel (with its focus on ordinary life), arguing that Chekov's attempts at writing modern tragedy demonstrate that "the impossibility of modern tragedy is the greatest modern tragedy" (120). See also Moretti on the differences in dialogue and the event between the tragedy and the novel.

[4] Critics are divided about how to account for the similarities between the novels; some see *Mrs. Dalloway* as derivative of *Ulysses* (see Wyndham Lewis and Robert Weninger), while it's easy to conclude from Woolf's diaries and non-fiction essays that she hated Joyce and tried to distinguish her work out of disdain for his shortcomings (see William Jenkins). The interpretation that falls between these extremes and considers their common regard for the dramatic form argues that *Ulysses* was an inspiration to Woolf and she considered him, as Suzette Henke writes, "a fellow genius and an innovative modernist" ("Woolf, Joyce, Prime Minister" 4). See also Bonnie Kime Scott "Introduction" (l-lv) and "A Joyce of One's Own," as well as Johanna Garvey, James Heffernan, Molly Hoff, Hilary Newman, and Harvena Richter. See White for my related article on dramatic poetics in *Ulysses*.

Woolf's 1920 review in *Athenaeum* of T. S. Eliot's *The Sacred Wood*, so it is plausible that she would be aware of Aristotle's dramatic theories during this time, especially considering she composed *Mrs. Dalloway* during the span of years 1923-27 in which she was studying Greek and Elizabethan drama for essays in *The Common Reader*.[5] As Steven Putzel asserts, "Woolf continued to search for a way to incorporate the evocative power and the immediacy of drama in her own narratives" ("VW and Distance" 440).

One challenge for Woolf is that certain characteristics of modernity have changed the modern mind, and genre must respond accordingly. In "Poetry, Fiction and the Future" (1927), she argues that prose is the genre best suited to that mind, and she imagines in the future a new kind of novel that has "the exaltation of poetry,...the ordinariness of prose. It will be dramatic, and yet not a play. It will be read, not acted" (80), but will take advantage of "the explosive emotional effect of drama" (83-84). Here she draws a distinction between a play that is performed and a dramatic quality or effect, which can be achieved as well, or perhaps better, in the read dramatic text. Putzel explains that Woolf preferred reading a play to seeing it performed, in part because she "doubts the theater's ability to lead to full audience complicity or intellectual interaction" ("VW and Distance" 438). Moreover, the performed version necessarily departs from the solitary reader's imagination of the characters, setting, and other features, and instead imposes the authority of that staged interpretation. When "contrasting the theatrical text on stage with the dramatic text in her own mind" (438), Putzel says, Woolf prefers the reader's version to the performed one. Her trace through English literary history in "Anon" emphasizes that the unique modern moment is best served by the prose writer and the solitary reader: "That theatre must be replaced by the theatre of the brain. The playwright is replaced by the man who writes a book. The audience is replaced by the reader" (*E6* 599). The modern age lends itself to a shift from the communality of the theater audience to a work where the dramatic novel invites a collaboration with the reader. *Mrs. Dalloway* is a relatively early example of the kind of prose work that protects the autonomy of the reader's imagination—its freedom from the authority of either stage director or narrator—while still bringing life to the reader as a play can.

To suggest that Woolf reconstitutes narrative using a modified dramatic poetics is to suggest a new frame for reading *Mrs. Dalloway*—a novel considered to be primarily interested in interiority—and to provide a broader context for the role that dramatic theory played in her changes to narrative form. The first section examines the changes that Woolf makes to narrative discourse itself, reframing what scholars already widely accept about her stream of consciousness style—that it shows rather

---

[5] See diary entries from August 28, 1922 (and n. 21); September 3, 1922; October 4, 1922; January 7, 1923 (*D2*). See also her letter to Barbara Bagenal dated September 21, 1922 (*L2* 558).

than tells—in terms that address the degree of narrative mediation. Although, for Aristotle, direct character speech produced for the audience the greatest likeness to life, while the poet's voice had a more distancing, *telling* effect—tragedy is "performed by actors, not through narration" (10)—Woolf's narrative discourse navigates between the two: it offers a depth of character interiority not available in direct speech, while retaining the quality of directness, of mimetic *showing*, by presenting a minimally intrusive narrator. In this way, Woolf's work brings the reader into more direct relation with the experience at hand, a formal closeness that I call "narrative intimacy," which converts the isolated, passive reader of the didactic novel into a reader who privately but actively collaborates in the reading experience.[6] The emotional effect of that readerly intimacy echoes Aristotle's own investment in the emotional experience of the audience. The second section, then, builds on this echo of Aristotle by establishing that her adaptation of the classical unities of time, place and action reflects her belief in the value of formal constraints as an alternative to the often sprawling diegesis of the realist narrative. Though widely understood in expansive terms of streaming consciousness, plentiful flashbacks and readerly alienation, *Mrs. Dalloway* is oriented—even in its flashbacks—to the present moment (in time and place), which produces an immediacy that evokes Aristotle's unities without neatly reproducing them. Reading the novel through this lens suggests that the actions of Clarissa and the Smiths are linked with an internal logic and causality to this particular day, offering a distilled critique of dominant public narratives and celebrating the integrity of individual privacy in the story world. Woolf's mimetic economy—by which I refer to the constraints of time, place and action in *Mrs. Dalloway*—resists a fully satisfying closure to action; instead, the novel's end offers a paradoxical closing and reopening that reflects an interpretation of modernity in which strangers reach across lines of otherness to forge fleeting but surprisingly generative connections with one another. Thus, Woolf's engagement with the classical theory of the dramatic—in terms of narrative discourse and of constraints on time, place, and action—enables her to advance a philosophy about the integrity of the private individual that pushes against public normativity in the story world, and to imagine how the dramatic novel enables the reading audience to engage actively and intimately with the unmediated work of art.

[6] Molly Abel Travis understands this transition from passive to active reader in the context of a shift toward modernism (2). My argument about the effect on the reader joins a substantial body of scholarship about Woolf's readers, which includes considerations of the kind of reader Woolf imagined engaging in her non-fiction essays (see Kate Flint, Melba Cuddy-Keane, and Mark Goldman), the invitations to engagement expressed narratologically in Woolf's work (see Alessandro Giovanelli, Molly Hite, and Jim Phelan), and the pleasures and difficulties of reading Woolf's work (and modernism more broadly): Vicki Mahaffey, for example, argues for the intellectual and ethical value of reading challenging modernist fiction, and Jessica Berman addresses the ethical implications of the characters' interactions in *Modernist Commitments* and "Woolf and the Private Sphere."

A Narrative Intimacy

Woolf's evocation of the dramatic poetics reflects what for Aristotle are the primary distinctions between tragedy and epic: magnitude, length, and the relationship of verse-form to accessibility of action. According to Aristotle, "Tragedy is an imitation of an action that is admirable, complete and possesses magnitude; in language made pleasurable, each of its species separate in different parts; performed by actors, not through narration; effecting through pity and fear the purification of such emotions" (10). For him, this ideal drama offers a congruity of action with time, where the length of time corresponds to a unified whole plot, while an equivalent unity of place offers the most efficient presentation of action. Though Aristotle is not prescriptive about the unities of time and place—those constraints are developed and codified much later—he writes, "tragedy tries so far as possible to keep within a single day, or not to exceed it by much, whereas epic is unrestricted in time, and differs in this respect" (9).[7] The unities distill the drama's tragic content, where the audience experiences *mimesis*, or the closest likeness to life. For Aristotle, mimesis is a direct form that shows likeness to the audience through the dramatization of actions and direct speech of characters. By contrast, Aristotelian *diegesis* refers to the narrative form in which the poet's voice, by telling the story, distances the audience from the action and characters.[8] That distance lessens the emotional impact on the audience, whereas the direct presentation of mimesis—its closeness—is superior for its greater emotional effect. Unlike Plato, Aristotle valued emotion, but he also valued emotional balance, endorsing the Apollonian idea that tight form can create that balance in the audience. The most efficient and direct mimetic presentation (the dramatic immediacy) brings about the ideal emotional effect on the audience, a mix of terror and pity that leads to the pleasure evoked by the satisfying resolution.[9]

Like Aristotle, Woolf prefers a likeness to life over a distancing, telling narrative voice. Some modernist scholars refer to works like Woolf's as offering a new

---

[7] Unities of time and place were concretized in Italy and France in the sixteenth and seventeenth centuries. See Andrew Bongiorno and Bernard Weinberg on those developments.
[8] Malcolm Heath suggests that Aristotle's mimetic likeness is neither reducible to a set of conventions nor synonymous with "representation"—both of which are linked to a particular form—but rather is more like mimicry, denoting similarity or evocation rather than a strict copy (xiii). In narrative theory the term "diegetic" refers to the world described in the primary narrative storyline; information from outside that narrative world is therefore considered extradiegetic. This usage connects to Aristotle's "diegesis" in its relation to the narrator—in both cases diegesis refers to that which is told by a narrator.
[9] On emotion and characteristic pleasure see Aristotle (21, 38, 48). See Heath on Aristotle's concept of catharsis and its relation to the pleasure specified (xxxviii-xliii).

realism,[10] while the term "mimesis" remains a dirty word because it is equated with the diegesis that characterizes narrative realism. As an alternative, Woolf's use of dramatic theory to reframe narrative form produces mimesis of a different kind. Woolf imports the idea of likeness or closeness to life through formal efficiency, but modifies the Aristotelian relationship between form and emotion in light of modernity, effectively revising mimesis. Instead of using form to regain emotional equilibrium in service of release and closure, as Aristotle does, in *Mrs. Dalloway* Woolf's economy of form conveys the dynamic chaos of modern human relations, which is evident in both the action and the style of the novel. Woolf's economy of form brings the audience in close relation to the unreconciled emotions of life in the story world and beyond, and the lack of resolution troubles both the status quo and the very notion of a fixed reality that can be objectively described and upheld. In reimagining narrative as dramatic to achieve the desired impression, Woolf reclaims and revives Aristotle's concept of mimesis from its association with realist representation.[11] As opposed to a conception of the novel in which the name "mimetic realism" conceals what amounts to excessive diegesis, Woolf gravitates toward the showing effects of Aristotle's mimesis and the potential for immediacy offered by the conventions of tragedy.

The questions of what constitutes "life" or reality and in which form to produce its likeness best are, of course, intimately linked. Woolf's novel troubles the implicit association in the realist project between a *content* that reflects existing conditions and norms, and the diegetic narrative *style* that upholds the status quo by privileging an authoritative voice and its claims to present authentic reality. As her essays "Modern Fiction" (1919) and "Mr. Bennett and Mrs. Brown" (1923) attest, Woolf seeks a narrative discourse that departs from the informing voice of the Edwardian writer who merely conveys material details upon which the reader must rely to imagine the character that might match those facts. She refers to that materialism as "the alien and external" ("Modern" 288), arguing that their "wrong" tools "have laid an enormous stress upon the fabric of things" ("Mr. Bennett" 207)

---

[10] Henke calls the new Georgian style "psychological realism," "psychological verisimilitude," and "psychological fiction" ("Virginia Woolf" 623 & 626, 625). Similarly, Susan Sontag argues that Woolf's (and Joyce's) novels are simply mimetic of a different kind of content. This very "form of mimeticism" constitutes part of Rita Felski's critique of the dominant narrative about masculine modernism (25-26).

[11] See Brian Richardson on narration in drama (151). The association of mimesis with social or material realism in the novel is a corruption of Aristotle's original conception. In presenting a likeness by trying to recreate physical reality through narrative detail, that mimetic realism looks more like extended diegesis, losing its "showing" quality because excessive narrating time dilates reading time indefinitely. In effect realism delinks likeness from showing because that which appears before the reader is familiar but presented through telling—diegesis—rather than mimetic showing.

in trying to "prov[e] the solidity" ("Modern" 287) of that material.[12] The inherited subject matter and practices of social realism (re)present a *what*—a material world, an object, character, scene, or even a transcript of the mind—and rely on a narrator to tell, preach or persuade that the *what* shows reality. It follows from the logic of the relationship between content and its representation that, if realism bolsters the status quo by offering a fixed and knowable version of reality, then a formal alternative to realism, one that instead emphasizes the phenomenology of experiencing, offers the potential to upset the status quo.[13] In a diary entry in 1916, Lytton Strachey articulated that phenomenology succinctly by privileging an experiential authenticity of looking "as one *does* look at it" and an immediacy of looking "when it happens" over the disdained inherited conventions, the "beautifying arrangements" and "selected realisms," of "Poets and Novelists" (141). Woolf's alternative to realism's material *what* is a hard-to-define effect, that way of experiencing that she calls "life" or "spirit," which is best described in terms of a *how to* verb: how to convey, how to express, how to bring closer, how to read.[14] Instead of telling about a *what*, Woolf's novel offers an alternative modern reality—in which the world is not materially static, tragedy is neither sad nor public, and the private experience is honored—in an alternative narrative form that is informed by dramatic directness and therefore conveys the reality—the experience—of experiencing (a *how*, as both verb and noun) to the reader. Stephen Kern calls it "dramatiz[ing] the phenomenology of encounter" (*Culture of Love* 50).

The notion of *how* is therefore bound up with the effect of inherited genres and formal innovation on the reader, and, more specifically, how directly or closely the form brings the reader to experiencing the life of the work. Strachey cried out hopefully for the modern novel "To come close to life!" (141), but the novel form that Woolf has inherited is the easiest and least concentrated form to write—it

---

[12] In light of developments in narrative theory that describe the narrative situation in more complex and nuanced terms than Woolf's author/reader and Aristotle's poet/audience binaries, I use the term "narrator" to describe that "telling" device that Woolf equates with a preaching or persuading authorial voice. See her discussion of Arnold Bennett "telling us facts" in "Mr. Bennett and Mrs. Brown" (205). See also Henke's synthesis of these two essays in "Virginia Woolf (1882-1941)" (622-28).

[13] Christopher Reed argues persuasively that Woolf's feminism and Bloomsbury formalism align in their rejection of the realist mimetic project, though Reed notably does not use the term "realism" to describe the literary modes against which Woolf develops her most formalist works (25-28). Rachel Bowlby defends realism against the dominant tendency in literary studies to dismiss it on the grounds that its reality is static (395). See also Linden Peach on Woolf's realist aesthetics.

[14] Woolf gives other descriptors of "life or spirit, truth or reality, this, the essential thing" ("Modern" 287), "a luminous halo, a semi-transparent envelope surrounding us," also called "this varying, this unknown and uncircumscribed spirit" (287-88) that makes a "vivid,... overmastering impression" ("Mr. Bennett" 207) on the artist—and, ideally, if conveyed well, on the reader.

can be taken up and put down more easily than a play or poetry,[15] she claims, and it benefits from assuming its audience to be a quiet, careful reader and re-reader ("On Not Knowing Greek" 31). It is therefore insufficiently rigorous, by formalist standards, compared to the tighter and more direct dramatic form where "every sentence had to explode on striking the ear" (31). The constraint of form produces that explosive, or dramatic, effect. Bowen's praise of Woolf's "dramatic Now" emphasized that the dramatic comes precisely from closeness, that is, from "things… happening close to each other." Woolf notes a praiseworthy negotiation of closeness and distance in Greek dramatist Aeschylus's work: "By the bold and running use of metaphor he will amplify and give us, not the thing itself, but the reverberation and reflection which, taken into his mind, the thing has made; close enough to the original to illustrate it, remote enough to heighten, enlarge, and make splendid" ("On Not Knowing Greek" 31). "[T]he thing itself"—a re-presentation of a *what*—is distinct from the impact (*how*) of its "reverberation and reflection" on the reader's mind, and Aeschylus's success lies in his ability to balance the closeness needed for illustration with the distance that enables dramatization, i.e., the spectacle of "mak[ing it] splendid." For Woolf, the closer the reader to the experience, the more affected, and she sought any form that would enable that closeness. "Any method is right," she writes in "Modern Fiction," "that brings us closer to the novelist's intention if we are readers. This method has the merit of bringing us closer to what we were prepared to call life itself" (289). The closeness achieved in narrative through dramatic directness produces narrative intimacy.

Dramatic mimesis offers the audience the most direct, close access because, for Aristotle, it is "performed by actors, not through narration" (10); action conveyed directly, rather than mediated (and therefore distanced) by a narrator, offers the best likeness. As Aristotle said of dramatic verse-form of both tragedy and good epics, "[t]he poet in person should say as little as possible" (41). For Woolf to rely only on character speech, however, would achieve directness but would sacrifice the breadth of information about thoughts and emotions that come with interiority but are often narrated diegetically. Spare fiction like Ernest Hemingway's is arguably the least mediated kind of fiction—and therefore most like drama—because it privileges character speech and reduces the narrator's role to attributions and minimal story world details. Woolf's narrative discourse, by contrast, offers a more complex, multilayered and far more intimate experience that includes character interiority while still reducing the telling voice of the narrator. In this way, her style navigates between the formal choices of direct speech and direct poet statement. She develops the least intrusive and least mediated form of narration, such that the

---

[15] "Women and Fiction" 46. On the novel as a passé, inferior, or insufficiently strict form, see also *A Room of One's Own* (66-69), Bell (105), and Eliot's "*Ulysses*, Order and Myth" (372). Reed notes that the first phase of Bloomsbury formalism "explicitly opposed itself to literature" (22).

narrator recedes from the reader's consciousness.[16] The relation of the narrator's mediation to the reader's closeness to the story world is therefore an inverse one: that is, the more explicitly self-conscious or overt the narrator, the more mediated the experience, whereas the more covert the narrator, the closer or more immediate the reader is to the text. Instead of just passively receiving information, the reader is affected directly, unencumbered by any imposition of authority from the narrator, much as Woolf imagines the reader of the drama to be free from the authority imposed on the live audience of a staged production. Molly Hite describes this change to the narrator as arising from a "calculated refusing or perplexing of authoritative directions" that denies readers the ability "to assign what they perceive to be authorially sanctioned feelings and thus values to the main events and characters" (250).

On the page, Woolf's alternative form includes the direct "speech" of interiority (the spare style known to critics and readers as interior monologue, stream of consciousness, or free indirect discourse) but offers it as part of a blend of discourses—a variable focalization—that reduces the intrusiveness of narrative mediation. Such focalization can be seen on the page throughout *Mrs. Dalloway,* and it is characterized by the indistinct shifts between free indirect discourse, character focalization, and minimal external focalization (the latter of which conveys attribution, physical actions and movement in the story world). The following passage (from Clarissa and Peter's reunion in *Mrs. Dalloway*) exemplifies this intimate discourse throughout the novel, juxtaposing narrative tags (in regular font) with direct speech (in *italics*) and direct thought (quoted "speech" in thoughts, <u>*underlined and in italics*</u>), indirect speech (***bold and in italics***), and free indirect discourse (in **bold**, with speech patterns particular to certain characters also <u>**underlined**</u>)[17]:

> **She flattered him; she fooled him,** thought Clarissa; shaping the woman, the wife of the Major in the Indian Army, with three strokes of a knife. <u>**What a waste! What a folly!**</u> **All his life long Peter had been fooled like that; first getting sent down from Oxford; next marrying the girl on the boat going out to India; now the wife of a Major in the Indian Army—<u>thank Heaven she had refused to marry him!</u> Still, he was in love; her old friend, her <u>dear Peter,</u> he was in love.**

---

[16] Hite argues of several of Woolf's novels that the narrators "provide insufficient or contradictory tonal cues" (250), measuring the effect of that narration in terms of impact on "us," i.e., the reader (254).

[17] I use the term "external focalization" not in the sense proposed by Genette—an outside view "reporting what would be visible and audible to a virtual camera" (Jahn 98)—but rather in the sense developed by Mieke Bal, which combines and subsumes Genette's ideas of external and non-focalization. For discussions of experimental forms including Free Indirect Style in *Mrs. Dalloway,* see Diane Blakemore, Gloria Jones, and Herman's "1880-1945: Re-Minding Modernism." On the difference between direct and indirect speech and thoughts, see Herman "Cognition" 248-49.

> *"But what are you going to do?"* she asked him. **Oh the lawyers and solicitors, Messrs. Hooper and Grateley of Lincoln's Inn, they were going to do it, he said. And <u>he actually pared his nails</u> with his pocket-knife.**
>
> *For Heaven's sake, <u>leave your knife alone!</u>* she cried to herself in irrepressible irritation; it was his <u>silly unconventionality, his weakness;</u> <u>his lack of the ghost of a notion what any one else was feeling that annoyed her, had always annoyed her; and now at his age, how silly</u>!
>
> *I know all that*, Peter thought; *I know what I'm up against*, he thought, running his finger along the blade of his knife, *Clarissa and Dalloway and all the rest of them; but I'll show Clarissa*—and then to <u>his utter surprise</u>, suddenly <u>thrown by those uncontrollable forces thrown</u> through the air, he burst into tears; wept; wept without the least shame, sitting on the sofa, the tears running down his cheeks. (45)

The direct speech is dwarfed by the complex, multiple features that make up what might qualify as Aristotelian narration or poet's voice. The fluid and unmediated movement between direct speech, indirect speech, and free indirect discourse expands the levels of consciousness, the methods of communication, and the waves of emotion. The moderately-revealing snippets of speech and thought are augmented by the speech patterns, or *expressivity markers*, of particular focalizers—Clarissa and Peter—within free indirect discourse: Clarissa's markers include (a) exclamations about waste and folly, (b) the *formulaic locution* of "thank Heaven" and "lack of the ghost of a notion," and (c) the *evaluative appraisals* implicit in "silly," "weakness," and the shocked, "he actually pared his nails."[18] Likewise, Peter's *expressivity markers* appear in his "utter surprise," while his emotional state can be seen in the repetition of the word "thrown" amidst the "suddenness," "uncontrollable" and "burst." In episodes such as this one, the complexity conveys an intersubjective communication, where one character's indirect thoughts accurately respond to those indirect thoughts of another, as when Peter's thoughts respond to Clarissa's own as if part of a dialogue[19]:

> "But he never liked any one who—our friends," said Clarissa; and could have bitten her tongue for thus reminding Peter that he had wanted to marry her.
> Of course I did, thought Peter; it almost broke my heart too, he thought; and was overcome with his own grief... (41)

---

[18] The italicized narrative terms come from Herman "Cognition" 248.
[19] On intersubjectivity in *Mrs. Dalloway*, see Miller, Annalee Edmondson, and Berman's *Modernist Commitments*.

This style offers the greatest degree of access to both interior and exterior expression using the least explicitly diegetic form of narration. The variable form therefore conveys the characters' compatibility or connectivity at a psychic level despite their feeling disconnected and lonely at conscious and social levels. This example demonstrates how dramatizing immediate subjective experience (rather than narrating it diegetically) produces a close narrative intimacy, between the reader and the scene. The reader is not merely audience to the experience, but actually an active participant in his or her own understanding of the complex relations in the story world.[20]

Woolf's adaptation of a dramatic poetics—in its narrative discourse and, as we will see, its mimetic economy—converts the isolated novel reader, who passively receives information from the explicit, telling narrator, into an active participant in meaning-making. "Mr. Bennett and Mrs. Brown" expresses the writer's obligation to produce a recognizable likeness as part of an intimately reciprocal contractual relationship with the reader: "The writer must get into touch with his reader by putting before him something which he recognizes, which therefore stimulates his imagination, and makes him willing to co-operate in the far more difficult business of intimacy" (206). Her modernist novel is neither a fixed object nor representing a fixed reality—nor idealizing formal or social stability—but rather offers a way of experiencing that comes from the difficulty of accessing or becoming familiar with the text and its world. That difficulty falls to the reader who must actively engage with Woolf's dynamic mimesis.[21] Vicki Mahaffey has argued that modernist literature challenges the implied contract between author and reader that presumes the author has the responsibility and authority for meaning-production, "forcing readers to face and make interpretive choices that narrators used to make for them, and it also helps readers to come to terms with the meaning of those choices. Modernist literature erodes the sharp distinction between writer and reader, and in so doing presents readers with interpretive ethical dilemmas" (7). In contrast to a narrative style in which excessive mediation distances the reader by telling, and thus forcing, what the understanding should be, in *Mrs. Dalloway* Woolf's modified dramatic narrative style livens form, conveying a strategy rather than a focus on content. Woolf's formal constraints generate an intimate exchange between reader and text: just as the narrator (or poet) does not hand meaning to a reader, neither does the reader actively wrest meaning from the text. The reader and text share a push/pull relationship, where familiarity comes from letting, or cooperating, rather than trying. *Mrs. Dalloway* offers a far more immediate, interactive conception of

---

[20] Cuddy-Keane articulates especially effectively the relationship between reader and narrative mediation (in discussing Woolf's nonfiction) 137.
[21] Other scholars have described this kind of active reader in the context of Woolf and modernism: see Flint 198 and Travis 19.

the *way* the written work conveys than that which relies on information from an intrusive narrator.

The irony of this familiarity is that its directness does not promise fixed or explicit meaning. On the contrary, the style can be off-putting because its scarcity of mediation makes it difficult to read; as Mahaffey argues, "such literature forces readers to face and make interpretive choices that narrators used to make for them" (7). Woolf's aim to make an impression or retain "the quality of a sketch in a finished and composed work" (*D2* 312) accounts for the dearth of orienting information in *Mrs. Dalloway*. Instead of describing London and its landscape for the passive reader to see, Woolf offers a place where the universal experience of living is nevertheless rooted, and to know it the reader must bring it into him or herself, as an audience member might emotionally experience the immediacy of action onstage. To name this or that encounter between two people is to evoke not a particular meeting in 1923 London but rather a sense of familiarity, the feeling of meeting or even knowing someone—anyone. In this way the novel privileges the reader's individual relationship to the work over a fixed meaning; as we will see in the analysis of the mimetic economy, the action of the novel celebrates a similar individual privacy for characters over normative public narratives. The encounter Woolf might have in mind, or any particular association in the reader's mind, is immaterial to the feeling of familiarity evoked, a feeling that is unconscious yet enabled by the immediacy of form. Bowen refers to this as a "general imaginative truth, about life, about experience, about human persons" which gives certain novels their durability over time: "A novel which survives, which withstands and outlives time, does do something more than merely survive. It does not stand still. It accumulates round itself the understanding of all these persons who bring to it something of their own. It acquires associations, it becomes a form of experience in itself" (141-42). Woolf's narrative intimacy assumes, creates, and relies on this "form of experience," privileging it over any question of the artist's message, the narrator's control, or the reader's comfort. This formal defamiliarization might seem, to critics or readers deterred by stylistic difficulty, like a cynical or elitist choice on Woolf's part. Paradoxically, however, that defamiliarization produces an intimate familiarity in the reader who is willing to let the unmediated narrative act on her or him. Thus Woolf's adaptation of the dramatic form produces for the private reader of the novel a sense of intimacy and emotional stakes historically experienced by the public, collective audience of the theater.

A Mimetic Economy: Time, Place and Action

In *Mrs. Dalloway*, the economies of time, place, and action serve as constraints whose effects compound each other, and have a causal relationship to Woolf's experiments with narrative discourse. Some scholars have addressed *Mrs.*

Dalloway as a novel of one day, and the prevailing interpretation is that the day simply offers a slice of life. Laura Marcus, who argues that the one-day novel is characteristically modernist, draws her conclusion in part from Woolf's proposal in "Modern Fiction" to examine "an ordinary mind on an ordinary day" (287), while Joseph Frank considers Bloomsday of James Joyce's one-day novel to be "a typical Dublin day" (233).[22] The words "ordinary" and "typical" suggest the length of time is significant as a microview of the macrolife, implying any such day would do. When considered with place and action, however, the single day actually serves an essential constraining function that brings the audience closer to the experience by contributing to the impression of a play. Aristotle refers to the productive constraints of time and place as 'concentrations,' saying, "the end of imitation is attained in shorter length; what is more concentrated is more pleasant than what is watered down by being extended in time" (47). No one would argue that everything in *Mrs. Dalloway* could be contained in audience memory, but neither is it "watered down by being extended in time"—on the contrary, the concise limitation of time to one day is directly related to the economy of action that echoes Aristotle's mimetic ideal.

Moreover, in *Mrs. Dalloway*, time and place operate together to establish this dramatic mimesis; that is, the concentrating effect of compressed time is more significant when compounded with the unity of place—the confinement of the action to London's city center—just as the action legitimates the setting on one day.[23] Though Erich Auerbach argues persuasively that, in modernist novels, objective reality sometimes disappears—in a way that a stage never does—when characters mentally travel over years in time and distances in space not covered physically in the story world, *Mrs. Dalloway* maintains a sense of rootedness in physical space, even during flashbacks.[24] In her diary entry for October 15, 1923, Woolf herself uses a spatial metaphor—"my tunneling process"—to describe her method of "tell[ing] the past by instalments, as I have need of it" (*D2* 272). The unity expressed by the

---

[22] The fact that Woolf's *Mrs. Dalloway* and Joyce's *Ulysses* share these same constraints has attracted scholars of the novel of one day, also sometimes called the "circadian novel." Higdon argues that the circadian novel has a particular appeal in the "time-obsessed twentieth century" (57), while Bryony Randall, Chiara Briganti, and Elizabeth Covington each associate it particularly with the quotidian and the rhythms of one day. See also James Schiff.
[23] That "Dalloway Day" (as Julia Briggs calls it in *An Inner Life* 144) is punctuated at certain hour markers by the chiming of London's Big Ben and the bells at St. Margaret's church makes explicit the importance not just of this place, London, but also of time measurements even within the finite constraint of the single day (Briggs, *Reading* 117-24). On time and *Mrs. Dalloway* see also Adam Barrows, James Miracky, and Kern's *Culture of Time and Space*.
[24] Auerbach describes in some writers of this period "a method which dissolves reality into multiple and multivalent reflections of consciousness" (551), using Woolf's *To the Lighthouse* and *Mrs. Dalloway* as two examples. Frank asserts that certain modern works demand to be read spatially, not sequentially (225, 233).

confinement to London's city center is exemplified by the events experienced by multiple individuals, such as the exploding tire of the motor car (13-19) and the airplane overhead, as well as the shared impulses to glean the identity of the car's passenger, or the message in the airplane's smoke (19-28).[25] According to Aristotle, such simultaneities are features specifically of the narrative epic, enabled by its particular discourse, but in Woolf's poetics they also indicate spatial proximity, as the actions are confined to an immediate area. Bowen describes the exploding tire scene in *Mrs. Dalloway* as "an extraordinary drawing together in the moment, in the actuality of the Now, of the fortunes and the thoughts and the destinies of persons who gradually we are to follow as the day and the book goes on" (138). Though David Bradshaw rightly reads these instances of shared experience as examples of collectivity and communality in *Mrs. Dalloway* ("Introduction" xli), they also reveal the compact city space covered by the novel's action.

Woolf achieves such concision of space by the "staging" of characters' bodies, akin to actors in a play. Though for Aristotle the staging is literal—"the imitation is performed by actors" (10)—he notes that it does not have to be performed: tragedy's effect can come just from reading (47). Woolf preferred the solitary reading of a play over seeing it performed, not least because as an audience member at a live performance, she was subject to the authority of the performed interpretation (seen in the direction, casting, acting, costuming, setting, etc.) which supplanted whatever she, as a reader, might have imagined it to look like. In *Mrs. Dalloway*, the staging is less literal, enacted through the characters' consciousness of their own bodies and the narrative presentation of those bodies in space. The novel never loses sight of the physicality of its "actors" for very long; even during narrative forays into interiority, Clarissa retains a consciousness of her body, for example, when reflecting that "since her illness she had turned almost white" (36), and when going up to her room: "she knew, and felt it, as she paused by the open staircase window which let in blinds flapping, dogs barking, let in, she thought, feeling herself suddenly shriveled, aged, breastless, the grinding, blowing, flowering of the day, out of doors, out of the window, out of her body and brain which now failed" (30).[26] The novel stages the city's "body" by regularly reorienting the reader to physical space and consistently coordinating characters' physical location such that their movement enables verisimilar mapping; for example, during Clarissa's morning walk to the florist's, the narrative follows her from the "kerb" in Westminster (4), entering and passing through St. James's Park (5-8), to Piccadilly (8), "walking towards Bond Street" (9) and finally up Bond Street to "Mulberry's the florists" (12). A similar

---

[25] On the phenomena of simultaneity or parallax in *Mrs. Dalloway*, see Kern's *Culture of Love*, Miracky and Benjamin Hagen.
[26] See Richardson on intersections between drama and narrative in terms of bodies in space, and Briggs on Clarissa's consciousness of her body (*An Inner Life* 138).

type of orientation could be claimed for the passage that follows Elizabeth, first on the omnibus and then walking, from Victoria Street to Chancery Lane, in the Temple, looking up Fleet Street (131-36). The intersections of characters' paths also attest to the compactness of the staged area of the city. When Peter receives a letter from Clarissa upon his return to the hotel (after having met her just seven hours before), his surprise at how quickly the letter has reached him—registered in exclamatory punctuation that conveys his discovery in real time: "Oh it was a letter from her! This blue envelope; that was her hand. And he would have to read it" (151)—demonstrates how much time has passed and how little space had to be covered for the letter to reach him by 6:00 pm. This mimetic treatment of London, where Woolf uses meticulous mapping to produce an accuracy of place in terms of walking time,[27] creates verisimilitude that equates more with dramatic staging than with the mimetic realism of a novel. The London that Woolf maps in the novel matches the London—the place itself—that she and her contemporaries would have known, lending credibility through the treatment of time and space to allow a reader to imagine those bodies moving.

Moreover, when that verisimilitude offers the spatial distance covered by characters, it also conveys the experience of walking in London. The narrative expresses the focalizer's sense of his or her body moving through space—blocking—which also maps the city, as references to everyday landmarks of London trace the character's physical movement.[28] The link between movement through space and passage of time, combined with the plausible connection of embodied focal shifts through a physical property—such as the sound of a siren or the sight of a car, airplane, or person—lays out the blocking of the novel's actors and attests to the rootedness of the focalizers in space. When the focalization shifts in Regent's Park between the Smiths, Maisie, and Mrs. Dempster—all strangers to each other, as indicated by their use of pronouns and impersonal descriptors in their references—their physical proximity in space locates them within each other's line of sight: the focalization shifts from a conversation between Rezia and Septimus to "Both seemed queer, Maisie Johnson thought. Everything seemed very queer.... this couple on the chairs gave her quite a turn; the young woman seeming foreign, the man looking queer" (25). Then, on the next page, it shifts again from Maisie to the nearby Mrs. Dempster: "That girl, thought Mrs. Dempster...don't know a thing yet" (26). The line of sight that connects them, indicated by the definite

---

[27] See the map "Mrs. Dalloway's London" (front matter, Harcourt edition, 2005) and Bradshaw, "Woolf's London, London's Woolf."
[28] The term "focalizer" (instead of the "narrator" that merely tells and "point of view" that merely sees) refers to the perspectival filter of narrative information that expresses the opinions, attitudes, experiences, and even voice of the focalized character; see Gérard Genette (161-211) and Manfred Jahn (94-108). See also ongoing developments of the terms "narrator" and "focalization" online in *The Living Handbook of Narratology*.

articles "this" and "that" (as in "this couple" or "that girl"), legitimates the focal shift between them, as if there were a camera handed off from one character to the next.

Like a line of sight, the sound of an ambulance connects the scene of Septimus's suicide to Peter nearby, attesting to their spatial closeness: "One of the triumphs of civilization, Peter Walsh thought. It is one of the triumphs of civilization, as the light high bell of the ambulance sounded. Swiftly, clearly the ambulance sped to the hospital, …the light high bell could be heard down the next street and still farther as it crossed the Tottenham Court Road" (147-48). That spatial closeness is also evident in the time-space congruity when Peter then walks from the Bloomsbury district to Clarissa's house for the party: "Bedford Place leading into Russell Square...and Whitehall...And here in Westminster...it was her street, this, Clarissa's" (159-60). That movement can be imaginatively mapped by a reader familiar with London, and because of the time-space congruity, that mapping does not require the readerly suspension of disbelief needed for a work covering long stretches of time or distances in space. While a realist novel might describe a character's experience at relatively great length (i.e. lots of page time), Woolf's mimetic tracing of Clarissa's, Peter's, Richard's, or Elizabeth's movements often observes a congruity between page time (in the text) and walking time (in the story world),[29] as if the timing and blocking are simply transferred onto the page of the novel. Certainly this congruity cannot be claimed for all parts of the novel; for example, during the scene in which Peter and Clarissa first reunite, the dilation of interior focalizations lengthens the page time of what would in real time be a much briefer interaction (39-47). In other parts, however, story world time equals page time (what narrative theorists call "story"), and space could be measured out in the time it takes to read. Words on the page create the space to imagine the body's movement through it. The constraints of time and place, and especially the congruity between them, produce a verisimilitude that allows the reader to envision the layout of the landscape (staging) and the characters' movements (blocking) without overt narrative mediation. In this way, the reader is freer in its experience of the work than a theater audience would be: a staged play must be confined to a space in which the audience can literally see the actors, and that audience is subject to the authority of a directorial interpretation. By contrast, the constraints on the world of the novel and its attendant verisimilitude lend it credibility—a body could move that distance in that amount of time—enabling the reader to experience a plausible likeness to life without what Woolf saw as potential drawbacks of live theater.

---

[29] Brian McHale also addresses "a transition from one perceiving mind to another by way of mutually-perceived sound" (101). Teresa Bridgeman theorizes the relationship between space and page time; see also Genette's "duration," which refers to relations between time span, story tempo, and textual space. See David Herman's *Story Logic* on cognitive mapping of fictional worlds.

The congruity of time passage and movement through space establishes a dramatic mimesis that also operates in conjunction with an economy of action. For Aristotle, action was the most important and complex—if also the defining—component of tragedy: "Tragedy is not an imitation of person, but of actions and of life…So the events, i.e. the plot, are what tragedy is there for, and that is the most important thing of all" (11). Woolf's action is no less complex and, indeed, more subtle, given her expressed resistance to the "unscrupulous tyrant" who would insist she "provide a plot" ("Modern" 287). The Aristotelian unity of action (or plot) begins with the hero's error of ignorance (*hamartia*), which leads to a change of fortune from good to bad that is manifest in suffering (*pathos*) within the family (or *philos*) relation, where the suffering is arguably most pitiable because of the familial affinity (23). The plot is unified in that each of the actions proceeds in a necessary and probable order, leading—in a complex plot—to a reversal (*peripeteia*, where the hero expects one thing but circumstances prove otherwise) and a recognition (*anagnorisis*, a change from ignorance to knowledge) that, at the end, "effect through pity and fear the purification [*katharsis*] of such emotions" (Aristotle 10). In Woolf's version, not all events in the novel contribute to a classical unity of action, as interior digressions seem to make the novel endlessly inclusive.[30] Reading Woolf's novel through an Aristotelian lens, however, highlights particular events whose accumulated significance develops a complex action, which in turn establishes the significance of *this* day, the June day of Clarissa's party and of Septimus's suicide, as more than just a slice of everyday life. Aristotle wrote, "As for the art of imitation in narrative verse, it is clear that the plots ought (as in tragedy) to be constructed dramatically" (38); Woolf's use of restricted form, such as the constraint of the single day, constructs the narrative dramatically.[31] Moving away from the single hero, *Mrs. Dalloway* reflects a life that is particular to modernity and reframes Aristotle's cathartic resolution as a dualism, while adapting and complicating the classical emphasis on suffering in the *philos* relation by giving the acquaintance or stranger a fundamental role in bringing about recognition.

The crucial events occur in the storylines of Septimus and Clarissa who, like the classical tragic hero, balance virtue with weakness, and the events in both storylines develop the action in the following way: the choice to conform

---

[30] Moreover, it is widely asserted that modernist novels do not have a plot; Auerbach argues, "in Virginia Woolf's case the exterior events have actually lost their hegemony, they serve to release and interpret inner events" (538). See also Mahaffey (5).

[31] Woolf constructs her plot in terms of this crucial day, using flashbacks to convey the significance of beginning and intervening events rather than starting the discourse with Clarissa's decision to marry and offering every event since. Aristotle praises Homer for his verse-form (a high proportion of direct speech) and for similarly constructing the plot in terms of a single action, Odysseus' homecoming, rather than the whole war (38-39).

to a conventional Britishness (with attendant norms of social convention, gender performance, and nationalist feeling) leads to a change of fortune for each which can be seen in suffering within close relationships, while the reversals and recognitions take place, unusually, in relation to the stranger or other. This action advances a theory of the dignity of individual privacy and of death as a legitimate expression of that privacy, in contrast to a life based in public performance according to social convention.[32] Berman argues that this development in the private sphere has important implications for the politics of the public sphere: "Woolf's attention to the intricate significance of human relationships presents a model of ethics that is built upon intimacy rather than radical alterity, and that ultimately changes the way we view the politics of the public sphere" ("Woolf and Private Sphere" 467). Though Septimus and Clarissa navigate the story world separately, the convergence of their storylines contributes directly to Clarissa's recognition, which in turn echoes and revises Septimus's own recognition forty pages earlier: in light of an inauthentic life defined by social convention, death is not a disaster to fear or regret.[33] Woolf's economy of action thus frames the tragic, emotionally and philosophically, in modern terms.

The *hamartia* for both Septimus and Clarissa centers around the erroneous but common belief in implied narratives about the necessity of living according to conventional behaviors. As a result, they make personal choices—made before the day on which the novel is set but that reverberate through the day's events—based on a public sense of nationalism that is inextricably bound up with gender performance. That nationalism that leads Septimus to volunteer for the war and then marry impulsively during the panic of a postwar lack of feeling ("he became engaged one evening when the panic was on him–that he could not feel" 85) stems from a culturally English manhood that is fashioned from his aesthetic sensibility—particularly, his love of Shakespeare's work—and his connection with a woman, his teacher, Miss Isabel Pole: "Septimus was one of the first to volunteer. He went to France to save an England which consisted almost entirely of Shakespeare's plays and Miss Isabel Pole in a green dress walking in a square" (84). The personal, particular associations lead him to identify with a generalized public ideology and subsequently to make life-altering decisions based on that identification, with

---

[32] On Clarissa critiquing the social system, see Lucio Ruotolo.

[33] Most of the focalizers' experiences in the novel—Peter's, Richard's, Elizabeth's, Miss Kilman's, and Sally's—ultimately serve Clarissa's plotline, their interiorities developing Clarissa's character and order of action. Peter's focal view connects Clarissa to Septimus; though he knows Clarissa and not Septimus, at different points in the novel he shares page time and story world space with both of them. The convergence of seemingly distinct plotlines suggests the novel does not follow an Aristotelian double plot structure (as the *Odyssey* does), which produces good outcomes for bad characters and bad outcomes for good characters, and does not produce the appropriate pleasure of tragedy (Aristotle 22).

disastrous consequences. He later most acutely experiences suffering and, on this day, a reversal and recognition in a scene that combines his artistic sensibility with another woman: his wife, Rezia. Similarly, in marrying Richard, Clarissa effectively chooses the conventional path for the upper middle class British woman, which promises the security of the known over other, less certain paths (to "love" with Peter, or to experience the exquisite, though momentary, "turn[ing] upside down" of the whole world with Sally 35). Though that choice reflects her fear of pushing the boundaries of expectation, born of a narrative equating social convention with personal comfort, it also lays the groundwork for her burgeoning reverence for individual integrity and privacy in the face of death. On this day, the time spent in her room resting because of her illness from influenza (30-37) introduces her to the value of privacy—not just of one's room but also of one's routines and thoughts—and the right not to have to face conversion to love, to religion, or to any set of prescribed behaviors or narratives (123-24; see fuller treatment of the quotation on pages 124-25). Clarissa's private philosophy means accepting and appreciating others as they are, rather than forcing conformity. This honoring of the other's experience effectively prepares the reader for Septimus's suicide. Though Septimus errs because of his true ignorance in equating the personal with the national, while Clarissa errs by more consciously electing a conventional path, she nevertheless genuinely believes that social convention is valuable for providing security, and therefore both of these heroes make a choice out of ignorance that begins the Aristotelian action.

The events on this day establish the falseness and insufficiency of the public narratives that contribute to their choices to serve in public roles; the resulting change of fortune produces suffering—for Aristotle, "an action that involves destruction or pain" (19)—in the familial relations for both Septimus and Clarissa. For the Smiths, for example, the Regents Park scenes reveal that Septimus's aesthetic sensibility has been reduced to a publicly visible, and therefore shameful, expression of insanity: "It is I who am blocking the way, he thought. Was he not being looked at and pointed at; was he not weighted there, rooted to the pavement, for a purpose? But for what purpose?" (15). Those park scenes demonstrate the tension between the privacy of the individual mind and the social pressure of public visibility; Rezia worries, for example, that "People must notice; people must see" (15). That same tension surfaces with the doctors' conflicting treatment suggestions for Septimus's condition: Bradshaw prescribes isolated rest in one of "*my* homes" (95), while Holmes suggests he "take an interest in things outside himself" (21). The inability to reconcile public expectation with Septimus's private experience produces the greatest suffering between Septimus and Rezia.

As a result of her own conventional choices, Clarissa similarly suffers in several close relationships over the course of the day, during events that underscore the inauthenticity of a life based on a public role and that culminate significantly in her party. As we have seen, her encounter with Peter reveals the congruency between them of which neither is aware—shown in their focalized thoughts rather than told by an external focalizer—while at the same time it exposes their miscommunication, and thus implies a missed opportunity for connection between them, foreclosed upon initially by her marriage and, more immediately, by their emotional withholding from each other (39-47). Richard's judgments about gifts for Clarissa reveal a seemingly harmless gap in his knowledge of her: he decides not to buy jewelry because he "did not trust his taste in gold," i.e. she did not wear the bracelet that he chose for her last time (111-12). His choice to buy flowers instead, however, suggests a misunderstanding of her in a different way; after all, she said (to Lucy) "she would buy the flowers herself" (3), and therefore his gift is not only redundant but also misses that small but significant assertion of independence that begins the novel. Together with the fact that he does not follow through with his intention to tell her he loves her (the novel repeats a version of "he could not bring himself to say he loved her; not in so many words" three times 115, 116), the gift suggests that the marriage she chose is no more connected or symbiotic than her relationship with Peter is or likely would have been; Peter himself thinks their marriage would not have been successful (152). Since both Peter and Richard "criticised her very unfairly, laughed at her very unjustly, for her parties" (118), these two encounters reveal the degree to which her relationships even with men who love her are characterized by disconnection and criticism. Meanwhile her encounters with Miss Kilman and Elizabeth and, later at the party, with Sally, recall the other love—between women—also foreclosed upon by her conventional choice. Each of these events hints at the discontent and loneliness that can come from making decisions based on the projection of a public self.

As elements of Woolf's version of Aristotelian action, those events also anticipate the revelations that occur at the party: despite the expectation that a conventional version of life would bring a sense of success, thoughts and conversations during the party reveal that, in the time since Clarissa's decision to marry, Richard, Peter, and Sally have all made decisions that diverged from their earlier plans and even foreclosed on certain desired possibilities. Richard has never gained a position in the Cabinet (so note Lady Bruton 175, and Sally 182). Peter has, Clarissa thinks, "never done a thing they had talked of; his whole life had been a failure" (8); he has no wife, no children and never became a writer (175, 183, 185, 187). For her part, Sally has become wealthy by marrying, an action she likely would not, in her youth, have considered taking, and of which she suspects Clarissa subtly disapproves (183, 185). Clarissa's square look at her own fear of social failure—that is, that the party will be "a complete failure" (163)—introduces an important irony: the success of the party by social standards ultimately becomes a form of personal infidelity, because it is a public, rather than private, success. The suffering Septimus and Clarissa each experience in their relationships has its roots in the inauthenticity of adhering to a public standard, and in the discrepancy between public performance and both protagonists' private impulses.

The reversals and recognitions in both storylines, which for Aristotle make the plot complex, constitute the culmination of the economy of action and also reflect changes particular to the modern age. The *peripeteia* for Septimus and Clarissa, where they expect one thing but circumstances prove otherwise, demonstrates the inadequacy of public narratives and the value of death as a private experience that offers possibility. Indeed, in the discrepancy between public life and the individual private life lies the potential for resolution or a change of fortune back to the good. Against the backdrop of their suffering in the personal realm—the *philos*, particularly spousal, relationships—both Septimus's and Clarissa's realizations are brought about by acquaintances or strangers, achieved when they reach beyond the modern, atomized self to care about, acknowledge, and honor difference and otherness. In these encounters, they experience unexpected versions of identification and reciprocity that transform them. Septimus's transformative encounter is with his wife who is distanced from him both because of his mental illness and because of her outsider status as a foreigner. After several scenes in which the couple clearly experiences suffering (the word "suffer" even appears when Rezia is focalizer [23]) and they have been unable to bridge their differences—Septimus too engulfed in his irrational fantasies and paranoia, Rezia too rational to comprehend and too preoccupied by how they are perceived by others—their final scene together presents a brief return to pre-shellshock normalcy for them and, for him, to rationality. Therein lies the heart of the reversal in this storyline: Septimus and Rezia both imagine that the rational can save him, and in a way, it does, but not as they expect. While in their flat, Septimus applies his intact reason ("he could add up his bill; his brain was perfect" [86]) to think his way out of madness by perceiving objects and rooting himself in the sensory, real world: "he looked at the sideboard; the plate of bananas; the engraving of Queen Victoria and the Prince Consort; at the mantelpiece, with the jar of roses. None of these things moved. All were still; all were real" (138-39). His lucidity restores his connection with Rezia, who has in the past consistently defended his creative work—his "diagrams, designs" (144), "Some things were very beautiful; others sheer nonsense" (137)—from his own impulse to destroy them. In this final scene, seeing a return to his rational self, she engages his artistic sensibility through hat-making (141), her family's creative vocation in Milan, which brings them together as a fortification against the doctors who might separate them: "Even if they took him, she said, she would go with him. They could not separate them against their wills, she said" (144). Though Septimus begins to see his connection to reality fade—"directly he saw nothing the sounds of the game became fainter and stranger and sounded like the cries of people seeking and not finding, and passing further and further away. They had lost him!…That was it: to be alone forever" (141-42)—he now knows he is not alone: "no one could separate them, she said" (145). His fleeting rationality thus dissolves their previous isolation from one another and their connection restores his prewar, feeling sense of self that first associated a guiding female figure (Isabel Pole) with literature (Shakespeare) and motivated the sense of nationalism that led him to volunteer. In these last minutes of his life, Rezia becomes that guiding figure and, by preserving his aesthetic sensibility and honoring his particular condition, she connects with him as his unique self rather than as a psychically damaged soldier, a husband, or an Englishman. As Septimus thinks, "She was a flowering tree; and through her branches looked out the face of a lawgiver, who had reached a sanctuary where she feared no one; not Holmes; not Bradshaw; a miracle, a triumph, the last and greatest.…Over them she triumphed" (144-45). In this way, Rezia ushers in his movement from ignorance to knowledge, a form of Aristotelian *anagnorisis*, from the terrible feeling of being alone to having her on his side of beauty and truth.

In the Smiths' storyline, Woolf brings the satisfying, righteous death of tragedy to bear on the particularly modern circumstances of shellshock and suicide. That the rational Septimus chooses death by suicide revises the expectation that a return to rationality signals a return to sanity and a rescue from his insane death wish. The end of the scene reveals, however, that rationality actually enables him to choose death. Rather than saving him from death, then, rationality makes his death righteous, in the tragic sense. This scene and the Smiths' relationship offer, therefore, a rereading of public narratives about death and suicide that, as we will see, anticipates Clarissa's own reflections at the end of the novel.[34] Even in his rational consideration of his options for committing suicide, Septimus himself recognizes his actions as participating in the tragic genre: "There remained only the window, the large Bloomsbury-lodging house window, the tiresome, the troublesome, and rather melodramatic business of opening the window and throwing himself out. It was their idea of tragedy, not his or Rezia's (for she was with him)" (145-46). He identifies but does not buy into a melodramatic notion of tragedy, though—or perhaps because—"He did not want to die. Life was good" (146). Septimus's consideration defies rational thought about the opposition between life and death; even his exact reasons for throwing himself out of the window remain private (from the reader as from those around him), an assertion both of his individuality and his unconditional connection with Rezia, who "was with him." Rezia herself preserves the significance of his death as a personal choice; her response when standing by

---

[34] Christopher Ames reads Septimus's suicide as the tragic result of living according to conventions (104). By contrast, J. Hillis Miller sees in suicide the possibility for communion in contrast to the failure of the party.

him, even after death, underscores her acceptance: "'He is dead,' she said, smiling at the poor old woman who guarded her" (147). His suicide, and her acceptance of it, are markers of their togetherness, signaling *anagnorisis*, the movement from ignorance toward the knowledge that their fundamental connection is cemented by, and ongoing after, his death. Furthermore, death is a private, rational choice and an assertion of individuality rather than, as public narratives and genre dictate, the sad, selfish, isolated and cowardly act of a madman (the latter judgment expressed so clearly by Dr. Holmes, who calls Septimus "The coward!" 146). In the context of Aristotelian tragedy, Septimus's death arguably constitutes an ending that is both pitiable and righteous, since it is the culmination of the causal development of action and, though a suicidal death, is framed as restorative and affirming. This event denies Aristotelian closure, however, because Septimus's personal end is not the novel's end, and the Smiths' storyline is also significant for Clarissa's storyline: the resolution of the Smiths' storyline—where normalizing public narratives give way to an appreciation of privacy that comes from the eradication of difference and distance between the couple—anticipates Clarissa's own reading of suicide and death.

The importance of the Smiths' storyline for Clarissa lies in honoring individual autonomy: just as the events of the day lead Septimus and Rezia to personal redemption when they turn away from public expectations, so do the events in Clarissa's plotline lead her to realize the inadequacy of the social conventions on which she has based her own decisions and expectations. In her own version of *peripeteia*, she expects to find meaning throughout the day in her existing relationships—with Hugh, Peter, Richard, Elizabeth—and in the public social setting of her party, but her moments of greatest identification and empathy occur when she connects as a private individual rather than a public figure with the unfamiliar other. The identification with strangers—as Clarissa thinks, the "Odd affinities she had with people she had never spoken to" (152-53)—departs from Aristotle's assertion that the most pitiable suffering occurs in close, usually familial, relations. He notes that, between enemies, "there is nothing pitiable either in the action itself or in its imminence, except in respect of the actual suffering itself. Likewise with neutrals" (23). Woolf offers a set of interactions where the parties are neither enemies nor family, but not neutral, either; their affinity stems from a mix of proximity and sympathy in the modern city. Thus, *Mrs. Dalloway* conveys an experience of modernity in which traditional bonds based on shared nationality, nationalism, religion, social status, and even domestic space no longer necessarily connect individuals, leaving them unmoored. Both storylines, together, address the problem of isolation in modernity, especially in the face of a normalizing public context. The alternative connection between strangers is enabled in the crowded modern metropolis by relative anonymity, manifest for Clarissa in a "privacy of the soul" (124).[35] Though the resulting atomization could be read as a sad paradox—that the only thing shared is a sense of isolation—Clarissa's experience especially at the end of the novel implies the opposite: it is precisely that shared sense of isolation and those common everyday experiences, routines, familiar objects and physical details of place that generate intimate identification. Clarissa even goes so far as to frame marriage in terms of honoring the separateness of two individuals: "And there is a dignity in people; a solitude; even between husband and wife a gulf; and that one must respect, thought Clarissa, watching him open the door; for one would not part with it oneself, or take it, against his will, from one's husband, without losing one's independence, one's self-respect—something, after all, priceless" (117). The emotional effect of experiencing this kind of connection while retaining autonomy is distinct from that in Aristotle's poetics (which emphasizes the *philos* relation): for Clarissa, familiar identification with the unknown other produces an affinity between strangers, a more extreme version of the Smiths' overcoming differences. That connection calls attention to the value of individual privacy and thereby writes against public sameness, reaching across lines of otherness.[36]

This intimate identification, which leads for Clarissa to her *anagnorisis* about the privacy of death, becomes clearest in the passages in which she is, significantly, alone and away from the party, when she observes the unknown neighbor's exercise of individual privacy (123-24, 181-82) and unexpectedly learns of Septimus's suicide. During her initial observation, when the old lady is unconscious of being watched, Clarissa concludes,

> Had she ever tried to convert any one herself? Did she not wish everybody merely to be themselves? And she watched out of the window the old lady opposite climbing upstairs. Let her climb upstairs if she wanted to; let her stop; then let her, as Clarissa had often seen her, gain her bedroom, part her curtains, and disappear again into the background. Somehow one respected

---

[35] Hana Wirth-Nesher argues that anonymity actually enables this connection ("Impartial Maps" 58), negotiating intimacy and distance in the urban setting (*City Codes* 206). See also Berman's *Modernist Commitments*, which considers the political and ethical implications of the private moment facing the other, framing the old lady as a neighbor rather than intimate or stranger.

[36] Miller sees alienation as a shared condition (171), as opposed to Cristina Delgado García, for whom alienation denies connection (19-22). Olson addresses the emphasis on modernism on the value of the ordinary (as an experience, activities, things, and a style). For Woolf on characters' ordinary rituals in the *Odyssey*, see "On Not Knowing Greek" (38). This valuing of the private individual and even the connection between strangers arguably reflects the intimacy among members of the Bloomsbury Group, as well as their ethical stance toward the autonomy of the individual, expressed in their political views, critical and artistic works, and intimate, personal lives. See Christine Froula and Jesse Wolfe.

> that—that old woman looking out of the window, quite unconscious that
> she was being watched. There was something solemn in it—but love and
> religion would destroy that, whatever it was, the privacy of the soul. (123-24)

This passage fleshes out a cooperative and non-intrusive interchange, where the neighbor is solemn in her activities as she is merely "being herself," unconscious of being watched. For her part, Clarissa identifies herself with verbs such as "respect" and "let" as opposed to "convert," where as a watcher she does not try to control, possess, or judge the individual before her. This connection is reaffirmed by the significant fact that Clarissa's recognitions occur while she is in a private room separate from her party, even though, in a classical plot, the crucial event of the action would be the party itself. Instead, *Mrs. Dalloway* offers a form of closure through enclosure that is also, ironically, an opening up. Plagued as she has been all day by a fear of death and a nagging awareness of oppressive social conventions and public narratives about love and religion, the news of Septimus's death initiates her private reflection. In this way, his storyline contributes centrally to her recognition, while the inverse is also true: Clarissa's ultimate recognition frames Septimus's story as he would have seen it, articulating how to read his ending outside of conventional understandings of suicide, which would reduce Septimus to a sacrificial figure. Just as he reflected, "It was their idea of tragedy, not his or Rezia's" (146), so does Clarissa believe that Septimus's death is not sad:

> A thing there was that mattered; a thing, wreathed about with chatter,
> defaced, obscured in her own life, let drop every day in corruption, lies,
> chatter. This he had preserved. Death was defiance. Death was an attempt
> to communicate; people feeling the impossibility of reaching the centre
> which, mystically, evaded them; closeness drew apart; rapture faded, one
> was alone. There was an embrace in death. (180)

Death is transformed in her consideration of Septimus's final act into something that preserves the thing that matters, that defies, tries to communicate, and offers an embrace. Though she does not know him, she understands him and grants him the dignity of honoring his private conception of death and what it offers. Instead of converting his narrative to something conventional, she takes from it an opportunity to exercise her theory about the soul's privacy. Just as she comes to this realization, she is prompted by a speculative exchange with the old lady to acknowledge her own position relative to that theory:

> [Clarissa] parted the curtains; she looked. Oh, but how surprising!—in
> the room opposite the old lady stared straight at her! She was going to
> bed....She was going to bed, in the room opposite. It was fascinating to

> watch her, moving about, that old lady, crossing the room, coming to the window. Could she see her? It was fascinating, with people still laughing and shouting in the drawing-room, to watch that old woman, quite quietly, going to bed. (181)

Though Clarissa has been the self-conscious subject holding the neighbor as the object of her gaze, this moment of visual exchange makes clear that Clarissa is equally object—a familiar but mostly unknown, ordinary woman—to the neighbor's subjective view. The privacy of her own moment is every bit as accessible to the neighbor as that neighbor's bedtime routine is to her. Berman reads this second encounter as a moment in which they "engage in a relationship of mutuality," as opposed to the first encounter, in which Clarissa has an option to maintain a "laissez-faire" attitude toward the neighbor (*Modernist Commitments* 61). This mirroring insinuates that the old lady might equally honor Clarissa's private self, reinforcing that Clarissa's value does not lie solely in the publically visible role of hostess, which leaves her punished and passively stuck in a performance: "Somehow it was her disaster—her disgrace. It was her punishment to see sink and disappear here a man, there a woman, in this profound darkness, and she forced to stand here in her evening dress" (181). Rather, she is valuable as a private, ordinary self. Significantly, in each of these encounters with the stranger—when she initially looks at the old lady, when she contemplates Septimus's death, and when the old lady looks back at her—Clarissa's language disparages the public, conventional sphere: the conversion mechanisms of love and religion destroy that something solemn (124), and "the thing that matters" is surrounded, damaged, hidden, and lost in "corruption, lies, chatter" (180). She most explicitly contrasts the old lady's private routine with the sounds of her party nearby and she metonymically references her own participation as she is "forced to stand here in her evening dress" (181). Clarissa's significant recognition takes place privately, during but outside of the party, a setup that makes explicit the contrast between the public social events and the private everyday actions.[37] The party proves to be not the climactic event but instead a mere background for the crucial, though private, climax of action, defying expectations about the setting of a classical plot resolution.

The spectacular emotional climax of the end of action, then, is neither spectacular nor the end. Whatever release Clarissa (and the reader) feels is fleeting and not part of the final scene or episode of the novel. Rather, the understated joy of Clarissa's realization is bracketed at physical, emotional, and narrative levels. In the private room she is physically separate from the party, and her brief emotional connection to the neighbor and Septimus is bracketed by her obligatory return to it:

---

[37] See also Briggs *An Inner Life* 137 for an alternative reading of the scene.

"She felt somehow very like him—the young man who had killed himself. She felt glad that he had done it; thrown it away. The clock was striking. The leaden circles dissolved in the air. He made her feel the beauty; made her feel the fun. But she must go back" (181-82). She applauds his liberated surrender, a fearless pushing away of life (implied by the phrase "thrown it away") and gives credit, ironically, to he (who could not feel) for "ma[king] her feel the beauty...the fun." Clarissa's realizations are, after all, juxtaposed with the defeated surrender that she "must go back to them," registered in the word "but." Her private moment is closed off in a room she must leave because of a social obligation she must meet. The moment is also bracketed at the level of narrative discourse, as the shift to focalizers Sally and Peter, who are back in the main room, effectively return the reader to the party before Clarissa herself returns. J. Hillis Miller remarks, when "she returns from her recognition of her kinship with Septimus to bring 'terror' and 'ecstacy' to Peter" she also comes back "into the language of the narration" (183). Woolf's design early in her composition of the novel was to "knit...together everything" by allowing Peter, Richard and Sally "to sum up Clarissa" (*D2* 312), producing a paradoxical circumstance in which Clarissa is at the center of the novel while also decentered and complicated by the multiple views and narratives about her. This explains why the novel ends not with Clarissa's interior voice or her private realization, but rather with others' speech and thoughts about her. Such a move emphasizes the fleeting and unresolved nature of her recognition by showing that the party goes on without her, and notably not showing how or whether she is changed in the long run. Though Clarissa experiences a form of recognition that satisfies the arc of the action, hers is not the last word.[38]

The shift in *Mrs. Dalloway* from the Aristotelian theory—in terms of what the recognition is, who brings it about, and where it takes place in both the story world and the narrative itself—produces an ambivalent emotional conclusion. The ending incorporates a paradoxical condition like the terror and pity of *katharsis*, but tempers the "characteristic pleasure" (Aristotle 38) of classical resolution and release. Instead, the recognition that Clarissa achieves through her connection to strangers—from both seeing and being seen, and sharing the embrace of death with Septimus—actually amounts to a loving close without full closure. Thus, in the endings of both Clarissa's and the Smiths' storylines, Woolf's novel offers an

---

[38] Critics disagree about whether this constitutes a happy or a bleak ending. Miller sees Clarissa as rejuvenated and returning to life, while Thomas Beattie asserts that Clarissa overcomes the failure to which Septimus has succumbed, though against the backdrop of an "unfathomable cosmos" (529). Others, by contrast, read the ending as not rejuvenating (Laurence Scott) and offering no clear future (Delgado García). What these readings have in common is a sense of a resolved ending, while I am interested in how the narrative discourse denies full closure by juxtaposing brief resolution with uncertain continuation. See also Hite on this ending as dynamic and continuing (267).

awakening or opening, and the seemingly closed end as more of an arrival at a place of pause or a concentration of possibilities. Some might read the resistance to narrative or emotional closure in the ending as typically modernist, but so often such endings connote indifference at best, and hopelessness at worst. By contrast, the emotional tension of the narrative action in *Mrs. Dalloway* produces a condition that is best characterized as a "dualism," where contrasting concepts and emotions—success and failure, familiar and stranger, alienation and connection, conclusion and continuation—coexist without order or reconciliation, and without the domination of one over the other. Peter expresses that dualism at the end of the novel: "What is this terror? what is this ecstasy? he thought to himself. What is it that fills me with extraordinary excitement?" (190). It is Clarissa, of course, who has finally reappeared at the party, and so her last appearance in the novel is as the object of another's gaze, producing a yin and yang of feeling in Peter. She is still central, but no longer the focalizer. At the level of action there is implicitly more to come—she has privately resolved her philosophy, but then returns to the party, and the challenges and conflicts in her public life remain unresolved because they are unwritten. Even the return itself carries a double connotation: it constitutes a going or coming back, a reversion to before, and yet also holds the promise implicit in entering a room, of new space, new interactions, new moment, new scene. The positing of unwritten possibilities leaves that active reader suspended, neither trapped in an implausible and static conclusiveness nor abandoned to a formless open-endedness. Instead, this reader is empowered to experience the likeness to life, to the reality at least in modern times, of living with and through the chaos of irreconcilable opposites.[39] The dramatic quality that Woolf adopts—in her narrative discourse and in the constraints of her mimetic economy—makes this possible. The private reader, free from the authority of the narrator, of the performance and of the communal live audience, can experience the recognition that comes from intimate closeness to a life with which she can truly identify.

Works Cited

Ames, Christopher. "The True Self: Parties in Woolf." *The Life of the Party: Festive Vision in Modern Fiction*, Georgia UP, 1991, pp. 83-115.

---

[39] This dualism of happiness with sadness, joy with terror, echoes Friedrich Nietzsche's early philosophy of the ideal tragedy from *The Birth of Tragedy*, where the Apollonian impulse to order is tempered by the more chaotic, dynamic impulse of the Dionysian. Although Newton argues that most high modernists do not embrace Nietzsche's idea of tragedy and are only influenced by his assertion that art is not about reality or mimesis (121-22), Woolf's novel seems to adapt the formal constraints of Aristotle's poetics to a Nietzschean philosophy of life.

Aristotle. *Poetics*, edited by Malcolm Heath, Penguin, 1996.
Auerbach, Erich. "The Brown Stocking." *Mimesis: The Representation of Reality in Western Literature*, Princeton UP, 1953, pp. 525-53.
Bal, Mieke. "Narration and Focalization." *On Story-Telling*, Polebridge, 1991, pp. 75-108.
Barrows, Adam. "'The Shortcomings of Timetables': Greenwich, Modernism, and the Limits of Modernity." *MFS: Modern Fiction Studies* 56.2, 2010, pp. 262-89.
Beattie, Thomas. "Moments of Meaning Dearly Achieved: Virginia Woolf's Sense of an Ending." *Modern Fiction Studies* 32.4, 1986, pp. 521-39.
Bell, Clive. "The Artistic Problem." *A Bloomsbury Group Reader*, edited by S. P. Rosenbaum, Blackwell, 1993, pp. 102-6.
Berman, Jessica Schiff. *Modernist Commitments: Ethics, Politics, and Transnational Modernism*, Columbia UP, 2011.
———. "Woolf and the Private Sphere." *Virginia Woolf in Context*, edited by Bryony Randall and Jane Goldman, Cambridge UP, 2012, pp. 461-74.
Blakemore, Diane. "Parentheticals and Point of View in Free Indirect Style." *Language and Literature: Journal of the Poetics and Linguistics Association.* 18.2, 2009, pp. 129-53.
Bongiorno, Andrew, ed. *Castelvetro's Commentary on Aristotle's Poetics 1447-1459: An Annotated Translation*, Cornell UP, 1935.
Bowen, Elizabeth. "Truth and Fiction." *Afterthought: Pieces About Writing*, Longmans, 1962, pp. 114-43.
Bowlby, Rachel. "Untold Stories in *Mrs. Dalloway*." *Textual Practice* 25.3, 2011, pp. 397-415.
Bradshaw, David. Introduction. *Mrs. Dalloway*, Oxford UP, 2000, pp. xi-xlv.
———. "Woolf's London, London's Woolf." *Virginia Woolf in Context*, edited by Bryony Randall and Jane Goldman, Cambridge UP, pp. 229-42.
Bridgeman, Teresa. "Time and Space." *The Cambridge Companion to Narrative*, edited by David Herman, Cambridge UP, 2007, pp. 52-65.
Briganti, Chiara. "Giving the Mundane its due: One (Fine) Day in the Life of the Everyday." *English Studies in Canada* 39.2-3, 2013, pp. 161-80.
Briggs, Julia. *Reading Virginia Woolf*, Edinburgh Press, 2009.
———. *Virginia Woolf: An Inner Life*, Harcourt, 2005.
Covington, Elizabeth. "Splitting the Husk: The Day Novel and Storm Jameson's A Day Off." *Genre: Forms of Discourse and Culture* 46.3, 2013, pp. 265-84.
Cuddy-Keane, Melba. *Virginia Woolf, the Intellectual, and the Public Sphere*, Cambridge UP, 2003.
Delgado García, Cristina. "Decentring Discourse, Self-Centred Politics: Radicalism and the Self in Virginia Woolf's Mrs. Dalloway." *Atlantis:*

Journal of the Spanish Association of Anglo-American Studies. 32.1, 2010, pp. 15-28.

Edmondson, Annalee. "Narrativizing Characters in Mrs. Dalloway." *Journal of Modern Literature* 36.1, 2012, pp. 17-36.

Eliot, T. S. "Tradition and the Individual Talent." *Selected Essays, 1917-1932*, Harcourt, 1932, pp. 3-11.

———. "*Ulysses*, Order and Myth." 1923. *Modernism: An Anthology of Sources and Documents*, edited by Vassiliki Kolocotroni, Jane Goldman, and Olga Taxidou, Chicago UP, 1999, pp. 371-73.

Felski, Rita. *The Gender of Modernity*, Harvard UP, 1995.

Flint, Kate. "Reading Uncommonly: Virginia Woolf and the Practice of Reading." *Yearbook of English Studies* 26, 1996, pp. 187-98.

Frank, Joseph. "Spatial Form in Modern Literature: An Essay in Two Parts." *The Sewanee Review* 53.2, 1945, pp. 221-40.

Froula, Christine. *Virginia Woolf and the Bloomsbury Avant-Garde: War, Civilization, Modernity*. Columbia UP, 2005.

Garvey, Johanna. "'A Voice Bubbling Up': *Mrs. Dalloway* in Dialogue with *Ulysses*." *Virginia Woolf: Themes and Variations*, edited by Vara Neverow-Turk & Mark Hussey, Pace UP, 1993, pp. 299-308.

Genette, Gérard. *Narrative Discourse: An Essay in Method*. Translated by Jane E. Lewin, Cornell UP, 1980.

Giovannelli, Alessandro. "In and Out: The Dynamics of Imagination in the Engagement of Narratives." *Journal of Aesthetics and Art Criticism* 66.1, 2008, pp. 11-24.

Goldman, Mark. "Virginia Woolf and the Critic as Reader." *PMLA: Publications of the Modern Language Association of America* 80.3, 1965, pp. 275-84.

Hagen, Benjamin D. "A Car, a Plane, and a Tower: Interrogating Public Images in *Mrs. Dalloway*." *Modernism/Modernity* 16.3, 2009, pp. 537-51.

Heath, Malcolm. Introduction. *Poetics*. By Aristotle, Penguin, 1996, pp. vii-xxi.

Heffernan, James A. W. "Tracking a Reader: What Did Virginia Woolf Really Think of *Ulysses*?" *Parallaxes: Virginia Woolf and James Joyce Seventy Years After*, edited by Marco Canani and Sara Sullam, Scholars, 2014, pp. 1-22.

Henke, Suzette. "Virginia Woolf (1882-1941)." *The Gender of Modernism: A Critical Anthology*, edited by Bonnie Kime Scott, Indiana UP, 1990, pp. 622-28.

———. "Virginia Woolf, James Joyce, and 'The Prime Minister': Amnesias and Genealogies." *Virginia Woolf Miscellany* 68, 2005, pp. 4-5.

Herman, David. "1880-1945: Re-Minding Modernism." *The Emergence of Mind:*

Representations of Consciousness in Narrative Discourse in English, edited by David Herman, Nebraska UP, 2011, pp. 243-72.
———. "Cognition, Emotion and Consciousness." *The Cambridge Companion to Narrative,* pp. 245-59.
———. *Story Logic: Problems and Possibilities of Narrative,* Nebraska UP, 2002.
Higdon, David Leon. "A First Census of the Circadian or One-Day Novel." *Journal of Narrative Technique* 22.1, 1992, pp. 57-64.
Hite, Molly. "Tonal Cues and Uncertain Values: Affect and Ethics in Mrs. Dalloway." *Narrative* 18.3, 2010, pp. 249-75.
Hoff, Molly. "The Pseudo-Homeric World of *Mrs. Dalloway.*" *Twentieth Century Literature: A Scholarly and Critical Journal* 45.2, 1999, pp. 186-209.
Jahn, Manfred. "Focalization." *The Cambridge Companion to Narrative,* pp. 94-108.
Jenkins, William D. "Virginia Woolf and the Belittling of 'Ulysses'." *James Joyce Quarterly* 25.4, 1988, pp. 513-19.
Jones, Gloria. "Free Indirect Style in Mrs. Dalloway." *Postscript* 14, 1997, pp. 69-80.
Kern, Stephen. *The Culture of Love: Victorians to Moderns*, Harvard UP, 1992.
———. *The Culture of Time and Space: 1880-1919,* Harvard UP, 1983.
Lewis, Wyndham. *Men Without Art*, Cassell, 1934.
Mahaffey, Vicki. *Modernist Literature: Challenging Fictions*, Blackwell, 2007.
Marcus, Laura. "The Legacies of Modernism." *The Cambridge Companion to the Modernist Novel*, Cambridge UP, 2007, pp. 82-98.
McHale, Brian. "Modernist Reading, Post-Modern Text: The Case of *Gravity's Rainbow.*" 1.1-2 *Poetics Today*, 1979, pp. 85-110.
Miller, J. Hillis. "Mrs. Dalloway: Repetition as the Raising of the Dead." *The J. Hillis Miller Reader*, edited by Julian Wolfreys, Stanford UP, 2005, pp. 169-84.
Miracky, James J. "A Simultaneous Flow: Diachronic, Psychological, and Synchronic Time in the Novel and Film Versions of *Mrs. Dalloway.*" *Interfaces: Image Texte Language* 19-20.1, 2001, pp. 225-40.
Moretti, Franco. "The Moment of Truth: The Geography of Modern Tragedy." 1986. *Contemporary Marxist Literary Criticism*, edited by Francis Mulhern, Longman, 1992, pp. 114-24.
Newman, Hilary. "Echoes of *Ulysses* in *Mrs. Dalloway.*" *Virginia Woolf Bulletin of the Virginia Woolf Society of Great Britain* 11, 2002, pp. 40-47.
Newton, K. M. *Modern Literature and the Tragic*, Edinburgh UP, 2008.
Nietzsche, Friedrich. *The Birth of Tragedy: Out of the Spirit of Music*, edited by Michael Tanner, translated by Shaun Whiteside, Penguin Classics, 1994.
Olson, Liesl. *Modernism and the Ordinary*, Oxford UP, 2009.

Peach, Linden. "Virginia Woolf and Realist Aesthetics." *The Edinburgh Companion to Virginia Woolf and the Arts*, edited by Maggie Humm, Edinburgh UP, 2010. 104-17.
Phelan, James. "Character and Judgment in Narrative and in Lyric: Toward an Understanding of the Audience's Engagement in *The Waves*." *Style* 24.3, 1990, pp. 60-73.
Puchner, Martin. *The Drama of Ideas: Platonic Provocations in Theater and Philosophy*, Oxford UP, 2010.
Putzel, Steven D. "Virginia Woolf and 'The Distance of the Stage.'" *Women's Studies: An Inter-Disciplinary Journal*, vol. 28, 1999, pp. 435-70.
———. *Virginia Woolf and the Theater*. Fairleigh-Dickinson UP, 2012.
Randall, Bryony. "A Day's Time: The One-Day Novel and the Temporality of the Everyday." *New Literary History: A Journal of Theory and Interpretation* 47.4, 2016, pp. 591-610.
Reed, Christopher. "Through Formalism: Feminism and Virginia Woolf's Relation to Bloomsbury Aesthetics." *Twentieth Century Literature: A Scholarly and Critical Journal* 38.1, 1992, pp. 20-43.
Richardson, Brian. "Drama and narrative." *The Cambridge Companion to Narrative*, pp. 142-55.
Richter, Harvena. "The *Ulysses* Connection: Clarissa Dalloway's Bloomsday." *Studies in the Novel* 21.3, 1989, pp. 305-19.
Rosenbaum, S.P. *Edwardian Bloomsbury: The Early Literary History of the Bloomsbury Group,* vol. 2, Palgrave Macmillan, 1994.
Ruotolo, Lucio. "Mrs. Dalloway: The Unguarded Moment." *Virginia Woolf: Revaluation and Continuity*, edited by Ralph Freedman and Maria DiBattista, U of California, 1980, pp.141-60.
Schiff, James. "Rewriting Woolf's Mrs. Dalloway: Homage, Sexual Identity, and the Single-Day Novel by Cunningham, Lippincott, and Lanchester." *Critique: Studies in Contemporary Fiction* 45.4, 2004, pp. 363-82.
Scott, Bonnie Kime. "A Joyce of One's Own: Following the Lead of Woolf, West, and Barnes." *Rereading Modernism: New Directions in Feminist Criticism*, edited by Lisa Rado, Garland, 1994, pp. 209-30.
———. Introduction to *Mrs. Dalloway*, edited by Mark Hussey, Mariner Books, 2005, pp. xxxv-lxviii.
Scott, Laurence. "Petrified Mermaids: Transcendence and Female Subjectivity in the Aesthetics of Virginia Woolf's *Mrs. Dalloway* and André Breton's *Nadja*." *Textual Practice* 28.1, 2014, pp. 121-40.
Silver, Brenda. *Virginia Woolf's Reading Notebooks*. Princeton UP, 1983.
Sontag, Susan. *Against Interpretation: And Other Essays*, Picador, 2001.

Strachey, Lytton. *Lytton Strachey By Himself: A Self-Portrait*, edited by Michael Holroyd, Vintage, 1994.
Sullam, Sara and Emily Kopley, eds. *Woolf and Literary Genre* special issue of *Virginia Woolf Miscellany* vol. 83, 2013, pp. 1-34.
Travis, Molly Abel. *Reading Cultures: The Construction of Readers in the Twentieth Century*, Southern Illinois UP, 1998.
Weinberg, Bernard. "Scaliger Versus Aristotle on Poetics." *Modern Philology: A Journal Devoted to Research in Medieval and Modern Literature* 39.4, 1942, pp. 337-60.
Weninger, Robert. "Days of Our Lives: The One-Day Novel as Homage à Joyce." *Bloomsday 100: Essays on Ulysses*, edited by Morris Beja & Anne Fogarty, UP of Florida, 2009, pp. 190-210.
White, Siân. "*Ulysses,* the Poetics of Tragedy, and A New Mimesis," *PLL: Papers on Language and Literature* 51.4 2015, pp. 334-72.
Wirth-Nesher, Hana. *City Codes: Reading the Modern Urban Novel*, Cambridge UP, 1996.
———. "Impartial Maps: Reading and Writing Cities." *Handbook of Urban Studies*, edited by Ronan Paddison, Sage Publications, 2001, pp. 52-66.
Wolfe, Jesse. *Bloomsbury, Modernism, and the Reinvention of Intimacy*. Cambridge UP, 2011.
Woolf, Virginia. *A Room of One's Own*. 1929, Harcourt, 1989.
———."Anon." *The Essays of Virginia Woolf vol. 6 and Additional Essays, 1906-1924*, edited by Stuart N. Clarke, Hogarth, 1986, pp. 580-99.
———. *The Diary of Virginia Woolf*, edited by Anne Olivier Bell and Andrew McNeillie, 5 vols, Harcourt, 1977-84.
———."The Dramatic in Life and Art." *The Virginia Woolf Manuscripts from the Monks House Papers at the University of Sussex*. Microform, Harvester Microform, 1985. Reel 2, MH/A26.
———. *The Letters of Virginia Woolf*, edited by Nigel Nicholson and Joanne Trautman, 6 vols, Harvest Books, 1982.
———. "Modern Fiction." 1919. *The Virginia Woolf Reader*, edited by Mitchell A. Leaska, Harcourt, 1984, pp. 283-91.
———. "Modern Novels (Joyce)," Woolf's Reading Notes on *Ulysses* in the Berg Collection, New York Public Library, edited by Suzette Henke, in *The Gender of Modernism: A Critical Anthology*, edited by Bonnie Kime Scott, Indiana UP, 1990, pp. 642-45.
———. "Mr. Bennett and Mrs. Brown." 1924. *The Virginia Woolf Reader*, edited by Mitchell A. Leaska, Harcourt, 1984, pp. 192-212.
———. *Mrs. Dalloway*, edited by Mark Hussey, Harcourt, 2005.

———. "On Not Knowing Greek." *The Common Reader*, Harcourt, 1984, pp. 23-38.

———. "Poetry, Fiction and the Future." 1927. *Virginia Woolf Selected Essays*, Oxford, 2008, pp. 74-84.

———. *Virginia Woolf "The Hours": The British Museum Manuscript of* Mrs. Dalloway, edited by Helen M. Wussow, Pace UP, 2010.

———. "Women and Fiction." 1929. *Women and Writing*, edited by Michèle Barrett, Harcourt, 1979, pp. 43-52.

Woolf, Leonard. "Back to Aristotle." *Athenaeum* 4729, 17 December 1920, pp. 834-35.

Virginia Woolf's Egyptomania: Echoes of *The Book of the Dead* in *To The Lighthouse*
Brett Rutherford

To the Lighthouse is many things to many readers and critics. Acknowledged as the most autobiographical of all Virginia Woolf's novels and an elegy for her parents, it is also seen as a confrontation with Freud's Oedipal theories anticipating a feminist psychology (Abel), an oblique satire of imperialism/colonialism (Seshagiri), an aesthetic debate of Moore *versus* Fry (Ingram), a battleground of materialism *versus* spiritualism (Gaipa), and a struggle against the negation of mental illness (Rubenstein). Part of the novel's staying power is that while all these characterizations can be true, the whole is always larger than the scholars' interpretive findings.

To the Lighthouse has yet another layer, imbued with images, symbols, characters, and narrative elements taken directly from Egyptian myth and from *The Book of the Dead*, a reflection of Woolf's classical reading and of the rampant "Egyptomania" of the 1920s. Woolf's overlay of Egyptian gods on the Ramsay family requires a re-examination of her treatment of Freud's Oedipal complex, a concept she resisted even while employing it. Further, Woolf's allusions to the matrilineal culture of ancient Egypt and the international cult of Isis demonstrate her search for an alternate discourse, less patriarchal than Greco-Roman, Judeo-Christian, and Freudian modes. Finally, there is the question—perhaps unanswerable—of whether Woolf's "Egyptianizing" of her novel during its writing constituted a private coding of the text for her literary friend and lover, Vita Sackville-West.

The Osiris-Isis-Horus Myth

Since Egyptian mythology is far less familiar than that of the Greco-Roman pantheon, the following paragraphs should serve to provide a basic overview of the Isis-Osiris-Horus-Set mythology that pervades *To the Lighthouse*. The characters in the Egyptian death-and-resurrection myth revolve around Isis as wife, sister and mother. After being betrayed and murdered by his brother Set, Osiris becomes the god of the underworld, akin to Hades/Pluto. The savior of Osiris is his sister-wife Isis, who uses her magic spells to assemble his scattered body parts, and to revive him, to a point. She then turns into a kite, and:

> She made light [to appear] from her feathers, she made air to come into being by means of her two wings...She made to rise up the helpless members of him whose heart was at rest, she drew from him his essence, and she made therefrom an heir (see Figure 1) (Budge, *Osiris*, 99).

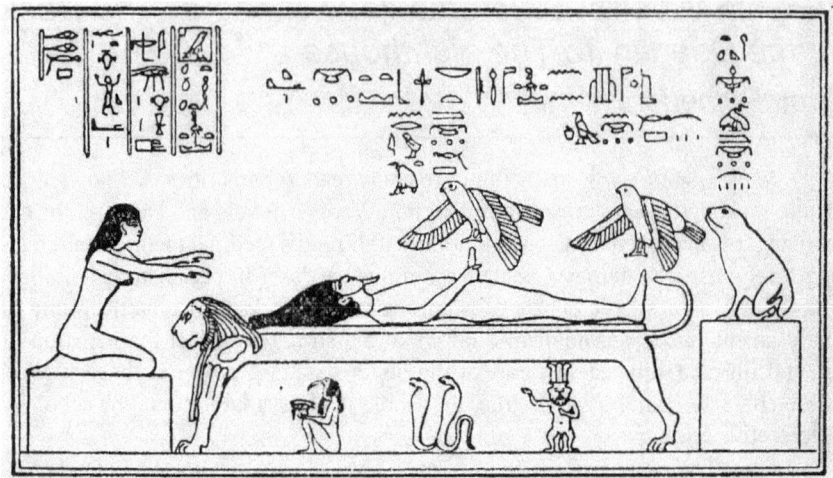

*Figure 1: Osiris impregnating Isis, who is in the form of a hawk. The second hawk is Nepthys. At the head of the bier sits Hathor and at the foot, the frog-goddess Heqet. (*Budge, *Osiris, 280).*

The product of this necrophiliac mating is the falcon-headed god Horus, protected and reared in secret, raised to become his father's avenger. Young Horus has several setbacks, including a traumatic encounter with a black pig (Set in disguise), and death by scorpion bite; he is revived by his mother and the wisdom-god Thoth. Later, Horus captures Set and leaves him guarded by Isis; she inexplicably releases their enemy. Horus finally triumphs over Set, but only after losing and regaining an eye (the symbol of his life force). Set, although vanquished, continues to hold a place in the pantheon of Egyptian gods, warlike, Satan's prototype; he is even depicted riding in his own separate boat to the land of the dead, in the guise of a black pig (Budge, *Osiris* 42).

The text known in English as *The Book of the Dead (The Book of Coming Forth By Day* to Egyptians), was buried with every Egyptian wealthy enough to have it copied, a personalized scroll with the owner's choice from hundreds of available prayers, spells, and instructions (Goelet 14). This text, used alike for Pharaoh and commoner, relates the journey of Osiris to the underworld, or Land of Reeds, where he is judged, found blameless, and then becomes Lord of the Dead. The owner of the scroll expects to make a similar journey: if he is a Pharaoh, he *becomes* Osiris at the completion of the journey; other subjects use Osiris's spells to join the ranks of ghosts free to come and go among the living and the dead. The name of the dead subject becomes a suffix of Osiris, *e.g.,* Osiris-Ani, Osiris-Ramses.

The journey, in a boat, transports the *ba*, the double of the physical body, and the *ka*, or spirit. The *ba* appears in Egyptian art as a mummy, immobile, its legs wrapped together; the *ka* is depicted as a bird-like figure. After a "negative confession" of sins not committed, the subject's heart is weighed on a scale against a feather. Judged by Thoth, god of wisdom, the good soul is freed; the bad soul is instantly consumed by Ammit, the Eater of the Dead, a creature conglomerated of lion, hippopotamus, and crocodile.

The journey of the resurrected god Osiris, surrounded by other gods and threatened by various monsters, is a simple allegory of the sun's daily journey above, and its night journey below, the horizon. As ritual, the symbolic text serves god, Pharaoh and Everyman. The text, despite its male-gendered protagonist, is generic: the subject can be man, woman or even a beloved animal. Isis stands as an undying mother figure for all, a literal mother in the case of a dead Pharaoh (McDermott 89).

Names and Allusions

The Lighthouse. The iconic symbol of Alexandria, Egypt's seaport on the Mediterranean, was the great Pharos Lighthouse, built by the Greek ruler Ptolemy II in 323-290 BCE (El-Abbadi 38). One of the wonders of the ancient world, the tower of the lighthouse stood for over a thousand years. Evelyn Haller connects the Lighthouse in turn to Mrs. Ramsay, suggesting, "Mrs. Ramsay is to be understood primarily as Isis Pharia, that is, as Isis as Guardian of the Lighthouse" ("Anti-Madonna" 100). The iconic nature of this lighthouse is conveyed by E. M. Forster, in a book published by the Woolf's Hogarth Press: "Never, in the history of architecture, has a secular building been thus worshiped and taken on a spiritual life of its own. It beaconed to the imagination, not only to ships, and long after its light was extinguished memories of it glowed in the minds of men" (*Pharos* 17).

Woolf names her lighthouse keeper Sorley, an allusion to Charles Hamilton Sorley,[1] a young soldier-poet who died in the trenches in 1915. Some of Sorley's most memorable poems evoke rain and wind, so much so that Robert Graves wrote a poem proposing to dash out into a rainstorm to meet Sorley's ghost (Graves 24). By employing Sorley's name, Woolf suggests that the rain- and wind-swept location of the lighthouse is inhabited by ghosts, compatriots to the Ramsays' dead soldier son, Andrew.

The Hebrides. The Ramsays' westward boat journey from the Hebridean island of Skye has an Outer Hebridean lighthouse as its destination. Woolf's choice of the Hebrides, instead of the actual Cornwall location of her childhood summers, presents another Egyptian connotation. The Outer Hebrides, the westernmost part of Scotland, are also known as "The Western Isles." In Egyptian myth, the land of

---

[1] Sorley, Charles Hamilton. *Marlborough and Other Poems.* 1916. Cambridge UP, 1932.

the dead, and all burials, are in the west, the direction of sunset, Osiris, and death. In this way, Woolf places her novel at the near shore of the realm of the dead.

Mr. Ramsay. As first noted by Evelyn Haller, "Ramsay" sounds like "Ramses," the most famous line of Egyptian Pharaohs ("Anti-Madonna" 100). By using a Pharaonic name, Woolf invokes the multivalence of *The Book of the Dead:* a subject not commoner but Pharaoh. As stand-in for a king, Mr. Ramsay makes a journey toward death that is not personally tragic: he moves toward his apotheosis as Osiris-Ramsay, the justification of his life and work.

Woolf gives Mr. Ramsay an Egyptian code of ethics resembling her own father's stoic and agnostic philosophy, in a long paragraph that parallels an important ritual speech in the Egyptian negative confession. The description of Mr. Ramsay's code, "What he said was true. It was always true" ends with a reference to "the passage to the fabled land where…our frail barks founder in darkness" (*TTL* 4). Truth-telling is mandatory for the Egyptian: the dead subject, passing before the tribunal of the gods, must make statements including, "I have not done wrong…I have not stolen…I have not told lies…I was not sullen…I have not caused (anyone) to weep…I have not dissembled…I have not discussed secrets" (Budge, *BOTD*, 347-48).

Mr. Ramsay's metaphor of his philosophical career as an incomplete alphabet expresses frustration that he has only attained the letter "R"—his own initial—which he repeats obsessively (*TTL* 33-35). The isolated "R" is also the Egyptian phoneme for Rā, the sun god, making the repetition of "R" a ritual incantation. The boat-journey of the dead subject cannot commence without Rā's consent (Budge, *Osiris* 139). Mr. Ramsay envisions a Sphinx-like death as he stands "stock-still" by an urn: "Yet he would not die lying down: he would find some crag of rock, and there, his eyes fixed on the storm, trying to the end to pierce the darkness, he would die standing. He would never reach R" (*TTL* 35). His self-monumentalizing evokes the massive basalt statues of Pharaohs from the early dynasties; the urn refers to canopic jars inside which the organs of the mummified dead were placed. The sweeping prose that follows, citing "isolation and waste of ages and the perishing of stars" (36), suggests the dizzying 6,000-year span of Egyptian history. This alphabet fixation also echoes the A-to-Z *abecedarium* that Sackville-West included in a letter to Woolf sent from Egypt (Sackville-West 93).

Mr. Ramsay and his wife are denied Christian names throughout the novel, or, as Evelyn Haller puts it, have "an Egyptian-sounding surname without a Christian name" ("Anti-Madonna," 100): throughout the novel, they are simply "Mrs. Ramsay" and "Mr. Ramsay," and no one addresses them using first names. At the commencement of Woolf's holograph manuscript, the names "David" and "Lucy" head the names list (*Holograph* 3); "Dan" is crossed out once in favor of "Mr.

Ramsay" (6); and Mrs. Ramsay might be "Sara" (6). The suppression of first names contributes to the elevation of both characters to a mock-royal or mythical status.

Mrs. Ramsay. At the heart of the novel is Mrs. Ramsay as the goddess Isis. The worshipful men believe that "she had the whole of the other sex under her protection" and despite her age, "she was now formidable to behold" (*TTL* 6). Mrs. Ramsay provokes a religious enthusiasm appropriate to Isis-worship, culminating with Lily Briscoe's ecstatic ghost-vision or memory: "Mrs. Ramsay! Mrs. Ramsay! ...There she sat" (202).

Although Woolf explores the flaws and lack of communication in the Ramsay marriage, other characters idealize or even mythologize the couple's relationship. As Lily Briscoe sees it: "Directly one looked up and saw them, what she called 'being in love' flooded them. They became part of the unreal but penetrating and exciting universe which is the world seen through the eyes of love." (*TTL* 46-47). It is as though the happiness of the gods, demanding nothing, could inspire happiness by the mere contemplation of it. Briscoe makes this even more manifest as love "that never attempted to clutch its object; but like the love which mathematicians bear their symbols, or poets their phrases, was meant to be spread over the world and become part of the human gain" (*TTL* 47). Of such raptures are made the descriptions of Mrs. Ramsay; Lily Briscoe concludes the near-apotheosis:

> [T]here was Mrs. Ramsay...clear as the space which the clouds at last uncover—the little space of sky which sleeps beside the moon. . . . [S]he imagined how in the chambers of the mind and heart of the woman who was, physically, touching her, were stood, like the treasures in the tombs of kings, tablets bearing sacred inscriptions, which if one could spell them out, would teach one everything (*TTL* 50-51).

The long depiction of the dinner party with all its abrupt shifts of point-of-view, includes Egyptian references: Mrs. Ramsay imagines herself as a ghost returning to old friends elsewhere (like the Egyptian ghosts permitted to "come and go"), evoked by their memories of her (*TTL* 87); Mrs. Ramsay's matchmaking as a magic spell (101); and, most significantly, an instant during which Mrs. Ramsay assumes the Isis-kite form:

> [She] hovered like a hawk suspended...[in] the still space that lies about the heart of things...[she] could then, like a hawk...flaunt and sink on laughter easily, resting her whole weight upon what at the other end of the table her husband was saying (*TTL* 104-5).

In her survey of "anti-Madonna" figures in Woolf's fiction, Evelyn Haller finds even more Egyptian allusions in these domestic scenes in *To the Lighthouse*, including references to the sistrum, to Isis's association with fruit-bearing trees, and depictions of Isis suckling the figure of a full-grown Ramses ("Anti-Madonna" 101).

James Ramsay. The Ramsays' son James, who becomes Horus in this telling, cuts out pictures of household objects from a mail-order catalog. The tombs of the Pharaohs were crammed with household goods, full-size and models, to accompany the dead soul on its journey. James arranges the pictures in "his private code, his secret language," his hieroglyphics. Woolf describes the boy almost as a wall painting of a somber Egyptian king: "[H]e appeared the image of stark and uncompromising severity, with his high forehead and fierce blue eyes, impeccably candid and pure" (*TTL* 3, 4).

Charles Tansley. Tansley is the name of an English village, but it also suggests an important Egyptian place name, Tanis (Hart, xiv). Charles Tansley, Mr. Ramsay's obsequious student, attaches himself as acolyte to Mrs. Ramsay, seeking her mother-goddess approval: "He would like her to see him, gowned and hooded, walking in a procession" (*TTL* 11) and despite her age "she was the most beautiful person he had ever seen" (14). He sees her with "stars in her eyes and veils in her hair," a matronly Isis (14).

Mrs. Ramsay subordinates Tansley as a sacrificial victim: "If her husband required sacrifice (and indeed he did) she cheerfully offered up to him Charles Tansley, who had snubbed her little boy" (*TTL* 16). If this seems out of tune with a conception of Egypt as too civilized for human sacrifice, one need only consult Budge, who documents horrific sacrifices of captives to Osiris in some of the earlier dynasties (*Osiris*, 197-210).

Minta and Paul Rayley. The guests Minta Doyle and Paul Rayley, for whom Mrs. Ramsay plays matchmaker, are aptly named. "Min" is the Egyptian god of fertility, Woolf adds the final "t," an Egyptian female diminutive; Rayley refers to Rā (or Amon-Re), the sun god. After they marry, Minta and Paul raise hares, certainly a symbol of fecundity (*TTL* 174).

Lily Briscoe. The painter Lily Briscoe's name has two allusions, one of them Egyptian. "Lily" refers to the water lily, or lotus, the iconic Egyptian flower. Although the lotus is not, botanically, a lily, Budge conflates the two, and translates the flower hieroglyphic sign as "lotus/lily." Arthur Briscoe (1873-1943) was a noted painter and etcher of nautical scenes whose work was widely shown in London and featured in the *Illustrated London News* (IFPDA).[2]

William Bankes. Lily Briscoe's admirer, William Bankes, offers yet another link, this time to Egyptology. Woolf does not include the surname Bankes in her list of "Names to be used" at the beginning of her holograph manuscript (Woolf,

---

[2] At the time Woolf was writing *To the Lighthouse*, Arthur Briscoe had acquired some notoriety for the inflated prices being paid at auction for his works (Salaman 3). In Woolf's artistic circle, Briscoe might have been resented and frowned upon as a traditional artist and dilettante, so that Woolf's use of the name is ironic.

Holograph 1.7). Bankes, not earlier mentioned as one of the house-guests, abruptly appears in Chapter 4 of "The Window," ostensibly to provide a conversation-partner for Lily Briscoe as she paints. Bankes, an elderly widower, imagines himself as a kind of mummy, "like the body of a young man laid up in peat for a century" (*TTL* 21), a resemblance Woolf repeats in a flashback about Bankes's interrupted friendship with Mr. Ramsay: "he must have dried and shrunk" (22).

As Heidi Stalla has observed, Woolf's choice of this name is a direct allusion to Egyptology: William John Bankes (c. 1768-1855) was one of the best-known early British travelers to Egypt, accumulating the largest collection of Egyptian antiquities in private hands anywhere in Britain (Fagan 266), including the famous obelisk of Philae whose inscriptions in Greek and hieroglyphics complemented the Rosetta Stone and may have helped Champollion crack the Egyptian writing system (Usick 78). Bankes was also the first to record the inscriptions and paintings at Abu Simbel, the largest temple of Ramses II (Fagan 104).

The historical William Bankes may have been known to other members of the Bloomsbury group. Lytton Strachey would doubtless have known about the homosexual scandals that drove Bankes from England (Usick 171-75). Roger Fry, Duncan Grant, and Vanessa Bell, with their focus on art and interior décor, also may have known Bankes as a legendary Regency art collector who filled his Dorset mansion with antiquities and paintings, and anticipated their views about the primacy of the aesthetics of the home. The other source where Woolf might have encountered biographical information about Bankes is her father's *Dictionary of National Biography* (Benson, 124).[3]

Bankes, despite his periods of exile to Venice and other locales, continued to rebuild and decorate his English country home, despite being subject to an open arrest warrant: taking advantage of a loophole in British law, he moored his yacht offshore and visited home on Sundays from sunrise to sunset, hours during which he could not be arrested (Rowse 124-25). The weekly boat-journey "home" by Bankes, is also apt in the context of the Ramsays' interrupted boating trip.

In "The Lighthouse," Woolf describes Bankes as an art connoisseur, and though Lily "loved William Bankes," their relationship was apparently platonic, he a man of "disinterested intelligence" (*TTL* 176), and a case of failed matchmaking on the part of Mrs. Ramsay, who insists: "William must marry Lily" (104).

Quentin Bell speculates that the personality of Mr. Bankes was based on that of an eccentric classical scholar and family friend, Walter Headlam (118), whose gap in age with Woolf paralleled that between the fictional William Bankes and Lily Briscoe. Woolf's Bankes, however, seems more akin to the historical Bankes.

---

[3] The *Dictionary* article skirts Bankes's more scandalous activities, and all that is said of his Egyptian adventures is that "he discovered an ancient Egyptian obelisk in the island of Philae, and had it brought to England for the purpose of erecting it in his own grounds at Kingston Hall" (Benson 124).

He is flamboyant. He travels with a valet, and Briscoe's awed take on him, "generous, pure-hearted, heroic" (*TTL* 24), echoes the admiration the explorer William Bankes garnered (before his disgrace) from his schoolmate Lord Byron and from the Duke of Wellington (Usick 13, 156-57).

Augustus Carmichael. Another character in *To the Lighthouse,* the almost immobile Augustus Carmichael, has two Egyptian connotations. The Temple of Augustus at Denderah commemorates the birth of Isis (Hart 106); Carmichael echoes Karnak, another sacred site. The remaining clues about Carmichael come from his physical description. At the beginning of the novel he is "basking with his yellow cat's eyes ajar" (*TTL* 10). Ammit, The Eater of the Dead, matches the various descriptions of Carmichael that Woolf provides during the novel. This goddess (gender is irrelevant here) is an amalgam of lion, crocodile, and hippopotamus. She waits at the final judging, with reptilian patience, to swallow the souls found wanting. Carmichael is like this creature, "puffing and blowing like some sea monster" (191) "surging up, puffing slightly...looking like an old pagan god, shaggy, with weeds in his hair ... swaying a little in his bulk" (208). Lily imagines that Mr. Carmichael's poetry is about "the desert and the camel ... the palm tree and the sunset ... it said something about death" (195). In the holograph manuscript, Woolf calls Carmichael "this gorged alligator who lay on her lawn" (*Holograph* 17).[4]

Mrs. Bast and Mrs. McNab. The two women who come to the empty house to supervise its cleaning in "Time Passes" are Mrs. Bast and Mrs. McNab. Although Bast is a perfectly respectable English name, it is also the name of the cat goddess Bast or Bastet. Bast, in particular, is associated with the beneficent, warming rays of the sun (Budge, *Mummy*, 288). Woolf writes: "Mrs. McNab, Mrs. Bast, stayed the corruption and the rot," carrying household objects into the sunlight to restore them. The author underscores the feline reference by adding, "George, Mrs. Bast's son, caught the rats" (*TTL* 139).

The name McNab, although properly Scottish, is also a compound of *mak* and *nebt*, two Egyptian words, which combined, mean, "Behold the Lady." Since the character is a charwoman, there is some irony here, although Mrs. McNab does have full dominion over the house, so long as it is untenanted. "Behold the Lady" could also refer to the charwoman as a voyeur of the Ramsays' domestic affairs; she uses a telescope and spies, unseen, as Mr. Ramsay approaches (*TTL* 139-40).

Children's Names. The Ramsays' son Jasper is named after a semi-precious stone prized by Egyptians for ornamental jewelry, and known as the "blood of Isis" (Hart 101; Budge, *Egyptian Magic* 43-44). Woolf's reduction of some of the children's names to monosyllables prompts a search for similar Egyptian words. Mrs. Ramsay's daughter is "Cam"—the ancient name of Egypt is "kem"; her other

---

[4] Mr. Carmichael plays the role of Poseidon in a different mythological reading of *To the Lighthouse,* that has Mrs. Ramsay as Demeter and Lily Briscoe as Persephone (Barr). This is a further elaboration on the Persephone symbolism described by Blotner in 1956.

daughter is Prue—the phoneme "pr" means "house" (McDermott 21). (Vowels are absent in Egyptian writing, and some vowels are just educated guesses based on surviving Egyptian words in Coptic.)

"Time Passes": The Feather on the Scale

The weighing of the heart against a feather in *The Book of the Dead* is the climactic moment in the passage of a human soul from life to the world beyond. In "Time Passes," Woolf makes, and repeats, in two adjacent paragraphs, a reference to this Egyptian rite:

> For now had come that moment, that hesitation when dawn trembles and night passes, when if a feather alight in the scale it will be weighed down. One feather, and the house, sinking, falling, would have turned and pitched downwards to the depths of darkness...
>
> If the feather had fallen, if it had tipped the scale downwards, the whole house would have plunged to the depths to lie upon the sands of oblivion. (138-39)

This twice-repeated clue is the cardinal point of Woolf's Egyptianizing. For the reader familiar with Egyptian mythology and *The Book of the Dead*, coming to these passages provides a thrill of recognition. The house itself, personified, sits at the moment of judgment before Thoth and the watchful Eater of the Dead.

In "Time Passes," the cataloging of the contents of the house, with wind, sand, and time working their slow decay, recalls Howard Carter's listing of the contents of Tutankhamen's tomb, an impersonal list of objects resisting entropy, becoming numinous by the act of rediscovery. Reading this part of *To the Lighthouse* with archaeological cataloging in mind adds a new context to the largely-depopulated central portion of the book. Here, Woolf inserts the names of the dead family members—Mrs. Ramsay, Prue, and Andrew—inside square brackets, starkly brief descriptions of their passing. Typographically, they resemble editorial insertions by a hand other than the author's. In Budge's edition of *The Book of the Dead* and in his other works, missing and speculative passages are always shown in square brackets, a common practice in classical texts. The name-insertions also recall the personalization of each copy of *The Book of the Dead.*

The figure of Mr. Ramsay, reaching out with his arms to the absent spouse (*TTL* 128), also suggests the hieroglyphic of two extended arms, representing an embrace, or, if turned upward, representing the *ka* or spirit (McDermott 33).

A Doubting Freudian: The Shawl and the Skull

Because the Woolfs' Hogarth Press was the British publisher of Sigmund Freud's works, it is tempting to search for Freudian elements in *To the Lighthouse*. Woolf overtly employs the Oedipus complex in her portrayal of the hatred young James feels for his father, an emotion that reaches a reconciliation only at the end of the novel. Woolf, however, was not at that period of her life interested in Freud. In 1924, after glancing at one Freudian excerpt, she wrote, "these Germans think it proves something—besides their own gull-like imbecility" (*L3* 135). As late as 1932, Woolf insisted "I have not studied Freud or any psychoanalyst—indeed I think I have never read any of their books; my knowledge is merely from superficial talk. Therefore any use of their methods must be instinctive" (*L5* 36). Woolf searched for her own understanding of the child mind. Nigel Nicolson recalls being interrogated by Woolf in 1926, when he was a boy of nine years, about "What is it like to be a child?" (1), and speculates that he was part of her psychological research for the character of the boy James Ramsay.

Nonetheless, Woolf both employs and resists Freudian concepts in overlaying the Oedipal triangle of Mrs. Ramsay-Mr. Ramsay-James with the Isis-Osiris-Horus family triad. The mother-centered world of Isis resists patriarchy, and the details of the Egyptian myth undermine the primacy of sexuality and castration fear in Freud's theory. Woolf's characterization of James, however, forces her to displace and merge characters in the Egyptian myth, situating Horus and his nemesis Set, in more Freudian terms, as James's ego and infantile id.

When Mr. Ramsay approaches his wife for a gesture of kindness and sympathy, Woolf depicts his approach using curious language: "into this delicious fecundity, this fountain and spray of life, the fatal sterility of the male plunged itself, like a beak of brass, barren and bare" (*TTL* 37) and, later, "James, as he stood stiff between her knees, felt her rise in a rosy-flowered fruit tree laid with leaves and dancing boughs into which the beak of brass, the arid scimitar of his father, the egotistical man, plunged and smote, demanding sympathy" (38). This passage is rife with Oedipal conflicts (son against father); it is also written to include the approach of a god with his hawk-totem-head (beak of brass) to the life-giving tree which is Isis. Mrs. Ramsay responds to the approach of her consort in magical terms: "[T]here throbbed through her, like the pulse in a spring which has expanded to its full width and now gently ceases to beat, the rapture of successful creation" (38). As Mr. and Mrs. Ramsay harmonize their minds together, Woolf reminds the reader of mortality by twice interrupting with the stand-in for The Eater of the Dead: "Augustus Carmichael shuffling past ... Mr. Carmichael shuffled past" (38). Mrs. Ramsay guards James as the protective mother Isis guards her son Horus: "Oh, but she never wanted James to grow a day older!" (58).

While Woolf sets her human characters on a Freudian life-path, she interposes and, in effect, performs psychoanalytic work on the Egyptian myth. The author sets two counter-currents in motion in her explicit revelations of James's childish hatred for his father. She seems willing to let her plot explore this conflict and resolve it at the end of the novel, yet at the same time, the Osiris/Isis/Horus myth undermines many Freudian premises. In the Egyptian myth, the father has been dismembered/castrated/reassembled, and the son's struggle is against the fratricidal uncle (Set). The mother (Isis) is healer, mediator, opposing yet sparing her son's potential killer. Set makes a dramatic appearance in the Ramsays' house, when Mrs. Ramsay peeks in on her children at bedtime and uses her shawl to cover an animal skull, mounted on the wall, that alarms her daughter Cam: "[S]he quickly took her own shawl off and wound it round the skull, round and round and round" (*TTL* 114-15). Her son James, on the other hand, admires the deathly object and insists that it stay visible through the night.

By wrapping the skull but not removing it, Mrs. Ramsay hopes to placate both children. Cam will no longer recognize it as a monster, while James will know it is still there under the wrapping. Mrs. Ramsay then assures Cam that the skull, after all, only comes from a *black pig*, like the ones they had seen on a farm (*TTL* 114). In Egyptian depictions of the soul's boat-journey to the afterlife, Set is sometimes a black pig, riding in his own small boat. This brings us to Woolf's profound displacement of the Egyptian myth: James-as-Horus should be terrified of the black pig, which is the symbol of Set and the most-detested animal in the Egyptian mythos.

This displacement leads to the splitting of James/Horus's personality. The mythical figure of Horus is one of unalloyed virtue, as Set is of evil. At some moments, Mrs. Ramsay regards James as a figure of virtue, who will grow up to be a judge (*TTL* 4). Mr. Tansley, on the other hand, gives James the epithet of "the Ruthless" (22), and Mrs. Ramsay herself at another point confesses James and Cam "demons of wickedness, angels of delight" (58). The violent thoughts of six-year-old James against his father (4), to which the reader is privy but Mrs. Ramsay is not, and his continued ambivalence as an adolescent in "The Lighthouse," are not Horus-like: they are Oedipal. To make James a realistic character in light of Freudian psychology, the author gives him characteristics of *both* Horus and Set, of ego and of infantile id. To do this, she must contradict the Egyptian myth.

This joining of Horus and Set speaks to the most enigmatic episode in the Isis-Osiris-Horus narrative: Isis's decision to release Set from captivity, after the evil god was placed in her guardianship (Budge, *BOTD*, li). Woolf's penetrating insight, which she expresses by having James-as-Horus identify with the symbol of Set, is that there can be no Horus without Set, no Set without Horus: they are halves of the same personality. The ego withers with nothing to struggle against, no evil thoughts to repress; the id has no purpose or direction without an authority figure to subvert. Thus, Woolf performs an act of psychoanalysis on Egyptian myth, or, more provocatively, argues that the id-ego barrier is essentially and irreparably permeable.

The shawl and skull return in "Time Passes" (*TTL* 140), the shawl working its way free. This image, amid the cataloging of the empty house, calls to memory one of the most powerful photographs from the opening of Tutankhamen's tomb: the Anubis shrine, draped with a linen shawl (see Figure 2): "[F]astened around his neck was a long leash-like linen scarf ... adorned with a double fillet of blue lotus and cornflowers…twisted into a bow at the back of the neck" (Carter Vol III, 41). The jackal sits on a golden chest covered with *tyet* symbols representing Isis (Reeves 133).

The Leg and the Foot

The leg is central to Egyptian myths of resurrection. A pivotal spell in *The Book of the Dead*, "The Chapter of Walking with the Two Legs, and of Coming Forth Upon Earth" (Budge, *BOTD*, 320) insures that the subject will regain mobility of the feet and legs, without which coming forth among the living and the dead would be impossible. In the famous "negative confession" the dead subject's demonic interrogators do not sit in judgment: almost all "come forth," and some have epithets such as "thou whose strides are long ... whose legs are of fire…who dost stride backwards" (347-48). In the other Osiris texts, the mobility theme is reiterated in lines like "Thy leg is great, thy leg is mighty, it strides to the great throne" (Budge, *Osiris,* 141) and "Thy legs are thine, Osiris…his legs are to himself…He approaches heaven in his strides" (117). In hieroglyphics, the ideograph of two legs walking is an unvoiced determinative used with every verb expressing walking, running, or related actions (McDermott 33).

During her walk to the village with Tansley, Mrs. Ramsay pauses to watch a one-armed man ascend a ladder to put up a circus poster (*TTL* 11). This foreshadows the spectacle of amputees after World War I, but is also an indication that Woolf may have read the early versions of the Osiris myth, in which the revived god needs a celestial ladder, and a boost from Horus and Rā, to find his way to the land of the dead (Budge, *Osiris* 75; *Egyptian Magic* 51-53).

Woolf employs leg imagery as the "vast flapping sheet" of a circus poster (resembling a long papyrus scroll) shows animal and human legs first as it is glued onto a billboard (*TTL* 11). William Bankes stands awkwardly next to Lily Briscoe, studying her shoes (18). Mr. Ramsay "strides" (20); Mrs. Ramsay makes stockings for the lighthouse keeper's son and measures them against her son's leg (27-28, 30). Mr. Ramsay tickles, then prods, his son's bare leg (31, 32). Mr. Ramsay imagines he is on a horse while taking a long walk, although he has no horse (43-44).

Figure 2: The Anubis shrine. (Carter Vol III, Plate II).

Lily, on the beach, imagines herself at Mrs. Ramsay's knees (51). Mr. Ramsay is angry, "marching up and down the terrace" (146), then "bearing down" on Lily (148, 150). The awkward interlude in which the tongue-tied Lily can only talk to the widowed Ramsay about his boots (153-54) acquires special poignancy in its Egyptian context: Ramsay asks not only for sympathy, but for the magic words to give him the power of mobility. James describes himself and his father as two sets of footprints, and poses a hypothetical question in which someone's feet are crushed (184-85). Mr. Ramsay leaves for the lighthouse with a "firm, military tread" (154), marching as in a procession (182), and finally, at the Lighthouse, "he sprang, lightly like a young man" (207).

It might be argued that a similar list of ambulation events could be compiled from almost any work of fiction. Yet aside from some splashes of eye-color and Lily Briscoe's inexplicable "Chinese eyes," and some general descriptions of physique, Woolf is sparing of other references to the body. Eyes, mouths, hands, arms, shoulders, breasts, hair, give place to this work's insistent iterations of legs and feet. Heide Stalla notes this, too, and compares Lily's apostrophe on Mr. Ramsay's boots to the monumental sculptural ruin in Shelley's poem, "Ozymandias" (Stalla 32).

The Knot

Lily Briscoe considers the problem of her unfinished painting, and uses the word "knots" in an intriguing way. Woolf's style might be called a knotted narrative, and there is an Isis association too: the symbol of Isis is a buckle in the form of a knotted *ankh*—like the ankh of Osiris except that the arms extend downward. This turned-upon-itself figure is called a *tyet* (Hart 101; Budge, *The Mummy* 256; Budge, *Egyptian Magic* 43). Lily's artistic problem is expressed thus:

> There was something ... she remembered in the relations of those lines cutting across, slicing down, and in the mass of the hedge with its green cave of blues and browns, which had stayed in her mind; which had tied a knot on her mind so that at odds and ends of time, involuntarily ... she found herself painting that picture, passing her eye over it, and untying the knot in imagination (*TTL* 157).

Then Lily Briscoe has a rapturous recollection of Mrs. Ramsay and how everything seemed to cohere and make sense under her influence, "Mrs. Ramsay saying, 'Life stand still here': Mrs. Ramsay making of the moment something permanent ... this was of the nature of a revelation" (161). In the book's very last gesture, as if to underscore Woolf's identification, artist to artist, with Lily Briscoe, Lily completes her painting: "With a sudden intensity, as if she saw it clear for a second, she drew a line there, in the centre. It was done; it was finished" (209).

Another photograph from Tutankhamen's tomb vividly conveys both the idea of narrative tied in "knots," as well as the idea of a structure divided by "a central line down the middle." It shows the unbroken seal of the tomb-shrine's door (see Figure 3). Seals, elaborate knots, and a length of rope are all that hold closed the two halves: the gap between the doors, the inky blackness inside which the king and all his mysteries rest, is a vertical line, a "central line down the middle."[5]

Figure 3: The seals, the knots, the "line down the middle" sealing the door to the shrine containing Tutankhamen's sarcophagus and mummy. (Carter Vol II, Plate LX.)

[5] Woolf meant "Time Passes" to be a connecting structure in the middle of *To the Lighthouse*, and this notion was derived from Roger Fry's "An Essay on Aesthetics" in his 1920 book, *Vision and Design*. Fry describes one class of simple paintings that can be analyzed using "a balancing of the attractions of the eye about the central line of the picture." But Fry immediately moves on to larger works, such as Chinese landscape scrolls, which can only be viewed in segments, yet which form a unity. "Such a successive unity is of course familiar to us in literature and music, and it plays its part in the graphic arts. It depends upon the forms being presented to us in such a sequence that each successive element is felt to have a fundamental and harmonious relation with that which preceded it." (21-22). Fry says that drawings can be viewed in this successive way, looking at parts of a drawing

The Boatman and the Journey

Woolf conveys the Ramsays' boat-journey with unremitting, eerie parallels to the ancient text. Mr. Ramsay, piloted by a boatman named MacAlister, heads toward the Lighthouse. In *The Book of the Dead*, the boatman who carries the soul is named Maa-ha-f, "he who sees what is behind him." The ferryman is also given authority by Rā to deny passage to manifestly unworthy souls (Budge, *Osiris* 134). MacAlister describes a shipwreck in the channel between Skye and the lighthouse (*TTL* 205-6), implying that not all travelers complete their journeys. Like a lighthouse, there is even a lamp waiting for the dead on the other side: "O thou his father Tem in the darkness...He has lighted for thee the lamp" (Budge, *Osiris*, 135).

The Egyptian book specifies offerings one must take, and Woolf asks, "What does one send to the Lighthouse?" (*TTL* 146). The dead subject receives ritual words for the boatman. James echoes this: "Now they would sail on for hours like this, and Mr. Ramsay would ask old MacAlister a question" (163) as if all that ensued was preordained. James resents the fact he and his sister are forced to take part, "carrying these parcels, to the Lighthouse; take part in these rites he went through for his own pleasure in memory of dead people" (165). Menacing fish, water animals, and serpents appear in *The Book of the Dead*; for lack of sea serpents, Woolf has the boatman's son catch a fish and cut it up (169). Cam looks back at the Skye shore, where, she thinks, people "were free to come and go like ghosts. They have no suffering there" (170). In *The Book of the Dead,* all the directions are invoked in the boat journey and there is a spell against getting the directions mixed up (Budge, *BOTD*, 106); Mr. Ramsay castigates his daughter for not having a sense of direction (*TTL* 167). Horus is at the helm of the mythical boat (Budge, *BOTD*, 248-49); Mr. Ramsay lets his son steer for most of the journey, and that act, accomplished and acknowledged, marks the Oedipal turning point of father-son reconciliation. Finally, Mr. Ramsay reads from a book throughout most of the journey, as though he were carrying and consulting his own coffin-text papyrus.

Woolf narrates the instant of arrival, and nothing more, but the feeling of ritual enactment is unmistakable, even though a Bloomsbury avowal of atheism is thrown in:

> "Bring those parcels," he said, nodding his head at the things Nancy had done up for them to take to the Lighthouse. "The parcels for the Lighthouse men," he said. He rose and stood in the bow of the boat, very straight and tall, for all the world, James thought, as if he were saying, 'There is no

---

in succession without requiring the visual unity we expect of a painting (22). Where Woolf takes Fry's concept in this linear sense, Lily Briscoe takes the dictum literally: she does not see an imaginary line at the center of her painting, but instead *draws* a literal line there.

God,' and Cam thought, as if he were leaping into space, and they both rose to follow him as he sprang, lightly like a young man, holding his parcel, onto the rock (*TTL* 207).

The Ramsay family's completed boat trip in "The Lighthouse" is a ritual without a clear set of rules: "What's the use of going now…What does one send to the Lighthouse?" (146). We are made to understand that it is a journey in memory of their mother's previous charitable gifts to the lighthouse keeper (151). In the Egyptian context, however, the journey is Mr. Ramsay's, who, like every subject in Egyptian thanatology, perishes alone and stands alone before the judges, accountable only for his own words and actions. Mr. Ramsay repeats "perished" and "alone" as a litany throughout "The Lighthouse." The reluctance to make the journey in the first part of the book, like the reluctance to move past the letter "R," is mortality denied. Under the spell of Osirian values, James's reconciliation with his father is the understanding that both their sets of footprints lead finally to the same place, to annihilation or rebirth.

Seen as a self-therapeutic dream-work employing myth, *To the Lighthouse* is Mr. Ramsay's own solitary journey to a private afterlife, and the author's letting-go of a perplexing and daunting father. The mother's death, on the other hand (and despite Woolf's assertion to the contrary) is not resolved except through apotheosis, or, as Haller suggests, she persists symbolically as the Lighthouse itself ("Anti-Madonna," 100). If Mrs. Ramsay becomes Isis, she is a figure untouched by time, change, or death, hailed ritually by Lily Briscoe on the shore. In that guise, Mrs. Ramsay sits at the center of a matrilineal, mother-centered antiquity, contending against evil while knowing she cannot destroy it. Healing the good souls left behind on the near shore, she is the goddess, venerated, trusted, indestructible.

Woolf on *To the Lighthouse*

Did Woolf admit to any Egyptian content, overt or covert, in *To the Lighthouse?* Woolf's correspondence with Vita Sackville-West includes Egyptian references from Sackville-West, cues to which Woolf does not respond in her letters. Sackville West, after commencing an intense love affair with Woolf, wrote to her on 29 January 1926 from Luxor, Egypt:

> I went down into the bowels of the earth and looked at Tut-ankh-amen. At his sarcophagus and outer mummy-case, I mean. This is merely of gilded wood. The inner one is at Cairo, (I saw it,) and is of solid gold. You know, the Valley of the Kings is really the most astonishing place. Tawny, austere hills with a track cut between them; no life at all, not a bird, not a lizard, only a scavenger Kite hanging miles high; and undiscovered Kings lying lapped in gold. (Sackville-West 94)

The letter expresses the wish that Woolf could see Egypt for herself, and includes a word game, a playful *abecedarium* (A-to-Z word list) of Egyptian images and names (93).

Woolf finished "Time Passes" on 25 May 1926 (Bell 122). Sackville-West returned from her Egyptian-Persian travels sometime in mid-summer, which may have provoked "a whole nervous breakdown in miniature" (123) at the end of July. The novel was not completed until early 1927, and was published on 5 May 1927 (127).

From May 1926 to January 1927, Woolf and Sackville-West saw one another intermittently, but passionately, based on their letters. Yet there is not a word in their extant letters about the *content* of *To the Lighthouse*. Sackville-West departed for a second journey to Persia in January 1927, and by February was imploring Woolf to undertake a journey to Greece, hoping they could meet up there. In February, Woolf writes somewhat disparagingly of her work-in-progress:

> . . . laboriously correcting two sets of proofs. My goodness how you'll dislike that book! Honestly you will—Oh but you shan't read it. Its [sic] a ghost between us. Whether its [sic] good or bad, I know not: I'm dazed, I'm bored, I'm sick to death: I go on crossing out commas and putting in semi-colons in a state of marmoreal despair. I suppose there may be half a paragraph somewhere worth reading: but I doubt it. (*L* 3 333).

In May, Sackville-West was back in England, and Woolf sent her a bound copy of *To the Lighthouse,* with a mock inscription calling it the best work she had written: it was a "dummy" copy with blank pages—like an empty Pharaoh's tomb. By May 12, a week after the book's publication, Sackville-West had read the novel, and she wrote a letter to Woolf praising it, but there is no indication that she grasped any Egyptian references. Sackville-West is afraid of Woolf's "penetration and loveliness and genius" (196). Woolf's letter in reply only talks about the characters in the novel. If she hoped and intended that Sackville-West would see her playful use of Egyptian names and motifs as a personal response to the letter from Egypt, or the common passion they might have shared for things Egyptian, there is no clue here.

Woolf reveals even less to others. When Roger Fry writes to her, "I suspect for instance that arriving at the Lighthouse has a symbolic meaning that escapes me" (qtd Bell 129), Woolf answers, perhaps providing a fellow formalist with the answer best-suited to him:

> I meant *nothing* by *The Lighthouse*. One has to have a central line down the middle of the book to hold the design together. I saw that all sorts of meanings would accrue to this, but I refused to think them out, & trusted that people would make it the deposit for their own emotions—which they

have done, one thinking it means one thing another another. I can't manage Symbolism except in this vague, generalised way. Whether its [sic] right or wrong I don't know; but directly I'm told what a thing means, it becomes hateful to me (*L3* 385).

Woolf here wishes to take credit for the plot structure and form of her book, just as Lily Briscoe wants to reduce the mother and child in her painting to pure forms, refusing to sentimentalize or symbolize her work's literal content. "A central line down the middle" explains structure as an architect might describe a keystone by drawing its shape without explaining what it does.

Since some of the Egyptian elements were already in place in *To the Lighthouse* prior to 1926-27, perhaps the most that might be said, then, of the Woolf-Sackville-West correspondence is that it may have served to *intensify* Woolf's use of Egyptian name allusions, and her exploration of the plot and character elements of the Isis-Orisis-Horus myth. An examination of Woolf's holograph manuscript, published in a typescript transcription in 1982, reveals that Woolf changed the names of characters as her work progressed. Near the beginning of her work, in March 1925, Woolf listed the names she intended to use in the book (*Holograph* 3). These already include the Ramsay family name, and "Araminta" Doyle is already nicknamed "Minta." The surname Briscoe is in place (sans "Lily"'), but there is no sign yet of William Bankes, Paul Rayley, Augustus Carmichael, nor of Mrs. Bast, or Mrs. McNab. The children's names do not yet include Jasper or Prue. Mrs. and Mrs. Ramsay are "David" and "Lucy": Woolf would monumentalize the couple by using only their last names in the novel. Between March and September, the first 31 pages of manuscript were completed, sketching in Augustus Carmichael, Charles Tansley (changed from Tansy), and naming daughter Prue. On page 16, the name "Lily" is attached to Miss Doyle; Sophie Briscoe becomes Lily Briscoe between pages 29 and 30. Sometime between 21st and 26th January, 1926, Woolf makes a marginal list of all the Ramsay children, adding Cam and Jasper (48).

Woolf's silence about symbolic or allusive content in the novel might also constitute a conspiracy of one. Like the Dreadnought Hoax, in which Woolf donned blackface and passed as an Abyssinian diplomat (Lee 278-83), Woolf's Egyptian gods masquerade in plain sight as the Ramsays and their guests. Patricia Maika, making her own case for Greek and Isian allusions in *Between the Acts,* notes Woolf's admiration for Sylvia Townsend Warner's *The True Heart,* a novel based upon the story of Psyche and Cupid from Apuleius. Although Warner did not reveal the critically-undetected model for her novel until 1978, Maika postulates that Woolf *did* perceive it, and understood that "Warner's clues to the identities of her characters lay in their names...[an] ingenious game" (Maika 78). Is Woolf engaged in a similar game in *To the Lighthouse,* in which the reader's failure to detect the hidden content is her measure of success?

Another novel employing critically-undetected allusions to mythological figures is Rebecca West's 1918 *The Return of the Soldier,* which plays on *The Odyssey.* In West's novel, an amnesiac soldier does not recognize his "Penelope" on returning home to his wife, recalling only an earlier love, who is now "Mrs. Grey." Mrs. Grey, summoned to help, must choose to be either Calypso, helping him to forget altogether, or Athena, making him know the truth. Less overt allusions to classical literature underlay Ford Madox Ford's Promethean hero Tietjens, in his trilogy *Parade's End* (1924-26), modeled on the Roman poet and reluctant soldier Tibullus and his destructive lady-love Nemesis. Like Warner, West, and Ford, Woolf uses a palimpsest pen. The hieroglyphs peep out from beneath the English letters.

Egyptomania

Egypt was not just on the minds of specialist scholars in the 1920s: it was one of the peak decades of "Egyptomania."[6] The discovery of the tomb of Tutankhamen in 1922 by Howard Carter and his sponsor Lord Carnarvon, initiated a frenzy of popular interest in Egyptian art and religion, as well as a wave of Egyptianized design. After the electrifying discovery of Tutankhamen's gold-filled tomb, Egyptian images and design motifs exploded into architecture and monuments; the interior design of restaurants, nightclubs and theaters; clothing and accessories, cosmetics and perfume packaging (Curl 211). The entire Art Deco design movement owes a large debt to Egyptian archaeology of the period (Pantazzi 508-14).

The writing of British and Continental Egyptologists, much of it for non-specialist readers, had planted seeds of interest in Egyptian myth since the 1880s. Budge's 1895 translation of *The Book of the Dead* was followed by numerous other books, his own and those of Gaston Maspero (translated from French, 1901-1906) and James Henry Breasted.[7] Shaw's 1898 play, *Caesar and Cleopatra,* had its first London staging in 1907. Woolf dressed as Cleopatra for a fancy-dress party and attended a revival of Verdi's 1871 Egyptian-themed opera *Aida* in 1909 (Lee 235). Egyptian-themed dance came from Diaghilev's company (*Cléopâtre,* Paris 1909, London revival 1918) and from individual dancers like Ruth St. Denis, Maud Allen, and Sent M'ahesa, who staged Egyptian programs (Pantazzi 508). Egyptomania was much "in the air" among British literati of the 1920s.

---

[6] Far from being a passing fad of the 1920s, Egyptomania has influenced Western art and literature in waves, initiated successively by the Roman annexation of Egypt, the Napoleonic invasion and subsequent publication of the monumental *Description de l'Egypt* (1809-29), the French and British protectorates that followed the building of the Suez Canal, and, finally, the opening of King Tutankhamen's tomb. The literature of European art history has acknowledged the priority and significance of Egypt since Winckelmann's landmark study, *History of Ancient Art (Geschichte des Kunst des Altertums)* in 1764.
[7] Breasted, James Henry. *Ancient Records of Egypt: Historical Documents from the Earliest Times to the Persian Conquest.* London: Luzac, 1906. 5 vols.

Woolf's Egyptian Sources

The casting of Mrs. Ramsay in terms of Isis, given the adoration accorded her by almost all the novel's characters, male and female, invokes not just Egyptian mythology, but also the later, and long-surviving Greco-Roman classical cult of Isis. Isis worship spread across North Africa to Carthage, and Isian temples existed in Greece and Rome before either nation had occupied Egypt (Jones & Pennick 57, 73). Many of the attributes of Isis transferred directly to the later veneration of Mary in Catholicism, one of Frazer's most discomforting assertions (118-19).

Woolf, tutored privately in Greek, read Xenophon and Thucydides in the original (Lee 141, 217). The Greek sources for knowledge about Egypt, however, were Herodotus (*An Account of Egypt*) and Plutarch (*On Isis and Osiris*). Woolf may have read these authors in Greek as part of her studies, but both were also readily available in translation. Budge reprints most of the Plutarch text with his own annotations (*Legends* 198-248).

Herodotus limits himself to geography and political history for the most part, avowedly skirting issues of religion. By Woolf's time, Herodotus had been discredited as an authority on Egyptian history (Godley xxi). Plutarch presents the Isis-Osiris-Horus-Set story in detail, but does not describe the worship of Isis in practice. Plutarch anachronistically subsumes Egyptian deities into similar figures in Greek myth, even attempting to make etymological connections between Greek and Egyptian deity names.

The only other source of Isis lore from antiquity is the second-century CE North African writer Lucius Apuleius, whose Latin text, *The Golden Ass*, details the cult of Isis, the dress and habits of its believers, and offers a self-censored account of initiatory rites. The author, an Isian priest, writes from personal knowledge. The 1566 Adlington translation, still highly readable, was available in a new London edition in 1893. Woolf possessed a copy (Haller 118) of this book, in which Isis speaks thus:

> I am she that is the naturall mother of all things, mistresse and governess of all the Elements, the initial progeny of worlds, chiefe of powers divine, Queene of heaven, the principall of the Gods celestial, the light of the goddesses...my name, my divinity is adored throughout all the world in divers manners, in variable customs and in many names...Queene Isis. (Apuleius 233)

In Apuleius's text, Isis claims unity with Minerva, Venus, Diana, Proserpina/Persephone, Ceres, Juno, Bellona, and Hecate, a syncretism with goddesses of love and fertility, lunar and seasonal change, the growing of grain, marriage, war, and magic. Apuleius's descriptions of Isian rites find their way almost verbatim into Walter Pater's *Marius the Epicurean,* where Isis is "the Great Goddess, that new rival, or 'double,' of ancient Venus" (105). Pater does not conceal his source: he cites Apuleius (106).[8]

The most conspicuous Egyptian-themed book found in London parlors in Woolf's time would certainly have been the sumptuous, elephant-folio size edition of *The Book of the Dead.* This lithographed color facsimile of one instance of the *Book of the Dead,* the "Papyrus of Ani" in the British Museum, was published in 1890.[9] The companion English translation by E.A. Wallis Budge was published separately in 1895. This made it possible for curious readers to pore over the mysteries of the art and hieroglyphs of more than 60 spells, prayers, and rituals that had come to be called *The Book of the Dead.* Budge's edition established the Egyptian text in the popular mind, however erroneously, as a fixed literary work. In reality, no two copies of *The Book of the Dead* were alike, with chapters tracing back to "Pyramid texts" as old as 2400 BCE, and later "coffin texts," which developed into a set of 192 (known) chapters that could be assembled to order for a burial (Goelet 14). In the context of modern "Egyptomania," Budge's romantically-titled translation—taking its name from *Totenbuch,* an 1842 German translation by Karl Richard Lepsius—provided the most coherent glimpse into the mythology of Osiris, Isis, Horus, and other Egyptian gods. This, and Budge's other books on Egyptian myth, magic, and mummies, have seldom been out of print since their original publication. In 1898, Budge published a 190-chapter version of *The Book of the Dead* in English, collated from numerous papyri, in the version known as the "Theban Recension."[10]

Travel literature about Egypt available to Woolf in 1927 included books by Lane (1835), Thackeray (1846), Florence Nightingale (privately printed, 1854),[11] and Lady Duff-Gordon (1866). Thackeray demotes the Pyramids to three oversize exclamation points (228). Fascinating as the travel books are, they contain little trace of the actual mythology, other than Duff-Gordon's thrilled discovery of surviving rites, and they offer little evidence of the appeal of Isis for hundreds of years into the Common Era. It must have been in some of this literature, though, that Woolf encountered the name and career of William Bankes, the first English Egyptomane to travel up the Nile to Nubia.

---

[8] Biographer Hermione Lee notes that reading Pater was part of Woolf's preparation for her trip to Greece (VW, 22), but she does not specify the titles. Both the 1885 Marius and the 1895 *Greek Studies* were available to her.

[9] *The Book of the Dead: Facsimile of the Papyrus of Ani in the British Museum.* London: British Museum, 1890. A sumptuous full-color facsimile of the scroll with no translation.

[10] *The Book of the Dead: The Chapters of Coming Forth By Day: An English Translation with Introduction, Notes, Etc.* Translated by E.A. Wallis Budge. London: Kegan, Paul, Trench, Trübner, 1898.

[11] Nightingale, Florence. *A Journey on the Nile, 1849-1850.* 1854. New York: Weidenfeld & Nicholson, 1987.

Matrilineal, Feminist Egypt

The work of French Egyptologist Gaston Maspero became more widely available to English readers in the 1903-1906 twelve-volume translation, *History of Egypt, Chaldea, Syria, Babylonia and Assyria*, where the historian describes, with some horror, the early Egyptians' matrilineal society, where there was "no family, in the sense in which we understand the word, except as it centered around the mother...the woman, to all appearances, played the principal part. ...Children recognized the parental relationship in the mother alone" (64-65). Feminists would take interest in this female autonomy, including property inheritance, and separate homes for wives, a "room of one's own" indeed!

The self-command, power, and authority of Isis, and the flourishing of her cult, is understandable in a culture where women were not denigrated. Frazer asserts that this "archaic system of mother-kin...based on the example of Isis" lasted through the Roman occupation of Egypt (*Adonis* 213-14). Erman's 1894 *Life in Egypt* uses everyday Egyptian documents and artifacts to elaborate on this matrilineal (if not feminist) picture of Egypt, so contrary to the patriarchal impression made by tomb art.

Despite the Christian suppression of the Isis cult after 390 CE (Jones & Pennick 58), Lady Duff-Gordon, in her 1863 visit to Egypt, insists that Egyptian women, counter to Christian and Islamic strictures, still re-enacted ancient seasonal and funerary rituals:

> Among the gods, Amun-Ra, the god of the sun and great serpent-slayer, calls himself Mar-Girgis (St. George), and Osiris holds his festivals twice a year as notoriously as ever at Tanta, in the Delta, under the name of Seyyid-el-Bedawee. The fellah women offer sacrifices to the Nile, and walk around ancient statues, in order to have children. The ceremonies at births and burials are not Muslim but ancient Egyptian. The women wail for the dead, as on the sculptures; a practice which is directly contrary to the injunctions of the Koran. All the ceremonies are pagan, and would shock an Indian Muslim (Duff-Gordon 94-95).

It is intriguing that an intrepid woman traveler discerns the persistence of pagan antiquity, while the estimable Edward William Lane, three decades earlier, reported that Egyptian Muslims regarded pyramids and temples with ignorance and superstitious horror:

> The ancient tombs of Egypt, and the dark recesses of the temples are commonly believed, by the people of this country, to be inhabited by 'efreets. I found it impossible to persuade one of my servants to enter

the Great Pyramid with me, from his having this idea. Many of the Arabs ascribe the erection of the Pyramids, and all the most stupendous remains of antiquity in Egypt, to Gánn Ibn-Gánn [son of the line of the pre-Adamite Solomons], and his servants, the ginn; conceiving it impossible that they could have been raised by human hands (Lane 226).

The misogyny of Classicists and Egyptologists resulted in the denigration of goddess-worship, and of Isis in particular. Evelyn Haller proposes that E.M. Forster's writings on Egypt, including a history of Alexandria that scarcely credits Isis,[12] challenged Woolf to make a stand for the long Isian tradition in her writing, "to set right, what she considered the misappropriation of the classics by Cambridge educated Apostles" ("Alexandria" 173-74). Since the Hogarth Press published Forster's second Egyptian-themed book, *Pharos and Pharillon*, in 1923, Woolf would have been well aware of Forster's lack of interest in pre-Hellenic Egypt, and his omission of any reference to the long survival of the Isis cult, even where he writes at length about the later syncretist Sarapis cult, in whose temples Isis was portrayed as that god's consort.

Prior Discoveries of the Egyptian Connection

Did readers notice Woolf's Egyptianizing? Finding allusions to myth in *To the Lighthouse* is not a new enterprise, but until the early 1980s it was limited to Greek and Roman associations, including the myths of Demeter and Persephone (Blotner) and Ovid's version of the Orpheus and Eurydice story (Goldman 40). Woolf's study of Greek language and literature was deep enough to assure that she could hold her own in this kind of symbolism. William Herman calls the classics "a matrix of patriarchal power" and proposes that Woolf "saw, in the depth of her imaginative being, that the classics could inform and empower her works" (258, 259).

The most persistent critic affirming the Woolf-Egypt connection has been Evelyn Haller. Writing in 1983, she traces Egyptian influences in *Between the Acts*, noting Woolf's reading of Pater's *Marius the Epicurean*; her tours of the British museum with its "tiers of Isis and Horus statues" (Haller, "Isis," 111); and Woolf's familiarity with other Egypt-related literary sources. In another article that year, Haller focuses intently on the Isis symbolism in *To the Lighthouse,* casting Mrs. Ramsay/Isis as "anti-Madonna," to wage "aesthetic war on imperialism, Christianity, and patriarchy" ("Anti-Madonna," 96). Patricia Maika also elaborates on the Isis allusions in *Between the Acts* in a 1987 study.

In 1988, Woolf biographer Hermione Lee suggests, "*To the Lighthouse* continually hovers on the edge of becoming a fairy tale, or, more ambitiously, a mythical

---

[12] Forster, E.M. *Alexandria: A History and a Guide*. 1922. Woodstock, NY: Overlook Press, 1974.

or even Christian allegory, whose subject—a frequent subject of myth—is the conquest of death" (Lee "*TTL* Completed Forms" 19). Certainly, Woolf's vocabulary in *To the Lighthouse* support's Lee's observation. References to ceremonies, rituals, processions, royalty, and goddesses abound throughout the novel. This has a satiric effect when read against the characters' social status, locale, and period, but opens the book also to a symbolic reading. The characters seem to spend a great deal of their time imagining one another throned, robed and mitered, adored and adoring.

In 1998, Mitchell Leaska detects the Isis/Osiris marriage, dismemberment and coupling in *The Years*, and notes Woolf employing there the surname of Egyptologist E A. Wallis Budge (418-19).

In 2003, Evelyn Haller turns to the Woolf-Egypt connection in *To the Lighthouse* again, framing the novel's allusions to Isis and the Pharos lighthouse as Woolf's rebuttal to E.M. Forster's classically-blinkered, misogynist book about Alexandria, published in 1922. In *Pharos and Pharillon,* a volume of Egyptian essays and sketches the Woolfs published in 1923, Forster does not even mention Isis. Yet, as historian Peter Green asserts, "By the Graeco-Roman period Isis had become the most influential and emotionally potent deity known to the ancient world" (410). In 2008, the Egyptian connection to *To the Lighthouse* was opened further by Heidi Stalla, who spots Woolf's use, in *To the Lighthouse*, of the name William Bankes, the 19th-century British explorer and collector of Egyptian antiquities. Stalla speculates that more might be found. The dearth of subsequent studies of the Woolf-Egypt connection is startling, considering how good a foundation these critics laid. The case for deepening the connection between *To the Lighthouse* and Egyptian myth was there for all to see, like a pyramid uncovered in the sand.

Conclusion

I have attempted to demonstrate, using only sources available to Woolf herself, the presence, whether playful or serious, of connections between *To the Lighthouse* and the 1920s' cultural awareness of Egypt, Egyptology, and *The Book of the Dead.* Woolf gained a new kind of authorial empowerment by employing myths and symbols millennia older than those of the Greeks. Going beyond the mere use of symbolism (characters as stand-ins for gods), and deeper than the mere peppering of a novel with name- and place-allusions, Woolf's method is something different. Her un-self-conscious threading of Egyptian elements into the characters, relationships, psychology, vocabulary, and indeed, plot incidents, sound as an Egyptian voice, Memphis speaking in concert with Bloomsbury. If writers are the sum not only of their lives, but of everything they have read, could not Woolf have surrendered to a co-narrator, a created persona extracted from her study of Egypt, an alternate-discourse "I" to the "I" who protests she "meant nothing?" This is a fiction-writer's equivalent of the poet's "muse," the sense of writing with a second voice that seems already to know what it is going to say.

There is always the possibility that a too-close reading creates a scaffolding that conceals the cathedral. Jane Goldman grants some leeway in reminding us, "[E]very reader of *To the Lighthouse* is encouraged to curate, almost in the manner of an editor of a recovered ancient inscription, the text of the novel in all its numbered fragments, and parentheses, its frames within frames. Every such reading, every such curation, is unique" (32).

Doubtless *some* of the connections I have found are coincidental and speculative.

Considering how densely overlaid the novel is with these Egyptian allusions, however, it is hard to conceive of the novel's Egyptian layer as unintentional. That it is there seems certain; yet on this subject Woolf herself is as silent as the Sphinx. *To the Lighthouse* beams out with these Egyptian links and echoes, a triumph of palimpsestic concealment.

WORKS CITED

Abel, Elizabeth. *Virginia Woolf and the Fictions of Psychoanalysis*. U of Chicago P, 1989

Apuleius. *The Golden Ass of Apuleius*. 1566. Translated by William Adlington, London: David Nutt, 1893.

"Artist Profile: Arthur Briscoe." 2006. Biographical sketch. *IFPDA [International Fine Print Dealers Association]*. www.ifpda.org/content/node/372. Accessed Jan. 23, 2017.

Barr, Tina. "Divine Politics: Virginia Woolf's Journey toward Eleusis in *To the Lighthouse*." *boundary 2*. vol. 20 no. 1, Spring 1993, pp. 125-45.

Bell, Quentin. *Virginia Woolf: A Biography*. New York: Harcourt, 1972.

Benson, G. Vere. "Bankes, William John." *Dictionary of National Biography*. 1885. Vol III, London: Smith, Elder. p. 124

Blotner, Joseph L."Mythic Patterns in *To the Lighthouse*." PMLA 71, 1956, pp. 547-62.

Budge, E. A. Wallis, translator. *The Book of the Dead; The Papyrus of Ani in the British Museum*. 1895. New York: Dover, 1967.

———. *Egyptian Magic*. 1901. New York: Dover, 1971.

———. *Legends of the Egyptian Gods: Hieroglyphic Texts and Translations*. 1912. New York: Dover, 1994.

———. *The Mummy*. 1893. New York: Causeway Books, 1974.

———. *Osiris and the Egyptian Resurrection*. 1911. Vol. 1, New York: Dover, 1973. 2 vols.

Carter, Howard. *The Tomb of Tutankhamen: Discovered by the Late Earl of Carnarvon and Howard Carter.* Volume II. London: Cassell, 1927.
———. *The Tomb of Tut-Ankh-Amen: Discovered by the Late Earl of Carnarvon and Howard Carter.* Volume III. London: Cassell, 1933.
Curl, James Stevens. *Egyptomania: The Egyptian Revival, A Recurring Theme in the History of Taste.* Manchester: Manchester UP, 1994.
Duff-Gordon, Lucie (Austin), Lady. *Letters from Egypt, 1863-65.* 3rd ed, London: Macmillan, 1866.
El-Abbadi, Mostafa. "Alexandria: Thousand-Year Capital of Egypt." *Alexandria: The Site and the History.* Edited by Gareth L. Steen, New York UP, 1993, pp. 35-81.
Erman, Adolf. *Life in Ancient Egypt.* Translated by Helen Mary Tirard, London: Macmillan, 1894.
Fagan, Brian. *The Rape of the Nile: Tomb Robbers, Tourists, and Archaeologists in Egypt.* 3rd ed., New York: Westview Press, 2004.
Ford, Ford Madox. *Parade's End.* 1924-26. New York: Penguin Books, 1982.
Forster, E.M. *Pharos and Pharillon.* London: Hogarth Press, 1923.
Frazer, James George. *Adonis, Attis, Osiris: Studies in the History of Oriental Religion.* 3rd ed, Vol. 2, London: Macmillan, 1914. The Golden Bough: A Study of Magic and Religion.
Fry, Roger. *Vision and Design.* London: Chatto & Windus, 1920. 2 vols.
Gaipa, Mark. "An Agnostic's Daughter's Apology: Materialism, Spiritualism, and Ancestry in Woolf's *To the Lighthouse.*" *J of Modern Literature,* vol. 26, no. 2, 2003, pp. 1-41.
Godley, A. D. Introduction to Books I and II. *Herodotus.* Vol. 1, London: Heinemann, 1920, pp. xix-xxi. Loeb Classical Library.
Goelet, Ogden. Introduction. *The Egyptian Book of the Dead: The Book of Going Forth by Day.* Translated by Raymond O. Faulkner and Ogden Goelet, San Francisco: Chronicle Books, 1994, pp. 13-18.
Goldman, Jane. "*To the Lighthouse*'s Use of Language and Form." *The Cambridge Companion to* To the Lighthouse. Edited by Allison Pease, New York: Cambridge UP, 2015, pp. 30-46.
Graves, Robert. *Fairies and Fusiliers.* London: William Heinemann, 1917.
Green, Peter. *Alexander to Actium: The Historical Evolution of the Hellenistic Age.* Berkeley: University of California Press. 1990.
Haller, Evelyn. "Alexandria as Envisioned by Virginia Woolf and E.M. Forster: An Essay in Gendered History." *Woolf Studies Annual,* vol. 9, 2003, pp. 167-92.
———. "The Anti-Madonna in the Work and Thought of Virginia Woolf." *Virginia Woolf: Centennial Essays.* Edited by Elaine K. Ginsberg and Larua

Moss Gottlieb, Troy NY: Whitston Publishing, 1983, pp. 93-110.

———. "Isis Unveiled: Virginia Woolf's Use of Egyptian Myth." *Virginia Woolf: A Feminist Slant*. Edited by Jane Marcus, Lincoln, NE: U of Nebraska P, 1983, pp. 109-31.

Hart, George. *A Dictionary of Egyptian Gods and Goddesses*. London: Routledge, 1986.

Herman, William. "Virginia Woolf and the Classics: Every Englishman's Prerogative Transmuted into Fictional Art." *Virginia Woolf: Centennial Essays*. Edited by Elaine K. Ginsberg and Laura Moss Gottlieb, Troy, NY: Whitston Publishing, 1983, pp. 257-68.

Herodotus. "Book II." Translated by A. D. Godley. *Herodotus*. 1920. Vol. 1, London: William Heinemann, 1966, pp. 273-497. The Loeb Classical Library.

Ingram, Penelope. " 'One Drifts Apart: *To the Lighthouse* as Art of Response." *Philosophy and Literature*, vol. 23, no. 1, 1999, pp. 78-95.

Jones, Prudence and Nigel Pennick. *A History of Pagan Europe*. 1995. London: Routledge, 1997.

Lane, Edward William. *An Account of the Manners and Customs of the Modern Egyptians*. 1833-1835. 5th ed, London: John Murray, 1860.

Leaska, Mitchell. *Granite and Rainbow: The Hidden Life of Virginia Woolf*. New York: Farrar, Straus and Giroux, 1998.

Lee, Hermione. "*To the Lighthouse:* Completed Forms." *Virginia Woolf's* To the Lighthouse. Edited by Harold Bloom, New York: Chelsea House, 1988, pp. 9-26.

———. *Virginia Woolf*. 1996. New York: Vintage Books, 1999.

Maika, Patricia. *Virginia Woolf's* Between the Acts *and Jane Harrison's Con/ spiracy*. Ann Arbor: IMI Research Press, 1987.

Maspero, Gaston. *History of Egypt, Syria, Babylonia, and Assyria*. 1901. Translated by M. L. McClure, Vol. 1, London: Grolier Society, 1901-1906. 12 vols.

McDermott, Bridget. *Decoding Egyptian Hieroglyphics: How to Read the Secret Language of the Pharaohs*. San Francisco: Chronicle Books, 2001.

Nicolson, Nigel. *Virginia Woolf*. New York: Lipper/ Viking, 2000. Penguin Lives.

Pantazzi, Michael. "Tutankhamen and Art Deco." *Egyptomania: Egypt in Western Art, 1730-1930*. Edited by Linda Muir, Ottawa: National Gallery of Canada, 1994. pp. 508-14.

Pater, Walter. *Marius the Epicurean*. Vol. 2, London: Library Edition, 1910. 2 vols.

Plutarch. "Isis and Osiris." Translated by Frank Cole Babbitt. *Plutarch's Moralia*. Vol. 5, Cambridge, MA: Harvard, 1936, pp. 1-191. The Loeb Classical Library. 15 vols.

Reeves, Nicholas. *The Complete Tutankhamun: The King, The Tomb, The Royal Treasure*. London: Thames and Hudson, 1990.

Rowse, A.L. *Homosexuals in History: A Study of Ambivalence in Society, Literature and the Arts*. New York: Dorset Press, 1977.

Rubenstein, Roberta. " 'I meant nothing by The Lighthouse: Virginia Woolf's Poetics of Negation." *Journal of Modern Literature*, vol. 31, no. 4, 2008, pp. 36-53

Sackville-West, Vita. *The Letters of Vita Sackville-West to Virginia Woolf.* Edited by Louise DeSalvo and Mitchell A. Leaska. New York: William Morrow, 1985.

Salaman, Malcolm C. Introduction. *Arthur Briscoe*. London: The Studio, 1930. Masters of Etching.

Seshagiri, Urmila. "Orienting Virginia Woolf: Race, Aesthetics, and Politics in To the Lighthouse." *Modern Fiction Studies*, vol 50, no. 1, Spring 2004, pp. 58-84

Stalla, Heidi. "William Bankes: Echoes of Egypt in Virginia Woolf's *To the Lighthouse*." *Woolf Studies Annual*, vol. 14, 2008.

Thackeray, William Makepeace. *Notes of a Journey from Cornhill to Grand Cairo*. 1846. The Oxford Thackeray. 3rd ed, London: Oxford UP, 1865.

Usick, Patricia. *Adventures in Egypt and Nubia: The Travels of William John Bankes (1786-1855)*. London: The British Museum Press, 2002.

West, Rebecca. *The Return of the Soldier.* 1918. New York: Penguin Books, 1998.

Woolf, Virginia. *To the Lighthouse*. 1927. San Diego: Harcourt Brace, 1981.

———. *Letters of Virginia Woolf: Volume 3: 1923-1928.* New York: Harcourt Brace Jovanovich, 1977.

———. *Letters of Virginia Woolf: Volume 5: 1932-1935.* New York: Harcourt Brace Jovanovich, 1979.

———. *To the Lighthouse: The Original Holograph Draft*. Edited by Susan Dick. U of Toronto P, 1982.

H.M.S. Orlando: The Metamorphosing, Imperial Vessel
Darin Graber

The incomparably named Marmaduke Bonthrop Shelmerdine, Esquire, knows Orlando's name before she divulges it to him in the fifth chapter of her eponymous, fictional biography. "He had guessed it," he says, "[f]or if you see a ship in full sail coming with the sun on it proudly sweeping across the Mediterranean from the South Seas, one says at once, 'Orlando'" (184). In the vision of the lifelong sailor, Shel, Orlando's body, including its "full sail" adornment, becomes a vessel, an imperial vehicle in motion that connects two non-contiguous parts of the globe-spanning British Empire. In addition to multiple moments in which the novel's "biographer" describes Orlando's body with vessel-related language, the repeated, literal presence of ships in the novel warrants attention—particularly as it inflects the novel's interest in and experimentation with the historical progress of the Empire along the span of Orlando's life, with the problems that his, then her, metamorphosing body causes for that progress. Through a hyperbolically long lifespan marked by consistent incongruity between Orlando's body and the temporally-determined fabrics and fashions which adorn it in accordance with his and her roles as a literal and metaphorical vessel of imperial power, the incompatibility of Orlando's metamorphosing body with imperial work exposes as specious the historical narrative undergirding English imperialism.

The roughly 300-year span of Orlando's life coincides with the establishment and consolidation of the oceanic British Empire. In or about 1615—a few years into the historical setting of *Orlando*'s first chapter—Sir Walter Raleigh declared, "[w]hosoever commands the sea, commands the trade, whosoever commands the trade of the world, commands the riches of the world, and consequently the world itself" (qtd in Jowitt 3). By the time that Raleigh makes this comment, England is already driving for sea-faring domination, and the sailing vessel has taken on primary importance in the dream of the global British Empire. Further, the warship does not necessarily take precedence in this endeavor, but the merchant vessel, because control of trade will bring domination by pairing with military power. From the Renaissance through the nineteenth century, the British Empire attained its global power on the high seas with this two-pronged naval approach.

Without rehearsing an exhaustive history of British imperial expansion, I only wish to remind readers of the extent to which vessels occupied British thought in the context of empire. In *Modernism, Imperialism, and the Historical Sense*, Paul Stasi writes, "the imperial context within which Woolf wrote" dictated that "to be British was also to be imperial" and, in turn, to be "dependent upon events that took place elsewhere" which means that the "British national subject was stretched across time and space" (112). Stasi then argues that such temporal and geographical "stretching" necessitates that the imperial nation "fashion forms of continuity for itself" (112), despite that it exists as, in historian Claire Jowitt's words, "an oceanic entity" of constantly moving military and trade campaigns (4). The naval and merchant vessel would seem to help fill this role, as Paul Gilroy established in *The Black Atlantic*, explicitly including ships as a vital part of the ideology of an English nationalism. However, Gilroy shows in that work that a "cohesive" national English identity (*which the ship symbolizes*) falls in favor of what rings truer historically, a constant stream of interacting cultures that breaks down that ideological identity (*which the ship actually effects*). For Gilroy, ships are "micro-cultural, micro-political system[s] in motion" (4), "mobile elements that [stand] for the shifting spaces between the fixed places that they connected," and a way "to explore the articulations between the discontinuous histories of England's ports, its interfaces with the wider world" (17). As I will show, Woolf has already written ships in *Orlando* to be just such a chronotope for studying empire, as both a symbol for English empire and a vehicle for taking apart the ideology that fuels it.

Woolf's play with representations of English merchant and military vessels in prior works (if not also her role as an "Abyssinian" dignitary in 1910's "Dreadnought Hoax") shows that she took such vessels seriously as tools of colonial work and as objects deserving not necessarily to be satirized, but to be critically problematized. Several of her preceding novels and essays placed English vessels in their narrative foreground in a way that, according to Kathy Phillips, introduces a typical "constellation" of thematic concerns for Woolf—"Empire making, war making, and gender relations" (vii). Particularly in the relationship between imperial work and gender relations, as Sonita Sarker writes, in *The Voyage Out* and *Orlando* "sexual exploration and experimentation and emergent or flagrantly rebellious sexualities are often located in 'other' places," whose "otherness…is deeply marked by colonial histories" and which, I posit, English ships not only made possible but practically constituted (119). Furthermore, I argue that Woolf's understanding of this otherness rooted in English ships and shipping allows locations like London's docklands, even *Orlando*'s frozen Thames, to become such sites of problematization.

Others have explored Woolf's linking of English empire, gender relations, and representations of ships as well, though typically emphasizing them as investigating the concept of the "voyage"—a genre of English writing that Woolf herself traces to the sixteenth-century writings of Richard Hakluyt. Molly Hite argues that *The Voyage Out*'s Rachel not only aligns with the ship which carries her to the novel's colonial destination (not in the least because her father's shipping company owns it), but that it exposes the "peculiar process of social embodiment" which Rachel experiences through her "increased definition" aboard the ship and upon delivery to the colony, pointing toward the novel's thematic position that "something supremely important is lost in the voyage that brings this young girl from the state of being an inchoate subject of experience to the state of being visibly and acceptably delineated" (533). Likewise, E. H. Wright argues that Rachel's time on the *Euphrosyne* constitutes a kind of "epiphanic" voyage resulting from her inherently restrictive upper-class upbringing (twenty-four years of feeding rabbits, as Rachel puts it [Wright 83]). In this way, the ship which enables the voyage becomes "alternately…a symbol of freedom" but also of "isolation" (83). In this context, the sea itself offers "refuge from the people and rules that have dictated" Rachel's life and "from social pressures and behavioral expectations based on essentialist thinking" (83, 84). However, aboard the *Euphrosyne*, Rachel endures Richard Dalloway's unwanted, if not violent, sexual advance, which precedes Terence Hewet's ogling and sizing her up as a candidate for marriage—both of which set the stage for the newly female Orlando's experience on the *Enamoured Lady*.

Jeanne Dubino and Anna Snaith also focus on Woolf's consistent use of ship-bound voyages to explore the English cultural constructions of gender which accompany the colonial work carried out by them. Dubino argues that women's sea voyages are inherently gendered in Woolf, that "they become an educational occasion in which women learn about femininity" but, rather than producing actual freedom or change, reveal "straightjackets of conventional gender roles" (12).[1] In "Leonard and Virginia Woolf: Writing against Empire," Snaith posits that Woolf "defamiliarizes" the trope of "English (wo)man abroad" in order to "undercut narratives of imperial pride or superiority," setting the stage for Orlando's life and travels (24).

In order to enact such undercutting of proud narratives of English empire and superiority as Snaith posits, Woolf draws on the very same historical writings which she admired as a young reader. That is, she both invokes and then deconstructs the two perhaps most canonical works of English sea exploits of the sixteenth century, those of Richard Hakluyt—particularly *The Principal Navigations, Voyages, Traffiques & Discoveries of the English Nation*, first published in 1589 and reprinted in 1906.[2] Other critics have shown Woolf's repeated engagement with this and related works (Professor Walter Raleigh's *English Voyages of the Sixteenth Century* and James Anthony Froude's *English Seamen in the Sixteenth Century* [Fox 20]), and Stasi has argued that Woolf saw Hakluyt specifically as laying the groundwork

---

[1] Wright argues that "Rachel arguably dies to avoid this eventuality," whereas Orlando does not die at all, as if performing an inverse form of resistance (84).
[2] The other primary work of Hakluyt being *Divers Voyages Touching the Discoverie of America* (1582).

for the 19th-century English empire (122). Alice Fox documents Woolf's repeated readings of her reprint of *Principal Navigations* over several years.[3]

The way in which Woolf repeatedly engages with Hakluyt's works as a young reader and as an author suggests that she finds productive ambivalence in them. She praises his narratives' rhetorical qualities and even involves their geographical descriptions in her own writing (as Fox shows at some length). Nonetheless, in "The Elizabethan Lumber Room," she explicitly recognizes their potential to be "used effectively all through the West Country to decoy the apt men lounging by the harbour side to leave their nets and fish for gold. Less glorious but more urgent," she writes, "was the summons...to set foot on some intercourse between the merchants of England and the merchants of the East" (63). In other words, her admiration for captivating stories of the English on the high seas in Hakluyt comes paired with a wariness of their imperial utility.

In terms of Woolf viewing her representations of English vessels as something like Gilroy's empire-creating, yet imperial-narrative-deconstructing, chronotopes, Hakluyt works as an atlas for tracing their historical progress and for approaching new possibilities in terms of imperial action, English social hierarchy, and even gender relations. Fox writes that Woolf saw in Hakluyt's depictions of English vessels "a means of class mobility, rather than a perpetuation of a system that allowed the rich to salve their consciences while keeping down the underprivileged," particularly as his representations of sixteenth-century English sailors contrasted with that of her near-contemporary, Froude (36). Understanding Woolf's take on her own important source material in this way opens up the role of vessels in her narratives. Here they function as mobile sites that challenge the relationship between characters' socially-defined subjectivity, which in Stasi's argument, typically "must be rooted in place" to the extent that the closeness between place and subjectivity "effac[es]" possibilities of "allegiances" across social classes (134). Following Fox's position, however, Woolf's sense of Hakluyt's ships as "means of class mobility" leads her to depict vessels as spaces for novel actions or social formations. Moreover, Fox shows that such influence runs throughout the novels preceding *Orlando*. She demonstrates how Woolf's reading of Hakluyt's collected narratives of the "southern voyages" "had already informed her writing of *The Voyage Out*" and influenced her "thoughts about gender in relation to the phenomenon of voyaging" in *Jacob's Room* and *To the Lighthouse*. Her rereading in Hakluyt about both the "northern" and southern voyages then "enter[ed] into her last novel of that decade, *Orlando*" (39). Thus, in Woolf's fiction, as distilled into the title character and narrative of *Orlando*, as I will show, the English vessel

---

[3] *The Diary of Virginia Woolf* features two entries regarding Hakluyt, August 15, 1924 and December 8 1929, in which she reminisces about her embrace of his work as a girl, and reports spending much of her week rereading him, respectively.

moves between modes of meaning, geographical space, and social structures of class, gender, and imperial work.

Woolf's fiction consistently uses vessels in a literal, denotative sense to discuss merchant and colonial travel. More intriguingly, it also consistently makes and uses metaphors for people *as* vessels in order to enact more complicated examinations and experimentations with the aforementioned "constellation" of thematic concerns ("Empire making, war making, and gender relations"). Within such imagery, as part of Woolf's vessel-based experimentation in *Orlando*, fabrics play a surprisingly central role. For most of the three hundred-odd years of his and her existence alongside that of imperial England, fabric in the form of sails makes English ships go. Fabric, especially wool, is delivered by English ships to colonial and/or commercial destinations. Fabrics are brought home to England's docks by those same ships, at which point they take center stage in English fashions. Fabric inheres in Woolf's depicted, if not also in historical, English colonialism in *Orlando*, and previous works demonstrate her by-then established consideration of fabrics' particular roles in colonial economics and travel. In works like *The Voyage Out* and *The London Scene*'s "The Docks of London" and "Oxford Street Tide," she consistently specifies the nature and action of any pertinent ship's sails. Further, she insistently and specifically references fabrics as important trade and imperial commodities throughout these works. In so doing, she intentionally places fabrics as colonial commodities into contact with literal and metaphorical vessels, which results in an even wider constellation of concern for English bodies, predominantly, and the ceremonial and martial fashions that adorn them for particular roles in the imperial endeavor.

Prior to *Orlando*, Woolf developed a repertoire of metaphors that recast people as ships, and ships as people, to explore this nexus of bodies, fabrics, and colonial work. In "Oxford Street Tide," she describes barrows loaded with goods, and by association, the people pushing them, directly as "vessels" which "eddy vaguely across the stream of traffic" in their part of the "effort to persuade the multitude that here unending beauty…very cheap and within the reach of everybody, bubbles up every day…from an inexhaustible well" (24-25). In this effort, the "vessels" involved do not function as people but as tools. In the same way, but reversing the direction of transformation of ship-to-person, "The Docks of London" describes its "romantic and free and fitful" ships as "swimming" upriver to the port, where, after their "sails are furled," they "have no longer the proper perspective of sea and sky behind them" or "the proper space in which to stretch their limbs" (6).

Similarly, *The Voyage Out* both figures Rachel as a vessel and the ship, *Euphrosyne*, as a virgin bride-to-be, connecting, in Snaith's reading, the economics of colonial trade to those of "the marriage market" on which Rachel is a commodity ("Race, Empire" 207). In Chapter 1, just after readers are told that the *Euphrosyne* is one of her father's ten merchant ships, Rachel declares, "I'm going out to t-t-triumph in the wind!" as if she were a sailing vessel—emphasizing her individual connection to the material ship by taking her to its wind-blown decks. In the next chapter, the *Euphrosyne* becomes "a bride going forth to her husband, a virgin unknown of men," as an "inhabitant of the great world...travelling all day across an empty universe, with *veils* drawn before her and behind" (24-25, emphasis mine). That Woolf's narrator conflates the ship's sails with the veils worn by a bride, a virgin bride, no less, bears directly on *Orlando*'s descriptions of the relationship between the body and its adornment, to the social and political roles fabrics and fashions imply, and to the newly female Orlando's experience aboard the *Enamoured Lady*.

Such metaphors also link ships and shipping to the economic activities of British colonialism. When Woolf writes in "The Elizabethan Lumber Room" that much of the "charm" of Hakluyt's volumes "consists in the fact that Hakluyt is not so much a book as a great bundle of commodities loosely tied together, an emporium, a lumber room strewn with ancient sacks...huge bales of wool, and little bags of rubies and emeralds" and that reading it resembles "sitting down in semi-darkness to snuff the strange smells of silks and leathers and ambergris," she highlights this connection between English vessels and the commodities that inhere in imperial economics—fabrics being among the most prevalent, most important of them (61).[4] Thus, Hakluyt not only influences Woolf's rhetoric in describing ships, voyages, and colonial destinations in her fiction, it also draws her attention to the way that his narratives work as commodities that motivate colonialism as well as the commodities that system garners. They "remind" captains of "how necessary it is to find a market abroad for English wool" and to draw the "apt young men" to win "immortal fame...in search of markets and goods" ("Lumber Room" 63-64).[5]

When it comes to the economic products and work of British imperialism in Woolf's imagination, then, fabrics serve as both literal, historical markers of colonial trade and exploitation and as metonymic images for colonial attitudes (all

---

[4] While wool serves as an export in "The Elizabethan Lumber Room," in the "The Docks of London" it figures as one of the most important *imports*: "None of all the multitudinous products and waste products of the earth but has been tested and found some possible use for. The bales of wool that are being swung from the hold of an Australian ship are girt, to save space, with iron hoops; but the hoops do not litter the floor; they are sent to Germany and made into safety razors. The wool itself exudes a coarse greasiness. This grease, which is harmful to blankets, serves, when extracted, to make face cream. Even the burrs that stick in the wool of certain breeds of sheep have their use, for they prove that the sheep undoubtedly were fed on certain rich pastures. Not a burr, not a tuft of wool, not an iron hoop is unaccounted for," given "the aptness of everything to its purpose" (11-12).

[5] *The Voyage Out*'s Clarissa Dalloway echoes this sentiment from the decks of the *Euphrosyne*: "One thinks of all we've done, and our navies, and the people in India and Africa, and how we've gone on century after century, sending out boys from little country villages...it makes one feel as if one couldn't bear *not* to be English" (42).

of which Orlando and his and her body will trouble). Snaith takes the Flushings' practice of buying and selling of fabrics in *The Voyage Out* as an example of "the violent capitalist motivations behind colonialism in the search for cheap labour, new markets, and raw goods" ("Writing against Empire" 19). Mrs. Flushing gleefully explains to Rachel that she and her husband regularly obtain "shawls, stuffs, cloaks, embroideries" "cheap" around the world and then sell them to wealthy Londoners upon their return: as the unnamed, indigenous peoples, "don't know what they're worth,...we get 'em cheap," she says, "And we shall sell 'em to smart women in London" (*VO* 238).[6] Snaith points out that Mrs. Flushing essentially quotes from Leonard's *Empire and Commerce in Africa* here, as he describes the "universal," "dominating" "economic passion" of imperialism—"the passion of buying cheap and selling dear" (qtd in Snaith 22). Thus, in *The Voyage Out*, as a prelude to an extension of the same principle to Orlando's body, fabrics take up a primary place as problematic colonial commodity at the heart of its exploitative economics.

Orlando takes this issue further in the focus that begins in the novel's first line on the fabrics that adorn Orlando, both as a literal and figurative vessel of empire. The specificity of Woolf's descriptions of his and her adornment throughout Orlando's life tie the practices of fashion to those of empire, a theme with which Woolf also works in "The Docks of London." There she writes that the "only thing...that can change the routine of the docks is a change in ourselves," again using wool as an example, saying that if "we...took to using rubber instead of wool for our blankets, the whole machinery of production and distribution would rock and reel," and citing "our tastes, our fashions" as "mak[ing] the cranes dip and swing" and "call[ing] the ships from the sea" (14).[7] "Flocks upon flocks of Australian sheep have submitted to the shears," she continues, "because we demand woollen overcoats in winter" (14).

As others have shown, Woolf targets "the perpetrators of colonialism: the ideologies, systems, institutions, commodities, and exhibitions through which colonial power is maintained" (Snaith, "Race, Empire" 209), while using "juxtaposition and metaphor" to "orient the gaze...toward the background links among Empire, military, and gender relations, which together constitute a comprehensive imperial ideology" (Phillips xxix). I posit, then, that Woolf creates the character of Orlando as a multiply-signifying vessel. Orlando ties the colonial tool of the literal vessel (in her "full sail" and in her "launch" into London society, for example)

---

[6] The Flushings' economic exploitation corresponds with the apparently standard trip upriver from Santa Marina: "Every year at this season English people made parties which steamed a short way up the river, landed, and looked at the native village, bought a certain number of things from the natives, and returned again without damage done to mind or body" (*VO* 250).
[7] Again mirroring Leonard's statement in *Empire and Commerce* that people must change their own "beliefs and desires" to effect solutions to colonization and warfare, as Phillips shows (Phillips xxxiii).

to the colonial commodity (in the specification of fabrics reaped through colonial trade), and to the historical arc of culturally determined meaning of those elements toward the carrying out of British Empire (in his and her fashions and their bodies' relationship to them as signifying of class, gender, and imperial role)—or, in other words, to Stasi's "sense of continuity" that historical narratives build for the empire. Orlando's mutability and its slippery relation to that narrative then challenges any such continuity or coherence.

Initially, Orlando's masculine youth promises a future in the British ruling class under royal appointment—as introduced in the first lines depicting his boyhood pastime: slicing at a severed "Moor's" head with a sword in an attic room. The head has been handed down by some unknown, unnamed, paternal ancestor. Apparently as a matter of course, "Orlando's fathers had ridden…and they had struck many heads of many colours off many shoulders, and brought them back to hang from the rafters" (11). His paternal line constitutes a repeating process of colonial warfare more than a series of unique individuals, and Orlando stands at the end of it, willing to take on the head-lopping mantle.

However, an already-noticeable discrepancy between his body and its adornment complicates his seemingly predestined service to the Empire from the outset. Constructing the novel's opening lines so that the reader cannot determine whether or not his clothes are "appropriate" to Orlando's gender—because they partially "disguise" it—foreshadows the pattern of Orlando's failed imperial action, raising doubts about whether Orlando will be capable of serving as the continuation of the war-making paternal line. Thus, the novel's first parenthetical expression points out a critical junction for my argument: the inherently intertwined problem of Orlando's period-appropriate adornment, his somehow troubling body and sexuality, the fact that both adornment and sexuality are culturally regulated in the Empire's successive historical periods, and that his imperial role hinges upon this cultural regulation. The latter emerges in Queen Elizabeth's rewarding Orlando's family with an estate and Orlando himself with an appointment as Treasurer and Steward based upon his "implied…pair of the finest legs that a young nobleman has ever stood upright upon" (18). This investment with royal authority makes Orlando into a vessel of the queen's power, which he doles out in Scotland and other locales, though only briefly and unreliably as his youth and "boyishness" lead him to other pursuits, namely of women.

Orlando's interest in women ought to reinforce a sense of heteronormative masculinity. However, the places where he cultivates this interest violate the restriction of scope expected by his ruling class, inducing the social and political problems of his young, male life—and typified by the garments he must conceal as well as those he uses to do so. Along the banks of the Thames where sailors tell Hakluyt-esque tales of their voyages, Orlando finds captivating women who are "scarcely less bold" in speech or "free in their manners" than the men. On this fringe of society—the docklands upon which England's colonial trade depends—social mores appear more egalitarian than in the class from which Orlando comes (22). This license titillates him, but he feels compelled to remain anonymous—less for decorum's sake than for maintaining his own freedom of movement—and he dons "a grey cloak to hide the star at his neck and the garter at his knee" (22). The performative, imperial rigging of the garter and star pendant made of gold, enamel, and precious stones, would, if seen, bar his access to the common sailors' world, because it would denote the power the Queen has invested in him. Covering these two features of his adornment with grey cloak made of duffle (common, coarse woolen cloth affiliated with lower-class garb) enables a kind of class transvestism—an adoption of coarse fabric not meant for the "fine" figure of Orlando, with his curling hair and attractive "nobleman's" legs, and most importantly, imperial station. That Woolf names this fabric, "duffle," is an invocation of English colonial history, as the *OED* traces its etymology through English trade with the town of "Duffel" in Brabant, then later with American Indians and then with the New England and Virginia colonies through the eighteenth century. The fact that the fabric's name became synonymous with a cloak worn by lower-class subjects forms a contradiction to the authority vested in Orlando as the queen's appointee, covering the sartorial signs of that power.

This class transvestism grants Orlando access to the sailors and women, "eager" as they are "to come at the truth of the matter as Orlando himself" (22). The phrase, *the truth of the matter*, implies in one way that the nearer to his skin the women can go, the closer they draw to Orlando's true identity—as if his clothes function as protective layers hiding the kernel of truth, presumably his/her genitals. The other possible meaning of this phrase, as a euphemism for sex, posits a coexistence of "truth" with intercourse, in which a naked body cannot conceal gender or identity the way a cloak or other adornment might. Both meanings fail to account for a mutable body and contrast with Shel's later sighting of the apparently clearly female Orlando's "full sail" of English canvas which accurately announces her.

In any case, the three themes of Orlando's gender and sexuality, the role of his clothing in relation to them, and his decreasing utility to His or Her Majesty's Empire meet on the banks of the Thames, thanks to shipping's role in the Empire. Because the Crown relies on sea trade, it sanctions constant traffic into and out of London, even at the risk that such constant traffic provides opportune locations for otherwise forbidden or unsavory activity: "Every day sail[s] to sea some fine ship bound for the Indies; now and again another blackened and ragged with hairy unknown men on board [creeps] painfully to anchor" (*O* 22). Orlando's noble body does not belong with "ragged" ships and "hairy" men, but because the Empire lives via its ships and their constant comings and goings, he can hide himself among the river's on and offshore traffic, where "opportunity" is not "lacking," because "[n]o one misse[s] a boy or girl if they dall[y] a little on the water after sunset; or raise[s] an eyebrow if gossip ha[s] seen them sleeping soundly among the treasure sacks safe in each other's arms" (*O* 22). The bustling banks of the Thames offer freedom from class-based expectations, at once symbolizing imperial business and enabling Orlando to act without regard to, if not against, the imperial, cultural order that oversees this business. In this way, the larger context and dock-side locations affiliated with shipping echo Gilroy's view of the ship as a tool of empire that actually orchestrates interactions that undermine the cultural ideology behind the imperial venture. As Her Majesty's Treasurer and Steward, an ostensibly important post, Orlando can be found in post-coital slumber "among the treasure sacks" on the banks of the Thames. Compared to the "severely utilitarian" docks of Woolf's "The Docks of London," which find "mercantile value" for even the most seemingly odd or out-of-place materials lying among the "dingy, decrepit-looking" banks and warehouses, Orlando uses his lower-class fabric and fashion to flout his imperial role there, thus challenging his own "mercantile" or imperial value (7, 11).

Such is Orlando's state as he enters the reign of James I and meets Sasha, whose freezing of English trade and subsequent theft of Orlando's love inspires his abandonment of the Steward and Treasurer position for a poet's life. One cannot say that *despite* that Sasha first appears to Orlando to be a boy, but partially *because of* or *in relation to* it, she captivates Orlando. On first sight of her, Orlando stands "ready to tear out his hair with vexation that the person [is] of his own sex, and thus all embraces [are] out of the question," because his cultural location prescribes his sexuality (28). As the Queen's, then the King's, tool, his duty is to further the empire abroad and produce offspring with an appropriately well-bred woman. Nonetheless, Orlando's false but exciting initial identification of a male Sasha results from her athletic movement and attire, a "loose tunic and trousers," which (familiarly enough) "serve to disguise the sex" (27). As Orlando's indeterminate gender and sexuality trouble his utility to the throne, Sasha's own ambiguous body and fashion mark her as outside the class of women Orlando should seek.

Sasha's troublesome complementarity with Orlando's ambiguous gender (which "Queen Bess" had confidently identified, and based upon which his post was granted) performs a complete embargo on Orlando's work as Steward and Treasurer, and freezes the traffic of ships in and out of London that signifies the nation's trade. Their first meeting on the frozen Thames symbolizes this embargo, a stop to that "irresistible call" to merchant ships to enter London that coincides with the duration of Sasha's hold on Orlando (Woolf, "Docks" 6). In combination with her distaste for his class of monarchs and lords (she calls them a detestable "English mob"), Sasha's active distraction of Orlando from his appointed, governmental responsibilities constitute the less physically apparent embargo, or "freezing" of, England's imperial project. Only recently considered a masculine young man whom the Queen herself handpicked for service to the Empire, Orlando now speaks French while strolling among commoners with Sasha, his infiltrating Russian girlfriend, and schemes to "escape" from his homeland with her.

As Orlando waits with the horses on their proposed night of escape, however, Sasha executes his emasculating defeat by sailing off. Simultaneously, all that her frost has impeded in the Thames breaks loose, having "gained its freedom" (46). The thawing river rages out to sea behind the Russian ship bearing Sasha, wreaking havoc along the banks and killing a number of Londoners marooned on speeding slabs of ice. The Muscovite Embassy's ship escapes, while the French, Spanish, Austrian, and "Turk" ships incur damages or sink. The confirmation of his betrayal comes in the shape of "black eagles…flying from the mast head"—or, in maritime terminology, the ship's dressing (48).[8] As he stands knee-deep in the water, he accuses Sasha of "all the insults that have ever been the lot of her sex," including that she is "[f]aithless" and, ironically, "mutable" (48). That mutability damns her foretells how this same characteristic will also render him (as her) an incapable, imperial vessel. As Sasha's ship takes her away, the water "takes" Orlando's words and washes a broken pot, the picture of an impotent vessel, against his leg (40).[9]

Sasha's flight motivates Orlando's complete break with his role as Steward and Treasurer. He abandons the Thames and its traffic for his family home and poetry. After his subsequent literary betrayal, this time at the pen of the poet Nicholas Greene, Orlando concludes, "I have done with men" (71). Without realizing it, however, Orlando is not fully done with men, as he is courted by "Harriet," a man dressed in women's clothes in order to approach Orlando in a culturally condoned manner. During one lighthearted argument between them, Harriet attempts to fit a shin plate from one of Orlando's suits of armor to his leg. This gesture symbolizes an attempt to adorn Orlando with the martial tools of empire, the armor in which his male ancestors presumably struck heads from the bodies of differently-colored men. Orlando's leg and the plate do not fit each other, though, producing an almost

---

[8] Maritime use of the verb "to dress" means "to ornament a ship for a celebration by hoisting national ensigns at the mastheads and running a line of signal flags and pennants from bow to stern" (*Merriam-Webster*). The *OED*'s definition more generally emphasizes ships' "flags" set as decoration. Woolf mentions a similar usage of the "Blue Peter" in "The Docks of London," a flag which signaled passengers or crew ashore of impending departure.

[9] In "*Orlando* and the Tudor Voyages," Ian Blyth notes that, historically (which Woolf certainly knew via her reading), King James' reign saw the loss of potential trade pacts with Russia to the Dutch (190). He reads Sasha's betrayal of Orlando as representing that commercial loss. To that, Fox notes that Orlando's time with Sasha bears signs of influence from Hakluyt's accounts of the first Russian ambassador's visit to London in the mid-sixteenth century (46), while Orlando's thoughts about Russia itself and the insults he sends toward Sasha's fleeing vessel refer to Hakluyt's description of Russian people as "great talkers and lyers, without any faith or trust in their words, flatterers and dissemblers" (qtd in Fox, 48).

overwhelming sensation of love directed at Harriet. At first a pleasant sensation, this love turns out to be the "black...vulture," "Lust," which "disgustingly" lands on Orlando (87). He refuses the plate and rejects Harriet in the same moment. Thus, before Orlando sails off in another imperial capacity, we find a repetition of his inability to fit properly into his station as English gentry, because his body and the raiment handed down by that station simply do not match. His body cannot be made compatible to his role as the Empire's tool, like a vessel rigged with the wrong sails.

Contingent upon the king's approval, Orlando flees from the conflicted love that Harriet's gesture with the shin plate produces, as Ambassador Extraordinary to Constantinople. His proposed royal service (now to King Charles) begins as a voyage of escape, not as a mode for imperial progress. Perhaps due to this predisposition, Orlando's time as ambassador coincides with a successful rebellion there. This rebellion's climax also denotes the climax of Orlando's imperial, political career.

On the night in which *he* will become *she*, symbols of imperial power awarded to Orlando collide with his actions, which contradict the practice of colonial politics. Preparations for the celebration of Orlando's dukedom feature signs of imperial power, not least of which are "jellies made to represent His Majesty's ships," as if the night's Turkish guests are invited to ingest representations of the same vessels exporting English empire to their country (94).[10] Once he enters, Orlando's body—specifically his "leg," "countenance," and "princely manners"—add to the presentation of English power (96). While standing on the "centre Balcony... hung with priceless rugs" and accepting "the Collar of the Most Noble Order of the Bath," the "Star" pin, "the ducal robes,...the ducal coronet," and "the golden circlet of strawberry leaves," Orlando stands as the proxy body of the English monarchy inhabiting Turkish space—being crowned there under protection of six Turkish guards (96-97).

However, Orlando addresses the room in Turkish, rather than in the King's English, and when he places the circlet on his head, an atmospheric disturbance occurs which is said to be either the beginning of the revolution or some prophesied, mystical hailing of Orlando. Effectively, the placing of the circlet on his head announces the end of *his* imperial service to England, rather than his ascendency within it. Christine Fouirnaies argues that the possession of power and land within Constantinople that the coronet, or circlet, ought to symbolize, once stolen in the rebellion, precipitates, or at least precedes, his "turn[ing] into a woman" and that this change denotes a change of class as well, since a woman cannot wear it (35). I posit that the "disturbance" which accompanies the moment of that circlet's contact with Orlando's body already indicates a mismatch between the body and the

---

[10] Fox points out further reference to Hakluyt in this scene, from an account of the reception of the first English sailors at the Turkish court—with a "magnificence" of scale and fineness, including a hall "spread with carpets on the ground fourscore or fourscore and tenne foot long, with an hundred and fiftie severall dishes set thereon" (34).

power-infused adornment, so that it echoes Orlando's experience with the shin plate from his ancestors' suit of armor as his and her body refuses the adornment that grants investment of imperial power.

Afterwards, Orlando's covering or replacing of the new ceremonial garb by a "loose cloak or dressing gown" repeats the fabric-based transgression of class and imperial role that he practiced in the London docklands earlier. Dressed this way, Orlando hoists "a woman, much muffled, but apparently of the peasant class" to his chambers' balcony, after which they embrace and go inside (98). First, on the ceremonial balcony, Orlando's body, as a vessel, contains and strategically doles out the King's power overseas, showing the majestic reach of England's throne. On the second balcony, Orlando skirts public view completely while the rebellion heightens, and he forgoes any demonstration of his and England's power by publicly "taking" a woman from among the local upper-class to solidify their adherence to English rule. As with his earlier breaking of class barriers, the coarse, lower-class-affiliated gown he covers himself in symbolizes a rejection of imperial British power and demonstrates his lack of allegiance to the ideology that allows colonization to flourish—namely, that a peasant and a duke cannot exist as equals, let alone as lovers, and that a colonial "race" could not and would not love another which it colonizes. After their marriage, Orlando enters the week-long slumber that allows him to survive the successful rebellion by appearing dead. When he wakes, his embassy is ransacked and he is now a woman.

Tellingly again, this new, female Orlando escapes the city with the help of "those Turkish coats and trousers which can be worn indifferently by either sex," in which she conceals "several strings of emeralds and pearls of the finest orient which had formed part of her Ambassadorial wardrobe" (104). She has the aid of a group of so-called "gipsies" with whom, the narrator reasons, "she must have been in secret communication before the revolution" (105). Eventually, Orlando's values and views about nature make her unwelcome among them, and she finds "an English merchant ship, as luck would have it, *under sail* in the harbour" near Mt. Athos (112, emphasis mine). The "biographer" does not further specify the location (on a northern Grecian island) or how Orlando came there, but its relevance lies in that, regardless of where Orlando finds him or herself—and not "as luck would have it"—English maritime trade has already established its presence (112).[11]

---

[11] Paul Stasi similarly reads *The Voyage Out*'s fictional history of Santa Marina, where the *Euphrosyne* delivers Rachel to the same place where English ships had lain 300 years prior as "Woolf...highlighting the continuity of imperial relations" even if simultaneously hearkening back to "something of the newness of discovery, a feeling that she imagines existed before the discourses of both empire and gender were codified" (126). Moreover, the English Navy's Mediterranean Fleet redeploying toward home waters at the end of *Voyage Out*'s fourth chapter (at which Clarissa Dalloway exclaims—"Aren't you glad to be English!") reiterates the seeming omnipresence of English commercial and martial vessels (60).

Using pearls from the now-useless ambassador's costume hidden under the gender-neutral, "Turkish" adornment, Orlando outfits herself in "the dress of a young English woman" and buys passage home (113). Thus, the remains of her imperial post's sartorial component offer her the power to buy transport home on an English ship in a fashion appropriate to her new station. Where once the male Orlando had lain with various female companions among "sacks of treasure" along the Thames, the *Enamoured Lady* now transports her via the Thames into London along with such "sacks"—and dressed in a fabric that connotes the "selling dear" of textile trade. The vessel's name foreshadows Orlando's ensuing realizations about the new expectations of behavior and character she must meet, highlighted by the sailor who nearly falls to his death from the mast after seeing "an inch or two of calf" which she failed to cover and the captain's immediate desire to erect an awning over her on deck (116).

Over the duration of her voyage these new, concrete realities sink in. *He* used to insist "that women must be obedient, chaste, scented, and exquisitely apparelled" for his pursuit (115). Now *she* must "pay in [her] own person for those desires" while she protects herself, above all else, as a vessel for (English) procreation (115). "[C]hastity is (women's) jewel," Orlando thinks, while the *Enamoured Lady*'s captain arranges the awning to shade her and "the coil of skirts about her (once admired, once free) legs" make themselves felt (113). Her body's culturally prescribed adornment both contains her and announces the new rules by which she must play.

All the while, textiles as vital pieces of imperial economics and politics cover her three times over: the awning chivalrously rigged by the captain, the dress that marks her as "a young Englishwoman of rank," and, in a telltale move for Woolf, the ship's sails which conspicuously fall on their landing in Italy (113). In *The Art of Sail-Making*, David Steel explains that the sails under which Orlando rides, like all English sails for centuries, would have constituted a layer of English canvas regulated for their Englishness. That is, beginning under William III, English ships had to be rigged with sails produced in Britain, of British materials, as long as demand could be met, while any coming from overseas were taxed, examined, and if approved, stamped as English before being flown over English ships (187-88). Altogether, Woolf's orchestration of the female Orlando's return to England draws attention to the fabrics around her, as near to her body as stockings and as remote as the sails flying from the masts, as material connections between sartorial culture and colonial economics—with the variably gendered Orlando most problematically bearing them.

While Orlando ruefully takes in the limitations of being wrapped this way ("these skirts are plaguey things to have about one's heels," she thinks), she also finds that "the stuff (flowered paduasoy) is the loveliest in the world" and shows her "own skin...to such advantage" (114). Again, the word's etymology reveals a micro-history of English textile trade, as "paduasoy" refers to the Italian city of Padua from which the "strong, rich, silk fabric, usually corded or embossed" came (*OED* "paduasoy"). Furthermore, contrasted with the "duffle" used as concealment by the young, male Orlando or on the balcony prior to his empire-defying marriage, this fabric aligns Orlando with the "smart women" of London to whom *The Voyage Out*'s Mrs. Flushing sells colonial textiles. Moreover, while her role appears mostly unappealing to Orlando as an intelligent person who previously experienced the freedom men enjoy, she explicitly connects her skin to her adornment in an aesthetic way. This particular cloth, which Woolf clearly uses with intent, improves her own understanding of her appearance—not necessarily in that she appears more *genuine* but perhaps more *attractive*. Being attractive, consciously and assiduously pursuing an appearance that wins the interest of men, now constitutes the primary outlet designated by upper-class, English culture for Orlando.

When Sasha sailed away from Orlando and England, a broken pot washed against his leg. Now, landing in England via the Thames, Orlando must protect herself as a "chaste, threatened, weak, and fertile vessel," in Phillips' words, ready to be filled and to "meet the needs of an imperial state" by delivering a line of children into the throne's service (199). She may no longer strike a man, or curse him, make an oath, or "draw [her] sword and run him through the body," but she may express her expected and appropriate inner emptiness—her being a vessel—by pouring out tea and asking, "D'you take sugar? D'you take cream?" (*O* 116).[12] In her own argument for Orlando's change of "sex" as inherent in the loss of British influence in Constantinople, Phillips posits that the empire requires that Orlando become female in order to justify military intervention as the protection of female English subjects. This new, "imperial role" for Victorian women is to give their male counterparts a martial motive in guarding "the chastity which the bridal veils proclaim," then to fill the "bassinets (that) nurture the soldiers who will fill the ranks" (Phillips 197). Hence comes Orlando's understanding that "the British Empire came into existence" by each woman bearing fifteen children (*O* 229). The *Enamoured Lady* delivers this new vessel of the English gentry, the promise of a continued, imperial lineage, into the Victorian era, when she must fight her disinheritance for being either dead or a woman in a legal suit, which foretells her coming difficulty and ultimate failure to fill this vessel's role.

After moving to London to escape Archduke Harry's second attempt to woo her, now under the reign of Queen Anne, Orlando immediately makes the mistake

---

[12] Orlando's full lamentation of her loss of recourse to violence is strikingly thorough in its scope, while also invoking the element of imperial fashion, the coronet, that was placed on him just before he became she: "I shall never be able to crack a man over the head, or tell him he lies in his teeth, or draw my sword and run him through the body...or wear a coronet...or sentence a man to death, or lead an army" (116).

of walking in public alone—which ladies may not do.[13] And even in London's "miasma" which might seem more amenable to an incompletely-gendered woman, Orlando finds no clear place. Crucially, the "biographer" describes the attempt to introduce her there as the launching of a ship for its maiden voyage. "Orlando was launched without delay," he writes, "and with some splash and foam at that, upon the waters of London society" (141). Not only does this "launch" figure Orlando directly as an English ship, it does so similarly to the earlier works mentioned above, which use such metaphors to connect vessels to imperial work and commodities.[14]

The launching of the ship that Orlando ought to be fails, however. She does not "pass muster" as a proper female because "there was an absent mindedness about her which…made her clumsy" (143). Further, "she was apt to think of poetry when she should have been thinking of taffeta; her walk was…too much of a stride for a woman…and her gestures…endanger a cup of tea on occasion" (143). "Passing muster" as female, just as for a ship or a soldier, means appearing uniform, fitting the stipulated pattern of dress and decorum. To fulfill her role as an English lady, Orlando should focus on her own surface and its appearance to others' view—to move gracefully, to speak and listen congenially while entertaining or being entertained, to think of fabrics and fashions that complement her skin and body. She should not pursue self-determined, intellectual subjects—contemplating poetry or philosophy, nor moving her body willfully. Ultimately, the failure of the newly launched Orlando, who rudders constantly against the borders of condoned behavior, marks a failure of the expected coopting of her body for imperial expansion or continuity.

In a way that mirrors Orlando's male life, then, she cannot live up to what the country, crown, and culture demand of her female life. She does not function as an imperial vessel, which ought to deliver fighting men and merchants for service overseas, who will, themselves, later return with treasure and win decorations like the men of "Portrait of a Londoner." Nor was she successful when a male Steward (carousing with the lower classes and enabling the freeze on English trade) or Ambassador (losing Constantinople). Orlando's mutability, the lack of a clear match between his and her body and its adornment in the textiles that are also colonial commodities, both signal and help enact his and her incompatibility with any imperial role.

---

[13] An echo of Rachel Vinrace's realization about why she has never been allowed to go out alone, after Dalloway accosts her on the decks of the *Euphrosyne*.

[14] "Portrait of a Londoner" describes the reintegration of exported and then re-imported men into London society by Mrs. Crowe, which seems much less public, judgment-laden, and more personal than what Orlando experiences in a woman's return: "Travellers absent for years, battered and sun-dried men just landed from India or Africa, from remote travels and adventures among savages and tigers, would come straight to the little house in the quiet street to be taken back into the heart of civilisation" (74).

Not only does this failed combination repeatedly prevent the success of his, and then her, imperial activity up to the time of her return to England, but the Empire's progress through time also increasingly pushes Orlando's indeterminate nature further to the fringes of imperial usefulness and, thus, of social relevance. As the nineteenth century arrives—and the height of British colonial reach with it—Orlando finds it "antipathetic to her in the extreme" (178). Its most dire infringement upon her fluid nature is the predominant sartorial textile, crinoline, which is "heavier and more drab than any dress she had yet worn" (178). Not unrelated to the repressive Victorian mores concerning female physicality, Orlando finds that no other fabric "had ever so impeded her movements" (178). Her body develops a stronger affinity for nature during this time, specifically with the natural elements surrounding her home in Blackfriars, where she declares: "I have found my mate. It is the moor. I am nature's bride" (182). But Victorian England's fashions directly fight her natural attraction to nature as a "mate." Its plumed hat blows off as she walks (with difficulty, in the crinoline) and its thin shoes become "quickly soaked and mud-caked" as she attempts to tramp the moor (179). Because Orlando needs this communion with the plants, animals, and soil of her lands, the nineteenth century becomes another, stronger case in which Orlando's bodily and/or spiritual needs and history's gendered fashions cannot coexist. And any role in imperial work remains out of the question.

Similarly, the increased mechanization and ordering of life that Orlando first notes while passing the now-orderly Wapping Stairs on the *Enamoured Lady*'s arrival in London constitutes the latest form of imperial progress, and her refusal to live up to the late Victorian model of mechanistically bringing the "British Empire...into existence" by "marry[ing] at nineteen and [having] fifteen or eighteen children by...thirty" poses equal resistance to empire as refusing to adopt its modernization. However, as the Victorian period gives way to the twentieth century she proves (again, against gender expectations) to be an adroit driver. Where Orlando has never fit since his adolescence, Orlando continues not to fit—in the class of lords, dukes, and duchesses. Despite giving birth to one child (vowing it will be the only), Orlando falls out of the ruling class and its attention.

Where the adoption of a second or subsequent gender might often be thought of as the shedding of a sense of falsity in favor of a genuine identity, I posit that, in *Orlando*'s title character, such a removal of falsity is precluded by the mutability of the character. Orlando's metamorphosing body, gender, or "sex" renders the dichotomy of "truthfulness" and "falseness" moot. It is precisely this mootness which demonstrates the British Empire's ideology as fallacious in *Orlando*, as Woolf orchestrates it within the historical arc of British colonialism's vessel-based foundation and expansion—with Orlando's transformation directly at its midpoint. Woolf's use of the "biographer" foregrounds his history, like all histories, as a narrative construction, which combines with Orlando's continual fashion and gender-related social and political failures to refute anything like the narrative of continuity that Stasi describes.

However, his and her political and social failures do not expose Orlando as an incapable individual. They expose the fully arbitrary, temporally relative, but stringently reinforced cultural expectations foisted onto him and then her as such, which is given form on Orlando's body through the cultural regulation of fashion as performative of gender and sexuality *and* as both a tool and product of colonial economics. Regardless of gender and time, the versions of English culture which define sartorial, economic, and social mores throughout *Orlando* remain arbitrary, despite that the imperial business for which Orlando is to be outfitted as a literal or representative vessel depend on those regulations. Thus, the string of successive, present-moment failures surrounding Orlando's metamorphosing body constitute a critique of the very narrative motivating the continuation of English colonial history.

Works Cited

Blyth, Ian. "*Orlando* and the Tudor Voyages." *Locating Woolf: The Politics of Space and Place*. Eds. Anna Snaith and Michael Whitworth. Palgrave Macmillan, 2007, pp. 183-96.

"dress, v." *Merriam-Webster Online*. Britannica. 12 December 2012.

"dress, v." *OED Online*. December 2012. Oxford UP. 12 December 2012.

Dubino, Jeanne. "Engendering Voyages in Virginia Woolf's Fiction." *Voyages Out, Voyages Home: Selected Papers from the Eleventh Annual Conference on Virginia Woolf*. Eds. Jane de Gay and Marion Dell, Clemson U-Digital P, 2010, pp. 12-17.

"duffle | duffel, n." *OED Online*. September 2012. Oxford UP. 8 December 2012.

Fouirnaies, Christine. "Was Virginia Woolf a Snob? The Case of Aristocratic Portraits in *Orlando*." *Woolf Studies Annual*, Vol. 22, 2016, pp. 21-40.

Fox, Alice. *Virginia Woolf and the Literature of the English Renaissance*. Clarendon Press, 1990.

Gilroy, Paul. *The Black Atlantic: Modernity and Double Consciousness*. Verso, 1993.

Hite, Molly. "The Public Woman and the Modernist Turn: Virginia Woolf's *The Voyage Out* and Elizabeth Robins's *My Little Sister*." *Modernism/Modernity*, vol. 17, no. 3, 2010, pp. 542-48.

Jowitt, Claire. *The Culture of Piracy, 1580-1630: Literature and Seaborne Crime*. Ashgate, 2010.

"paduasoy, n." *OED Online*. September 2012. Oxford UP. 8 December 2012.

Phillips, Kathy J. *Virginia Woolf Against Empire*, U of Tennessee P, 1994.

Sarker, Sonita. "Woolf and Theories of Postcolonialism." *Virginia Woolf in Context*. Eds. Bryony Randall and Jane Goldman. Cambridge UP, 2012, pp. 110-22.

Snaith, Anna. "Leonard and Virginia Woolf: Writing against Empire." *The Journal of Commonwealth Literature*, 50:1, 2015, pp. 19-32.

———. "Race, Empire, and Ireland." *Virginia Woolf in Context*. Eds. Bryony Randall and Jane Goldman. Cambridge University Press, 2012, pp. 206-18.

Stasi, Paul. *Modernism, Imperialism, and the Historical Sense*. Cambridge UP, 2012.

Steel, David. *The art of sail-making, as practised in the Royal Navy, and according to the most approved methods in the merchant service, accompanied with the parliamentary regulations relative to sails and sail cloth. Illustrated by numerous figures, with full and accurate tables*. London, 1796. Eighteenth-Century Collections Online. Gale. 9 December 2012.

Woolf, Virginia. *The Diary of Virginia Woolf*. Ed. Anne Olivier Bell. 2 vols. Harcourt Brace Jovanovich, 1977.

———. "The Docks of London." *The London Scene: Six Essays on London Life*. Daunt Books, 2013, pp. 5-15.

———. "The Elizabethan Lumber Room." *The Common Reader*. Harcourt, Brace & Co., 1925, pp. 61-71.

———. *Orlando: A Biography*. Orlando, Harcourt, 2006.

———. "Oxford Street Tide." *The London Scene: Six Essays on London Life*. Daunt Books, 2013, pp. 19-26.

———. "Portrait of a Londoner." *The London Scene: Six Essays on London Life*. Daunt Books, 2013, pp. 67-74.

———. *The Voyage Out*. Penguin Classics, 2006.

Wright, E. H. "The 'girl-novel': *Chance* and Woolf's *The Voyage Out*." *The Conradian: The Journal of the Joseph Conrad Society* (U.K.), vol. 39, no. 1, 2014, pp. 80-97.

Guide to Library Special Collections

This list reflects updates or changes received in 2017. Readers are advised to check an institution's website for the most current information. Suggestions for additions to this list are welcome.

Name of Collection: The Beinecke Rare Book and Manuscript Library

Contact: Timothy Young, Curator of Modern Books and Manuscripts
Nancy Kuhl, Curator of American Literature

Address: Yale University Library
P.O. Box 208240
New Haven, CT 06520-8240

URL: http://beinecke.library.yale.edu/

Access Requirements: Registration required at first visit.

Holdings Relevant To Woolf: General Collection includes autograph manuscript of "Notes on Oliver Goldsmith." Comments on Edward Gibbon, William Beckford Collection. Letters from Virginia Woolf in the Bryher Papers, the Louise Morgan and Otto Theis Papers, the Rebecca West Papers, the James Lees-Milne Papers, and the Mary Smyth Hunter correspondence. Related material: 41 letters from Vita Sackville-West to Violet Trefusis; files relating to Robert Manson Myers's *From Beowulf to Virginia Woolf* in the Edmond Pauker Papers.

Yale Collection of American Literature includes typewritten manuscripts of "The Art of Walter Sickert," "Augustine Birrell," "Aurora Leigh," "How Should One Read a Book?" "Letter to a Young Poet," "The Novels of Turgenev," "Street Haunting." Dial/Scofield Thayer Papers: manuscripts of "The Lives of the Obscure," "Miss Ormerod," and "Mrs. Dalloway in Bond Street." Letters from Virginia Woolf in the William Rose Benet Papers, the Benet Family Correspondence, Henry Seidel Canby Papers, the Seward Collins Papers, the Dial/Scofield Thayer Papers, and the

Yale Review archive. Material relating to translations of Woolf in the Thornton Wilder papers. Related material: Clive Bell, "Virginia Woolf" (Dial/Scofield Thayer Papers); 43 letters from Leonard Woolf to Helen McAfee (*Yale Review*); 11 letters from Leonard Woolf to Gertrude Stein.

Name of Collection: The Henry W. and Albert A. Berg Collection of English and American Literature

Contact: berg@nypl.org for access procedures
Isaac Gewirtz, Curator

Address: New York Public Library, Room 320
Fifth Avenue & 42nd Street
New York, NY 10018

Telephone: 212-930-0802
Fax: 212-930-0079

Hours: Tue.-Wed. 11 am-6:45 pm
Thu.-Sat. 10 am-5:45 pm
Closed Sun., Mon. and legal holidays

Access Requirements: After acquiring Library card in room 315, check outerwear and all containers (briefcases, computer cases, handbags, folders, etc.) in Ground Floor cloakroom, and proceed to the Berg Collection. Traceable and photo identification required. Undergraduates working on honors theses need letter from faculty advisor to be sent to the Berg's Curator and to receive an affirmative response prior to scheduling an appointment with the Berg librarians. No books may be brought to the reading tables, including notebooks.

Restrictions: Virginia Woolf's bound MSS, because of their fragile condition, are made available on microfilm and CD. URL for Berg finding aid: http://www.nypl.org/research/manuscripts/berg/brgwoolf.xml. N.B. All the Berg's Woolf MSS are on microfilm and 90 percent of them are on CD, published by Research Publications and available at many research libraries.

GUIDE TO SPECIAL LIBRARY COLLECTIONS 187

Holdings Relevant To Woolf: Manuscripts/typescripts of all of the novels except *Orlando*, including: *Between the Acts, Flush, Jacob's Room, Mrs. Dalloway* (notes and fragments), *Night and Day, To the Lighthouse, The Voyage Out, The Waves, The Years*; 12 notebooks of articles, essays, fiction and reviews, 1924-1940; 36 volumes of diaries; 26 volumes of reading notes; correspondence with Vanessa Bell, Ethel Smyth, Vita Sackville-West and others. Su Hua Ling Chen's Bloomsbury correspondence; proof copy of *A Room of One's Own* (July 1929); ALS Vanessa Bell to Vita Sackville-West, April 29, 1941 [in Marler, *Selected Letters* 478-80]; Frank Dean, *Strike While the Iron's Hot: Frank Dean's Life as a Blacksmith and Farrier in Rodmell*, ed. Susan Rowland (S. Rowland, 1994) [includes map, accounts of search for VW's body and of her funeral]; Vita Sackville-West, *Marian Stranways*, autograph manuscript, [1913].

Name of Collection: The British Library Manuscript Collections

Contact: Manuscripts and Maps Reference Team

Address: 96 Euston Road
London NW1 2DB
England

Telephone: 0207-412-7513
Fax: 0207-412-7745
Email: mss@bl.uk

Hours: Mon. 10 am-5 pm; Tues.-Sat.: 9:30 am-5 pm

Access Requirements: British Library Reader Pass (signed I.D. required and usually proof of post-graduate academic status, or other demonstrable need to use the collections—see www.bl.uk). In addition, access to most literary autograph material only available with letter of recommendation.

Restrictions: Paper Copies, Microfilms, and Photography of selected items available upon receipt of written authorization for photo duplication from the copyright holder.

Holdings Relevant To Woolf:	Diaries 1930-1931 (microfilm); *Mrs. Dalloway* and other writings (1923-1925) three volumes (Add MS 51044-51046); letter from Leonard Woolf to H. G. Wells (1941) (Add MS 52553); two letters from Virginia Woolf and three letters from Leonard Woolf to John Lehmann (1941) (Add MS 56234); letters from Virginia Woolf (1923-1927) and one written on behalf of Leonard Woolf to S. S. Koteliansky (1946) (Add MS 48974); notebook of Virginia Stephen (1906-1909) (Add MS 61837); Stephen family papers (Add MS 88954); travel and literary notebook of Virginia Woolf (Add MS 61837); A sketch of the past revised ts (1940) (Add MS 61973); letters from Virginia Woolf in the correspondence files of Lytton and James Strachey (Add MS 60655-60734); letter from Virginia Woolf to Mildred Massingberd (Add MS 61891); letter from Virginia Woolf to Harriet Shaw Weaver(1917) (Add MS 57353); (in the same volume as the letter on behalf of Leonard); letter from Virginia Woolf to Frances Cornford (1929) (Add MS 58422); letter from Virginia Woolf to Ernest Rhys (1930) (Egerton MS 3248); correspondence of Virginia Woolf in the Society of Authors archive (1934-1937) (Add MS 63206-63463); letter and postcard from Virginia Woolf to Bernard Shaw (1940) (Add MS 50522); three letters (suicide notes) from Virginia Woolf (1941) (Add MS 57947). "Hyde Park Gate News" 1891-1892, 1895 (Add. MSS 70725, 70726). Letters of Virginia and Leonard Woolf to Lady Aberconway, 1927-1941 (Add MS 70775). Letters from Virginia Woolf to Macmillan Co. 1903, 1908 (Add MS 54786-56035). Collection of RPs ("reserved photocopies"–copies of manuscripts exported, some subject to restrictions).
Name of Collection:	Harry Ransom Center
Contact:	Head, Research Services
Address:	Harry Ransom Center The University of Texas at Austin P.O. Box 7219 Austin, TX 78713-7219

Telephone:	512-471-9119
Fax:	512-471-2899
Email:	reference@hrc.utexas.edu
Hours:	See web site for most current information: www.hrc.utexas.edu
Access Requirements:	Completed online research application; current photo identification.
Holdings Relevant To Woolf:	The manuscript collection includes the typed manuscript with autograph revisions of *Kew Gardens*, and the typed manuscript and autograph revisions of "Thoughts on Peace in an Air Raid." The Center holds 571 of Woolf's letters, including correspondence to Elizabeth Bowen, Lady Ottoline Morrell, Mary Hutchinson, William Plomer, Hugh Walpole and others. Further mss. relating to Virginia Woolf include letters to her from T. S. Eliot and reviews of her work. A substantial collection of the first British and American editions of Woolf's published works, as well as 130 volumes from Leonard and Virginia Woolf's library and a collection of books published by the Hogarth Press, is also housed.
	An art collection holds a landscape painting of Virginia's garden and a series of Cockney cartoons in a sketch book, signed "V.W." The center also has extensive holdings of materials related to Leonard Woolf, Ottoline Morrell, Mary Hutchinson, Lytton Strachey, Dora Carrington, E. M. Forster, Clive Bell, Roger Fry, Vanessa Bell, Bertrand Russell, Elizabeth Bowen, William Plomer, Stephen Spender and Hugh Walpole.
Name of Collection:	Houghton Library (Monk's House Photograph Albums)
Contact:	Houghton Public Services
Address:	Harvard Yard Cambridge, MA 02138 United States

Telephone: 617-495-2440
Fax: 617-495-1376
Email: houghton_library@harvard.edu

URL: http://hcl.harvard.edu/libraries/houghton/

Hours: Mon, Fri, Sat 9-5
Tue-Thu 9-7

Access Requirements: http://hcl.harvard.edu/info/special_collections/index.cfm

The Monk's House photographs are restricted due to fragility. Users should consult the digital surrogates linked from the finding aids below. Access to originals requires permission from the curator of the Harvard Theatre Collection.

Holdings Relevant To Woolf: Virginia Woolf Monk's House photograph album, MH-1
Virginia Woolf Monk's House photograph album, MH-2
Virginia Woolf Monk's House photograph album, MH-3
Virginia Woolf Monk's House photograph album, MH-4
Virginia Woolf Monk's House photograph album, MH-5
Virginia Woolf Monk's House photograph album, MH-6
Virginia Woolf Monk's House photographs

Users can also page through the albums by following the links on this website (http://press.pace.edu/woolf-studies-annual-wsa/)

Name of Collection: The Lilly Library

Contact: Joel Silver, Director and Curator of Early Books and Manuscripts
Erika Dowell, Associate Director and Curator of Modern Books and Manuscripts

GUIDE TO SPECIAL LIBRARY COLLECTIONS 191

Address:	The Lilly Library, Indiana University 1200 East Seventh Street Bloomington, IN 47405-5500
Telephone:	812-855-2452
Fax:	812-855-3143
Email:	liblilly@indiana.edu, silverj@indiana.edu, edowell@indiana.edu
URL	https://iub.aeon.atlas-sys.com/ (for registration and requests)
Hours:	Mon.-Fri. 9 am-6 pm; Sat. 9 am-1 pm; *Closed Sundays and Major Holidays*
Acess Requirements:	Valid photo-identification; brief registration procedure.
Restrictions:	Closed stacks; material use confined to reading room; wheelchair-accessible reading room and exhibitions (but no wheelchair-accessible restroom).
Holdings Relevant To Woolf:	Corrected page proofs for the American edition of *Mrs. Dalloway*; letters to Woolf from Desmond and Mary (Molly) MacCarthy; 77 letters (published in *Letters*) from Woolf to correspondents including Donald Clifford Brace, Robert Gathorne-Hardy, Barbara (Strachey) Halpern, Richard Arthur Warren Hughes, Desmond MacCarthy and Molly MacCarthy; "Preliminary Scheme for the formation of a Partnership between Mr Leonard Sidney Woolf and Mr John Lehmann to take over The Hogarth Press" (includes contract signed by Lehmann, Leonard Woolf, and Virginia Woolf and receipt for Lehmann's payment to Virginia Woolf to purchase Virginia Woolf's share in the Hogarth Press); photographs of Virginia Woolf, Leonard Woolf, Lytton Strachey, Strachey family, Roger Fry, and Vanessa Bell (Hannah Whitall Smith mss.); (Richard) Kennedy mss. (four hand-colored lithographs of Virginia Woolf: artist's proofs for RK's portfolio, VIRGINIA WOOLF: "AS I KNEW HER"; Sackville-West, V. mss. (10,529 items: includes the correspondence of Vita Sack-

ville-West, and Harold Nicolson); MacCarthy mss. (ca. 10,000 items: papers of Desmond and Molly MacCarthy); correspondence between LW and Mary Gaither regarding publication of *A Checklist of the Hogarth Press* (1976, repr. 1986); Todd Avery, *Close and Affectionate Friends: Desmond and Molly MacCarthy and the Bloomsbury Group* (The Lilly Library/Indiana University Libraries, 1999).

Name of Collection: Literature & Rare Books, Special Collections, University of Maryland Libraries

Contact: Amber Kohl, Curator of Literature and Rare Books in Special Collections and University Archives

Address: University of Maryland
2208 Hornbake Library
College Park, MD 20742

Telephone: 310-405-9212
Email: askhornbake@umd.edu

Hours: Dates and hours of operation subject to change. Regular hours are Monday-Friday, 10 am to 5 pm. Extended hours are available on select days during the academic school year.
Email askhornbake@umd.edu before planning a research visit.

Access Requirements: Photo ID.

Holdings Relevant To Woolf: Papers of Hope Mirrlees contain five autograph letters and postcards (1919-1928) from Virginia Woolf to Mirrlees. Also in the collection are 113 letters from T. S. Eliot to Mirrlees, and three letters from Lady Ottoline Morrell to Mirrlees. A finding aid is available at http://hdl.handle.net/1903.1/1536.

Name of Collection: Monks House Papers/Leonard Woolf Papers/Charleston Papers/Nicolson Papers

Contact: University of Sussex, Special Collections

GUIDE TO SPECIAL LIBRARY COLLECTIONS 193

Address:	The Keep Woollards Way Brighton & Hove BN1 9PB
Telephone:	01273 482349
Email:	library.specialcoll@sussex.ac.uk
URL	http://www.thekeep.info
Access Requirements:	By appointment. Identification to be presented on arrival. Registration and material requests can be made through our website.
Restrictions:	Photocopying strictly controlled.
Holdings Relevant To Woolf:	The University of Sussex holds two large archives relating to Leonard and Virginia Woolf: The Monks House Papers, primarily correspondence and MSS of Virginia Woolf, including the three scrapbooks relating to *Three Guineas*, and Virginia Woolf's engagement diaries from 1930 to her death in 1941; and The Leonard Woolf Papers, primarily correspondence and other papers of Leonard Woolf. (Monks House Papers are available on microfilm in many research libraries.) The Charleston Papers consist in the main of letters written to or by Clive and Vanessa Bell and Duncan Grant which had accumulated in their home; the library houses Quentin Bell's photocopied set; letters from Roger Fry, Maynard Keynes, Lytton Strachey, Virginia Woolf, Vita Sackville-West, E. M. Forster, T. S. Eliot, Frances Partridge and others. The Maria Jackson letters comprise some 900 letters from Maria Jackson to Julia and Leslie Stephen. The Nicolson Papers complement these three Sussex archives relating to the Bloomsbury Group, and consist of Nigel Nicolson's correspondence relating to his editorial work as principal editor of the six-volume *Letters of Virginia Woolf,* published between 1975 and 1980.

The Bell Papers. A. O. Bell's correspondence relating to her editorial work on Virginia Woolf's diaries, a parallel collection to the Nicolson Papers. Collection level description may be accessed at www.archiveshub.ac.uk

Name of Collection: The Morgan Library & Museum

Contact: Reading Room

Address: 225 Madison Avenue
New York, NY 10016

Telephone: 212-590-0315
Email: readingroom@themorgan.org

URL: www.themorgan.org

Access Requirements: Admission to the Reading Room is by application and by appointment.
See www.themorgan. org/research/reading.asp for application form.

Recent Acquisition: Virginia Woolf. Typed letter signed, dated London to R. W. Chapman, 1930 November 13. 1 item (1 p.). Concerning revisions to the criticism section of a bibliography of Jane Austen. Accompanied by carbon copy of a letter from Chapman to Woolf dated 1930 November 11. MA 8893. Purchased on the Drue Heinz Fund, 2017.

Holdings Relevant To Woolf: Virginia Woolf. Autograph manuscript notebook, 1931 Sept. 24. 1 item (52 p.); 265 x 208 mm. Contains drafts of "A Letter to a Young Poet," a brief letter to the press entitled "The Villa Jones" [ff. 3-5] and a monologue by a working-class woman [ff. 44-46]. MA 3333. Purchased on the Fellows Fund with the special assistance of Anne S. Dayton, Enid A. Haupt, Mrs. James H. Ripley, Mr. and Mrs. August H. Schilling, and John S. Thacher,1979.

Virginia Woolf. Autograph letters signed (2) and typed letter signed, dated London [etc.], to E. McKnight Kauffer, 1931 Apr. 4-23, and undated. 3 items (4 p.). Concerning a drawing of her and a bibliography of her works. MA 1679. Purchased in 1959.

Vanessa Bell. 84 autograph letters, 3 typed letters, 7 postcards, and 3 telegrams. Most, but not all, are written by Vanessa Bell to John Maynard Keynes. Concerning Duncan Grant, Roger Fry, Clive Bell, the Bell children, Leonard and Virginia Woolf, Lytton Strachey, John Maynard and Lydia Lopokova Keynes, David Garnett, Ottoline Morrell, and others. MA 3448. Items in this collection are described in 97 individual records (MA 3448.1-97). Purchased on the Fellows Fund, special gift of the Gramercy Park Foundation (Mrs. Michael Tucker), 1980.

Name of Collection: Jane Marcus Collection

Contact: Mount Holyoke College Archives and Special Collections

Address: Mount Holyoke College
50 College Streeet
8 Dwight Hall
South Hadley MA 01075

Telephone: 413-538-3079
Fax: 413-538-3029
Email: archives@mtholyoke.edu

Hours: Monday-Friday; 9:30am-noon and 1-4:30pm

Access Requirements: Please contact the staff to make an appointment for your visit. Researchers complete a registration form upon arrival.

Restrictions: The Jane Marcus Collection was received in December 2016 and is currently being reviewed. Please contact the Archives and Special Collections staff for updated access information

Holdings Relevant To Woolf: Jane Marcus, who died in May 2015, laid the groundwork for feminist studies to become a mode of inquiry within the academy and her work established Virginia Woolf as a major canonical writer. The collection includes several of Marcus's unpublished manuscripts, as well as her research files and correspondence.

Name of Collection: 1. Katherine Mansfield Papers
2. Arts Club of Chicago Papers

Contact: Martha Briggs, Lloyd Lewis Curator of Modern Manuscripts
Liesl Olson, Director, Scholl Center for American History and Culture

Address: The Newberry Library, 60 West Walton Street, Chicago, IL, 60610

Telephone: 312-255-3554 (Briggs)
312-255-3665 (Olson)

Email: briggsm@newberry.org
olsonl@newberry.org

Hours: Tuesday-Friday: 9-5
Saturday: 9-1

Access Requirements: The Newberry's reading rooms are open to researchers who are at least 16 years old or juniors in high school. Before using the collections, all researchers must apply for and receive a reader's card. Issued in the Reference Center on the third floor, cards require a valid photo ID, proof of current home address, and a research interest that is supported by the Newberry's collections.

Holdings Relevant To Woolf: The papers of the Arts Club of Chicago—since 1916, a private club and preeminent exhibitor of international art—contain material related to Bloomsbury artists and how they were received in Chicago. The papers of Katherine Mansfield contain manuscript copies of some of Mansfield's most important work, and outgoing correspondence—the bulk to artist Dorothy Brett and Lady Ottoline Morrell. There are a few incoming

GUIDE TO SPECIAL LIBRARY COLLECTIONS

miscellaneous letters, printed works, photographs, and memorabilia.

Name of Collection: University of Reading Special Collections

Contact: Special Collections Service

Address: Special Collections Service
University of Reading
Redlands Road
Reading RG1 5EX

Telephone: 0118-378-8660
Fax: 0118-378-5632
Email: specialcollections@reading.ac.uk

URL: http://www.reading.ac.uk/special-collections/

Access Requirements: Prior appointment suggested to consult material. Permission required to consult or copy material in the Hogarth Press, Jonathan Cape, and Chatto & Windus collections from Random House:

Random House Group Archive & Library
1 Cole Street
Crown Park
Rushden
Northants. NN10 6RZ
rushdenqueries@randomhouse.co.uk

Holdings Relevant To Woolf: Hogarth Press (MS 2750): editorial and production correspondence relating to publications of the Press including Woolf's own titles. Production ledgers 1920s-1950s. Correspondence between Leonard Woolf and Stanley Unwin about progress with his collected edition of the works of Freud. Order books—e.g. lists of booksellers, book clubs, and how many books they have ordered for a particular title. Newscuttings—press clippings of advertisements for Hogarth Press books including Virginia Woolf publications. Correspondence files regarding translation rights of Virginia Woolf's publications, 1924-1983, (MS 2750/C).

Chatto & Windus (CW): small number of letters 1915-1925; 1929-1931.Various letters and notes by Leonard Woolf; outgoing letters to Leonard Woolf: 22 November 1927 (CW A/119); outgoing letters to Virginia Woolf: 29 January 1936 (CW A/172), 22 December 1931 (CW A/135), 31 December 1931 (CW A/135), 15 December 1920 (CW A/100), 20 December 1920 (CW A/100).
George Bell & Sons (MS 1640): 5 letters from Leonard Woolf 1930-1966.

Routledge (RKP): Reader's report by Leonard Woolf on George Padmore's "Britannia rules the blacks" (1935); "How Britain rules Africa." 1 letter from Leonard Woolf (June 1941) from Miscellaneous publishing correspondence 1941-1942 Wi-Wy RKP 174/15. Draft introduction by Leonard Woolf to *Letters on India* by Mulk Raj (1942) and 1 letter to Leonard Woolf from Mulk Raj Anand 1942-1943 RKP 178/3. Correspondence concerning the publication of *The War for Peace* by Leonard Woolf, 1939-1940 RKP 160/5. 1 letter from Virginia Woolf declining an invitation from Routledge to write a biography of Margaret Bondfield, 25 May 1940 RKP 160/5.

Megroz (MS 1979/68): 2 letters from Leonard Woolf, 1926.

Allen & Unwin (MS 3282): Correspondence with Leonard Woolf c.1914-1918 (re. his book *International Government*), 1923-1924; 1939-1940; 1943; 1946; 1950-1951; 1953; 1965 (concerning ill-founded rumors about the Hogarth Press); 1967 (concerning a reprint of *Empire and Commerce in Africa*).

Jonathan Cape (MS 2446): All correspondence from file JC A43. Correspondence between Jonathan Cape and Virginia Woolf and Cape and A. C. Gissing concerning Virginia Woolf's introduction to George Gissing's *Ionian Sea* to which A. C. Gissing objects. 1 postcard (1935), 1 letter (1933), 2 letters (1932) from Virginia Woolf. 1 letter

(1932) from Virginia Woolf declining to write an introduction to Jane Austen's *Northanger Abbey*. 4 letters (1931) from Virginia Woolf declining to write an introduction to one of Miss Thackeray's books.

Letters from Vanessa Bell: 1 letter from Bell CW 152/2; 1 letter from Bell CW 171/10; 2 letters from Bell CW 578/1; 1 letter from Bell CW 59/9; 1 letter from Bell (1936) CW 61/10. Artwork by Vanessa Bell for various Virginia Woolf titles.

Artwork by Angelica Garnett, Philippa Bramson and others for various books in the Chatto & Windus archive.

Name of Collection: Frances Hooper Collection of Virginia Woolf Books and Manuscripts.
Elizabeth Power Richardson Bloomsbury Iconography Collection.

Contact: Karen V. Kukil, Associate Curator of Special Collections.

Address: Mortimer Rare Book Collection
Young Library
4 Tyler Drive
Northampton, MA 01063

Telephone: 413-585-2908
Email: kkukil@smith.edu

URL: www.smith.edu/libraries/libs/specialcollections

Hours: Mon.-Fri. 10 am-5 pm

Access Restrictions: Appointment to be made with the Curator.

Holdings Relevant To Woolf: The Hooper Collection emphasizes Woolf as an essayist but also includes many Hogarth Press first editions, limited editions of Woolf's works, and translations. The collection includes page proofs of *Orlando*, *To the Lighthouse*, and *The Common Reader*, corrected by Woolf for the first

American editions, a proof copy of *The Waves* that Woolf inscribed to Hugh Walpole, and the proof copies of *The Years* and of *Flush*. The Collection also has one of the deluxe editions of *Orlando* that was printed on green paper. Other items include twenty-two pages of reading notes from 1926, three pages of notes on D. H. Lawrence's *Sons and Lovers*, thirty- three pages of notes for *Roger Fry*, a six-page ms. "As to criticism," a five-page ms. of "The Searchlight," and a fourteen-page ms. of "The Patron and The Crocus." The Hooper Collection also owns 140 letters between Woolf and Lytton Strachey as well as other correspondence, including a 13 February [1921] letter to Katherine Mansfield and ten letters to Mela and Robert Spira.

The Richardson Collection is a working collection of books and materials used by Richardson in preparing her *Bloomsbury Iconography*. It includes Leslie Stephen's photograph album, ninety-eight original exhibition catalogs dating back to 1929, clippings and photocopies of such items as reviews of early Woolf works, and Bloomsbury material from British *Vogue* of the 1920s. The Collection also has three preliminary pencil drawings by Vanessa Bell for *Flush*.

The Mortimer Rare Book Collection also owns Woolf's 1916 Italian ms. notebook and her corrected typescripts of "Reviewing" and "The Searchlight." In addition, there is a 1923 photograph of Woolf at Garsington. Original cover designs for Hogarth Press publications include *The Common Reader, On Being Ill*, and *Duncan Grant*. The Mortimer Rare Book Room also has a Sylvia Plath collection that includes eight of Woolf's books from Plath's library, several of which are underlined and annotated, as well as Plath's notes from her undergraduate English 211 class at Smith (1951-1952) in which she studied *To the Lighthouse*. The collection also includes Woolf's 26 February 1939 letter to Vita Sackville-West, a 1931 bronze bust of Virginia Woolf by Stephen Tomlin, a 1923 Hogarth Press edition of T. S. Eliot's *The Waste Land*, a 1919 Hogarth Press edition of *Paris* by Hope Mirrlees and first editions of Vita Sackville-West and Katherine Mansfield publications. Additional Bloomsbury items include *Original Woodcuts* (Omega Workshops, 1918), Vanessa Bell's original woodcut for the cover of *Monday or Tuesday* (1921), and exhibition catalogs for *Manet and the Post-Impressionists* (Grafton Galleries, 1911), *Friday Club Members* (Mansard Gallery, 1921) *Paintings and Drawings by Vanessa Bell* (Independent Gallery, 1922). Additional photographs include the Mary L. S. Bennett (née Fisher) Family Photographs. A recent gift of the Henrietta Worth Bingham Papers (1905-1968) includes her correspondence with Stephen Tomlin and John Houseman, photographs, ephemera, books and research files. Online exhibitions are available on the Mortimer Rare Book Room's website.

Name of Collection: Woolf/Hogarth Press/Bloomsbury

Contact: Lisa J. Sherlock

Address: Victoria University Library
71 Queens Park Crescent E.
Toronto M5S 1K7
Ontario Canada

Email: victoria.library@utoronto.ca

URL: http://library.vicu.utoronto.ca/special/bloomsbury.htm

Hours: Mon.-Fri. 9 am-5 pm

Access Requirements: Prior notification; identification.

Restrictions: Limited photocopying.

Holdings Relevant To Woolf: This collection, the most comprehensive of its kind with nearly 5,700 items, contains all the work of Virginia and Leonard Woolf in various editions, issues, variants and translations; all the books hand-printed by Leonard and Virginia

Woolf at the Hogarth Press, including many variant issues and bindings, association copies and page proofs; a nearly comprehensive collection of Hogarth Press machine printed books to 1946 (the year Leonard Woolf and the Press joined Chatto & Windus) including presentation copies, signed limited editions, page proofs, variants as well as substantial amounts of ephemera, such as the Catalogue of Publications to 1939 with annotations by Leonard Woolf. The collection is also very strong in Bloomsbury Art and Artists, especially the decorative arts, including important examples of Omega Workshops publications and exhibition catalogues. Materials include the catalogue of the second post-impressionist exhibition, 1912; catalogues relating to Vanessa Bell and Duncan Grant exhibitions; bronze medal of Virginia Woolf by Marta Firlet; oil on canvas portrait of Amaryllis Garnett by Vanessa Bell (c.1958); Portrait sketch of Leonard Woolf by Vanessa Bell; portrait of Leonard Woolf by Duncan Grant; Duncan Grant and Vanessa Bell designed Clarice Cliff dinner plates; original Vanessa Bell and Duncan Grant sketches and designs for dust jackets, novels, and other special projects; Duncan Grant charcoal portrait of Virginia Woolf (1968); Quentin Bell set of five pottery plates based on the novels of Virginia Woolf (ca. 1979); Quentin Bell pottery figurine in aid of Charleston (ca. 1980); a selection of other pottery by Quentin Bell; bronze busts of Lytton Strachey and Virginia Woolf by Stephen Tomlin (1901-1937); as well as the Marcel Gimond bust of Vanessa Bell and the Tomlin bust of Henrietta Bingham. Book hand bound by Virginia Woolf. Wooden plaque from the Hogarth Press at 24 Tavistock. Examples of programmes, posters, and handbills relating to productions of plays, movies, and dance productions with content relating to Bloomsbury group members. Original correspondence and mss. material includes that by Vanessa Bell; Leonard Woolf; Ritchie family re: Anne Thackeray Ritchie/Stephen family; Duncan Grant; Quentin Bell; S. P. Rosenbaum mss. Letters from E. M. Forster, Bertrand Russell, James Strachey,

Raymond Mortimer, David Garnett, Nigel Nicolson and others in the Bloomsbury Circle; as well as biographers, scholars and bibliographers such as Joanne Trautmann, Carolyn Heilbrun, J. Howard Woolmer, Leon Edel, Leila Luedeking, P. N. Furbank, Noel Annan and others. Large Ephemera Collection includes items revealing Virginia Woolf's effect on popular culture.

Name of Collection: Library of Leonard and Virginia Woolf (Washington State University)

Contact: Trevor James Bond
Head, Manuscripts, Archives, and Special Collections

Address: Washington State University Libraries
Pullman, WA 99164-5610

Email: tjbond@wsu.edu

URL: www.wsulibs.wsu.edu/holland/masc/masc.htm

Hours: Mon.-Fri. 8:30 am-4:30 pm

Access Requirements: Letter stating nature of research preferred; student or other identification.

Restrictions: Materials must be used in the MASC area under supervision. Photocopying or photographing is permitted only when it will not harm the materials and is permitted by copyright.

Recent Aquisitions: Correspondence to Clive and Vanessa Bell (approximately 30 items), with most items addressed to Clive. Correspondents include Stephen Tallant, Eric MacLagan, John Pollock, H. J. Norton, Lyn Irvine (including one letter mentioning Mrs. Raven Hill), Sir George Grahame, Karen Costelloe, John Alford, Ivor Churchill, the Earl of Sandwich, George Lansbury, Clifford Sharp, F. H. S. Shepherd, Gilbert Seldes, Lord Evan Tredegar, C. E. Stuart, Max Eastman, E. Hilton Young, Col. Heward Bell.

Holdings Relevant To Woolf WSU has the Woolfs' basic working library including many works which belonged to Woolf's father, Sir Leslie Stephen, and other family members. Over 800 titles came from their Sussex home, Monks House, including some works bought at auction soon after Leonard Woolf died in 1969. Later additions include: 1,875 titles from his house in Victoria Square, London; 400 titles from his nephew Cecil Woolf; and over 60 titles from Quentin and Anne Olivier Bell. WSU has been actively collecting: all works in all editions by Virginia Woolf; all titles by Leonard Woolf; dust jackets; works published by the Woolfs at the Hogarth Press through 1946; books by their friends and associates, especially those by Bloomsbury authors and about Bloomsbury artists; relevant correspondence and original works of art. Original artwork by Vanessa Bell; scattered letters by Vanessa Bell, E. M. Forster, Roger Fry, Leslie Stephen, Lytton Strachey, and Leonard Woolf. Original artwork by Richard Kennedy for illustrations in his book *A Boy at the Hogarth Press*; scattered letters by Roger Fry, Leslie Stephen, Ethel Smyth, and Leonard Woolf. Virginia Woolf's initialed copy of *Cornishiana*; Leonard Woolf's annotated copy of *An Anatomy of Poetry* by A. Williams-Ellis; Leslie Stephen's copy of *Lapsus Calami and Other Verses*, inscribed by James Kenneth Stephen. Several letters from Virginia Woolf, including two written in 1939 to Ronald Heffer, and a letter to Edward McKnight Kauffer. New in the Hogarth Press Collection are a copy of E. M. Forster's *Anonymity, an Enquiry*, bound in cream paper boards, and what Woolmer calls the third label state of Forster's *The Story of the Siren*. The Library of Leonard and Virginia Woolf is once again shelved separately so that scholars visiting Pullman may see the collection apart from the other rare book collections.

Name of Collection: Yale Center for British Art

Contact: Elisabeth Fairman, Senior Curator of Rare Books and Manuscripts

Address:	1080 Chapel Street P.O. Box 208280 New Haven, CT 06520-8280
Telephone:	elisabeth.fairman@yale.edu
Fax:	203-432-2814
Email:	203-432-2814
URL:	https://britishart.yale.edu/visit
Hours:	Tue.-Fri. 10 am-4:30 pm
Access Requirements:	Permission needed in order to reproduce.
Holdings Relevant To Woolf	Rare Books & Mss Department: 94 letters from Vanessa Bell and Duncan Grant to Sir Kenneth Clark; Prints & Drawings Department: 4 drawings by Vanessa Bell; 4 drawings by Duncan Grant; 6 drawings by Wyndham Lewis; 1 drawing by Frederick Etchells; Paintings Department: 1 painting by Vanessa Bell, 4 paintings by Duncan Grant (including portrait of Vanessa Bell); 3 paintings by Roger Fry. 6 letters from Lytton Strachey (to Clive Bell, Siegfried Sassoon, et al.).

Reviews

Tense Future: Modernism, Total War, Encyclopedic Form. Paul K. Saint-Amour (Oxford: Oxford UP, 2015) xiii + 347pp.

Writing Against War: Literature, Activism, and the British Peace Movement. Charles Andrews (Evanston, IL: Northwestern UP, 2017) xii + 236pp.

It is rare that I read a book of literary criticism like a work of fiction: compelled to keep turning pages, unable to break away from the narrative force or engaging style long after the time for reading has ended. But such was my experience while reading Paul K. Saint-Amour's *Tense Future* (2015): I found myself captivated, rapt in a way usually reserved for fiction. *Tense Future*, awarded the Modernist Studies Association Book Prize and the Modern Language Association's first annual Matei Calinescu Prize, promised a robust reading experience but Saint-Amour exceeded my expectations with his wide-reaching and engaging analysis of "the relationship between warfare and futurity" (7). And yet, what could easily be heavy and cumbersome—total war and encyclopedic form—is proffered with such precision that the breadth and density of the analysis does not weigh down but rather fuels the reader, propelling her forward while demanding she attend keenly to the future imagined by the past. For that is Saint-Amour's subject in *Tense Future*: the past's understanding of its potential futures, bombed, war-torn, anxiety-ridden, or, at the least, shaped and saturated by the aftereffects of total war and the suspenseful anticipation of its return.

Evoking Walter Benjamin's ninth thesis from "On the Concept of History," Saint-Amour reframes the infamous angel of history in a manner that represents the project of *Tense Future*:

> And what if some of the most trenchant critiques of violence we possess were mounted by those faced with a future they believed already lost to violence? In response, the angel of history would need, while facing the past, to bear witness to the past apprehensions of the *future* as the disaster or the storm oncoming. This angel would be willing to look over the cold shoulder it gives to futurity, not to gaze in fealty at history's triumphant consummation but in the effort to catch the dissident glimpses of the future—as otherwise, as retrograde, as null—that have since been consumed by progress. (23)

In *Tense Future*, Saint-Amour assumes the positionality of this angel, "bear[ing] witness to the past apprehensions of the *future*" and in so doing, he offers modernist scholars a new framework for reading the interwar and its literature.

By leveraging what Saint-Amour calls critical futurities—"scholarship that takes as its object past and present conscriptions of 'the future'" (24)—he reimagines the interwar years, an especially important project for those who locate modernism's apex at 1922. Complicating the commonplace understanding of the interwar as a retrospective description mapped onto a period that during its unfolding was only postwar—"read[ing] the middle by the back light of its terminus" (34)—Saint-Amour contends that many conceived of the immediate postwar years as an interval between what was then the Great War and its anticipated sequel, even if the form its sequel would take on was still uncertain. Since the 1930s are already understood as a decade of increased anxiety about and mounting fear of a return to war, *Tense Future*'s most significant contribution to modernist studies is through its attention to the years most closely associated with high modernism, providing scholars of the interwar a way to read canonical modernist novels like *Mrs. Dalloway* and *Ulysses* as products of a war-wearied present that imagines its future as one already damaged, if not foreclosed, by the violence of total war. "What would happen," Saint-Amour inquires, "if we were to transperiodize the interwar condition forward, conceiving of it as interrupted rather than ended by the beginning of the Second World War?" (37). One thing that becomes strikingly clear: interwar modernism has much in common with future-obsessed fiction written during the Cold War. In other words, by refusing to confine war to "an event that either is or is not happening within a global frame" (37), the twentieth century is reimagined, not as modular periods of relative peace flanking finite episodes of war, but rather as the continuous duration of interwar occasionally interrupted by an always anticipated and ever memorialized war. As Saint-Amour provocatively queries, "What would it mean to stop waging interwar?" (37).

There is an important caveat to Saint-Amour's argument that must be addressed. Although he does examine canonical novels—as well as other literature unequivocally not modernist—he "does not advance a wholesale redefinition of modernism in relation to total war, traumatizing anticipation, or encyclopedic form" (38). Rather, modernism for Saint-Amour is associative, probabilistic, and connotative, functioning locally and provisionally throughout *Tense Future* (38). In this manner, *Tense Future* emerges as an exemplary text for understanding the efficacy of weak theory. As Saint-Amour explains, unlike strong theory which proffers a totalizing view of modernism, rejecting the possible in favor of surety and completeness, "weak theory tries to see just a little way ahead, behind, and to the sides, conceiving even of its field in partial and provisional terms that will neither impede, not yet shatter upon, the arrival of the unforeseen" (40). The weakening of the theory of modernism compels scholars to eschew definitional approaches and embrace "uses, models, questions, temperaments, and possible typologies" (41).

As its weak theory approach suggests, *Tense Future*'s bibliography is deep and its scope wide. Saint-Amour's argument touches on aspects of modernism and interwar writing as diverse as the archive, the epic, and encyclopedic form while also reaching forward into modernism's Cold War future. But of particular interest to Woolf scholars is his chapter "Perpetual Suspense: Virginia Woolf's Wartime Gothic." Saint-Amour encourages readers to attend to both the "radiant moment of presence" and the "rending moment of disaster" that Woolf's fiction highlights (92). Unlike Woolf scholarship that privileges the "luminous halo" of the present moment, to adapt a phrase from "Modern Fiction," *Tense Future* identifies and examines the sense in Woolf's fiction "that something terrible, even annihilating, is at hand" (93). Through this framework, Saint-Amour reads *Mrs. Dalloway* not as a novel reaching towards what it beholds as a possible future, but rather as a narrative seized, haunted by past shocks and the potential of future disasters (93). In this manner, Saint-Amour perceives Woolf's writing as cultivating an ethics of "perpetual suspense" that positions her novels as a "kind of second-generation sensation fiction…adapt[ing] the late gothic to the civilian's experience of world war" (96-97).

Beginning with "A Mark on the Wall," what emerges is an "air raid archipelago," tracing a path through scenes that explicitly and implicitly explore the experience of city-dwelling civilians in an age marked by the upturned gaze indicative of an emerging airmindedness (103). Of course, airmindedness—a phrase for which Valentine Cunningham credits Elizabeth Bowen (*British Writers of the Thirties* 167)—is more than the cultural obsession with new forms of air travel; after the German Gotha raids on England beginning in 1915, airmindedness carried with it the stress and apprehension of possible destruction. For Saint-Amour, this attention to the skies fueled not only awe and curiosity—what exactly is the skywriting airplane in *Mrs. Dalloway* penning in the sky?—but also fear and vulnerability—"The world has raised its whip; where will it descend?" (*MD* 14). The chapter thus brings a nuanced perspective to oft-cited scenes from Woolf's writing. *Mrs. Dalloway*, *The Years*, and "Thoughts on Peace in an Air Raid" constitute Saint-Amour's air raid archipelago through which he reads Woolf's pacifism as inseparable from the discourse of total war thus challenging Alex Zwerdling's claim that Woolf's pacifism constituted an "'involuntary revulsion for the whole business'" (qtd. in Saint-Amour 97). Rather, *Tense Future* reveals Woolf's deep engagement with the discourse of total war, thus undercutting her well known declaration that "We are all C.O.'s in the Great War" (qtd. in Saint-Amour 97). Instead of assuming the role of the objector, Saint-Amour argues, Woolf "asked what could be seen anew from inside the logic of total war" (98). In other words, Woolf's pacifism leveraged the discourse and doctrine of total war—its rhetoric, temporality, form, and vocabulary—as her vehicles for thinking through and beyond total war. Woolf, thus, hones her pacifist gender politics, on display most fully in *Three Guineas*. Instead of perceiving the male soldier and the female civilian as "opposed by nature and law," Woolf, according to Saint-Amour, is able to present them as "intimately connected through social webs, structures of feelings, and their shared legitimation by a reproductive view of a national future" (98).

Charles Andrews's monograph, *Writing Against War: Literature, Activism, and the British Peace Movement*, joins the scholarly conversation currently oriented by *Tense Future* with an engaging examination of the 1930s peace movement focusing particularly on experimental writing by a diverse set of authors including Aldous Huxley, Storm Jameson, Siegfried Sassoon, Rose Macaulay, and Virginia Woolf. As such a line up suggests, Andrews's book exists at the intersection of scholarship on 1930s literary modernism and pacifism in the British peace movement. Rather than pushing against the parameters of either 1930s literature or modernism—since both are often employed simultaneously as period designations and aesthetic programs— Andrews leverages their overlapping contexts in order to paint a complex portrait of interwar pacifism during the decade leading up to the Second World War. In order to do this successfully, Andrews first attends to the slipperiness of one of his main concepts: pacifism. I found this brief introductory discussion extremely productive as it helped illuminate a central tenet of *Writing Against War*: that pacifism is "more capacious and varied than is often supposed" (7).

In fact, if Andrews's argument across all five chapters has one thing in common, it is the commitment to challenging the overarching simplification that has commonly attended pacifist literature—and, by extension, the commonplace reduction of 1930s literature and modernism to flimsy, one-dimensional constructions that do not account for the way politically-engaged, experimental, pacifist writing emerged within their concomitant cultures. By "showing how literary works engage with matters of peacemaking and conflict resolution apart from explicit representations of violence"—or, for that matter, explicit representations of peace—Andrews offers scholars of peace studies, war writing, 1930s literature, and modernism ways of reading that counter the tendency to divide literature written in the decade before the Second World War into categories such as war, pacifist, modernist, or 1930s writing. And by foregrounding the British peace movement broadly, and the Peace Pledge Union particularly, *Against War* "reframes the notion of 'failure'" so often associated with pacifist writing and privileges the "long view" on peace activism, opening up the canon of pacifist writing to works by modernists, veterans, and activists. Consequently, *Against War* is poised to be useful to many scholars in modernist studies and beyond.

Of special interest to *Woolf Studies Annual* readers is Andrews's chapter, "Thinking as Fighting in Virginia Woolf's *The Years* and *Three Guineas*." The beginning of this chapter rehearses the evolution of Woolf's image from E. M. Forster's "the Invalid Lady of Bloomsbury" to Jane Marcus's portrayal of Woolf as an activist on the page (155), as well as her more explicit intellectual engagement with politics in the last decade of her life. Andrews highlights the political activism

Woolf engaged in through her lectures—about which she was often ambivalent—and the Hogarth Press. Taking the Peace Pledge Union as an example, central throughout *Against War*, Andrews illustrates Woolf's *proximity to*, as opposed to her involvement in, pacifist and anti-war politicking. And it is this "'of but not in'" positionality that motivates Andrews's readings of *The Years* and *Three Guineas*, which occupy the last third of the chapter.

Against War offers Woolf scholars a compelling reading of her nuanced political position that does not lean heavily on her declaration in *Three Guineas* that as a woman she has no country. Woolf did emphasize her outsider position, of course, in gender and also by way of her refusal to join political societies whose activist strategies require complicity with patriarchal ideologies. But Woolf was also deeply engaged in the political unfoldings of her time, as scholars have meticulously documented—and on this score, Andrews's chapter does not add anything particularly new to the conversation. Rather, the strength of Andrews's examination exists in the way he situates Woolf vis-à-vis the broader peace movement and diverse pacifist writers. In fact, the majority of the chapter is dedicated to this rich contexualization and Andrews's readings of *The Years* and *Three Guineas* productively employ context as a framework of analysis enriching the close readings of relevant and frequently studied passages. In this manner, *Against War* makes a compelling argument for reading Woolf's 1930s writing as demonstrating "literary peace witness," as opposed being a straightforward example of pacifist writing. As Andrews concludes, "As long as we remain fixated on whether Woolf *was* or *was not* a pacifist at the end of her life, we will reproduce the pacifism/antipacifism binary that plagues so many attempts to examine peace activism" (190). Ending, as most studies of Woolf's relationship to war do, with "Thoughts on Peace in an Air Raid," Andrews refuses to celebrate Woolf exclusively as a pacifist writer whose anti-violence and anti-war commitment earned her a place in his study. Rather, he chooses to address her legacy as it is represented by the memorials that populate Bloomsbury near Woolf's Tavistock Square home: the bust of Woolf erected by the Virginia Woolf Society of Great Britain stands in proximity to a statue of Ghandi, a cherry tree honoring the victims of Hiroshima, and an inscribed stone dedicated to conscientious objectors, and although her memorial "says nothing about peace activism," it "places her as a pacifist outsider working alongside the British peace movement" (193).

—Erica Gene Delsandro, *Bucknell University*

Works Cited

Cunningham, Valentine. *British Writers of the Thirties*. Oxford University Press, 1988.

At the Mercy of Their Clothes:
Modernism, the Middlebrow, and British Garment Culture.
Celia Marshik (New York: Columbia UP, 2016): xiii + 247pp.

Garments, writes Celia Marshik in her latest monograph, can "surprise, delight, or torment" (65). And torment they do. As she argues in *At the Mercy of Their Clothes: Modernism, the Middlebrow, and British Garment Culture*, garments assume surprising and sometimes troubling agency, becoming not only animate but aggressive. The book's title, which she adopts from the caption of a 1929 sketch in *Punch*, suggests the complex ways in which a garment—in this instance, an unruly evening gown—might "impinge and impose on its wearer" (25).

As each chapter demonstrates, wearers and their clothing "work in concert but seldom in harmony" (25). The evening gown diminishes a woman's subjectivity; the mackintosh levels and effaces, eroding individual identities into nameless casualties; fancy-dress costumes promise transformation, but reliably (and often brutally) break these promises; and secondhand clothing distributes and dilutes the subjectivity of its owners. These case studies comprise a fascinating and useful addition to accounts of fashion, material culture, and modernist studies by the likes of Jane Garrity, Elizabeth Outka, Jessica Burstein, and Ilya Parkins. In building her critical framework, Marshik pays tribute to key voices in the field of thing theory, namely Barbara Johnson, Bruno Latour, Alfred Gell, and Bill Brown. But where these writers tend to focus on "mechanical or technical objects that malfunction," Marshik attends instead to "soft technologies" that threaten their wearer even as they do not necessarily malfunction; indeed, they are often "perfectly functional at the very moment that texts represent them as most threatening" (13).

The book's structure is at once inviting and pragmatic: early chapters focus on singular garments, the evening gown and mackintosh, while later chapters turn to types and trends, namely fancy dress and secondhand clothing. In this respect, the book seems to widen in scope with each successive case study. Throughout, Marshik's focus is primarily British, with an archive that ranges from James Joyce and Jean Rhys to Dorothy Sayers and Daphne du Maurier. In each chapter, and for each type of garment, Marshik reads canonical works of high modernism alongside their middlebrow relations—from dress histories and *Punch* cartoons to biograph films and fashion periodicals. Such an approach, she explains, is essential: "we cannot understand the dynamic relation between clothing worn on the street and that figured in literature by looking to high modernism alone" (5). As a result, each chapter is richly varied in its array of primary sources, and peppered with lively and engaging visuals: photographs, cartoons, advertisements, posters, and portraits. In keeping with these aims, the book scales up and down the socioeconomic ladder, with two chapters focused on especially moneyed fashions (evening gowns and fancy dress) and two more that highlight the effects of thrift and frugality on fashion (the mackintosh and secondhand clothing).

Throughout, Woolf takes center stage. In fact, the book opens with the "all-but-unloved and -unlovable" Doris Kilman of *Mrs. Dalloway*, whose garments betray particular clues about her class and gender identity (1). Woolfians will appreciate Marshik's careful and capacious attention to Woolf's fiction—*Jacob's Room*, "The New Dress," *Mrs. Dalloway*, and *Orlando*—as well as diaries, letters, and even anecdotes about Bloomsbury larks. In writings by Woolf as well as her contemporaries, garments test and often thwart negotiations with self and self-fashioning. Marshik's readings uncover a pattern of "characters who are confused and shamed by selves that do not measure up to a coherent ideal" (17). Writers, of course, tend to fix on moments of delicious disgrace or single out sartorial miscalculations. And Woolf, as her readers well know, is particularly attuned but also sympathetic to the gauche, gawky, and graceless.

Chapter One addresses the evening gown, a lingering vestige of courtship rituals that allowed writers to examine the tense dynamics between women and their object worlds—in many cases, "explor[ing] the way in which women, too, are objects" (28). The evening gown, unusually resistant to mass reproduction, remained a singular form in the early twentieth century, one that "served to synthesize superior having and being" even as other clothing styles had become cheaper and more widely available (30). Modernists, Marshik explains, are particularly attuned to the evening gown's emotional pull—attentive to the "intense longing" and "profound yearning" entangled in such garments (27).

Woolfians will appreciate this chapter's account of young Virginia Stephen's skirmishes with evening dress. In reading Woolf's memoirs for clues about these debacles, Marshik takes care in navigating between the writer's past and present selves, noting that "we should not let the trajectory of Virginia Woolf's life obscure Virginia Stephen's sartorial mortification" (47). The mortifications of dress are nowhere more excruciating than in Woolf's "The New Dress," or in accounts of Lady Ottoline Morrell, whose attire was cruelly caricatured in the era's *romans à clef*. With each of these examples, Marshik demonstrates how garments can "express a form of material agency that diminishes human fantasies of power and control" (63).

In Chapter Two, readers will be happy to discover that Marshik has expanded the reach of her 2012 article "The Modern(ist) Mackintosh," a staple and well-loved piece of scholarship in modernist studies. The mackintosh, which she traces across a wide range of novels aimed at different audiences, persistently effaces individuality and "cloaks the unscrupulous, deadly, and cruel" (68). Particularly during and after World War I, argues Marshik, the mac transforms men and women into masses "where they were dismissed, disparaged, and killed in numbers"—a pattern that "testif[ies] to the fragility of human bodies, which moved (and continue to move) through an object world seemingly only partially of their, and our, own making" (101).

Especially illuminating is the third chapter's account of fancy-dress costumes of the upper and middle classes—or what Marshik describes as the "supreme sartorial form for projecting an idealized self" (105). But, as this chapter demonstrates persuasively, such an ideal seldom prevails. Wearers of fancy dress, seduced by promises of transformation, tend to find themselves disappointed, even shamed, by the results. This chapter's attention to *Orlando* may prove particularly useful for readers of Woolf. Here, Marshik surveys the various selves adopted and assembled by Orlando, from reader and gardener to nobleman, concluding that "Orlando's clothes, like fancy dress, do not disguise; they multiply possibilities and suggest that one *is* in part what one wears" (134-35).

The book's fourth and final chapter explores secondhand clothing in light of changing class strata, specifically the emergence of the "new poor," a population struggling to shore up uncertain class identifications in the wake of World War I. Selling one's clothes (and the private information encoded therein) seemed akin to dispossessing or distributing oneself, a consequence that would prove popular fodder for modernist and middlebrow fiction. In a brief coda, Marshik concludes her argument with the advent of World War II. "The war changed all," she writes. As the economy transformed, entire genres faded; fancy dress, for instance, "became an artifact of prewar life" (178). In its place emerged popular campaigns such as Make-Do-and-Mend, which framed conservation, preservation, and economy as national and cultural values.

At the Mercy of Their Clothes sheds light on the vexed relationships between garments and their wearers in the early twentieth century, and each chapter is engaging as well as versatile in its attention to modernist and middlebrow voices. Throughout, Marshik's research is thorough and absorbing, and her argument persuasive. But most compelling is the undercurrent of unease and disquiet that she uncovers, or to borrow her words once more, "a profound anxiety about the elision of subjects and objects—the ability of particular things to transform humans into passive matter" (181). Garments have indeed promised to transform lives and worlds, and in breaking these promises, they have shown little mercy.

—Emily James, *University of St. Thomas*

Modernism, Fashion, and Interwar Women Writers. Vike Martina Plock (Edinburgh: Edinburgh UP, 2017) vii + 246pp.

With the material turn in modernist studies, new work on the role of garments, clothing, and fashion is finding solid ground in discourses about identity, self-styling, and celebrity for women writers. The work of scholars such as Caroline Evans, Celia Marshik, Ilya Parkins, and Elizabeth Sheehan has recast fashion as a serious area of inquiry through their readings of sartorial codes and expectations in interwar literature. Now, we can add Vike Martina Plock's *Modernism, Fashion and Interwar Women Writers,* an engaging contribution, to both fashion and Woolf studies.

Plock's chapters on Edith Wharton, Jean Rhys, Rosamond Lehmann, Elizabeth Bowen, and Virginia Woolf address their relationship to fashion, the marketplace, and questions of dress. As a whole, her case studies possess a through-line rooted in the contradiction between originality of expression (differentiation) and acceptance into a community (assimilation). Plock's writers are aware of finding the balance between being too conspicuous and being swallowed up by the masses. These writers grapple with the complexity of determining a public identity through conscientious clothing choices, what Woolf termed "frock consciousness," while also maintaining a personal integrity about their work. Thus, Plock frames her discussion about fashion within the parameters of celebrity culture and publishing demands, showing how five writers "developed their novels and authorial personas in response to contemporary market demands" (2). During the interwar period, Plock observes, the marketing of books took a page from Hollywood and began to depend more on the image of the writer than the content of the pages. Thus, for women writers, in more problematic ways than their male contemporaries, the reception of their work was often dependent on what they looked like, how they dressed, and how they performed in public spaces.

Plock shows how each of these women writers incorporated the "feminine pursuit" of fashion choices into the serious work of literary production (16). It should be noted that fashion has historically been gendered a feminine pursuit, despite the reality that until the mid-century, more men than women filled the roles of *haute couture* fashion design and production, and while Plock does not enter into this historical terrain too deeply and at no detriment to her argument, it contributes to the sartorial problems her chosen writers face. By beginning with Edith Wharton, not typically included in studies of interwar literary culture, Plock is able to establish her as an early commentator on the tensions between economics and artistic production that later became central to modernism. While Wharton scholars have addressed dress, design, and garments in her life and fiction, Plock sets her study apart by reading Wharton's concerns about fashion as a way to challenge existing discussions about her "antagonistic relationship with literary modernism" (41).

Wharton saw mass-produced fashion as aligned with mass book production where marketing and celebrity image became more powerful forces on cultural economies than the individual's discerning artistic taste for good writing. Plock argues that Wharton saw fashion as a "destructive dynamic" that "unsettled the relationship between...deep-seated beauty and cheap originality" (47). The Wharton chapter introduces anxieties about uniformity and loss of individual expression that become central to the Woolf chapter that closes Plock's book, wherein uniformity is linked to fascist ideology, a more severe consequence.

The chapters on Jean Rhys and Rosamond Lehmann are complementary to each other as they focus on each writer's critique of modern fashion and the way that fashion shapes their own self-styling as successful, young, modern writers during the twenties. For Rhys, the experience of constructing herself as a writer is tinged with some darkness which filters into her characters, who are often lonely, without stable finances, and worried about appearances. Plock traces Rhys's critique of the fantasy the fashion industry produces and its tie to economic self-sufficiency through much of her Left Bank fiction. Rhys had a troubled experience with the literary marketplace, Plock contends, due to her idiosyncratic life and writing, which could not be turned into a "commercially viable fashion" until interest in postcolonial themes made *Wide Sargasso Sea* a success (77). This, of course, was well after most of Rhys's peers thought she had died in obscurity, confirming for Plock, that she was never really an accepted part of the fashionable café crowd that we associate with the moderns in Paris during the interwar years.

Like Rhys, Lehmann prioritizes women's professional and personal attempts at self-fashioning and the challenges they face. For Lehmann, assimilating into the literary marketplace meant attempting to align her work with highbrow women writers, a challenge to the prevailing consensus that she wrote specifically for readers with "middlebrow tastes and horizons" (113). By calling Lehmann's style "modish modernism," Plock positions Lehmann in an interesting space between highbrow and middlebrow literary production, which productively destabilizes the way that we look at writing by women and for women. In a sustained reading of *Invitation to the Waltz*, Plock makes an intriguing claim that the novel's "reverential imitation" of Woolf's *To the Lighthouse* shows Lehmann's concern with building relationships and community with other women writers (112). According to Plock, Woolf was an important role model for Lehmann. Plock describes some of the correspondence and interaction between the two women to develop her later reading of Woolf's thoughts on how to appeal to wider audiences and the complications of mainstream publishing.

The chapter devoted to Elizabeth Bowen, (a writer also inspired, mentored, and befriended by Woolf), argues that she carefully fashioned and then used her position as a serious writer to critique the trends and whims of mass literary production. In Bowen's novels, fashion's objects become central characters with just as much or more agency than the humans who wear them. The chapter's central text is *To the North*, which was courted and published by Victor Gollancz, thereby cementing Bowen's reputation as a serious and important writer. While Plock abandons to some degree the discussions about author image and celebrity that were prominent in earlier chapters, she focuses interestingly on Bowen's resistance to industry pressures of writing quickly and dwells on her fastidious and methodical craft. Bowen returns in Plock's concluding chapter, which further develops how fashion served as a vital creative force for both her writing and her long and full life.

The book's final case study on Virginia Woolf focuses on Woolf's thinking about uniforms, an increasingly common sight in the late 1930s, and her attitudes about uniformity in book publishing. With the rise of the British Union of Fascists (BUF)—the party led by Sir Oswald Mosley whose members were identifiable by their black uniforms (the Blackshirts)—uniformity in dress signaled more than a loss of individuality, but a dangerous kind of collectivity that sought to eradicate the individual entirely. Evidenced by an extensive collection of clippings she gathered in preparation for writing *Three Guineas* and *The Years,* Woolf was making observations and asking questions about this shift toward uniforms for daily dress in England and Germany. Plock offers a significant contribution in this chapter to discussions of Woolf's use of fashion as a way to critique women's roles and argues that her "critical focus on uniformity reveals Woolf's awareness of the political use to which fashion can be put" (183). In contest with scholars who have argued Woolf was categorically against uniformity in dress and in publishing, Plock suggests that Woolf realized a "tactical compromise with modern fashion as the initiator of uniform looks for bodies and books was essential in her attempt to reach her readers" (184). The chapter closes with a fascinating analysis that draws comparisons between sartorial codes of uniformity and how the uniform (and inexpensive) editions of Woolf's works from Hogarth Press made her feminist and anti-fascist perspectives available to a wider readership.

Plock's book is especially relevant to our current times when we should be aware that collective forms of dress like the "dapper" style adopted by white nationalists, the black tactical gear worn by Antifa's members, and hashtag slogan t-shirts initially produced by Black Lives Matter activists and now worn widely demonstrate that fashion is far from trivial and always political.

—Sarah E. Cornish, *University of Northern Colorado*

Cheap Modernism: Expanding Markets, Publishers' Series, and the Avant-garde. Lise Jaillant (Edinburgh, UK: Edinburgh University Press, 2017) xi + 172pp.

In "Modern Fiction," Woolf famously describes her messy vantage point "in the crowd, blind with dust" and decrees that "it is for the historian of literature to decide" from a "sufficiently lofty pinnacle" about the state of modern fiction (*CR* 1). Lise Jaillant's brilliant new book attains this superior vantage point onto a vast throng of competing publishers' series and offers a thoroughly researched topographical view of the historical development and cultural importance of this phenomenon, while also giving a thick account of the "dust" on the ground kicked up by authors and publishers negotiating the bustling marketplace for cheap reprints of modernism. Jaillant attains this balance between a long, broad historical network and thick local examples through her ambitious structure of five archivally researched chapters, each featuring major avant-garde modernists and documenting those modernists' involvement in seven publishers' reprint series. Jaillant covers an impressive terrain and gathers together materials from a trove of geographically-dispersed archives: she situates the prefatory introductions by T. S. Eliot and Virginia Woolf commissioned by the Oxford's World's Classics Series; then she moves to the circulation of the subversive texts by James Joyce in the Traveller's Library and D. H. Lawrence in the New Adelphi Library; the third chapter focuses on the publication of Wyndham Lewis's *Tarr* in the Phoenix Library; the fourth chapter extends the focus to "the continental diffusion of Anglophone modernism" (19) through Tauchnitz and Albatross; and the final chapter focuses on the Hogarth Press's Uniform Edition of Virginia Woolf's works.

While there have been many excellent studies of individual series and on single publishing houses—Jaillant's first book on the Modern Library Series is a sterling example—Jaillant rightly claims that *Cheap Modernism* is "the first study of European uniform reprint series that widened the market for modernist texts" (1). Jaillant adds to the growing scholarly conversations about modernism's imbrication within the marketplace and fills an important gap by focusing on book publication rather than the bulk of this new work, which has focused primarily on periodical print cultures. Jaillant argues persuasively that the cheap reprint series she focuses on "sold modernism to a wide audience—thus transforming a little-read 'highbrow' movement into a mainstream phenomenon" (1). *Cheap Modernism* always helpfully quantifies its claims and clarifies its key terms: here Jaillant specifies that by "'wide audience', [she] mean[s] thousands of readers—much less than a mass-market readership, but much more than the small coteries that had read texts by Virginia Woolf, James Joyce and others in their original context of publication" (1). *Cheap Modernism* shows us how the readership for modernism expanded from "high" to "low" markets and also "spatial[ly]—since publishers' series were distributed within and outside metropolitan centres in Britain, continental Europe and elsewhere" (1).

Cheap Modernism demonstrates stylistic mastery of the book history genre—Jaillant avoids the dry recounting of costs and editorial ambitions and manages to convey an impressive amount of knowledge about each series she covers without getting bogged down in an avalanche of details. Jaillant keeps her reader engaged by continually drawing us back into her larger story and keeps the cultural stakes clear throughout. She also includes welcome moments of humor: when discussing the J. M. Dent's Wayfarers' Library, which focused on publishing 'clean' modern literature "excluding controversial or pessimistic texts" (14), Jaillant made this reader snort with laughter: "In other words, any middleclass household could display these books without anxiety: there was nothing too risqué to shock the vicar" (15).

The introduction provides useful context and positions the cheap reprint series of modernism into a larger narrative reaching back to the late eighteenth century to trace how a landmark copyright case and changes in printing technology and costs worked to establish the long history of the rise of the cheap reprint series. Jaillant connects the legal and technological developments with changes to education which paved the way for the shift from the more lurid, entertaining railway series to the more soberly packaged classics that were spurred by the shift in 1880: when "school attendance became compulsory for all children until the age of ten, opening up new markets" (8). While Jaillant's main focus is on series within Britain, she also incorporates the histories of cheap series in France and Germany.

Cheap Modernism continually attends to the material format of the books themselves to consider how their physical dimensions enhanced their links to cosmopolitanism and travel as "geographical mobility was linked to upward mobility" (9). For readers fascinated by the material forms of bookishness, Jaillant's carefully researched book constantly satisfied cravings for details about the dimensions and designs of the books she covers. I was thrilled by her continual linkage of these physical properties to advertising copy, which she argues often made use of the book's proportions and prettiness to sell these reprints as visible testaments to the consumer's cultural capital: "The World's Classics was described as 'the cheapest, prettiest, and handiest form in which you can obtain the great classics of literature' [… Readers] were encouraged to see the series as a coherent whole designed to be displayed on the shelf as a sign of taste and social respectability" (12).

Of most particular interest to Woolf scholars are the first and final chapters, which focus explicitly on Woolf's engagement with mass readerships and with growing canonicity through Publishers' reprint series. Chapter One focuses on introductions that Oxford World's Classics commissioned from Woolf and Eliot that made older books "new" and modernist by association, while also "transforming the image of these modernist writers from obscure avant-gardists to members of the artistic establishment" (18). Jaillant shows how Woolf's introduction to Sterne's *Sentimental Journey* in 1928 conferred a doubleness of prestige: "The 'consecration' process worked in two ways: writers of introductions brought new prestige to old books (and to the World's Classics series), and in turn, these classics increased the cultural aura of already-distinguished authors" (26). Jaillant argues that this kind of introduction was only useful to Woolf at that particular point in her career—in the late twenties when she was still trying to reach a wider audience of common readers especially in America—as afterwards she and Leonard both rejected subsequent opportunities and instead developed their own cheap series to help Woolf's work circulate to larger markets. In Chapter Five, Jaillant focuses on the Hogarth Press's "Uniform Edition" as an understudied development in Woolf's reaching a wider transatlantic readership. The Hogarth Press had offered Woolf "exceptional creative freedom," but had also made her books initially only available in "the sphere of small presses with limited market opportunities" (120). Leonard and Virginia used the Uniform Edition to lower the price point and used the "collected"-ness of the series to rebrand Woolf and re-circulate her work more widely and also to solidify her status "as a canonical author whose work deserved to be collected and preserved" (121). Jaillant places this achievement within a meaningful larger context by showing how many of Woolf's modernist contemporaries failed where Woolf succeeded—she documents the struggles of Ford Madox Ford, James Joyce, and Gertrude Stein here to control their own canonicity through a collected edition: "While other modernists depended on publishers to market them as important writers, Woolf used her own press to canonise herself" (122). Jaillant documents how "among her modernist peers, Woolf was therefore in the unique position to directly shape the literary canon—not as an author, but as a publisher (134).

While Jaillant's book is much more informative than it is polemical, she does insistently challenge critical discussions about modernism as a "Battle of the Brows" and wants to make the interaction between "high" and "low" a lot more fluid and uses Hogarth Press advertisements of Woolf's "high" modernist works alongside popular genres like detective fiction to show how "Woolf's positioning in the literary field was characterised by hybridity rather than radical separation from lower cultural forms" (128). Jaillant fights against a misguided view of the Hogarth Press as only a coterie publishing house and to reconsider how "Woolf—as author and publisher—fully exploited the commercial opportunities offered by the 'middlebrow' cultural sphere" (129).

Cheap Modernism is ambitious and impressive: Jaillant's archival work traces a global network of cheap reprint series and places them into a larger history of mass market editions—from the Railway editions of the nineteenth century to the rise of Penguin and paperbacks that took over afterwards. This book makes a substantial contribution to modernist studies with its historical scope, the number of presses and authors it covers, and the range of archival materials that it collects. These materials—including advertisements, letters from authors and publishers and printers, dust jackets, and early reviews—allow her to consider multiple facets of the print marketplace as she moves with dexterity between production, circulation, and reception. *Cheap Modernism* is a valuable resource to scholars and students of Woolf and of modernism more broadly—an informative study of the reprint series that helped modernism become "mainstream" (3).

—Jennifer Sorensen, *Texas A&M-Corpus Christi*

Ordinary Matters: Modernist Women's Literature and Photography.
Lorraine Sim (London: Bloomsbury, 2016) 228 pp.

When American photographer and war correspondent Lee Miller posed in Hitler's bathtub within days of the Third Reich dictator's suicide (and directly following a visit to Dachau), she enlisted surreal methods to reveal harrowing realities to a *Vogue* readership accustomed to photo spreads on fashion and beauty trends. Elsewhere, in her contributions to *Grim Glory: Pictures of Britain Under Fire*, Miller extinguishes reassuring perceptions of a far-off front line. Lorraine Sim argues, "Positioning the viewer as a London civilian implicated in the daily trauma of survival, Miller disrupts any complacent gaze on the part of her American audience as war has here moved into the space of the home and private experience" (165). In Miller's work in Normandy and across France to Nazi Germany, distinctions between agents and victims, sites of horror and shelter, continue to be clouded: a GI casually chats with two smiling German POWs at a U.S. evacuation hospital, presenting a compassionate but unfamiliar tableau. Nurses eat, bathe, do laundry, and enjoy leisure time even as some of the war's most vile perpetrators are rounded up in a nearby village. Miller approaches the unfolding events from an unconventional perspective, positing that war is not just a spectacle of death, but an event whose currents extend to small things and intimate moments. Power hierarchies shift and evil-doers display human qualities.

In her introduction to *Ordinary Matters: Modernist Women's Literature and Photography,* Sim takes aim at the marginalization of women's contribution to modernist studies' "everyday life theory," arguing that such a position overlooks the rich theoretical interpretations of the ordinary, the daily, and the mundane. *Ordinary Matters*, she declares at the outset, "focuses on conceptions of the ordinary and how particular forms of modernity shaped modernist women's personal, artistic and ethical investments in the ordinary and daily" (15). With broad use of the work of Henri Lefebvre, Maurice Blanchot, Michel de Certeau, and a host of other male scholars, Sim establishes that male sociologists, philosophers, and theorists have long had a corner on everyday life theory. Through case studies of Dorothea Lange,

Dorothy Richardson, Helen Levitt, Gertrude Stein, Virginia Woolf, Lee Miller, and Margaret Monck, Sim sets out to establish the ethical value of attention, empathy, intersubjective relations, and intimacy in women's considerations of the everyday.

Dorothy Richardson's positive treatment of London's nexus of "streets and by-ways" constitutes the first chapter, "'I am part of the dense smooth clean paving stone': The Street in Dorothy Richardson's *Pilgrimage*." In these pages, the protagonist, Miriam Henderson, cultivates a sense of appreciation and self-reliance in wandering through neighborhoods, granting urban space a positive value and finding delight in simple human interactions. As Sim explains, Henderson engages with the cityscape, building awareness of others, finding consolatory meaning, and securing independence: "Miriam imagines the street not only as a companion but as a part of her own being, that is, as connected to her in kind" (22). Sim explicates Miriam's relationship to the street through various lenses—"ontological, intersubjective, epistemological and effective—foregrounding how the street takes on existential value in her life" (25).

Before she traces the street's animating effect on Miriam, Sim summarizes the long, dreary history of the streets that poets, novelists, and scholars have illustrated in their work, preparing the reader for the radical inversion of Miriam's "positive city consciousness" (27). Sim begins with Richardson's predecessors and fellow modernists who, expressing prevailing currents of Western thought, depict London as a city of vice, endangerment, and moral deterioration. Sim presents a roll call of writers who perpetuate visions of a purgatorial city populated by human husks: "Such dystopian renderings of the city can be found in the work of Charles Dickens, Charles Booth, Henry Mayhew, George Gissing, H. G. Wells and T. S. Eliot" (24).

But for Miriam, exploring the London streets builds a sense of self-awareness and social empathy, personal and social gratification. Moving against the human current becomes a way of pushing back at traditionally and normatively sanctioned power. Miriam's perceptions contradict traditions of masculine flânerie, in which perspectives are often "panoramic and detached" (33). Miriam moves through a lyrical London as twilight gives way to lamp-lights, and "'the sudden glare of yellow shop-light'" (36). Noises and sudden irruptions are a "'happy symphony'" and kerbs are "friendly." Miriam and the street enjoy a metaphorical embrace, and London is a "'mighty lover.'"

In the late 1930s and 1940s, American photographer Helen Levitt documented inhabitants of New York streets, capturing people *in medias res*—at play and at rest, climbing a tree or following bubbles floating through the air. Her improvisational images of everyday life convey a guileless beauty, "an aesthetics of the everyday" (42). Countering agreed-upon standards of interest, Levitt saw her subjects through an apolitical lens and was "non-interventionist in approach" (44). Her graceful presentation of "poor neighbourhoods, the working classes, women and children, and often African-American and immigrant subjects" offers social commentary on urban life during her historical moment (47). In her candid shots of children climbing trees, jumping rope on sidewalks, playing tag, and laughing, Levitt "challenges cultural histories of the street by figuring it as a rich, positive and dynamic social sphere, not, as was historically the norm, a site of alienation, depopulation or social degeneration" (59). Her warm and quirky photos document human expressiveness without condescending interpretations of heroism and silent dignity.

Sim turns her attention to the value of modest objects and ingenuous human encounters in Chapter Three, "Homely Things: Gertrude Stein and Virginia Woolf." In these pages, Sim adds to modernist studies' growing interest in objects and "ordinary things" and the effort to liberate them from "'the cultural logic of capitalism'" (68). In this effort, Sim examines "how the writing of familiar things in [*Tender Buttons* and *To the Lighthouse*] contributes to the reanimation and revaluation of the object world…" (69). Stein is deeply invested in the vitality of everyday objects—the things that populate her carefully curated domestic world. In sections titled "Objects," "Food," and "Rooms," Stein flouts patriarchal discourse's denigration of "'the female domain'" (22), delighting in an intimate, intersubjective relationship to objects, redefining them for her own purposes, and engaging in a private dialogue that often defies readers' efforts to translate. By way of example, Sim offers: "Prose-poems like 'a *purse.*' indicate how Stein rejects modernity's proscription of objects to their material or instrumental value, instead transforming this object—which is normally associated with economies of money—to object-subject economies that are private, pleasurable, embodied and interpersonal" (78).

In *To the Lighthouse,* Virginia Woolf affirms the value of intimate attention to domestic objects "knitted stockings, shawls, boots, jewellery, [and] chipped tea cups" (82). Where some characters experience reciprocal relationships with objects, others remain detached. "Thus, in the early stages of the novel, contrasting perceptions of and modes of relation to the object world are set up via the characters of Mr Ramsay (philosophical/abstract), James Ramsay (child's wonder and fascination) and Lily Briscoe (the artistic)…" (82). Objects not only stir subjective feelings and create private vectors of meaning, they also operate as psychic fulcrums between people, "serv[ing] as an affective bridge connecting the interior worlds of different characters" (83). The objects that occupy domestic space in *To the Lighthouse* are both inner-directed and outer-directed; they are intermediaries for human connection.

Sim continues to make inroads into "everyday life theory" with "Mrs. Brown and the Face-to-Face," Chapter Four, the second chapter dedicated to Woolf's work. Here, Sim draws on Emmanuel Levinas's phenomenological method, in particular, its refusal to reduce the Other to the same. To Levinas, the Self and the Other must have absolute, irreducible distinction. As Sim explains, Woolf and Levinas share a disdain for totality as a social structure that denies the humanity of Other and as a political structure that culminates in fascist regimes. Readers unfamiliar with Levinas will find the second section to the chapter ("Totality and Infinity") informative; unfortunately, this explication results in an overly long chapter. But the discussion of *Mrs Dalloway* at the chapter's end refocuses the study, concluding that "the framework of Levinas' account of the face-to-face, that the ordinary…assumes an important position in Woolf's ethics, particularly her account of self-other relations and responsibility, as well as in her account of the ethics and aesthetics of characterization in the modern novel . . ." (119).

To today's viewer, Dorothea Lange's iconic photographs present both human despair, frozen time and wide-frame, expressive commentary on the economic, political, and environmental conditions that their human subjects endured. Sim cites key ideas from Susan Sontag's *On Photography* to criticize received opinions of the medium's inherent "aestheticization of the banal and simple" (122) and the questionable ethics therein. Sim adopts Sontag's argument for her own purposes, announcing that her chapter "examines the relationship between photography and the everyday…and considers [Lange's] work in the context of some of Sontag's claims about the moral risks and limits of photography" (123). (As an aside, the almost-rote invocation of Sontag in scholarship on photography warrants some critical assessment.)

Reproducing nine of Lange's photographs, Chapter Five, "Dorothea Lange: On Photographing the Familiar," documents pea-pickers, migrant laborers, drought refugees, and children—destitute, dust-coated, with faraway eyes. Lange had early success as a portrait photographer but her exemplary *White Angel Breadline, San Francisco* placed her work squarely in the social documentary genre. Soon Lange was photographing victims of Depression-era, rural America living "in appallingly squalid and dangerous conditions, in makeshift dwellings with no running water, sanitation or adequate food" (127). With human subjects, Lange's framing balances intimacy and acknowledgement of the Other.

"Everyday life theory" receives its final treatment with Sim's chapter on Miller's war photography (though there is also a coda on Margaret Monck). Sim convincingly concludes that Miller's "photographs possess a semantic and moral ambiguity and complexity that distinguishes them from most Allied photojournalism of Germans and Germany post-victory" (173). Though the chapter could have done without reference to Hannah Arendt's "famous thesis on the banality of evil" (175) (which Holocaust scholars have almost unanimously discredited), Sim draws together many the disparate themes of her study here.

Ordinary Matters demonstrates how themes of everydayness yield "positive value and sufficiency" (206). In the work of modernist women writers and photographers, ordinary objects and themes of everydayness transform into media of mutual appreciation, points of attention, modes of intervention, and bases for ethical contemplation. Sim's study makes persuasive inroads toward bringing the value of these contributions to light.

—Annalisa Zox-Weaver, *Independent Scholar*

Fresca: A Life in the Making. A Biographer's Quest for a Forgotten Bloomsbury Polymath. Helen Southworth (Brighton: Sussex Academic Press, 2017) xvii + 373pp.

Helen Southworth's project to discover the story of British-German Jewish Francesca Allinson, whose autobiographical novel, *A Childhood*, was published by the Hogarth Press in 1937, is a "biography-in-action." Instead of a seamless portrait and study of the ways in which the story of Fresca's life intersected with the lives and artistic endeavors of better known and, equally, forgotten contemporaries, it is "a life in the making," as the title highlights, a tale that maps out its own processes. This meta-methodology is indicated very clearly at the outset, from the subtitle to the preface and acknowledgements page, "A Tale of Research or Biography as Detection and Jigsaw" (vii). As Southworth outlines, the "biography" is structured where possible in terms of the order in which items such as books, photographs, and wills "presented themselves to me," including "leads that did not pan out, that did not produce gold, as well as, of course, those that did, and details and anecdotes that pertain only peripherally to Fresca's life story" (viii). So the reader is introduced to Southworth's virtuoso and occasionally vertiginous exposé of the practices and processes of an archival researcher and biographer who works, in the footsteps of Woolf herself, on the lives of the obscure. In the absence of a single Fresca archive, Southworth takes to traditional archive and standard library research, e-mails, and interviews, as well as pursuing new resources and methods facilitated by the internet—Google Maps, Google Books, crowd sourcing, and more—to build an archive of her own. Inspired by other biographers, to "show the folds of a life" (viii), this is not only an unconventional biography about an unconventional life tragically cut short, but also about a specific period in English cultural history glimpsed through unexpected vistas that the search for Fresca recovers.

Who was Fresca, what did she write, whom did she know, and what were her connections with Bloomsbury? Included in a checklist of Bloomsbury publications, the reference to Francesca Allinson's only novel, *A Childhood*, sends the author on a series of textual quests through which a reading of her novel is interwoven. Clues to Fresca's childhood, the illness she struggled with all her life, her education, her life as a writer and as a musician who made significant contributions in the field of choral work, her largely unacknowledged scholarship on the music of Henry Purcell, and her keen interests in folk music, theatre and puppetry, are necessarily traced through the lives and writing of others. Their letters, poetry, autobiographies, musical dedications and compositions, and several obituaries following her suicide are tracked down, retrieved and often quoted at length. In composer Michael Tippett's autobiography, *Those Twentieth Century Blues*, Southworth finds her first story of Fresca, a complex story of shared interests—music, social justice—and unrequited love "which has a beginning, a middle and a tragic end" (2). The story of Tippett's life, his homosexuality and pacifism, and the history of some of his compositions closely connected with Fresca as further excavations reveal, his letters and papers more broadly, continue to be central sources. This is especially so following the discovery in the Tippett archive of a misidentified document that is in fact Fresca's diary. It is a revelation: "These intimate notes provide a map of Fresca's soul, a very troubled soul, and give a sense of the landscape of literary resources available to an educated, intellectually curious woman of the 1930s. The diary is a reader's diary" (207).

Fresca's reading choices, carefully identified and often quoted, included Woolf's writing, another connection with Tippett: "Woolf appears to represent a shared language, a shared passion" (6). Painstaking explorations of other significant friendships offer further insights into brief crossings with Bloomsbury and an explanation for the appearance of her only novel in the Hogarth publications list. Enid Marx, who emerges as a fascinating figure in her own right, a protégée of Paul Nash who became best known for her textile and other industrial design work as well as her book illustrations (140), has a double connection it turns out. Adrian Stephen is Marx's analyst, as well as Fresca's, for a period. The Hogarth Press considers Fresca's manuscript thanks to Marx's friendship with Alice Ritchie, "a Hogarth Press insider" (134) and sister of Trekkie Ritchie Parsons. In turn, Fresca's request that Marx illustrate her novel ensures further collaboration between Marx and the press. In search of further details, Southworth's visit to the Hogarth Press Archive at the University of Reading reveals a series of exchanges between Fresca and Leonard Woolf about the manuscript and its forthcoming publication, also pointing to a meeting between Virginia Woolf and Fresca. Disappointingly for biographer and reader, there is no record of that interview. What is fascinating here, however, and indicative of the riches of the entire project, is where attention to the conventional focuses of scholarship, Woolf, Bloomsbury, and the Hogarth Press bring to the fore alternative and hitherto unexplored groupings, the other side of a conversation.

Teasing out Fresca's complex relationship with Judy Wogan, close friend and for a time lover, reveals another productive period for Fresca in the realms of both literature and music, and mutual interests in social engagement. It also brings to light the Arts League of Service and the array of affiliated writers and artists, its council members ranging from Wyndham Lewis and T. S. Eliot to Tagore and E.

McKnight Kauffer (97). Among the many striking details surfaced are Judy Wogan's association with a travelling theatre troupe allied to the Service that saw her performing in a play that Constance Markievicz and her husband took on tour. Wogan went on to establish the Grafton Theatre in London, an extraordinary avant-garde project that Southworth's explorations bring to light.

While the accumulation and careful documenting of material, the tracking of correspondence, the meeting with biographers, relatives, and friends described in depth, the handing over of letters on pavements next to Tube stations, and wild goose chases might threaten to distract a reader who wants to get on with the story, these details offer the thrill of recognition to any scholar who has undertaken this kind of research. Dilemmas—an offer of a photograph torn from an album, guilt about letters returned to a generous scholar but in a muddle, the discovery of a diary and doubts about invading the privacy of another—are also examined. And just when, at times, the tracking of minute details of Francesca's life or of her relatives and friends becomes almost overwhelming, an unexpected fact, a connection illuminated, sparks a revelation. The radical feminist and anarchist *Freewoman* and *New Freewoman* as well as the socialist *New Age* carried advertisements for *A Book for Married Women*, written by Fresca's father "early whole foods, vegetarian and natural prescriptions guru Dr Thomas Richard Allinson" (13), for example. Fresca's brother Adrian Paul Allinson, Slade School trained, occupied the margins of "the lives of several famous Slade Art School graduates, including Bloomsbury figures Mark Gertler and Dora Carrington, as well as Edward Wadsworth, Christopher [C.R.W.] Nevinson, and Stanley Spencer" (16). Author of an unpublished biography, *A Painter's Pilgrimage*, held, intriguingly, with the Dorothy Miller Richardson papers at the University of Tulsa (n. 11, 336), Adrian Allinson's links with Bloomsbury were more tangential than Southworth initially imagined, but his connections with other literary and aesthetic circles are equally fascinating. These circles are glimpsed early in the research project—the composers Philip Heseltine, the writers Jean Rhys and Dorothy Richardson, the artists Alan Odle (Richardson's husband) and Nina Hamnett (18-19). Adrian Allinson's "Café Royal" painting features, among others, Nancy Cunard, Iris Tree, and Augustus John. Adrian Allinson's connections anticipate the carefully mined details about intersections among Fresca, Bloomsbury, and other often overshadowed pacifist, experimental and avant-garde circles of the interwar and early period of the Second World War, the creative friendships and collaborations that later excavations reveal. Southworth brings to light additional literary and musical contributions, such as Fresca's book of nursery rhymes illustrated with woodcuts by Marco (Enid Marx) and, most intriguingly, an unpublished folk song monograph, a collaborative project begun with Michael Tippett, "The Irish Contribution to English Traditional Tunes." Discovering a version of the monograph in the Ralph Vaughan Williams archive, Southworth finds that the subject of the monograph proved problematic for Vaughan Williams and others who wanted to safeguard the Englishness of English traditional tunes. She finds a letter to Leonard Woolf asking whether Hogarth Press would be interested in her "highly controversial" book (273). In search of an understanding of Fresca's project, its history, and the story of its failed publication offer another unexpected angle on the cultural history of the period.

In the true spirit of archival and biographical researchers who set out with a plan and a focus but find themselves waylaid or side-tracked down unexpected avenues, readers who might be tantalized and drawn to read this work through the titular reference to Bloomsbury will discover familiar territory from new perspectives alongside entirely unexamined terrain. For researchers interested in literary, artistic, musical, pacifist, and other networks of the interwar years, this "biographer's quest" is a cornucopia. Not always an easy reading experience because layers of textual excavation and complex networks need to be navigated, the narrative is necessarily circuitous and fractured at times; it is, however, a richly rewarding one, full of surprises and illuminations.

—Kathryn Laing, *Mary Immaculate College, University of Limerick*

Virginia Woolf's Modernist Path: Her Middle Diaries & the Diaries She Read. Barbara Lounsberry (Gainesville: UP of Florida, 2016) ix + 286 pp.

The middle section of any trilogy is where the action happens, where the plot thickens, where the stakes are raised. This is probably as true of life as it is of art, and Barbara Lounsberry's *Virginia Woolf's Modernist Path: Her Middle Diaries & the Diaries She Read*, the second volume of a three-volume work, creates a quiet drama of Woolf's life, but also of the diary that is the record of that life. The time period it covers—1918 to 1929—is arguably the most fruitful creative period of Woolf's life, and Lounsberry convincingly situates the diary as an integral part of Woolf's developing modernist aesthetic, and as a work worthy of study in its own right. In this volume, we see Woolf move from the "passionate apprentice" of the early diaries (discussed in Lounsberry's first volume, *Becoming Virginia Woolf: Her Early Diaries & the Diaries She Read* [2014]) to the confident modernist author of *Mrs. Dalloway*, *To the Lighthouse*, and *Orlando*.

It has long been one of the oddities of Woolf scholarship that the diary has received such scant academic attention. It has been plundered for decades for its insights into Woolf's creative process and for biographical details, but rarely has it been read as a stand-alone work. A few books have addressed Woolf's diary in the larger context of diaries in general (Thomas Mallon's *A Book of One's Own* [1984], Harriet Blodgett's *Centuries of Female Days* [1988], Judy Simons's *Diaries and Journals of Literary Women from Fanny Burney to Virginia Woolf* [1990],

Elizabeth Podnieks's *Daily Modernism: The Literary Diaries of Virginia Woolf, Antonia White, Elizabeth Smart, and Anaïs Nin* [2000], among others), while assorted dissertations have examined various aspects of Woolf's diary, often alongside discussion of Anaïs Nin. Prior to Lounsberry's work, only one book-length study—Joanne Campbell Tidwell's *Politics and Aesthetics in The Diary of Virginia Woolf* (2012)—existed. But Barbara Lounsberry, a professor emerita of English at the University of Northern Iowa and the author of numerous works on creative non-fiction, holds the distinction of being one of the first Woolf scholars to have published on the diary as a text.

Lounsberry's current project has its roots in the essays she published in the 1990s in the conference proceedings of the International Virginia Woolf Conferences: "The Art of Virginia Woolf's Diaries" (1994), "What the Diary Can Tell Us" (1995), "The Diaries vs. the Letters: Continuities & Contradictions" (1996), and "Virginia Woolf and the Community of Diarists" (1999). Having done extensive work on Woolf's diaries myself, I have often found it easy to get lost in a text which seems to have no real order apart from the dailiness of its structure, and one of the best things about Lounsberry's approach is her ability to impose order on apparent chaos: she chooses to see Woolf's diary as divided into three major periods—early, middle, and late—and rather interestingly frames her argument with analysis of the published diaries Woolf read in each period. Indeed, future scholars of Woolf's diary should be grateful for the research Lounsberry has done in tracing the scores of diaries Woolf read—and there were far more than I realized—and summarizing their content and the ways in which they may have influenced Woolf's own method. (The diarists who people these pages include John Evelyn, Anton Chekhov, James Boswell, Anne Chalmers, Lady Anne Clifford, Jonathan Swift, Beatrice Webb, and Katherine Mansfield, among others.)

In *Becoming Virginia Woolf*, Lounsberry establishes a structure which she continues in *Virginia Woolf's Modernist Path*: she begins her chapters with descriptions of the physical books in which Woolf kept her diaries (a great resource for Woolf scholars unable to access the originals in the Berg Collection at the New York Public Library, where all but one of the manuscripts are housed, and I can vouch for the accuracy of Lounsberry's descriptions), followed by astute analysis of each diary's contents. Next, she provides discussion of the diarists whom Woolf was reading at the time the diary in question was kept. Interestingly, there is little sense of "the anxiety of influence" at work here: Woolf seems not a bit tormented or dismayed by the diarists who preceded her. On the contrary, in Lounsberry's account, Woolf is grateful for these models which provide her with such a rich diaristic tradition. Stylistically, Lounsberry's method allows readers to dip into a section on an individual diary or year and read a self-contained study of that particular text and its influences, a feature that will no doubt prove useful to future students and scholars. In the broader sense, Lounsberry's practice of situating Woolf's diary in the greater stream of diarists allows her to attain a grasp on this vast, otherwise slippery mass of material.

At the beginning of her book, Lounsberry discusses at length the differences between Woolf's Asheham and Hogarth diaries of 1918, arguing that the experimentation between the two books—the Asheham entries spare and compact descriptions largely of the natural world, the Hogarth entries more in the mode of standard diary-writing—feeds and shapes the work that is to come. When Woolf begins then to move more inward in her focus, Lounsberry sees a concurrent shift in the form of the diary: "Formal experiment—another modernist focus—occurs alongside the taut inward turn" (3). The drift towards a modernist sentence, a modernist aesthetic, begins for Lounsberry in the diary: "Fragments...resist any single, dominating narrative. Instead they offer a series of contingent states. Woolf's diary allowed her to experiment semiprivately with nonlinear narration, to search beyond accepted patterns of order and significance. This was practice for her modernist works" (5). In chapter after chapter, Lounsberry shows that the flowering of Woolf's diary—particularly in 1926, which Lounsberry sees as the period of headiest expansion in the diary's form—corresponds to a flowering in her published literary output, both in that output's form and quantity.

Lounsberry aptly proposes that Woolf's diary was not only what almost all diaries are—a place to record one's thoughts, one's feelings, one's trials and tribulations—but also a site for working out literary and creative difficulties: "Can a diary help heal and restore? Emphatically. Virginia Woolf's 1921 diary reveals—more explicitly than any of her other diary books—her use of her diary (when necessary) as a treatment center for literary distress of several sorts" (51). (Let me say for the record how delighted I am by the phrase "literary distress.") During this period, Woolf increasingly began to use her diary to work her way out of literary conundrums, particularly when she was writing *Mrs. Dalloway* and *To the Lighthouse*. Lounsberry does not delve deeply into the composition of these works here, as this is not her project. Instead, she seeks to reveal the ways in which the changing process of diary-writing informed Woolf's writing as a whole, and thus leaves an enticing opening for future scholarship on the ways in which Woolf's developing use of modernist techniques in the diary lines up with her public, published writing. Though Elizabeth Podnieks examines Woolf's diary's modernist attributes in *Daily Modernism*, Lounsberry's books present the fullest examination of the topic to date.

One of the most pleasant surprises about Lounsberry's first two books in the project—a surprise that will no doubt persist in the third volume—is the sheer readability of Lounsberry's prose. The volume of her research would lead the reader to expect a clotted, knotty, footnote-laden style, but each of Lounsberry's chapters unfolds in clean, elegant, stripped-down sentences. The introduction of each new diary that Woolf read is handled expertly, and there is never confusion or doubt as to who this diarist is or why he or she is important to the story of Woolf's evolution as a diarist. Lounsberry's sure hand as a stylist is always in evidence, which will make her project appealing to anyone interested in the practice of diary-writing or its history in the twentieth century.

—Drew Patrick Shannon, *Mount St. Joseph University*

Scholarly Adventures in the Digital Humanities: Making the Modernist Archives Publishing Project. Claire Battershill, Helen Southworth, Alice Staveley, Michael Widner, Elizabeth Willson Gordon, Nicola Wilson (Palgrave Macmillan, 2017) xvi + 182

Why do we spend so little time discussing in print the material and social forms that produce books on Woolf, or for that matter the forms that supported Woolf's books themselves? Why so little published discussion of the role of specific archives, institutions, libraries, technical materials, publishers, chance encounters at the Hogarth Press? These material and archival actors and forms are at the heart of this deeply collaborative, heteroglossic, engagingly subversive book. Written for the most part in a lively scholarly first-person plural, *Scholarly Adventures in the Digital Humanities* takes as its subject the process and materials of production that many scholarly works attempt to conceal. The pretext is the creation of a digital humanities project, the *Modernist Archives Publishing Project (MAPP)*, but that project's creation is the main interest of the book. The tone and argument of the book are thus usefully figured (by the authors themselves) as an extension of Woolf's depiction of feminist collaboration in "A Society." That story, like this one, chronicles a highly messy, punctuated, and consciously gendered work of research and discovery, moving from libraries to group meetings to the interruptions of "birth, death, illness, and divorce" (59). The volume thus stakes a wager on radical epistemological and professional vulnerability, on the grounds of Woolf's practice and the requirements of the project itself.

The authors begin by telling the story of the Hogarth Press as determined by an acute awareness of the "material ecologies and economies of space, place, and method that went into turning narratives into readable, distributable objects" (2), an awareness that the *Modernist Archives Publishing Project* aspires to rediscover. That project is a "critical digital archive of early twentieth-century publishing history," which aims to be a hub of information on presses and publication archives like those of the Hogarth Press held at the University of Reading (see http://www.modernistarchives.com/content/about-the-project). The book adds a book-historical and digital dimension to existing work on the Hogarth Press, including an important predecessor book edited by Helen Southworth (also one of the authors of the present volume), *Leonard and Virginia Woolf, the Hogarth Press and the Networks of Modernism* (Edinburgh: Edinburgh University Press, 2012). The book's introduction situates its work between the field of book history, in particular the social text model associated with Donald McKenzie and Jerome McGann, and the burgeoning tools, platforms, and provocations of the Digital Humanities. If the publication records, printers' bills, errata, and Leonard Woolf's handwriting all turn out to be determinative for the history of the Hogarth Press, as McKenzie would argue, but those same records are scattered across institutions from Sussex to Washington State, then MAPP aims to build a digital bridge between collections in the service of a material history of modernist book publication.

After providing the theoretical and material sources for the project, the authors describe who they are and how they produced the project, and here we have heteroglossia: a variety of voices and scholarly trajectories emerge, united by conference conversations, shared questions, and a love of Hogarth Press first editions. The inevitable scholarly critique imagined here is surely: but where is the unified arc of a career? How could all these voices unite in one intellectual project? Isn't this just chance and contingency? To which the authors stirringly reply: love, contingency, and feminist collaboration are precisely the basis of the project itself.

This particularly comes through in their "Reflections on Collaboration" chapter, which challenges the "tyranny of the monograph," and its model of individual performance and evaluation, with a rich account of collaboration as a practice already at play in the humanities classroom: "we have noticed that our teamwork at its best replicates a successful pedagogy as when, in a good seminar, process, curiosity, and imitative commentary—the polyphony of the group—generates smarter, cumulative insights precisely because one person is *not* deputized the authoritative leader" (56). Many of their conclusions will be helpful to those engaged (often for the first time) in collaborative scholarly projects: learning to write memoranda of understanding on the obligations and roles intrinsic to the project; prioritizing in-person meetings and retreats alongside software for distant collaborations; approaching grant-writing as a way to form group identity; defining goals; and setting deadlines. Perhaps their book's most important lesson is the example of the book itself: *write it down,* even and especially the mangle of practice, both for your own sake and to help others in the future.

The primary audience for *Scholarly Adventures in the Digital Humanities* is likely to be other humanists with a particular set of needs and questions. The authors carefully define all terms and tools for the absolute beginner, but certainly those already engaged in Digital Humanities projects have a great deal to learn. Their discussion of the "critical digital archive" as a form deals with previous examples in the field, like the *Rossetti Archive* and the *Women Writers Project*, addresses roads and platforms not taken, and describes the intellectual work that underlies their choice of a Drupal database: "building an archive is itself a form of scholarship that can be generative of new scholarly thinking and writing," they argue (75). They make a compelling case for using open-source code whenever possible, rather than customized one-use applications, and employing a data structure that aims at linked open data conventions like those employed in leading projects (such as the ARC Collex group aiming to unify eighteenth- and nineteenth-century metadata collection). The book also records an amazing range of pedagogical experiences with MAPP, and admirably preserves the various successes and failures to connect familiar to all digital humanists.

Scholarly Adventures in the Digital Humanities sustains throughout the note of the venture sounded in the title, and marks an important new stage of maturity in modernist digital humanities projects (along with the established *Modernist Journals Project* and other important ventures). Many potential objections to the projects' heterogeneity and provisionality are fully addressed within it, as we have seen. A few other criticisms of the book should be lodged: the reference to "traditional" research methods at times seemed to indicate anything non-digital, even as the book indicated its intellectual origins within rather avant-garde theories of book history; such notions of a cultural split between the "traditionalists" and "digital moderns" are always questionable in digital humanities scholarship, particularly so when the subject is book history. The book often hints at something that could be even more directly confronted: learning, theorizing, and building with entirely new methods derived from other disciplines, especially in conjunction with the appalling spread of contingency and job insecurity in the humanities, represents an enormous burden of stress, uncertainty, and worry; this is a burden often shouldered by the most vulnerable early-career members of a team.

Yet to their credit, the authors manage to make this methodological hurdle appear not only surmountable but energizing. This book sounds the call for new ways of both doing and representing collaborative scholarship, and indeed the reader quickly imagines ways of using and expanding on their work (why don't we have a physical map of where the Woolf or Beckett or Futurist "archive" is variously located, and also of the aporias where those archives are incomplete?). The unveiling of the project at the University of Reading during the 2017 conference on Virginia Woolf was an important event in Woolf Studies and modernist digital scholarship. But the authors have recorded a different mode of scholarly experience in this volume. In the midst of a transatlantic project, created in difficult times, they demonstrate the power of "that vital force that Woolf saw as the core of a literary experience: 'the more exciting intercourse of friendship'" (128).

—Gabriel Hankins, *Clemson University*

The Sky of Our Manufacture: The London Fog in British Fiction from Dickens to Woolf. Jesse Oak Taylor (Charlottesville, VA: U of Virginia P, 2016) 260 pp.

Edward Burtynsky's *Manufactured Landscapes* (2006) evokes the aesthetic sublimity of quarry vistas lit crimson by the sunset, the spangled play of light in recycling yards, and the rhythmic intervals of repetition in a Chinese manufacturing plant. The aesthetic effect is a conscious one on Burtynsky's part as the film instigates confrontation with the ways in which aestheticization is a necessary means of rendering visible the monstrous evidence of industrial impact. Similarly motivated, though with fictions of air rather than photographs of the earth, Jesse Oak Taylor's *The Sky of Our Manufacture: The London Fog in British Fiction from Dickens to Woolf* is concerned with the difficult process of "learning to see the smog and the discomfort produced by finding it beautiful" (167).

The Sky of Our Manufacture joins a fruitful discussion about modernism and ecological history that includes Jennifer Ladino's *Reclaiming Nostalgia: Longing for Nature in American Literature* (2012), Jeffrey McCarthy's *Green Modernism: Nature and the English Novel, 1900 to 1930* (2015), Joshua Schuster's *The Ecology of Modernism: American Environments and Avant-Garde Poetics* (2016), and Kelly Sultzbach's *Ecocriticism in the Modernist Imagination: Forster, Woolf, and Auden* (2016). Part of the University of Virginia's "Under the Sign of Nature: Explorations in Ecocriticism" series, *The Sky of Our Manufacture* charts in Victorian and modernist novels a developing awareness of the atmospheric changes rendered by industrial pollution. Therefore, for Taylor, smog, climate, and atmosphere are significant interrelated terms. Bracketing his period of study between Dickens and Woolf, Taylor tracks in the aesthetic shift from realism to modernism literature's increasing ability to describe the weirdness of the changing climate. This literary historical epoch fits more or less alongside two events of cultural and environmental significance: the Great Exposition of 1851 and the Great Smog of 1952 (the latter reaches somewhat beyond the scope of the authors in this study, but is relevant since it is an epochal event, signifying the emergence of environmental policy).

Cognizant of one of ecocriticism's challenges when working with historical rather than contemporary material, Taylor anticipates accusations of presentism or anachronistic ideological interpretation. Acknowledging that such terms as nature-culture (put into circulation by Bruno Latour and Donna Haraway) or posthumanism ill fit this period, Taylor rightly identifies in Victorian and modernist imaginative works the prehistory of these concepts. Taylor regards novels as cyphers or containers of historical thinking that capture the "contingency of the present by way of the alterity of the past" (9), which is a way of saying that the Victorian and modernist novels discussed in *Sky of our Manufacture* present early instances of writers grappling with some of the first recognizable signs of anthropogenic climate change. The novel, or any imaginative work of literature for that matter, does not, of course, stand in for actual soil samples or barometric pressure gauges or the like, and Taylor is quick to make it clear that he is interested in the novel as a model of thinking, specifically climate thinking. Novels imagine worlds by drawing from the stuff of everyday of life. What Taylor finds in Dickens, Conrad, Woolf, and others is keen observational insight into the complex interplay of the human and nonhuman worlds. Since these novels were written before the widespread understanding of the effects of pollution, the novels are not expressions of environmentalism. In fact, in direct acknowledgment of the period's lack of eco-awareness, Taylor interestingly suggests that the novel by its fictive nature, "encourage[es] readers to imagine themselves as participants in broader, unplanned collectives [and thus] may have actually encouraged the kinds of behavior that enabled the human species to take on hitherto unknown agency" (202). This observation on literature's ability to collude with as well as resist detrimental social, political, and ecological policies, is refreshing, to say the least.

The study unfolds across three sections. The first recasts Victorian realism in George Eliot and Dickens by emphasizing the Victorian novels' reliance on new technological innovations for measuring climate as ways of metaphorically representing character and cityscape interaction and the ways in which climate shapes events. Taylor introduces the term "abnatural" to describe the persistence of nature as it mutates in response to anthropogenic climate change. Smog, existing at the intersection of nature and culture, is a combination of moisture, cool and warm air, and particulate matter ejected into the atmosphere by industrial activity. Smog is a prime example of the abnatural. The discussion of *Bleak House*'s opening smog scene is rather brilliantly executed, but it becomes apparent that the rest of the novel is of far less importance to Taylor than it is as a means of presenting a cultural history of smog. To be fair, *The Sky of Our Manufacture* is upfront about one of its aims, which is to link humanities and meteorological discourses for the purposes of inspiring environmental citizenship. The consequence of this purpose is that the salvific portions of this book are quite inspired and likely more significant than specific readings of some of the individual texts. The comprehensive effect, however, is valuable for scholars of specific authors as well as for more broadly-situated ecocritics.

Whereas the first section dealt with the novel as "climate model," the second section introduces abnatural supernaturalism. Here, attention shifts from realism to fin de siècle works that embrace the uncanny and the weird. Taylor reads *Dr. Jekyll and Mr. Hyde* and *Dracula* alongside popular Victorian cartoons that personify a "Fog Demon" in order to make a case for an aesthetic of the supernatural which departs from High Victorian realism. The third section, "Climactic Modernism," examines literary modernism as witness to climate change in Joseph Conrad and Virginia Woolf as well as less well-known figures like poet and essayist Alice Meynell and nature writer Richard Jefferies. Again, Taylor excels at recovering the environmental-historical moment out of which these novels were written. He elaborates on a widely held summation that the realism that characterized the Victorian novel is replaced by modernist impressionism. Literary Impressionism, or departure from traditional mimetic form, draws attention to the processes of perception.

In his discussion of Woolf, Taylor turns to *Mrs. Dalloway* and *Orlando*, particularly to Woolf's experimentation with nonlinearity. Discussing *Mrs. Dalloway,* Taylor argues that the novel operates through an atmospheric temporality that shifts between local limited perspectives and explains that the city of London links these moments spatially. Although there is no smog in *Mrs. Dalloway,* the collapse of time recalled through London's spaces produces a haunting nonlinear atmospheric effect figured as a "mist," or an equally appropriate atmospheric image of ebb and flow. Taylor relates Woolf's narrative technique to our contemporary awareness of the ways in which petroculture links the present day to deep time, effectively dissolving the fiction of historical linearity. With *Orlando*, Taylor describes a Woolfian satire of "climactic determinism" (209). This reading, as with Taylor's other readings of Woolf and Conrad, brilliantly raises one of the most difficult questions of our time: "What does it mean to imagine an artificial climate? To live beneath a sky of our manufacture and conceive of the weather as in no small measure our own handiwork?" (1).

—Margaret Konkol, *Old Dominion University*

Virginia Woolf Writing the World: Selected Papers from the Twenty-fourth Annual International Conference on Virginia Woolf. Pamela L. Caughie and Diana L. Swanson, eds. (Clemson: Clemson UP, 2015) xviii + 228 pp.

In their introduction to *Virginia Woolf Writing the World: Selected Papers from the Twenty-fourth Annual International Conference on Virginia Woolf*, editors Pamela L. Caughie and Diana L. Swanson present a map of the globe denoting the countries from which conference participants traveled. All in all, 18 countries were represented, including Argentina, Australia, Brazil, Colombia, Mexico, Norway, Poland, Qatar, South Korea, Sweden, and Taiwan. "The conference theme, Writing the World, was motivated by our desire to see what kinds of answers people… would have to the question of whether and how Woolf still matters in the world," Caughie and Swanson explain (xii). Presentations by the scholars, students, teachers, artists, creative writers, and common readers who responded demonstrate that Woolf is, unequivocally, very much a part of our global twenty-first-century world. Co-sponsored by Loyola University Chicago and Northern Illinois University, the conference and its attendant special events "allowed us to move through the city, across the campus, and into the community," the editors write, "as well as to virtually travel the world through the conference presentations" (ix).

The editors have divided the papers into four sections: War and Peace, World Writer(s), Animal and Natural Worlds, and Writing and Worldmaking. Fascinating in their own right, papers in each section also establish important dialogues with each other, as we see the unique topics driving each presenter's work along with how myriad ideas complement or worry one another. The War and Peace section opens with one of the conference's three keynote events, a roundtable discussion on Woolf and Violence chaired by Mark Hussey and with remarks by Sarah Cole, J. Ashley Foster, Christine Froula, and Jean Mills stemming from several suggested prompts, such as, *"What are the sources of violence and war?"* and *"Does Woolf's 'thinking is my fighting' (D5 285) really make a difference now?"* (4). Cole finds "that violence in Woolf's writing impedes change; it disrupts and derails the narrative of life, movement, thought" (5). Foster notes Woolf's understanding that "fighting…is a 'habit,' something cultivated and taught, and therefore can be either socially encouraged or sublimated." She also points to *Three Guineas*'s revelation that "while the capacity for violence may always already be embedded within us, the use of force is not inevitable. There is a choice" (8).

Froula discusses the German zeppelin bombings of civilians in England during the First World War and Woolf's comments upon them in her diaries and letters, indicating Woolf's consideration of aerial warfare long before writing of the "ruined houses and dead bodies" of the Spanish Civil War. Mills takes up the question of whether Woolf's "thinking is my fighting" is "something we can usefully claim for ourselves today" (15). Her answer is a resounding "yes." Like Foster, she finds Woolf articulating alternatives to war when those in power would have us believe in warfare as the only suitable response to injustice or military aggression. "Violence is not everywhere," Mills writes. "And war is not inevitable" (16). It is imperative, Mills argues, that we share histories of nonviolence with our students—for instance that "Nonviolent actions have achieved historic gains for African Americans, for women, for farmworkers" (16).

In the same section, Judith Allen explores modes of control and surveillance in both Woolf's time and our own. "Woolf's writings," Allen states, "express and enact a different mode of surveillance, as her narrators prompt readers to 'see,' to observe, to expose, but also to be aware that much is hidden or re-named in an Orwellian sense. As citizens, as readers, we are urged to doubt, to think critically, to question everything" (26). Erica Delsandro's paper on modernism and memorials finds important affiliations between Woolf and Christopher Isherwood, writers often placed in opposition to one another given the discrepancies in their lived experiences of war. Delsandro brings together *Jacob's Room*, *To the Lighthouse*, and Isherwood's 1932 novel, *The Memorial*, to highlight each work's critique of "national memorialization through the use of absence and distance" (32). Christine Haskill discovers a strong Victorian strain in *Three Guineas* as she locates "the affinities rather than the radical ruptures between New Woman writers and Woolf" (43).

Additional papers in this section continue to highlight Woolf's understanding of war's incursion into virtually every facet of human life and the natural world. Ann Martin studies the car industry's involvement with warfare and munitions, while Eleanor McNees explores the 1914 "expurgated chunk" of *The Years*, particularly its array of civilian responses to war, excised from the published novel. The War and Peace section concludes with Maud Ellmann's keynote on Woolf and Sylvia Townsend Warner in which she considers "war and how it reverberates in Woolf's and Warner's fiction" along with "news and how it travels across the airwaves" (76). Ellmann also "examines how Woolf and Warner remind us of the atmosphere of war—an atmosphere in which the thunder and lightning of the bombing raids can scarcely be distinguished from the weather" (77).

In devoting significant attention to this first and longest section of the book, I hope to demonstrate the wide-ranging yet interconnected nature of the papers, evoked by the editors' careful selection and arrangement. The same holds true for papers in the subsequent sections of the book. In the World Writer(s) section, David J. Fine parses that much-bandied term "global citizenship" to render it more meaningful to his students than slogans and sound bites allow. Fine analyzes how *Three Guineas* in particular "productively complicates students' engagement with communities both local and global" (93). He assigns *Three Guineas* to foster in his students "a more rigorous interrogation of their privileges" (93) and to "reorient their vision toward their implication in political systems that systematically and historically privilege certain groups of insiders" (96). Teaching women students in the Middle East, Erin Amann Holliday-Karre finds *Three Guineas* valuable for "explor[ing] the limits of Western feminist ideology in the Middle East." Reading *Three Guineas*, her "students are introduced to the kind of argumentation that allows them to challenge an all-too-common tenet of liberal humanist feminism that insists upon the oppression of women in the Middle East" (99).

The Animal and Natural Worlds section reminds us of Woolf's deep engagement with nonhuman life. Elizabeth Hanna Hanson, for example, traces the hundreds of references to donkeys throughout Woolf's oeuvre and finds that "Woolf associates their work with the work of the writer—but generally the less significant, more difficult work, the work less facilitated by ease and inspiration" (136). Vicki Tromanhauser explores "dogmanity" in *Three Guineas*, arguing that the "sisters and daughters of educated men have been cultivated" like pets "to support their male companions" (141). Tromanhauser discerns how Woolf "endows her narrator with canine aptitudes in order better to navigate the fraught terrain of contemporary social life and sniff out its repressive structures" (142). In his paper on *The Waves*, Michael Tratner explains localization theory, a late-nineteenth and early-twentieth-century concept that "broke down the distinction between mind and body" (154) and "suggested physical analogues for functions that were previously considered the expression of nonphysical, mental, or vital powers" (Smith qtd. in Tratner 154). Reading *The Waves* "as presenting a localized view of consciousness," Tratner writes, "the six characters may then be not six separate individuals but six substructures within one body" (155).

Papers in the final section, Writing and Worldmaking, consider "how Woolf's writing directs our attention to writing itself" (Caughie and Swanson xvi). For instance, Amy Kahrmann Huseby considers Woolf and genre, noting "that Woolf's prose transformed into something different, something which no longer was purely the 'novel'" (191). Woolf infused *Between the Acts*, Huseby writes, with "Anglo-Saxon alliterative meter, and so I chose euphonic prose as the name for Woolf's project": words that "are simultaneously poetry and prose" (192). Kelle Sills Mullineaux engages composition theory to discuss Woolf and matters of audience. Citing Peter Elbow's controversial injunction to writers to, "at least in the beginning stages of drafting, ignore their audience" (197), Mullineaux delves into Woolf's myriad writings on audience as an alternately energizing and inhibiting force. Most famously, Woolf described "how her own imaginary audience member, 'The Angel in the House,' haunted her early writing" and had to be killed (197). "Because Woolf explored such a wide variety of audience insecurities," Mullineaux states, "her theories on the subject are comparable to those of modern composition scholars" (198).

The volume closes with a paper by Madelyn Detloff, who seeks to "reassert the value of the imaginative, the well-wrought, the beautiful, to the common weal—the public good" (204) using Woolf as her touchstone. Detloff quotes one of *New York Times* columnist David Brooks's many hand-wringing editorials about academia's abandonment of the humanities in favor of political correctness. "But," Detloff asks, "*who says* the two concerns (truth and beauty/social justice) are mutually exclusive? One could ask Brooks: For whom are questions of race, class, gender merely external matters?" (204). Detloff explores Woolf's attention to similar matters along with how academia, material conditions, and those daughters of educated men can perpetuate systemic injustice and "compromise intellectual freedom" (206). Virginia Woolf, Detloff asserts, in her "aesthetically complex and intellectually challenging" writings (207), in her deep and sustained social critiques, and in her continually reminding readers of the "perilous consequences of lockstep thinking" (208), remains vital for cultivating the "habits of mind" that can lead to meaningful social change. *Virginia Woolf Writing the World* presents an important body of work on the power of literature—Woolf's works in particular—to delight,

trouble, inspire, and instruct, and, as Detloff phrases it, to "enter into that experience of openness and transformation" (209).
—Kristin Czarnecki, *Georgetown College*

Virginia Woolf and Her Female Contemporaries: Selected Papers from the Twenty-Fifth Annual International Conference on Virginia Woolf. Julie Vandivere and Megan Hicks, eds. (Clemson: Clemson UP, 2016) xx + 234pp.

The latest volume in the Virginia Woolf Selected Papers Series arrives at a distinctive moment in scholarship on Woolf and the broader networks of modernist literature and culture in which the author moved. As many readers will know, it follows special issues of such journals as *Modern Fiction Studies* ("Women's Fiction, New Modernist Studies, and Feminism," edited by Anne Fernald, Summer 2013) and *Literature Compass* ("The Future of Women in Modernism," edited by Tory Young and Jeff Wallace, January 2013) whose contributors investigate the status and achievements of feminist subjects and methodologies in the field across the last two decades, offering new arguments to circulate, new paths to follow. This volume, and the conference from which it springs, precede just-launched publications and venues for the study of women's writing, gender, and modernism, such as the Feminist inter/Modernist Association and its affiliated journal, *Feminist Modernist Studies*, along with the forthcoming collection, *Teaching Modernist Women's Writing in English* (edited by Janine Utell). *Virginia Woolf and Her Female Contemporaries* offers a valuable account of facets of the present state of research on Woolf and in the wider field.

Editors Julie Vandivere and Megan Hicks open with a unique introduction that focuses primarily on the experience of organizing the volume's conference, which took place at Bloomsburg University in the Pennsylvania town of the same name in mid-2015. They discuss the particular challenges and benefits of hosting an international conference in a comparatively small university and town, highlighting strategies for acquiring financial support, engaging local media, and developing sustained points of contact among the university, schools, and readers in the Bloomsburg community. The editors provide a vivid sense of place in their writing. We are given views of events held at the nineteenth-century St Paul's Episcopal Church, for example, and the juried, public art exhibition that drew lively audiences along with a revenue stream that enabled scholarships for conference delegates. The reflections on organizing the conference in this part of book do limit its room for discussion of the conference's animating questions and themes. The introduction begins with an observation about Vandivere and other "scholars of lesser-known female modernists...sitting in a bar" and striking up the conversation that led directly to the 2015 conference, but the text promptly moves to the planning of the event rather than lingering over what must have been a spirited group discussion about women's writing and feminism in modernist studies (and our classrooms). However, Vandivere and Hicks point us to future publications including a standalone volume of essays about women modernists, not centered on Woolf, by the conference's plenary speakers. And this introduction usefully turns our attention to issues of labor and infrastructure that are crucial to successful scholarly gatherings but infrequently discussed.

Stimulating essays populate the volume's four central sections: "Who are Virginia Woolf's Female Contemporaries?"; "Virginia Woolf's Cultural Contexts"; "Virginia Woolf's Contemporaries Abroad"; and "Virginia Woolf's Contemporaries at Home." In this review, I consider seven of the volume's twenty-nine essays to give readers a sense of the collection's scope. It begins with Mary Jean Corbett's "Considering Contemporaneity: Woolf and 'The Maternal Generation,'" which cracks open two of the volume's key terms by addressing Woolf's encounters with writing by numerous women, teasing out understandings of how individuals and generations exist together in and across time. Corbett attends to Woolf's affinities with and disavowals of writers of her lifetime, most of whom (Vernon Lee, Alice Meynell) were notably older than her and provoked varied responses from Woolf as her own public, cultural status developed. Jeffrey M. Brown also explores "the peculiar values of contemporaneity" in his argument about how Woolf's writing about Ellen Terry's life and career on the stage suggests the author's awareness of "the forms of female cultural production that remained invisible and fleeting, resistant to the ossification and enduring life of print" (29). Kristin Bluemel juxtaposes Woolf's writing and personal, physical performance of gender with those of Gwen Raverat, an artist close to her in age and family history but different in the content and reception of her work. As Bluemel observes, Woolf's written responses to Raverat's body and representations of feminine experiences and identities in her engravings comprise a limited view of modern beauty. In "The Outsider as Editor: *Three Guineas* and the Feminist Periodical," Alyssa Mackenzie uses Woolf's writing about establishing a feminist journal that never came into print as a springboard for her study of how that imagined journal nonetheless illuminates some of the author's ideas about ideal conditions for disseminating polemics that are informed by her encounters with periodicals of her time, particularly *Time and Tide, The Freewoman*, and *The New Freewoman*. Jessica Kim is one of numerous contributors who traces the interplay between Woolf's work and texts by younger authors with whom she was contemporary. Here, Kim reads "Street Haunting" and Una Marson's "Little Brown Girl" together, identifying their varied representations of *flâneurie* to assert that the two further "a larger self-reflexive commentary... on the precarious status of British women writers as newly arrived observers, urban or otherwise, within a patriarchal imperial complex" (102). Part of the same section of the volume as Kim's work, Urvashi Vashist and Kristin Czarnecki situate their respective essays in geomodernist realms. Riffing on Rachel Blau Duplessis's evocative image, Vashist creates a 'woolfenstein' by bringing together Woolf and Cornelia Sorabji, associating them through not only Woolf's review of the latter's *Between the Twilights: Being Studies of Indian Women by One of Their Own* for the *Times Literary Supplement* in 1908, but also the parallels between its "uneasy union of [Sorabji's] selves, character, and author" and Woolf's approaches in her own life writing (141). Czarnecki's essay, "'In My Mind I Saw My Mother': Virginia Woolf, Zitkala-Ša, and Autobiography," takes up the proximity between the two authors' explorations of central intimate relationships and critiques of patriarchal and colonial paradigms in their texts. Setting "A Sketch of the Past" beside the Sioux writer's "Impressions of an Indian Childhood" (1900), Czarnecki identifies their similar longings for their mothers in addition to their resistance to the constraining social structures of their time. These and other papers indicate the robust qualities of the conference and this collection, as does the conference program assembled by the editors and other members of the committee, printed at the end of the volume.

Virginia Woolf and Her Female Contemporaries also is a remarkable contribution to the Selected Papers Series because of its final three pieces of writing, tributes to the groundbreaking Woolf scholar Jane Marcus by three women who first delivered them during the conference's memorial event for Marcus. Former students of Marcus, Linda Camarasana, J. Ashley Foster, and Jean Mills articulate the significance of their mentor's scholarship and teaching across several decades. Though they represent her singular impact on studies of Woolf and feminist modernism, they also turn readers' attention to the sprawling communities to which Marcus belonged. These final texts enrich the coherence of the collection. Their emphases on multigenerational dialogues and passionate intellectual pursuits gesture back to the cover image, a collage of photographic portraits of Woolf and women writers of multiple centuries, along with the photographic collage of delegates that ends the editors' introduction and together suggest the heterogeneous features of Woolf studies and the contours of feminist modernist scholarship.

—Kathryn Holland, *MacEwan University*

Virginia Woolf & Heritage: Selected Papers from the Twenty-Sixth Annual Conference on Virginia Woolf. Jane de Gay, Tom Breckin, and Anne Reus, eds. (Clemson, SC: Clemson UP, 2017) xiii + 285pp.

The collection of papers presented in this edited volume arises from the twenty-sixth Annual Conference on Virginia Woolf held at Leeds Trinity University (UK) in June 2016. The essays presented here analyze a two-way dynamic in which Woolf's often tense relationship with her own late-Victorian literary heritage is explored, and in which Woolf's legacy resonates in contemporary cultural frameworks. In this sense, the core preoccupation of the volume looks in two directions and constructs a conversation between both.

"Heritage" is a duplicitous term with a range of invested meanings, and the essays remain alert to the several problems that the theme presents, not only in its own terms, but also in connection with Woolf whose responses to the concept were ambivalent at best. The opening editorial statement, "Heritage: A Debate," does not attempt to evade these issues and sensibly identifies several of the problems that the contributors faced in thinking through the term and in drawing Woolf's writing into an analysis of what "heritage" (and, by association, "legacy") may mean.

The volume is divided into seven main sections, each considering heritage from a different perspective: the first block of essays, "Heritage, Education, and Mentoring," interrogates issues of a feminist heritage and of Woolf's conflicted responses to her own mentors. David Bradshaw's superb extended essay, "'The Very Centre of the Very Centre': H.A.L. Fisher, Oxford, and 'That Great Patriarchal Machine,'" offers a characteristically percipient and immaculately researched analysis of Woolf's relationship with her esteemed cousin. A further feature of this establishing section of essays is the double tribute to mentoring as heritage formed through two contributors' memories of their relationships with eminent Woolf scholars: essays by Jean Mills and Marion Dell discuss their debt to Jane Marcus and Julia Briggs respectively in terms that reflect on the vigorous echoes of Woolf's role as mentor-in-chief to generations of scholars, students, and common readers. Such essays confirm Woolf's claim in *A Room of One's Own* that "we think back through our mothers if we are women."

One of the great strengths of this volume is that contributions loosely connected by a theme nestle alongside each other to produce arresting changes of pace, methodology, and style: topics, and the approaches to them, are permanently on the move. Readers of any level remain constantly alert and aware that they are learning a great deal that they may not have expected to learn as they proceed.

However, not all essays or all topics are of equal interest or quality, and some contributions required more editing to justify their place here: the title of the volume promises selected papers and there is sometimes the sense that selection could have been more rigorous. Though each of the sections contains several original and compelling pieces, each also contains at least one weak essay. Occasionally, this is because the focus of the paper is too limited: "Silence, Darkness and Dirt: Mysticism and Materiality in *The Years* and *Between the Acts*" falls into this category, as does the opening essay of the volume, Jane Goldman's "'Her-it-age!': Virginia Woolf and Syllabic Intervention—Or, '*Heritage* is a Kim Novak word,'" a piece in need of more ruthless editing. In other cases, the essay's place in the volume is questionable because the discussion presents already well-rehearsed material (Gaura Narayan's "Sex and Literary History in *Orlando*" falls into this category), or explores a topic only tenuously connected to Woolf and her work (for example, Jeanne Dubino's "Kenya Colony and the Kenya Novel: The East African heritage of 'A Very Fine Negress' in *A Room of One's Own*"). Any edited collection of conference papers will struggle to maintain consistent quality whilst engaging as diverse a range of research interests and including as many voices as possible, so this is perhaps an inevitability of this type of publication. The editors of this volume have done well to limit the weaker essays and to produce a collection where outstanding essays greatly outnumber (but accentuate) less compelling or original contributions.

There are, indeed, too many fascinating essays to list here, though honorable mention must go to Marlowe A. Miller's, "Through the Arch: The Country House and the Tradition of English Tyranny in Woolf's *Between the Acts*," and Leslie Kathleen Hankins's knowledgeable discussion of Woolf's desks and the implications of her move from a "standing desk" to more conventional writing surfaces. Both pieces provide valuable research perspectives. In such essays, it is notable how "heritage" can connect with such a wide variety of debates concerning physical spaces, material objects, and familial legacies.

Section four, "Queer Pasts" is slim in comparison to the other sections. but Matthew Clarke, Kathryn Simpson, and Mary Wilson compensate by producing new readings demonstrating that this field is not yet exhausted. Clarke's discussion of the link forged by Queen Elizabeth between Lytton Strachey and Virginia Woolf (and the awkward rift marked by her as well) utilizes the concept of contiguity and explores "Queer Elizabeth" through the writing of the two friends. Simpson reads "Queer Pasts" in a productive comparative splice between Austen's *Persuasion* and Woolf's "maiden" novel, *The Voyage Out*; there is fresh insight here even for readers intimate with both novels. Wilson also produces new readings from familiar texts in her analysis of the domestic space in *Between the Acts* by charting "women's queering vision" through the "performance of domesticity" (154). All three essays are detailed, original, and written with admirable clarity.

An important strength of this absorbing collection is its range of research topics and connections. The section titled, "Writing Lives and Histories" contains excellent reflections on Woolf's diary production and life writing, as well as three astute essays on Woolfian biofictions. The section "Modernism and Heritage" presents a sophisticated undergraduate roundtable discussion of biopolitics in *Three Guineas* which connects suggestively with Diane F. Gillespie's riveting essay in the same section, "Virginia Woolf and the War on Books: Cultural Heritage and Dis-Heritage in the 1930s." Woolf's friendships, her passions, her artefacts, her responses to her heritage, her contexts, her legacy to diverse cohorts from Polish writers and readers to Las Vegas lap-dancers, and a range of associated topics besides, combine to produce a volume that presents an engrossing essay collection of significant use to several reading communities.

The work concludes with Laura Marcus's extended essay exploring Woolf's frequently asserted sense of bodily shame: "'Some ancestral dread': Woolf, Autobiography, and the Question of 'Shame'" includes a critical overview of shame and probes Woolf's letters to Ethel Smyth as well as the famous revelations of sexual abuse at the hands of Woolf's half-brother in "A Sketch of the Past." The superb essay, justifiably described as a "*tour-de-force*" by the editors, completes the collection with an emphasis on "legacy" in terms of "identity, memory, the exposure of the self's intimacies, and the practices of writing" (277).

Ella Ophir's subtle essay, "'Writing the history of my own times': Virginia Woolf and the Diary," contains a quotation from Barbara Lounsberry who describes diaries as a "hospitable space for disparate matter" (198). It is also a fitting summary of this volume. The collection as a whole achieves what seems to be an impossible combination; clear, authoritative, judicious readings that are accessible for students but that simultaneously offer even the most seasoned Woolf expert the opportunity to identify new connections. The volume is a fine legacy of the twenty-sixth Annual Conference on Virginia Woolf and it is truly a "hospitable space" where all students of Woolf's "hawkish inheritance" (257) will find intriguing new critical spaces.

—Madeleine Davies, *The University of Reading*

Notes on Contributors

Robin Adair is a visual artist, art educator, and PhD candidate at the University of Saskatchewan. In his doctoral work, he is examining Virginia Woolf's negotiation of the aesthetic theories and practices of the Bloomsbury Group, and is tracing connections between Woolf's fiction writing and the phenomenology of Maurice Merleau-Ponty. Robin has presented papers on these subjects at the 22nd and 25th *Annual Conference on Virginia Woolf.*

Matthew Cheney is a doctoral candidate at the University of New Hampshire, writing a dissertation on the melding of fiction and nonfiction in the works of Virginia Woolf, Samuel R. Delany, and J.M. Coetzee. He is the author of *Blood: Stories* (Black Lawrence Press, 2016).

Darin Graber earned his PhD in English at the University of Colorado Boulder in December, 2017, with the dissertation, "Flow Dynamics in Nineteenth-Century British Literature and Culture." His research uncovers problematic interactions between hydrological science and literary, economic, and social practices in nineteenth-century Britain. A current piece explores intersections of London's crises of urban drainage and water provision, epidemic disease, and management of the River Thames in the penny novel, *The Wild Boys of London* (1864-1866). Previous work appeared in *Studies in Romanticism*, and an exploration of competing biopolitical and disciplinary systems for regulating alcohol consumption and movement in Charles Dickens's *Our Mutual Friend* appears in *Dickens Studies Annual* (2018).

Margot Kotler is a doctoral student at the CUNY Graduate Center. Her work explores the relationship between affect, temporality, and identity in feminist and queer modernisms.

Ann Martin is an Associate Professor in the Department of English at the University of Saskatchewan. As well as publishing articles on British, American, and Canadian modernisms, she is the author of *Red Riding Hood and the Wolf in Bed: Modernism's Fairy Tales* (UTP 2006), co-editor of *Interdisciplinary / Multidisciplinary Woolf* (CUP 2013), and editor of *Virginia Woolf in the Modern Machine Age*, a special issue of the *Virginia Woolf Miscellany* (Fall 2015/Winter 2016).

Paulina Pająk is a doctoral candidate at the University of Wrocław and is writing a dissertation on gendered memory in Virginia Woolf's oeuvre, under the supervision of Professor Teresa Bruś. She has obtained an MA in British Literature and an MA in Psychology from the Jagiellonian University in Kraków. Her research interests include modernist, comparative and reception studies. Currently, she is working with Professor Jeanne Dubino on the book *Virginia Woolf and the World*.

Brett Rutherford retired in 2016 from the University of Rhode Island, where he was Coordinator of Distance Learning and a part-time instructor in the Gender and Women's Studies Program. He is editor and founder of The Poet's Press (since 1971), and Yogh & Thorn Books, two independent small press imprints, which he continues to operate from Pittsburgh, PA. He has published annotated editions of Matthew Gregory Lewis's *Tales of Wonder*; the collected poetry of Charles Hamilton Sorley; and the banned World War I novel *Despised and Rejected* by A.T. Fitzroy. His own published literary works include two novels, three plays, three poetry anthologies, and sixteen collections of poetry, the most recent being *Trilobite Love Song* (2014).

Siân White is Associate Professor of English at James Madison University, specializing in British and Irish modernism, narrative theory, Irish studies and gender studies. Her work explores the relationship between modernist form and transformations of intimacy in the modern age. In addition to her scholarship on Virginia Woolf, she is currently working on projects that address Irish modernism and its echoes in contemporary Irish women's fiction. Her articles on James Joyce and Elizabeth Bowen have appeared in *Texas Studies in Literature and Language*, *Textual Practice*, the *Journal of Narrative Theory*, *Papers on Language and Literature*, and *Genre*.

Submission Guidelines

Woolf Studies Annual invites articles on the work and life of Virginia Woolf and her milieu. The *Annual* intends to represent the breadth and eclecticism of critical approaches to Woolf and particularly welcomes new perspectives and contexts of inquiry. Articles discussing relations between Woolf and other writers and artists are also welcome.

Articles are sent for review anonymously to a member of the Editorial Board and at least one other reader. Manuscripts should not be under consideration elsewhere or have been previously published. It is strongly advised that those submitting work to *WSA* be familiar with the journal's content. Among criteria on which evaluation of submissions depends are whether an article demonstrates familiarity with scholarship already published in the field, whether the article is written clearly and effectively, and whether it makes a genuine contribution to Woolf studies.

Preparation of Copy

1. Articles are typically between 25 and 30 pages, and do not exceed 8,000 words. This is a guide rather than a stipulation, and inquiries about significantly shorter or longer submissions should be sent to the Editor at woolfstudiesannual@gmail.com.

2. A separate file should include the article's title, author's name, address, phone number, and email address. The author's name and any other identifying references should not appear on the manuscript to preserve anonymity for our readers.

3. All submissions must include an abstract of no more than 250 words.

4. Manuscripts should conform to the most recent MLA style.

5. Submissions should be sent as Word files by email to woolfstudiesannual@gmail.com.

6. Authors of accepted manuscripts are responsible for any necessary permissions fees and for securing any necessary permissions.

All editorial inquiries should be addressed to woolfstudiesannual@gmail.com.

Inquiries concerning orders, advertising, reviews, etc. should be addressed to PaceUP@pace.edu.

Other Woolf titles available:

Virginia Woolf and Communities: Selected Papers from the Eighth Annual Conference on Virginia Woolf, edited by Jeanette McVicker and Laura Davis

Virginia Woolf and Trauma: Embodied Texts Ed. Suzette Henke & David Eberly (2007)

Virginia Woolf Out of Bounds: Selected Papers from the Tenth Annual Conference on Virginia Woolf, edited by Jessica Berman and Jane Goldman

Virginia Woolf Turning the Centuries: Selected Papers from the Ninth Annual Conference on Virginia Woolf, edited by Ann Ardis and Bonnie Kime Scott

Women in the Milieu of Leonard and Virginia Woolf: Peace, Politics and Education Ed. Wayne K. Chapman and Janet M. Manson (1998)

Woolf Across Cultures Ed. Natalya Reinhold (2004)

All volumes of *Woolf Studies Annual* are available, including:

Woolf Studies Annual 6 (2000): The *Three Guineas* Correspondence, edited by Anna Snaith

Woolf Studies Annual 8 (2002): The Fawcett Library Correspondence, edited by Merry Pawlowski

Woolf Studies Annual 9 (2003): *Virginia Woolf and Literary History Part 1*, edited by Jane Lilienfeld, Jeffrey Oxford, and Lisa Low

Woolf Studies Annual 10 (2004): *Virginia Woolf and Literary History Part 2*, edited by Jane Lilienfeld, Jeffrey Oxford, and Lisa Low

Woolf Studies Annual 12 (2006): *"Letters to Readers From Virginia Woolf"* edited by Beth Rigel Daugherty

Woolf Studies Annual 19 (2013): *Special Focus Virginia Woolf and Jews*, edited by Mark Hussey

TULSA STUDIES IN WOMEN'S LITERATURE

Subscribe now for
Spring 2018, Vol. 37, No. 1

@TSWLjournal
Utulsa.edu/tswl
Like us on Facebook!

Mosaic
an interdisciplinary critical journal

Upcoming Issues

51.3 (Sep. 2018): Scale

Given the scale of such issues as climate change and of factors contributing to it, must theory, too, undergo a transition from local and individual to global perspectives? In what might a global imaginary consist, and how might it relate to existing critiques of globalization as but a label for the hegemony of Western culture? This issue considers "greening" theory, ecocriticism, the Anthropocene, climate change, and environmental and animal ethics.

51.4 (Dec. 2018): *Living On* Symposium proceedings

This issue comprises papers presented at *Mosaic*'s 50th-anniversary *Living On* symposium, held at the University of Manitoba on March 9-11, 2017. Taking its theme and title from Jacques Derrida's "Living On/Borderlines," the issue reflects on the continuing life of tinterdisciplinary research.

52.3 (Sep. 2019): Numbers

How pervasive is the rule of numbers? What are the challenges to calculability? Out of what set of variable examples will the limits to the rogue power of numbers emerge? As a supplement to its own special issue on Letters, *Mosaic* invites submissions on numbers in literature, art, music, theoretical texts, and the world at large. Possible themes include: finitude, multitude, technics, contingency, and economy.

Mosaic, an interdisciplinary critical journal
University of Manitoba
208 Tier Building
Winnipeg MB R3T 2N2 Canada
Email: mosasub@umanitoba.ca
Submit: umanitoba.ca/mosaic/submit

The twenty-fourth volume of *Woolf Studies Annual*
was published in Spring 2018
by Pace University Press

Cover and Interior Layout by Elliane Mellet
The journal was typeset in Times New Roman and Arial
and printed by Lightning Source in La Vergne, Tennessee

Pace University Press

Director: Sherman Raskin
Associate Director: Manuela Soares
Marketing Manager: Patricia Hinds
Design Consultant: Sara Yager

Graduate Assistants: Elliane Mellet and Bryan Potts
Student Aide: Erica Magrin

www.ingramcontent.com/pod-product-compliance
Lightning Source LLC
Chambersburg PA
CBHW061439300426
44114CB00014B/1747